THE GOSPEL ACCORDING TO JOB

D0880579

THE GOSPEL ACCORDING TO JOB

Mike Mason

CROSSWAY BOOKS

A DIVISION OF
GOOD NEWS PUBLISHERS
WHEATON, ILLINOIS

The Gospel According to Job.

Copyright © 1994 by Mike Mason.

Published by Crossway Books
    a division of Good News Publishers
    1300 Crescent Street
    Wheaton, Illinois 60187.

All rights reserved. No part of this publication may be reproduced, stored in a retrieval system or transmitted in any form by any means, electronic, mechanical, photocopy, recording or otherwise, without the prior permission of the publisher, except as provided by USA copyright law.

Cover design: Russ Peterson
Desert photo: William Warren / Westlight
Water drop photo: H. Wagi / SuperStock, Inc.
Art Direction: Mark Schramm

First printing, 1994

First trade paperback edition, 2002

Printed in the United States of America

Scripture taken from the *Holy Bible: New International Version®*. Copyright © 1973, 1978, 1984 by International Bible Society. Used by permission of Zondervan Publishing House. All rights reserved.

The "NIV" and "New International Version" trademarks are registered in the United States Patent and Trademark Office by International Bible Society. Use of either trademark requires the permission of International Bible Society.

Library of Congress Cataloging-in-Publication Data
Mason, Mike, 1952-
  The gospel according to Job / Mike Mason.
    p. cm.
  ISBN 1-58134-449-X
  1.Bible. O.T. Job—Meditations. I. Title.
BS1415.4.M37   1994
223'.106—dc20   93-42371

15	14	13	12	11	10	09	08	07	06	05	04	03	02
15	14	13	12	11	10	9	8	7	6	5	4	3	2	1

CONTENTS

For Bob Gemmell
Palma non sine pulvere

"I will never admit you are in the right; till I die, I will not deny my integrity. I will maintain my righteousness and never let go of it; my conscience will not reproach me as long as I live."

Job 27:5-6

"It is for freedom that Christ has set us free. Stand firm, then, and do not let yourselves be burdened again by a yoke of slavery."

Galatians 5:1

Introduction

O nce I met a man who, like Abraham, had moved his entire household halfway around the world on the strength of a vision from God. When I asked him to tell me the story, he answered that there were three versions of that story, and which one did I want to hear? First, there was the version of the story that he told to Christians. Then there was the version he told to non-Christians. Finally, there was the truth.

Job is a book that tells things from the third point of view. Probably, along with *Ecclesiastes*, it does this better than any other book in the Bible. Not that the other Scriptures do not tell the truth. But *Job* tells the truth in a way that makes it almost impossible to pervert the truth into pious pabulum.

A few years ago I went through a difficult time. Never mind what the problem was. It was nothing compared to the trials of Job. In fact, it was nothing at all compared to the sufferings of many of my neighbors right there on the quiet street where I lived. But pain is pain, and suffice it to say that my pain was enough to drive me to my knees, totally defeated, half-crazy at times, and crying out for relief. Month after month the battles raged on, thick, dark, agonizing. I prayed, but somehow prayer did not "work." Usually nothing at all worked, except lying low and gritting my teeth until, for reasons entirely obscure to me, the straightjacket of oppression began to loosen a little—at least enough for me to get on with my life for another day or so before the screws tightened again. What else could I do? How was I to fight this? In retrospect I can see that a large part of my anguish was rooted in the fact that there really was *nothing I could do* to control what was happening to me. I was absolutely helpless, and it is this, perhaps, that is the soul of suffering, this terrifying impotence. It is a little taste of the final and most terrifying impotence of all, which is death.

We Christians do not like to think about being absolutely helpless in the hands of our God. With all of our faith, and with all of His grace, we still prefer to maintain some semblance of control over our lives. When difficulties arise, we like to think that there are certain steps we can take, or attitudes we can adopt, to alleviate our anguish and be happy. Sometimes there are. But anyone who has truly suffered will know that when it comes to the real thing there is no help for it, no human help whatsoever. Simply put, when we are in a deep dark hole we cannot think our way out; neither can we hope, sing, pray, or even love our way out. In fact there is absolutely nothing either we or anyone else can do to better our situation. We can have faith, yes; but in itself faith will not change anything. Neither faith, nor any other good thing that a person might have or do, can actually lift the cloud, move the mountain, or bring about an end to the problem. Only the Lord Himself can do that, and when He does, as Exodus 6:6 puts it, "Then you will know that I am the Lord your God, who brought you out from under the yoke." How will we know? Simply because nothing and no one else could possibly have done it. In this kind of crucible, therefore, we come to a new understanding of what it means to be saved, what it means to be snatched away from the brink of destruction. Here we get down to the bedrock of the gospel.

During my night of anguish, I turned to the book of *Job*, and there I began to make contact with the gospel in a way that somehow I never had in studying the New Testament. Reading *Job*, I found myself experiencing in new and astonishing depth the reality of Jesus' promise in John 8:32, "You will know the truth, and the truth will set you free." Obviously this did not happen overnight. It happened over a period of about three years, and of course it is still happening. From the beginning of this process I took to writing little notes to myself. I had often kept a journal, but this was different. Now I was in desperate straits; my life was chaos. I did not have the time or the presence of mind to sit down at a desk and write coherently in the pages of a journal. Instead I would find myself waking up in the middle of the night, or at dawn, or I would jump up from having supper with my family, and frantically I would scribble something on any little scrap of paper I could lay hands on—an envelope, a corner of a newspaper, even toilet paper. I learned that I could write in pitch darkness, without being able to see the letters my hand was forming. For these thoughts I was having were as fleet as lightning, and they had to be caught and trapped or else they were gone. They were thoughts about the gospel as it was being revealed to me afresh in the pages of *Job*, and they had to be trapped and set down because they were setting me free.

At first I did not think of writing a book. But the little scraps of paper—these notes from the front of a horrific war that I was waging with the Devil, with myself, and with God—these notes grew into a stack, and gradually I saw that a pattern was emerging. After about a year of this scribbling I had sufficient composure to begin thinking about organizing my heap of notes into a series of short meditations on selected passages from *Job*. Going over and over the things I had written proved to be a therapeutic process in itself, and eventually, I think, I found myself actually listening to my own message and taking it to heart. I began, I suppose, to trust again. I began to trust, not merely God, but myself.

I do not mean this quite the way it sounds. As Jeremiah warned, "The heart is deceitful above all things" (17:9). But let me put it this way: when I became a Christian, God came to live in me. God lives in Heaven, but now He also lives in me. He lives in the deepest parts of me, and that means that as I walk with Him I can trust my deepest instincts. In fact, I *must* trust them, for they are the habitation of God. Knowing this gives a brand-new dignity to being human, and to all that being human entails. It gives one the sudden freedom to doubt, to be overwhelmed, to fail, to fear, to be angry, to have passions—in short, to be completely oneself. This is the kind of man Job was. What I discovered through my study of *Job* was that it is all right to be a human being. I found out that mercy is the permission to be human.

I have thought it important to set down something of how *The Gospel According to Job* came to be written. For I did not set out to write this book because I felt I understood *Job*; rather, in the act of writing, I began to understand. At the risk of sounding overly dramatic, I might even say that these chapters were written not with ink but with blood. Virtually every page was first composed under great pressure, at odd moments, on little scraps of paper. This writing was done not in an ivory tower but in an ebony hole. It records every inch of a tunnel that was dug with a teaspoon from barbed wire to freedom, and for that reason I hope and pray that it will speak directly to others who may be tunneling through spiritual crisis. I hope the message will be clear that there are no easy answers to suffering—that there is, for example, no such thing as getting a grip on oneself or pulling oneself up by the bootstraps. The only bootstrap in the Christian life is the cross. Sometimes laying hold of the cross can be comforting; but other times it is like picking up a snake.

Christ Himself found this out when He cried, "My God, my God, why have you forsaken me?"

Did I get angry at God during my struggles? You bet I did. I stood in the middle of my living room and screamed at Him. I pounded my fists on the floor. Once I slammed a door so hard that the molding shattered. I got far angrier with God than I have ever been with any human being. I do not defend this behavior. But in the course of it I did learn that such feelings are not at all incompatible with faith. On the contrary, faith involves our deepest passions engaged by the reality of God. Precisely because He is more real to us than anything else, He is able to sound both the top and the bottom of our registers in a way that no one and nothing else can. The person of faith is one who, like Job, knows what it is to be torn apart by the enormity of God.

Having said this, there is perhaps one note of caution I should sound about my interpretation of *Job*, which is that it is a highly personal and subjective one. Whether I have finally written more about Job and his God or more about myself, I do not know. What I do know is that much of the book is colored by a strong tendency to moodiness in my own temperament, and moreover by the stress and depression of a particular period in my life. In rewriting these chapters I have edited some of this out, but by no means all of it—for the simple reason that Scripture itself does not exhibit that sort of censorship. In people like Job, Jeremiah, the author of *Ecclesiastes*, and even in Jesus Himself, we see certain traits that may be very difficult for those blessed with naturally sanguine temperaments to identify with. Yet for the person who struggles and agonizes, the very blackness in the Bible is its gold. Just the presence in Scripture of a book so dark, chaotic, and thoroughly eccentric as *Job* should come as an immense comfort to any suffering believer. For the book says, in effect, "This is what faith is often like. Do not be surprised if you find yourself confused, doubting, afflicted, all but crushed. It does not mean you have lost favor with God."

To drive this message home, the book of *Job* does more than just address itself to the problem of suffering faith. It also addresses the problem of complacent faith, and it does this in the form of Job's three friends—Eliphaz, Bildad, and Zophar. Pharisees have trouble with this part of the story because it strikes too close to home. I say this out of personal experience, for as I came to write about Job's friends I found myself more and more strangely troubled about them. In many ways the characters of these men began to appear just as complex and puzzling as that of Job himself. What made them tick? I wondered. And where exactly did they stand with God? These were vital questions, I felt, and yet the more I thought about them and tried to reach some conclusions, the more disturbed and even angry I grew. Only gradually did it dawn on me that these feelings had less to do with Eliphaz, Bildad, and Zophar than they did with myself. What I mean is this: while I had begun this book thinking that I deeply identified with Job in his suffering, I ended by realizing that I identified just as deeply with Job's friends in their loveless pharisaism. Truly the Word of God is a two-edged sword! While *Job* is primarily a tale of one man's pain, there is also an implied sequel to the story, which concerns the peculiar suffering of the man's three friends as they are brought face-to-face with the treachery of their heartless rectitude.

Job, then, exposes and rails against religious hypocrisy just as Christ does in the *Gospels*. How significant it is that Jesus took His message not to the Gentile world, but rather to Jerusalem, straight to the heart of the highest and purest spiritual consciousness of His day. For the glorious beauty of the one true gospel shows up best not when it clashes with some obviously alien teaching, but rather when it is brought into direct opposition with a subtle distortion of itself. And the subtler the distortion, the more brightly shines the matchless pearl of the gospel.

One final warning I should issue about *The Gospel According to Job* is that, while it fulfills some of the functions of a commentary, it is primarily a devotional book, and devotionals are written with the deliberate intent of slowing reading down, indeed of stopping it altogether. The goal of devotional writing is to transform reading into prayer, and especially into a kind of prayer that the reader may never have practiced before. Like most books this one is far too long; I know that. But I make no apology for the length because *Job* itself seems to us too long a book. Suffering is a long subject, insufferably long. Besides, I do not expect everyone to read my book from cover to cover. People who are suffering do not (or at least should not) read that way. Rather, in weakness we learn to be gentle with ourselves, and we accept the freedom to read any book desultorily, pausing here and there as the mood may strike. The gospel is such a simple and homely thing—the sort of message that any child can understand and that certainly does not require 450 pages to explain.

So when the message hits home, lay the book aside. It is not anything new we need to hear but rather, in the words of Hebrews 2:1, to "pay more careful attention to what we have heard."

During a time of particular spiritual oppression, when I could not seem to shake the sense that God was implacably disappointed in me, I was walking by the ocean one morning when I spied a child's valentine lying in the sand. The message read, "You're okay with me, Valentine." I took it home and showed it to my wife, who promptly wrote on it, "To Mike / Love, God." Isn't it funny how a person can be a Christian and not really know the gospel? Isn't it strange how Christ can live inside us without our really enjoying Him? But perhaps it is not so strange. After all, we have only had this gospel for two thousand years. That is not a very long time for a fallen race to assimilate the incredible reality of inexhaustible mercy and eternal life. This gospel, it turns out, is not only good news—it is much *better* news than any of us has yet imagined.

A Note on Translation

The Scripture quotations in this book are primarily taken from the *New International Version*. However, because *Job* is one of the most difficult Old Testament books to translate, and because Bible scholars often disagree on the translation of specific texts, I have occasionally, after careful study and reflection, used my own paraphrase of passages from *Job* and other Bible books to convey more fully the sense intended. In addition, parts of quoted verses are sometimes taken from the *Jerusalem Bible*, the *King James Version*, or the *New American Standard Bible* when those translations have a better rendering of the text. All non-NIV renderings have been set in italics.

Finally, the reader will note that throughout this book divine pronouns have been capitalized, but copyright law will not permit the practice in NIV Scripture quotations.

THE PROLOGUE
Job 1–2

Then the Lord said to Satan, "Have you considered my servant Job? There is no one on earth like him; he is blameless and upright, a man who fears God and shuns evil."

—JOB 1:8

There is now no condemnation for those who are in Christ Jesus.

—ROM. 8:1

The Wizard of Uz

In the land of Uz there lived a man whose name was Job. (1:1a)

The book of *Job*, more even than most other Old Testament books, is shrouded in mystery when it comes to questions of historical origin and authorship. Traditionally it has been thought to be the oldest of all the Scriptures, predating even Genesis, and this lends the book an enigmatic, primal, almost chthonic aura. It is fascinating to think that as we open this text we may be faced with the earliest of all written accounts of a human being's relationship with Yahweh, the one true God. Sadly, most modern scholars do not share this view. But certainly those who favor a later dating must offer some explanation for one very curious fact: there is no reference anywhere in the book to the nation of Israel, nor to its temple, nor to its law or covenant or kings or prophets or Scripture, nor to any of the other religious milieu in which the rest of the Old Testament is steeped.

So there is something raw and wild about this book, something that defeats the scholars, something as immense and untamable as the leviathan that erupts off the page in Chapter 41. Even the theology of this odd work is, in a sense, self-contained, self-referencing. When bound with the Bible it assumes all the richness of that context. But in another way it stands alone, as Job himself does, against the tide. Perhaps for this reason, *Job* sits easily on the shelf right alongside the greatest masterpieces of the world's secular literature, from Homer to Shakespeare. This is a book that can hold its own anywhere, whether in the university lecture hall or the beer hall, and its hero is one who can strike a chord with people who have never felt drawn to any other Biblical story or figure, including Jesus. Many reject Jesus, but no one rejects Job. Rather, the world respects Job, and not with the grudging respect accorded Christ, but with a deep affinity untinged by reserve or fear. In the eyes of the world Job is less a saint than a comrade in arms. He did not found a cult or a religion, and he has never commanded any kind of following. Who would want to follow him? No, he is not even a religious figure at all, particularly, but is simply a man, and more than that, simply a man who suffered. In fact, rather than preaching in favor of religion Job preaches against it, and this is something that every sinner understands. It is something that every secular person understands, and every poor and outcast person, and every Marxist, and every skeptic, and every outlaw and prisoner, and everyone who knows any kind of pain. Simply by suffering so enormously, and by hanging on for dear life through it all, Job has won the world's heart and has come to embody the struggling sublimity of all mankind.

So Job is for everyone. He is Everyman. He is both an eastern and a western man, and he even manages, like Abraham, to be somehow both Jew and Gentile, and therefore a kind of prophetic forerunner of what Paul calls the "one new man [made] out of the two" (Eph. 2:15). To the Gentiles, Job is one of them, for there is nothing remotely Jewish about him. But to the Jews he is also one of them, for his knowledge of Yahweh is deeper than their own, and his faith in Yahweh is one that is in no way borrowed or adopted but that oozes out of his pores.

Job, then, is a book that floats strangely free, unchained to any particular culture or epoch. This man lived "in the land of Uz"— but where was that? No one knows. It could have been anywhere in the vast tract of exotic territories that lay east of Israel beyond the Jordan. It might as well have been the land of Oz where dwelt the famous Wizard. To be sure, the figure of the Wizard of Oz may appear at first glance to bear little resemblance to that of the great Sufferer of Uz. Yet the moral of the children's story is that this seemingly powerful and glorious master of the Emerald City turns out in the end to be no real "wizard" at all, but a mere man—and a rather pitiful, forlorn little man at that. His only wizardry, in other words, consists in being profoundly human.

And so it is with Job: the greatness of his faith, as we shall see again and again in this book, lies in the greatness of his mere humanity. Like the Apostle Paul this man's spirituality did not thrive upon covering up his weaknesses, but rather upon glorying in them, and so his faith stood up to having all his miserable frailty and human failure exposed and dragged out before all the world. Right from the beginning Job seems somehow to have known in his bones (though certainly he struggled with this knowledge) what the Wizard of Oz had sheepishly to learn: God's "power is made perfect in weakness" (2 Cor. 12:9).

A Blameless Man

This man was blameless and upright;
he feared God and shunned evil. (1:1b)

Not only the entire book of *Job* but the whole of the gospel may be summed up in this second half of the first verse. In fact, everything is summed up by this one word "blameless." For the central question of religion is, "How can human beings get free of guilt?" How can we escape that sense, however vague, of gnawing insecurity that dogs our every step? Jesus asked His disciples, "Why are you so afraid?" (Matt. 8:26). We are afraid because of our lingering suspicion that it is impossible to please God. Oh, we know that God loves us (maybe)—but how can we be sure He *likes* us? In the Parable of the Prodigal Son, the father loved both the rebellious son and his straightlaced elder brother, but in the end only the younger son pleased him. Only the prodigal delighted his father's heart.

Of course God loves us. Everybody knows that. But that is precisely the problem we have in relating to God: He loves everybody, indiscriminately, even the people He is going to send to Hell. Who needs love like that? The real question is not whether God loves us, but whether He approves of us, whether we are pleasing to Him. One thing is certain: if we are not pleasing to God, He will never be pleasing to us. Why should we like someone who is forever condemning us? On the other hand, can we imagine what it would be like to so move and excite the heart of God that He would run to meet us, throw His arms around us and kiss us, dress us in His best robe, and put rings on our fingers? Can we picture the Lord Almighty killing the fattened calf for us and throwing a big party in our honor? Can we imagine having the Creator of the universe say to us, just as He said to Jesus Christ, *"You are My beloved son, and I like you"* (Mark 1:11)?

In short, do we know what it would mean to be, as Jesus was and as Scripture claims Job also was, beyond reproach in the eyes of God? Can we even imagine such a thing? For if we cannot, then surely all our faith is useless. If we cannot get past God's criticism and into His favor—indeed, if we cannot be good friends with Him—then what is the point of all our religion? On the other hand, if Job really was a living example of blamelessness in his relationship with God, then such a thing must at least be possible, and we had better pay attention to this man and find out what his secret was.

The secret begins with a solid grasp of the fact that being "blameless" is not quite the same as being "guiltless." Objectively these two conditions are identical; but they are attained through different routes. If someone is guiltless, it simply means that he has done nothing wrong. If he is accused of wrong, then he is accused falsely and that is all there is to it. But if someone is blameless it means something far more mysterious: it means that no matter how horrible his offenses may have been, all the charges against him have been dropped. Absolutely no blame attaches to him, because the very one he offended has exonerated him. In the words of Psalm 32:2, "Blessed is the man whose sin the Lord does not count against him." God's covenant with us in Christ is not that He will prevent us from ever again committing a sin, but rather that He will forgive us our sins. He will be faithful in forgiveness. Our part is to believe this—that is, to be blameless not so much in our outward conduct (though obviously we strive for this also), but in our faith, our trust in the Lord's faithfulness. "It is with your heart that you believe and are justified" (Rom. 10:10). If we are blameless in this respect, then all the credit for our righteousness will very plainly be not ours but the Lord's, who, as Jude assures us in his great doxology, "is able to keep you from falling and to present you before his glorious presence without fault" (v. 24).

In *Job* we read the remarkable story of an Old Testament believer who somehow intuitively grasped and accepted this astounding message—so much so that even when he was tempted to the very uttermost to let go of it, still he held to it firmly against all odds. Under attack Job groaned, he wailed, he doubted and fell into deep depression, he lashed out like an infuriated animal—and yes, he even sinned. Yet when it came to this one point regarding the settled fact of his status of irreproachable blamelessness before the Lord, he refused to give an inch. Having placed his trust totally in God, he violently resisted the notion that there might still be some other step he should take, something else he must "do," to gain God's favor under adverse circumstances. Like Abraham, "against all hope, [he] in hope believed" (Rom. 4:18). In short, he had "the righteousness that comes from God and is by faith" (Phil. 3:9).

Rich and Righteous

He had seven sons and three daughters, and he owned seven thousand sheep, three thousand camels, five hundred yoke of oxen and five hundred donkeys, and had a large number of servants. He was the greatest man among all the people of the East. (1:2-3)

The Prologue section carries a strong patriarchal flavor. Job was a man like Abraham, a kind of Yahwistic sheik so rich and influential that his private estate would have been virtually a self-contained town. In the case of Abraham we know that his traveling tent-city consisted of at least "318 trained men born in his household" (Gen. 14:14). This implies a community, including women and children, of a thousand at the very least, and Job's domain appears to have been even larger than that.

Massive wealth is such a common phenomenon in modern civilization that we may easily miss the significance of this inventory of Job's estate. In the western world today even those who are among the top 5 percent of the world's wealthy are called "middle-class," and most of us who inhabit this bracket have (not surprisingly) a somewhat schizophrenic attitude toward our affluence. On one level we take it for granted, thinking of it as something to which we have a right or even as a sign of God's approval. Yet at a deeper level we know that we are only kidding ourselves. We know we live in a fool's paradise.

It is not that there is anything inherently bad about being rich. If God had been an ascetic He would never have created the world. Asceticism is a simplistic answer to a complex problem. Paul exposes the folly of the "Do not taste! Do not touch" approach when he cautions, "Such regulations have an appearance of wisdom . . . but they lack any value in restraining sensual indulgence" (Col. 2:20-23). There is no spiritual value in poverty, per se, but there is great worth indeed in the godly management of a large number of worldly goods and affairs.

Perhaps our problem today is that not many of us have the attitude toward our riches that Job had. Much later in the book we will catch a glimpse of what Job actually did with his money, and with his time and energy: he rescued the needy; he cared personally for the handicapped and the dying; he brought orphans into his home; he even took the power barons of his day to court and argued the case for the underprivileged (see 29:12-17; 31:16-21). Moreover, all of this was done without any government programs or assistance and without any tax benefits or receipts for charitable donations. If Job did not follow the letter of Jesus' command to "sell everything you have and give to the poor," he did follow its spirit, by administering all his resources not for his own good but for the good of society. He was, one might say, a true communist in the best sense of that word, in that the principles and ideals of socialism welled up out of his heart. When Jesus warned, "How hard it is for the rich to enter the kingdom of God" (Mark 10:23), He was pointing to the tendency of lucre first to bury itself in a man's pocket, and then to bury the man. But Job's wealth did not cling to him—it flowed through him. He was not so much a collector of wealth as a distributor of it, not an owner but a steward. That is why he could say so readily, "*The Lord gives and the Lord takes away*" (1:21). Job was that rarest of millionaires—one who was not "filthy rich" but rather "clean rich," not rich as sin but rich as righteousness. In fact it is worth noting that he had a goodly measure of the very things with which the Devil would tempt Jesus in the wilderness—not fantastic wealth alone, but with it the political and spiritual power that money inevitably attracts. With great wealth comes great responsibility, and like the other Biblical patriarchs Job must have led a tremendously busy life, filled with hard work and practical cares. No hut-dwelling hermit or introverted pietist, he was an active man of the world, continually rubbing shoulders with other people and meeting the challenges and stresses of ordinary life. These will be important facts to remember as we come to reflect upon his approaching ordeal.

In contemporary terms, perhaps the gist of this opening character sketch is that here was the sort of man who could have been President of the United States without it turning his head. One might wonder whether there is one such person alive in the world today. It is a sign of Job's great faith that he was able to handle such an extensive empire and still remain "blameless and upright."

Job's Prayer Life

His sons used to take turns holding feasts in their homes, and they would invite their three sisters to eat and drink with them. When a period of feasting had run its course, Job would send and have them purified. Early in the morning he would sacrifice a burnt offering for each of them, thinking, "Perhaps my children have sinned and cursed God in their hearts." This was Job's regular custom. (1:4-5)

How precious are the few sketchy details we have concerning Job's daily life prior to his downfall. After this, everything we learn about this man will come by way of conversation, and our view of him will be colored by the opinions of others and by the stress of his altered circumstances. Yet here in the Prologue we see Job from a purely objective viewpoint, through the lens of omniscient narration. And what is it we see? In the last chapter we saw Job as a practical man immersed in the whirl of business and management; but in the verses above we learn something of his spiritual life in the midst of that whirl. In particular, we see him on his knees praying for his family. Job knew that family gatherings can be hotbeds of vice. Childhood wounds reopen, in-laws are treated like outlaws, and sibling rivalry has not changed much since the days of Cain and Abel. Perhaps no sin is more shameful and scandalous than that which regularly breaks out when families assemble and strive so frantically, so pathetically, so naively to have a good time together. Conversely, if one is charitable toward brothers, sisters, parents and cousins, then one is charitable indeed. Without a frank admission of the horror of family sin, Job's manner of prayer may seem almost ludicrously overscrupulous. But nothing says more about a person than the way he or she prays, and so this curious detail about the old patriarch's regular early-morning sacrifices suggests several important facts about his faith—facts which, while obvious, are worth spelling out:

First of all, Job believed in the efficacy of mediation with God. He had implicit faith in repentance, sacrifice, and forgiveness. He knew that such things worked. His God was not distant and unresponsive, but "compassionate and gracious . . . slow to anger, abounding in love" (Ex. 34:6).

Secondly, like the other patriarchs Job apparently served as his own priest. Thus this story takes us back to the original "priesthood of all believers," to that fearsome time before the law when all the children of God set up their own altars and got their own hands bloody and somehow found direct access to the throne of God, just as Christians do today.

Thirdly, Job practiced his priesthood not only on his own behalf but on behalf of others. His spiritual life was not confined to the state of his own soul before God, but his prayers included deep concern for other souls, and this shows how joyously confident he must have been in his own salvation. Only one who is himself secure and happy in the Lord can pray effectively for others. Job's devotions were outward-looking and people-loving, and he took it on faith that his intercessions had a practical effect upon the welfare of those he loved.

Finally, and most remarkably, Job's prayers extended even into the murky realm of inadvertent or unconscious sin. His prayer for his children is akin to Jesus' prayer from the cross, "Father, forgive them, for they do not know what they are doing" (Luke 23:34). Job's faith in forgiveness was comprehensive enough that it completely covered not just individual known acts of sin, but sin itself, and this shows a fundamental grasp of the gospel.

This last point is essential to a proper understanding of all that follows. For in the gospel according to Job a person is either righteous, or not. One cannot be a little bit righteous any more than one can be a little bit pregnant. Either one's sin is completely forgiven (including not just sinful behavior but the innate sinfulness of the heart) or it is not. Christ's great principle of prayer—"Believe that you have received it, and it will be yours" (Mark 11:24)—applies first of all to the unconditional forgiveness that is the basic promise of the gospel. If God accepts us at all, He accepts us wholeheartedly, and He covers us completely with the spotless robe of righteousness. This robe of divine acceptance does not come in gray, but only in dazzling white, and one either has the robe or not. One is either righteous or wicked. And anyone who is wicked can have that status quickly amended by a trip to the cross.

Satan

One day the angels came to present themselves before the
Lord, and Satan also came with them. The Lord said to
Satan, "Where have you come from?" Satan answered the
Lord, "From roaming through the earth and going back and
forth in it." (1:6-7)

Unlike Job, Satan has no responsibilities. All he has to do all
day long is go gadding about in the world. He is a restless,
shiftless, roving hoodlum. He is like the delinquent kid who
comes slinking home in the wee hours of the morning, his face ashen
with dissipation, and when asked by his dad what he's been up to
answers evasively, "Just cruisin' around, Pop. What's it to ya?" The
Father Almighty, however, will not settle for such insolent vagueness. Yet neither does He lose His temper. Instead the Lord sharp-
ens the focus of the conversation with a provocative gibe of His
own, saying (to paraphrase 1:8), "You ought to try hanging around
with Job. Now there's a kid who knows the meaning of respect."

There is certainly an odd informality about this interview
between God and Satan. While it is true that Satan must "present"
himself to the Lord, as servant to Master, once these two are
together they do not seem to stand much on ceremony, but instead
they come straight to the point. Satan sauces, and the Lord boasts.
Even in such a sketchy dialogue we are left with the distinct impression that here are two individuals who *know* each other—indeed
who likely know each other only too well, to the point of transcen-
dental nausea. The Lord knows Satan through and through, and
Satan too, after his own perverted fashion, knows the Lord like the
back of his hand. Is this not precisely the way things stand between
archenemies? After all, these two have cased each other since who
knows when. Sadly, seldom are two friends more mutually attentive
and solicitous than are a pair of inveterate foes.

But who, exactly, is this ancient rival of the Lord, and what is he
doing among the holy angels before the heavenly throne? From the
sound of things he seems just to blunder in right off the street,

almost as if he owned the place! Surely this is one of the deepest
enigmas in the story of *Job*—not just that such awesome power and
privileges are bestowed with such seeming casualness upon this cosmic hooligan, but that the man who suffers so monstrously at
Satan's hands is kept entirely in the dark as to the very existence of
his spiritual foe. Nowhere in the long and exhaustive dialogue
between Job and his friends is the idea of personal, supernatural evil
so much as broached as a possibility. The whole subject is a locked
room. Satan is mentioned only in these first two chapters, and even
here, as elsewhere in the Old Testament, the Hebrew word is not
even a personal name but rather a title or office. Literally it is "the
satan," a term meaning "accuser" or, as he might be called today in
a court of law, "the Prosecution."

Just as the term "Christ" (or "anointed one") does not come to
assume personal weight until the advent of Jesus, so only in the New
Testament does the shadowy figure of "the satan" step fully out of
the wings. This personalization of evil began to take shape during the
intertestamental period, but the revelation remained blurred until
Jesus met Satan face-to-face in the wilderness, and then proceeded to
expose the Devil's dark identity and all his evil works before the
world. Ever since then this work of unmasking the face of evil has
continued, and is due to climax in the revelation of what the New
Testament calls "the man of lawlessness" (2 Thess. 2:1-12)—that figure who in some unthinkable way is to be the incarnation of Satan,
the very "son" of the Devil, just as Jesus is the incarnate Son of God.
The whole story of the Bible might be summarized as the gradual
unveiling of the profoundly personal character of both good and evil.

What is so very strange about the Prologue of *Job* is that it seems
to take us back to a time when Satan presumed to occupy the rightful place of Christ as the favored son, to a time when Satan apparently had the very ear of God and could ask Him for whatever he
wanted. This picture gives new and pointed force to Jesus' triumphant assertion in Luke 10:18, "I saw Satan fall like lightning
from heaven!" If Job was kept in the dark about these things, it
could only have been because the personal knowledge of Satan, this
breathtakingly cunning and powerful enemy of his soul, would simply have been too terrifying, too searing a knowledge for any human
being to have borne, without at the same time having the full revelation of the saving victory of Jesus Christ on the cross and of His
ascent to the right hand of the Father forevermore.

The Lord's Boast

Then the Lord said to Satan, "Have you considered my servant Job? There is no one on earth like him; he is blameless and upright, a man who fears God and shuns evil." (1:8)

Worldly praise is one thing, but the praise that comes from Heaven is quite another. Job was great among men, but he was also great in the eyes of God. In the Lord's own words, "There is no one on earth like him." Job would have been among the top ten, perhaps, of the finest human beings who have ever lived, and without this fact firmly in mind the rest of the story will be out of focus.

This verse leaves no doubt that Job really was a "blameless and upright" man and that such was not simply the subjective opinion of the book's author. Job's righteousness was a divinely attested fact, and from the very beginning it is the Lord Himself—not Job or any other human being—who sets out to justify this man and to establish his innocence. Moreover, this is not a defensive reaction on the Lord's part, but an offensive initiative. It is the Lord who issues the first challenge, the first taunt, by aggressively boasting to Satan about Job. Thus the unimpeachable righteousness of Job is the very core of the book, the linchpin upon which the entire plot hangs. God's praise for His servant is so open and lavish, and His backing so unqualified, that if at any point in the ensuing struggle we are tempted to question the integrity of Job's faith (as his friends do, relentlessly), it will not really be Job we are questioning, but the Lord.

Is there not something shocking about this, something almost flatly unacceptable—that the holy and awesome Creator of the universe should declare of a mere man (a man obviously flawed) that He finds not the slightest fault in him, and that this same God should then deliberately set out to defend this man against any and all detractors? Yet right here lies the unsearchable mystery of the gospel. For this same condition of imputed, impeccable righteousness is not only humanly possible, but is an established fact for every believer in the Messiah of God (whether before Christ's actual coming or after it). And Job, as we shall see, was undoubtedly a believer in the coming Christ.

In Christian terms it is often explained that God "sees" believers as being righteous, even though we are not, because He sees us "in Christ." When He looks at us He sees not us, but Jesus. Yet how can this be? Does it make any real sense? Consider, for a moment, the analogy of a garden sown with seeds. No one sees these seeds, for they are hidden in the ground. But the gardener knows they are there, and so he tends them, waters them, fertilizes the soil, and perhaps even builds a fence around his little plot. Anyone who had no knowledge of plants would think the gardener was crazy, lavishing all this attention upon an empty, barren patch of ground. The mystery is that the gardener cherishes his invisible seeds no less dearly than he would if they had already produced the full and bounteous crop he is expecting from them. While seeds in their ungerminated state may appear virtually worthless, he regards them as being inestimably precious because he knows their potential. Though strictly speaking seeds are "imperfect" (in the sense of being incomplete), nevertheless the gardener handles them with just as much careful regard as he would the perfect, full-grown fruit or flower, for he is mindful (and he alone is mindful) that already these homely little specks contain the blueprint of perfection.

Just so does the mustard seed of true faith earn God's full respect. If the mature plant is going to be perfect—and it will be—then so must be the seed. In this first chapter of *Job* the *King James Version* actually translates the Hebrew word for "blameless" as "perfect" (both in 1:1 and 1:8), and it is a shame that modern translations shy away from this term. For does not the New Testament assure us that Christ "has made perfect forever those who are being *sanctified*" (Heb. 10:14)? And does not Jesus command, "Be perfect . . . as your heavenly Father is perfect" (Matt. 5:48)? Would God expect us to do the impossible? Surely not—except by His grace! And that is precisely the point: it is God's grace, and nothing else, that declares a person perfect. It is in God's eyes that people achieve perfection, not in their own or in the world's. In our Heavenly Father's garden perfection is by faith and not by sight.

The Duel

"Does Job fear God for nothing?" Satan replied. . . .
"Stretch out your hand and strike everything he has, and he
will surely curse you to your face." The Lord said to Satan,
"Very well, then, everything he has is in your hands."
(1:9-12)

Why does God allow Job's suffering? Why does He give in (and so easily!) to the capricious demands of Satan? Why does the Lord Almighty give Satan so much as the time of day? "Very well then," says God, like one gentleman to another. But what is so very well about it? Does the Lord have any idea of what He is doing? The first chapter of *Job*, without directly addressing this question of God's tolerance of Satan, does lay down two important principles concerning the mystery of evil.

First of all, it shows beyond any question that people of faith can and do experience terrible afflictions according to the will of God, yet through no particular fault of their own. "You incited me against him to ruin him without any reason," insists the Lord to Satan in 2:3, and this thought in itself should be a source of inestimable comfort to any suffering believer. In the words of Psalm 34:19, "A righteous man may have many troubles, but the Lord delivers him from them all."

Secondly, the Prologue clearly establishes that the real struggle in the book is not between Job and his God, but rather between God and Satan. It is a celestial battle, fought on earth, a sort of duel between good and evil. Now a duel, it should be noted, is not at all the same as a war. For in war, as in love, all's fair and anything goes. But not so in a duel. A duel is a highly formal, almost civilized contest between two combatants in which the circumstances are scrupulously controlled so as to make the odds as even as they can possibly be. Neither party is to have an unfair advantage, and to that end the duelists choose identical weapons and observe a strict ritual, a code of conduct. In a duel the point that is being proved has nothing to do with brute strength, nor even, in the final analysis, with skill or

marksmanship. Rather, what is on the line is that peculiar commodity known as *honor*. The entire rationale for the contest is the
defense of personal honor.

In the case of a spiritual quarrel between God and Satan, surely it
would be perfectly legitimate for the omnipotent Lord of the universe
simply to parade His superior strength and prowess by unleashing
his big cannons against the Devil's pea-shooter. But the problem, in
terms of honor, is whether such a triumph would prove anything.
Would it—as insane as this might sound—be fair? No, it would not
be fair at all, but lopsided. From the standpoint of honor such a fight
would be rigged, and so in the end it would prove nothing.

So what is fair? In an area as subtle and abstruse as the honor of
celestial beings, what are the ground rules? What possible code of
ethics might apply? Where is the common territory upon which
these two inscrutable adversaries can meet? And what common
weapon might they employ that would be truly equitable to both?

The answer, of course, is *man*. Human beings, soul and body, are
the dueling ground where heavenly powers clash. It is as though two
magnificent warriors were to strip themselves entirely of armor,
throwing aside not just weapons and shields but raiment itself, and
were to step forward stark naked and join in hand-to-hand combat,
wrestling in the mud. For this, finally, is the only way in which the
Lord Almighty can begin to prove moral supremacy over the Devil
without in any way drawing upon His infinitely greater resources of
brute strength.

God's omnipotence, remember, is never in question in this fight.
Like it or not, even Satan is compelled to bow before the throne of
God. But what *is* being disputed in dubious battle on earth is God's
moral *right* to omnipotence, His mandate to rule. It is a question of
honor that is at stake, and therefore the theater of conflict must be
one that is appropriate to the display of purely moral qualities.

Who will win the prize of humanity's allegiance and praise? Will
it be the Lord or the Devil? To whom, in the crunch, will man
entrust his soul? The test is an eminently fair one. Indeed if the
advantage falls either way it is to Satan, in that the duel ends up
being fought not in the full light of day, but in confusion and darkness, on the Devil's own turf. And so in bewilderment and in exquisite torment man, through the subtle moods and shades and turnings
of his own high-mettled spirit, selects the winner. He is the weapon
of choice between giants.

Feathers and Millstones

"Your sons and daughters were feasting and drinking wine at the oldest brother's house, when suddenly a mighty wind swept in from the desert and struck the four corners of the house. It collapsed on them and they are dead." (1:18-19)

The sudden calamities that befell Job are too numerous, too horrible, and almost too fantastic to need rehearsing. Suffice it to say that his whole world caved in overnight. He lost everything, and in one final, fell swoop his entire family of ten grown children was wiped out by a desert whirlwind. Moreover, thirty-six chapters of agonizing soul-searching will elapse before the Lord so much as lifts a finger to begin comforting Job in these devastating losses. What a contrast this presents to the former security of Job's life, which was precisely the object of Satan's complaint in 1:10: "Have you not put a hedge around him and his household and everything he has? You have blessed the work of his hands, so that his flocks and herds are spread throughout the land." We can see Satan chomping at the bit for a chance to break through this hedge of blessings and plant a forest of thorns.

Few Christians are called upon to suffer the crushing spate of disasters that Job did. But does this mean that the ordinary person, going through the ordinary struggles and setbacks of life, cannot identify with him? Not at all. For Job in his sufferings is essentially a figure like Christ on the cross, a person with whom all the world can identify in spite of his absolute uniqueness. We do not need to have nails driven into our hands and feet to know what a cross is. A cross is a cross. To be crushed is to be crushed, and we have all had a taste of it. Countless people have committed suicide with far less provocation than Job had, and what to one person seems a feather is to another a millstone. Even feathers, when blown about by the Devil, can stir up quite enough trouble of their own.

When Jesus said, "Sufficient unto the day is the evil thereof" (Matt. 6:34, KJV), He was talking about everyone's day. Yet who has not caught themselves wishing at times that they could fight more glamorous battles than the ones they actually face? Glamor is one of Satan's great drawing cards. Yet what is the good of beating the Devil at cancer only to lose out to the common cold? Is it not just as important to defeat him in the corner store as in the concentration camp? "When the devil had finished all this tempting," reads Luke 4:13, "he left [Jesus] until an opportune time." It is the timing of the Devil's attacks, as much as the magnitude of them, that can crush us.

There can even be a dangerous false humility (in other words, spiritual pride) in saying, "I really have nothing to complain about, especially when I think about so-and-so whose husband has just died, or about all the starving children in the world." For the real question has nothing to do with so-and-so or with all the starving children. The real question is whether I myself, in my own unique set of circumstances, am giving glory and thanks to God from my heart. If I am not, then it makes no difference whether the problem I face is a big thing or a little thing. For the smallest of complaints can spoil fellowship with God. Just one. We see this principle plainly illustrated in marriage, where it can happen that just one unresolved tension, just one episode of stubbornness, just one dirty sock or unmowed lawn can be enough to provoke a bitter argument. So the point is not how big or how little the problem is; the point is the quarrel itself, the wrecked relationship. The point is whether one's own particular burden is being borne in the bitterness and pride of the flesh, or in the grace of God.

So let us not get trapped into comparing lots, whether in terms of troubles or of blessings. As Paul put it, "Each one should test his own actions. Then he can take pride in himself, without comparing himself to somebody else, for each one should carry his own load" (Gal. 6:4-5). Whatever our trials may be, we are not to begrudge them; but neither let us make the opposite mistake of underestimating or belittling them. Jesus did not sing sprightly choruses on the cross; He hung there and suffered.

Worship

Job got up and tore his robe and shaved his head.
Then he fell to the ground in worship. (1:20)

The words of worship that flow from Job's mouth in this time of unspeakable tragedy form one of the most moving and exalted verses in all of Scripture. Whenever people talk of Job it is this very first utterance of his that is quoted, as he falls on his face in the dust and sings, "Naked I came from my mother's womb, and naked I will depart. *The Lord gives and the Lord takes away: Blessed be the name of the Lord!*" (1:21).

After the Prologue Job will appear to us to move very far away from these clear and simple statements of faith. Often he will seem even to repudiate them. Nevertheless, because he shows himself at the outset to be a man for whom worship is second nature, his faith is justly celebrated. Worship is his initial response, worship is the spontaneous reaction to tragedy that wells up out of his soul, and somehow everything he says later on must be judged in the light of this fact. For we know that under such circumstances worship does not come to a person naturally or spontaneously, but rather it is a practiced response, a fruit of long faith and discipline. Job could never have reacted as he did unless he had been practicing for this moment all his life.

Before we consider the actual words of Job's worship, we need to pause and take careful note of the attitude of heart in which they were offered. Was Job, in the midst of his grief and turmoil, somehow at peace? Was he filled with a strange spiritual joy? No, not at all. He was as broken and cast down as a man can be. Granted, he apparently summoned the presence of mind to shear off all his hair and then to take a straight razor and drag it across his scalp (no mean task, as anyone who has ever tried it can testify). But if Job's hand was uncannily steady just now, surely it was not from being cool and collected, but rather from being in a state of shock.

Can true worship really transpire when the heart is broken and the mind shocked and dulled with horror? Is there any place in worship for bitter tears and wailing? Just one chapter later we will hear

Job groan, "May the day of my birth perish" (3:1). Has his worship ceased by this point? Has mere self-pity overtaken him? Or can groaning be a part of worship too?

Think of Mary at the foot of the cross: was it a sweet and mystical experience for her to stand there and watch her son die? No doubt years later, looking back on that day, she had more tender feelings. But at the time, surely, it was hellish. And so it will be for us whenever we make direct contact in our daily lives with the central object of mystery in Christian worship, the cross. It is marvelous to meditate on the cross and to be flooded with peace and joy. But that is the Holy Spirit showing us the effects of the cross; it is not the cross itself. It is wonderful to be filled with mystical rapture at the thought of Calvary. But more wonderful still, because more worshipful, is the moment when the rough wood touches our flesh and the nail bites. Real worship has less to do with offering sacrifices than with being a sacrifice ourselves. "*Present your bodies as a living sacrifice, holy and acceptable to God,*" urges Paul, "*for this is your spiritual worship*" (Rom. 12:1).

How writers like Paul and the author of *Job* stretch our religious vocabulary! Reading their books, old words like *worship* and *faith* and *righteousness* begin to sound different to our ears; they grow bigger and broader and deeper than we have known them to be. They become like oceans, into which any number of pebbles, boulders, even whole mountains may be thrown, yet without altering their fundamental nature. Conversely, how easy it is to turn religious words into stagnant ponds or to dry them up altogether. But Job makes these words breathe for us, he brings them alive. And what does it mean when language comes alive? It means that human beings are set free. As definitions expand and broaden, so does our freedom of movement within them. Perhaps there is no better test of the presence of true faith than when a staid old word like *justification* gets off its duff and begins to sing and dance around, or when *patience* pulls faces and stamps its feet, or when *worship* tears its robe, shaves its head, and falls prostrate on the ground. Reading *Job*, we discover that this man's God is bigger than our own, and because his God is this big we too grow big—bigger and more mysterious than we ever imagined ourselves to be.

Nakedness

*"Naked I came from my mother's womb,
and naked I will depart." (1:21a)*

Job knew one of the great secrets of faith: the believer in God has
no worldly rights. The true believer is someone who has abdicated all rights, freely accepting the status of a slave and no
longer laying claim to any earthly chattel, whether it be "houses or
brothers or sisters or father or mother or children or fields" (Matt.
19:29). These are precisely the sort of things that Job has just lost,
and yet his initial response to their loss is not bitter complaint, nor
even mere acquiescence, but adoration.

In many places in the world today we see people fighting and lob-
bying under the banner of Christianity for all sorts of human rights
and freedoms, both personal and political. To what extent the Bible
actually recognizes such rights is a complex question. But in terms
of individual spirituality, at least, the mature Christian should know
that he has no right even to the shirt on his back or to his next meal,
let alone the right to vote, to have a pension, to enjoy good health,
or to get eight hours of sleep every night. Strictly speaking the servant of Christ does not even have a right to his own private thoughts
and feelings, whether they be good, bad or indifferent. As the Lord
pointedly put it to a sulking Jonah, "Have you any right to be
angry?" (4:4).

The fact is, Christians have abdicated one kingdom in favor of
another. They have released their hold on this world's elaborate system of amenities and expectations, in order to embrace something
infinitely higher. In practice this letting go can be a delicate process,
for as citizens of the Kingdom of Heaven we certainly do have
rights, but what we do not have is *worldly* rights. "Were you a slave
when you were called? Don't let it trouble you," advises Paul—
though at the same time he hastens to add, "If you can gain your
freedom, do so" (1 Cor. 7:21). Worldly freedom, in other words,
may be a good thing for the Christian, but it is not an entitlement.
The children of God have the Lord's own promise that "I will pay

you whatever is right" (Matt. 20:4); yet what is right is to be calculated not in earthly terms but in heavenly. As Jesus taught, "Any of you who does not give up everything he has cannot be my disciple" (Luke 14:33).

For a Christian to insist on having worldly rights and comforts is, plainly and simply, to be a grumbler. It is to be like the Israelites in the desert when they were continually murmuring against God. How often do we as believers waste precious time and energy trying to "claim" things that, as those whose lot in this life is nothing more than to share the cross of Christ, we have no right to claim? The tragedy is that meanwhile we neglect to claim the spiritual rights that are properly ours. In our pursuit of worldly contentment, we forfeit spiritual joy and peace.

Already we have made the point that God not only *loves* believers, He *likes* them. But what about our feelings toward Him? If we claim to love God, do we also like Him? Are we genuinely fond of the Lord? Do we like the way He does things? Do we approve of His methods of child-rearing? Or do we secretly resent Him whenever life does not go our way? Can we enjoy God, and yet not enjoy the life He has given us, not bless our own unique incarnation in all its fantastic variety and unpredictability?

We Christians are people who know in our bones that we never had any right to be created in the first place, let alone redeemed. We know we have no more inherent title to life and its goodness than a dead man has. For us the coffin lid has already been nailed shut on all the natural joys and privileges that earth can offer. Knowing this, we are set free to bless the Lord in all circumstances, whether we find ourselves clothed or naked.

When Adam discovered he was naked, he hid from the Lord. But when Job was faced with his nakedness he worshiped, and this is what sets the fallen man apart from the redeemed man. Even Christ, after all, when He came into the world, came naked. And He died naked too. The *Gospels* plainly state that soldiers divided Jesus' garments among them at the foot of the cross, including His undergarment. The pictures do not usually show this; it is almost as though the sight of God's nakedness would be somehow more appalling than His death. But in the full Biblical revelation it is clear that God became not only man, but man naked and helpless, and that both at the beginning and at the end of the Lord's earthly life His bare flesh had to be wrapped in rags like that of any other poor wretch.

Luck

"The Lord gives and the Lord takes away;
blessed be the name of the Lord!" (1:21b)

Job's remarkable statement here takes us back to the very primitive (and some would say pagan) concept of *chance* or *luck*. Job is basically saying that there is good luck and there is bad luck and that God administrates them both, and not only is it His divine prerogative to do so, but for every one of His seemingly arbitrary decrees He is to be praised. Whether in the casinos of Las Vegas or in the parliaments of the nations, it is God who picks up the roulette ball and places it wherever He will. It is He who shuffles the deck—even if He does not shuffle but rather arranges each card as carefully as He numbers the hairs on a head. Whether luck exists at all, from God's point of view, is a good question. But from the human standpoint, there is so much of the divine patterning that cannot be understood, that we might as well chalk it up to luck. Why does one person have red hair and another brown? Why is one sick and another well? Why does one die young and another live to see four generations—and all without any regard for individual spiritual beliefs? There are no good religious answers to these questions. There is only the nonreligious answer: the luck of the draw.

To believe in God is to accept the nonreligious answer. It is to allow for the fact that the Deity behind the strange and inexplicable façade of this world is a real, living person, and therefore a person with not only rational plans and ideas, but also with nonrational intuitions, feelings, and even whims of His own. To know the Lord in this way is, in some respects, just like knowing anybody else, for in our dealings with other people do we not inevitably run up against a large measure of pure unfathomable irrationality? People would not be people if they were entirely reasonable, and so it is with God. How reasonable is grace? Or love? Many cannot believe in God because they cannot stomach His whims. But to allow the Lord His whimsicalness—and more than that, to bless Him for it—is faith.

This topic turns out to be the the crux of a good deal of the long debate between Job and his friends. The friends could never have made the statement in 1:21. It would have been too arbitrary, too superstitious for their liking. Good religious people do not believe in luck; they believe in finding reasons for everything. They are always trying to figure out why they are having a bad day, or why they are sick, or why they are not more happy or prosperous. This type of thinking, which forever tries to appease and manipulate the god behind every bush and rock, is a kind of paganism. In this tight theology there is no room for the sheer arbitrary unreasonableness of the Lord. By contrast, the mind that is able to live with unanswerable questions, letting the roulette ball spin at will and yet still seeing the Lord's hand at work—this is the mind of true faith. This is the faith that can respond, whether in good luck or in bad, "Amen!"

The moment we start thinking that we can discern some pattern to the ways of the Lord, we begin to draw dangerously near to idolatry. We come to worship the pattern rather than the Person behind it. We see patterns everywhere, as in tea leaves, and so grow preoccupied with technique rather than relationship. Patterns become molds into which we try and squeeze all of reality, whether it fits or not. In modern times the most obvious example of this is science. Certainly there are patterns in God's universe to be discovered and legitimately exploited; but no pattern can encompass all of reality. When a pattern or system attempts to be all-inclusive, the final result is that it excludes the most vital factor of all: God. This is not to say that God is not rational, only that mere rationality does not completely define His being.

To the ancient Hebrews pure chance, far from being an idea opposed to God, was one of the very things that proclaimed His sovereignty. Why else would they have cast lots and employed the device of "Urim and Thummim" to discern the Lord's will (see Ex. 28:30)? "The lot is cast into the lap, but its every decision is from the Lord" (Prov. 16:33). Luck was just one more of the enigmatic channels through which God worked. The mere fact that we are alive at all—is that not lucky? That a loving Heavenly Father has preordained every detail of human lives does not mean that there is any discernible reason why the ball lands on 7 rather than 15. While there is much about God that can be known, this is not what the book of *Job* is about. *Job* is about the incomprehensible ways of God, and about the praise that is due Him in bad luck as in good.

Skin for Skin

"Skin for skin!" Satan replied. "A man will give all he has for his own life. But stretch out your hand and strike his flesh and bones, and he will surely curse you to your face." (2:4-5)

Just as in the temptation of Jesus in the wilderness, the Devil here quotes God's own law to Him: eye for eye, tooth for tooth, and "skin for skin." It is almost as though Satan, having overheard Job's lofty thoughts concerning man's humble status of utter nakedness before the Lord, determines to take him at his word and make him more naked still, tearing off even his bare flesh and flailing him alive.

When it comes to the topic of physical pain, people who are not actually experiencing such pain can entertain all kinds of noble theories about it. As long as it is happening to someone else, pain is but an abstraction, a theological conundrum, an unfortunate blight on an otherwise fairly tolerable world. But as soon as the Devil so much as touches a person's own body, the whole picture changes. Then suffering becomes the very opposite of an abstraction: it becomes an enormity, a concrete reality so overwhelming that it has the power to engulf all other reality, to eclipse all other thought except the thought of itself.

The Bible contains many graphic descriptions of what happens when strong, intelligent, self-assured people (and even some very godly ones) are caught suddenly in the grip of acute pain. Warns the Old Testament in one of its most oft-repeated images, *"Pangs of anguish will seize them, they will writhe like a woman in labor"* (Isa. 13:8). It is true that many believers are enabled by God's grace to bear enormous burdens of physical pain with dignity and even with radiant cheerfulness. Nevertheless a much smaller degree of pain, when applied to other believers who may be just as godly, can be enough to plunge them into depression or make them lose all control and whimper and scream for mercy. Even the great and good King Hezekiah, in one of the most piteous scenes in the Bible, when stricken with a mortal illness "turned his face to the wall" and "wept bitterly" (2 Kings 20:2-3). He simply could not take it.

At its deepest level, much of the meaning of *Job* revolves around the distinction between these two vastly different perspectives on suffering: on the one hand, the coolly considered outsider's view, and on the other hand, the view from inside the furnace. As for the latter, it is not really a "view" at all and even to call it that is to do the sufferer an injustice. One does not hold rational, articulate opinions when one is writhing in pain. Pure suffering has a consciousness, a tongue, a heart all its own, and even the memory of it is but a pale unreality when compared with the actual experience. Only the sufferer himself, in the moment of piercing torment, knows what it is really like, and his knowing is of a sort that drastically alters the very meaning of the verb "to know."

It could almost be said that the sufferer's knowledge of pain is of the same order as the believer's knowledge of God and that this is why the Devil exploits pain as a prime vehicle of temptation. Restlessly he casts about for something that will prove more compelling, more absorbing, more real than God Himself, for he believes that to find that something (and in this he is perhaps partly right) would be to dislodge God from His throne. After surveying all the possibilities, his final choice lights on physical pain. It is no accident that the place where the Lord and the Devil themselves join ultimate battle—the cross—is a rack of torture.

So the stakes are very high when Satan afflicts Job with "painful sores from the soles of his feet to the top of his head" (2:7). At this point the central question of the book subtly shifts from, "Can a man lose everything he has and still bless God?" to, "Can a man lose even what he *is* and still remain under God's blessing?" For enough agony, like enough joy, can alter a person's most basic makeup. How much pain can a human being take and still nurse the fond notion that *"nothing in all creation can separate us from the love of God"* (Rom. 8:39)?

On the Ash Heap

*So Satan went out from the presence of the Lord and
afflicted Job with painful sores from the soles of his feet to
the top of his head. Then Job took a piece of broken pottery
and scraped himself with it as he sat among the ashes. (2:7-8)*

Without attempting a medical diagnosis of Job's condition,
let us just listen to what he himself says about it at various stages in the book: "My body is clothed with worms
and scabs, my skin is broken and festering" (7:5); "My gauntness
rises up and testifies against me . . . my face is red with weeping, deep
shadows ring my eyes" (16:8, 16); "My whole frame is but a
shadow" (17:7); "Night pierces my bones; my gnawing pains never
rest. . . . My skin grows black and peels; my body burns with fever"
(30:17, 30).

Anyone who has ever had a severe skin disorder will know that
it is the sort of thing that can drive a person half-crazy. How
pathetic and heart-wrenching to read of the shard of pottery with
which Job scrapes his boils! Scratching is such pointless activity; it
only makes the infection worse. We all know this, and yet we cannot help but scratch, and scratch frantically, as though we were condemned to tear ourselves to pieces. Job's affliction may remind us
of one of the Bible's most dreadful prophecies: "This is the plague
with which the Lord will strike all the nations that fought against
Jerusalem: Their flesh will rot while they are still standing on their
feet" (Zech. 14:12). There is not much that is more personal to us
than our skin, or that more plainly reflects our mortal condition.
When the skin is diseased it can be a kind of living death, almost as
if the body had been turned inside out and the exposed soul covered
with the visible, tangible wrath of God. This is certainly how the
ancients viewed it. Disease of the skin was equated with disease of
the soul, and anyone afflicted in this fashion was automatically
judged to be spiritually unclean. Hence the stigma attached throughout the Bible to "leprosy"—a word which in Hebrew was applied
not to leprosy alone but to a wide range of skin infections, and also
more generally to anything that was ceremonially unclean.

When Job's three friends came to visit him, therefore, even before Job opened his mouth they would have formed a clear opinion as to what his problem was. Was it not plain to all the world that a man whose body was visibly rotting away must be a sinner? Job's physical affliction put him in a class not very different from that of the contemporary victim of AIDS. This torment was not just a private but a public one. More than painful, it was shameful. Listen to Leviticus 13:45-46: "The person with . . . an infectious skin disease must wear torn clothes, let his hair be unkempt, cover the lower part of his face and cry out, 'Unclean! Unclean!' As long as he has the infection he remains unclean. He must live alone; he must live outside the camp."

This is precisely what happened to Job: he was banished from society, run out of town on a rail, treated as an outcast. That is why the Prologue makes a point of telling us that he was sitting "among the ashes" and scratching himself with "broken pottery." Where does one find heaps of ashes and broken pots? At the garbage dump, naturally. Job was not lying at home in his own comfortable bed between crisp white sheets and being waited on by private nurses; no, he was where all the other lepers and pariahs would be found, quarantined in the town dump. At least there, rather than being a burden on society, such people could take care of one another (after a fashion) and scrounge around for their own food; besides, there would be lots of broken pottery to scratch themselves with. For all we know, even Job's wife and his friends would have treated him as an untouchable, keeping a safe distance and conversing with him through the pall of drifting smoke, like the poet Dante visiting with the shades in the *Inferno*.

As the dialogue between Job and his friends unfolds, we will do well to bear in mind this horrific picture of a reeking dump as the setting in which the long and rather abstract theological debate takes place. These men are not sitting in some elaborate conference room in a multi-million-dollar church complex, nor even around the kitchen table, but rather amidst heaps of ashes, smoldering fires, stench, buzzing flies, scampering rats and jackals, piles of rubble, and all the other ruins of civilization—not least of which were the human ruins, the broken men and women gibbering like ghosts in the smoky murk. All in all, is the stage not set for an apocalyptic drama?

Job's Wife

His wife said to him, "Are you still holding on to your integrity? Curse God and die!" He replied, "You are talking like a foolish woman." (2:9)

When a husband and wife are united, they find a measure of strength and mutual comfort that holds its ground against almost any amount of trouble. But when they quarrel, their troubles are aggravated tenfold. Job's wife appears only once in the book, in this one verse, and yet in her own way she is nearly as famous a person as Job himself. Unfortunately her fame is founded on rather dubious, even scandalous, grounds: she apparently deserted her husband, and her God, when the chips were down.

Just as in the temptation of Jesus in the wilderness, when one approach fails to break Job's faith, the Devil tries another and another, steadily increasing the pressure, the seductiveness, and the subtlety of his strategies. Since it did not work simply to kill off Job's children wholesale, when it comes to his wife the tempter adopts a different tactic: he sows strife and succeeds in turning the couple against each other. She ridicules his religion, and he calls her a fool. A degree of alienation sets in which, just in itself, would very likely have been the worst trial these two had ever passed through in their married life.

It is easy to blame all of this on the woman and to react to her conduct with horror—as if it were something surpassingly strange and appalling. And yet, is this not just the way things are? Most spouses will graciously support their partners through a certain degree of misfortune, but when the hardships and the complaints drag on and on, even the most saintly love will reach a breaking point. In the very best and strongest Christian marriages there will come times when either partner may view the other (however temporarily) as no longer a lovable or a godly person at all, but as a sniveling and self-centered little worm. Married couples make the vow "for better or for worse," but when worse becomes worst and one's spouse has a nervous breakdown or contracts some lingering terminal illness, then there are few wives or husbands who will find in themselves a natural desire to keep on being smilingly supportive.

By Chapter 2 we begin to notice that there is a pattern to the trials of Job, a pattern that is like the tightening of a noose as the Devil's onslaughts grow more and more personal, closer and closer to his victim's heart. First it was buildings and servants that were attacked; then the man's children were taken; next his body was struck with disease; now his wife has been alienated from him. Soon his closest friends will unwittingly become tools of the Devil as they assault him with cold comfort and shallow theology. From this point on Job's trials grow increasingly lonely and interior, for Satan is directly attacking his personal relationships.

The plain fact is, if you follow Jesus there will be times when you will find yourself absolutely alone, cut off from everyone. In spite of the glorious unity and love that are ours in the Body of Christ, there are bound to come times when the soul must stand utterly alone before God. For there are some traits of soul, some spiritual qualities, that can only be acquired and perfected in solitude—and not in the comfortable solitude we call "time to ourselves" and of which we all crave a certain amount, but rather in the grueling solitary confinement of real loneliness and desertion. There is just no way around it. Without tasting this experience no Christian can become fully Christlike. The *via dolorosa*, the path to the cross, must be trod alone. Like the dock before the very judgment-seat of God, this is a narrow place, wide enough for only one abreast. There is no marriage in Heaven, taught Jesus (see Matt. 22:30). We squeak through the pearly gates one by one.

Trouble from God

"Shall we accept good from God, and not trouble?" (2:10)

Teaching about His Father's impartiality Jesus said, "He causes his sun to rise on the evil and the good, and sends rain on the righteous and the unrighteous" (Matt. 5:45). But couldn't this thought easily be turned around to read, "He causes His hail to fall on the crops of the just and the unjust alike"?

From the outset Job blames no one but God for his problems. Of course he does not really "blame" God at all—he trusts Him. He trusts God enough to locate the final source and cause of all his adversity directly with Him, the Sovereign Lord of the universe, and yet still to hope in Him. And this remains the hallmark of Job's faith throughout the book. Always he looks directly to the Lord as the one ultimately responsible for everything that happens, and never does he get sidetracked into blaming his troubles on a multitude of more obvious, yet secondary causes such as the weather (1:16, 19), other people (1:15, 17), or the Devil (of whom he has no knowledge anyway). Most surprisingly of all, Job does not even blame himself.

Job refuses, in other words, to get bogged down in trying to understand all the "reasons" for his misfortune. God knows the reasons; he does not. To "accept trouble from God" implies the acceptance of a certain illogical dimension to life, a dimension so totally beyond human ken that even faith, by its own secret and darkly luminous wisdom, cannot really comprehend it. Here we need the kind of faith whose God is so big as to be not just unmanageable, but to a large extent (as paradoxical as this may sound to Christian ears) unknowable. "Who has known the mind of the Lord, or who has been his counselor?" quotes Paul from Isaiah on two different occasions (Rom. 11:34; 1 Cor. 2:16). True, in the latter case he follows this immediately by saying, "But we have the mind of Christ." Yet having the mind of Christ is not quite the same as having the mind of God the Father. Even Jesus during His time on earth apparently had limits to His supernatural knowledge.

When we first become Christians we feel that we have finally come to "know" God, and so we have. But as we progress in faith we go through times when we are less and less certain that we really know Him at all, and yet more certain than ever that He knows us. This is what must have happened to Abraham's concubine Hagar when, lying half-dead in the desert, she gave this name to the Lord who spoke to her: "You are the God who sees me" (Gen. 16:13). Real faith is not so much seeing God, as knowing that one is seen. Only this kind of faith is resilient enough to embrace "trouble from God." As King George VI said in his famous 1940 radio talk, "Go out into the darkness and put thine hand into the hand of God. That shall be to thee better than a light, and safer than a known way."

It is much easier to use one's mind to reduce God to understandable proportions than it is continually to accommodate oneself to the divine mystery. It is easier to diminish God than to enlarge one's own heart. The poet William Cowper, who was subject to fits of insanity, knew something of this. According to one account it was while slipping into one of his dark spells that he wrote the well-known hymn, "God moves in a mysterious way, His wonders to perform; / He plants His footsteps in the sea, and rides upon the storm."

In some ways Job's wise and simple words in 2:10 are the very last expression of clear-minded, unshaken faith that he will utter before he sinks completely beneath the waves. The best of people, after all, may exhibit great clarity and magnanimity one moment, and despair the next, and after this point in the story Job's suffering at the hands of Satan grows so intense and prolonged that everything he says will be laced with darkness and confusion, so that at times his very character will appear to have come unhinged. Yet however much this man's humble faith may seem to be dashed to pieces later on, here at the outset we see him as he really is. We see him, in spite of terrible strain and agony, still in his right mind, and we realize that here is a person whose nature was not characteristically of a pessimistic, brooding or morbid type, but rather steadfast and sanguine. Indeed these latter qualities were doubtless the very ones that so infuriated the Devil that he petitioned God, "Stretch out your hand and strike his flesh and bones" (2:5). Already we have seen Job's body afflicted all over with painful boils; henceforth we shall see the boiling of his soul.

Friendship

*When Job's three friends . . . heard about all the troubles that
had come upon him, they set out from their homes and met
together by agreement to go and sympathize with him and
comfort him . . . they sat on the ground with him for seven
days and seven nights. No one said a word to him, because
they saw how great his suffering was. (2:11, 13)*

What a blessing it would be to have just one friend like this
in time of need—one friend who would drop everything
at a moment's notice, travel any distance, and stick by
one's bedside night and day for an entire week! Job, apparently, had
not just one such friend-in-need, but three. Even in the Bible we do
not often hear of people having this many close friends. One memorable exception is the paralytic of Mark 2:3-4, who had no less
than four friends who loved him so much that they actually went to
all the trouble and embarrassment of carrying him through a large
crowd and then digging down through a roof in order to get him to
Jesus. In the New Testament, understandably, heart-to-heart friendship becomes an increasingly common phenomenon, and the long
genealogical lists of the Old Testament gradually give way to a very
different sort of list, such as the one in the last chapter of *Romans*
in which Paul gives us just a glimpse into the vast network of people who, far more than being mere friends, were his true family, his
brothers and sisters in the Lord. These are blood ties indeed, for here
the family tree is the cross.

Even the gregarious Paul, however, as his difficulties multiplied
towards the end of his life, was to find himself in situations where
he would feel abandoned and betrayed by almost everyone (see 2
Tim. 1:15; 4:16; etc.). So three good friends in time of affliction is
a very great number. And seven days is a very, very long time for
concerned people (especially religious sorts) to hold their tongues
and refrain from flapping around. What a moving scene it must have
been, therefore, as the three gracious friends of Job in simple and
quiet dignity sat with their suffering brother, wordlessly expressing
their heartfelt compassion and solidarity.

At least, it would be nice to think that was the way it was. Yet unfortunately this idealistic view of things is quickly shattered by what happens in the ensuing dialogue. For once these people open their mouths we begin to see what was really going on inside them during those seven extraordinary days of silence. And what was really going on was this: Job's friends were condemning him.

It is a distasteful fact, but a fact nonetheless, that the three dear friends who came "to sympathize with [Job] and comfort him" (2:11), far from actually comforting, were in their minds picking him to pieces, analyzing him up and down for faults, loopholes, and hidden sins, casting around in search of reasons for all the terrible things that had happened to him. And although we are told that these discreet gentlemen said nothing at all to Job for an entire week, is it not probable that they whispered confidentially among themselves?

The main problem with this mission of mercy was that no mercy was forthcoming. Certainly Job himself would derive no comfort whatsoever from his friends' visit. On the contrary we shall watch him grow increasingly angry and disconsolate, to the point where his friends, impatient with his uncooperative attitude, will find it impossible to sustain even the outward semblance of sympathy towards him. Instead of truly identifying with him, they will distance themselves and withdraw. Feeling overwhelmed, and scrambling to get a better fix on the problem, they will do the only safe thing: they will pull back and assume the stance of objective analysts. Naturally they will go about all of this in a very warm and godly way and with the best of intentions. They are like benign family physicians, kindly old docs faced with a tough case and scratching their balding heads. Yet without realizing it, by their clinical theorizing they are effectively withdrawing their human affections, their very friendship, and this at the very time when intimate friendship is most needed.

To be sure, none of this is spelled out quite so early in the story; but in later chapters it comes spilling out. Like all fair-weather friendship, and all flawed theology, Job's friends stop short of the cross.

Light to the Gentiles

When Eliphaz the Temanite, Bildad the Shuhite and Zophar the Naamathite . . . saw him from a distance, they could hardly recognize him; they began to weep aloud, and they tore their robes and sprinkled dust on their heads. (2:11-12)

The visit of Job's three friends suggests, obliquely, a kind of parody of the visit of the wise men to the Christ-child. It is a parody rather than a parallel, since Job's friends are going not as seekers to a wondrous birth, but as mourners to a mass funeral. There is no hint of adventure in this journey; it is undertaken in heaviness rather than in joyous expectation. And yet, perhaps there is no less a sense of epiphany about it. One wonders what might have happened if the Magi, rather than discovering an adorable child in Bethlehem, had arrived a few years later to find instead a full-grown man hanging on a cross. Would they still have bowed the knee and presented their gifts? Or would they have joined with the scoffers? Eliphaz, Bildad, and Zophar broke into sobs when they saw that Job's pain was so great that it had transformed him, that he was no longer the man he had once been. The great tragedy of the remainder of the book is that they never do succeed in discovering and ministering to the man he had now become: a man of sorrows, acquainted with grief.

Like both the birth and the death of Christ, the suffering of Job was a multicultural event. This man was a cosmopolitan, with close personal ties that transcended tribal, and perhaps even national, boundaries. The precise location of the Temanite, Shuhite, and Naamathite territories is uncertain, but it does seem clear that Job's friends came from some distance away. Almost like a miniature United Nations, they appear to have represented a cross-section of the various ethnic groupings of the ancient Near East, and this serves to remind us that in the ancient world the practice of monotheism was by no means confined to the Israelites. Just as Job's friends represented Gentile nations, they also represented Gentile religion—and not the run-of-the-mill pagan variety, but rather a very pure and sophisticated brand of moral monotheism. Not every

Gentile in the Old Testament was an idolater, and true faith was never a racially delimited phenomenon. Was Noah a Jew? Was Abraham a Jew? It was the patriarchs who spawned the Jewish nation, not the other way around. From early days there existed individuals such as Melchizedek, true God-fearers who somehow fell outside the bounds of the special covenant Yahweh planned for His people Israel, yet who enjoyed intimate relationship with Him. Job himself, apparently, was a person just such as this, a kind of free-lance Yahwist who was, to borrow the Apostle Paul's description of himself, like "one abnormally born" (1 Cor. 15:8). If Paul was the "Apostle to the Gentiles," then Job might almost be termed a "Patriarch of the Gentiles." Like Melchizedek, he was a founding father of all those outside the Jewish line who, from earliest times, would carry the torch of pure faith in the one true God.

But what about Job's friends? As lofty as their religious consciousness was, can we really say, on the basis of the ensuing dialogue, that their monotheism had advanced all the way to the throne of the living God of grace? Did these men truly know the same God Job knew? In some ways this is the central question of the next forty chapters, and it is not at all an easy one to answer. In any case, whatever Job's friends may have believed at the outset of their journey, the Epilogue makes it clear that by the end they were soundly converted (or else corrected or restored) to living faith in the God of Job (see 42:7-9). And how did this happen? It happened in the same way that people have always been converted: by being brought to the foot of the cross. It was the mystery of suffering, and especially the propitiatory value of the unmerited suffering of a righteous believer, that finally brought these reluctant magi to see the light.

And so it is possible to interpret *Job* as being essentially a book about the action of grace among Gentiles. (In this respect it bears a certain resemblance to the books of *Ruth* and *Jonah*.) This is a story of how revival breaks out because of the faith of one person, because of the suffering of one person, because one person has been humbled before the Lord. What power there is in the sacrifice of one righteous, broken, and penitent heart! In the humiliation of Job, the glory of God is seen in a way that it is not in all the eloquent theological speeches (including Job's own) that accompanied it.

THE DIALOGUE:
ROUND 1
(Job 3–11)

"Why is life given to a man whose way is hidden, whom God has hedged in? For sighing comes to me instead of food; my groans pour out like water."

—JOB 3:23-24

We do not want you to be uniformed, brothers, about the hardships we suffered in the province of Asia. We were under great pressure, far beyond our ability to endure, so that we despaired even of life.

—2 COR. 1:8

Calling a Spade
a Spade

*After this, Job opened his mouth and cursed
the day of his birth. (3:1)*

After seven days of saintly silence, seven days of commenda-
tory restraint and of *"not sinning by anything he said"*
(2:10), we may wonder why Job at the beginning of Chapter
3 suddenly cuts loose and "curses the day of his birth." Why does
he have to ruin everything by opening his big mouth and sticking
his foot in it? However much we may strive to sympathize with Job's
suffering, his expression of it now becomes so dark and shocking
that we cannot help but ask, What is really going on here? Must we
hold the whole of this chapter at arm's length, chalking it up to the
misguided ravings of a man who has essentially lost control of himself, a tortured mind gone haywire?

Yet surely one of the most distinctive impressions we have as we
read through the speeches of Job is that here is a man who has not
gone haywire at all, but who knows exactly what he is saying and
means every word of it. True, at the end of the day he will recant his
strong language and "repent in dust and ashes" (42:1-6). But this
latter perspective is gained under entirely different circumstances, as
the result of a direct encounter with the Lord, and it is difficult to
imagine that Job would ever have repudiated the process by which
he was drawn step-by-step into that transcendent experience. This
process, admittedly, was one involving various moods and mental
states that at times presented all the appearance not only of godless
despair, but of an unbalanced mind veering towards total breakdown. And yet, one of the grimmest aspects of this story is that Job
never does teeter over the brink into madness, but rather faces his
entire ordeal with eyes wide-open. Even when utterly broken, he
somehow retains not only his faith but his sanity, while at the same
time managing, at the cost of incredible anguish, to give voice to the
insanity and the denial of God that reside in us all.

In pondering, from this point on, the question of Job's lack of verbal restraint, one fact worth considering is that we have no way of telling exactly how long his trials may have lasted. The events narrated in the Prologue, we know, comprised at the very least ten days, and probably closer to two or three weeks (although the suggestion of "months" in 7:3 may point to an even longer duration). The poetic dialogue, on the other hand, while it occupies the vast majority of the physical space in the book, may easily have taken place over as short a period as a single afternoon. In that case we might more readily understand why Job, after a lengthy siege of silent agony, should finally have broken down and given vent to a one-day (or a one-hour) outburst. Even the Lord Jesus, after all, was known to give way to apparent bouts of frustration, as when He complained of His poor scruffy band of stupid and incompetent disciples, "O unbelieving and perverse generation, how long shall I stay with you? How long shall I put up with you?" (Matt. 17:17).

The fact is, there is a point at which any man simply throws in the towel. He does not abandon his faith, necessarily; he just gets thoroughly sick and tired of trying to put a good face on things, when the things he is facing do not have anything good about them at all. This is not sin; it is just plain honesty. It is calling a spade a spade. Job is a forthright and plainspoken man, the sort of person who is not afraid to say what is on his heart, and at the outset of the Dialogue section we need grudgingly to acknowledge that such uncommon honesty may be one of the greatest virtues a saint can possess.

The third chapter of *Job* may well be the bleakest chapter in all of Scripture—more so even than Psalm 88, which after eighteen bleak verses ends abruptly with the line, "Darkness is my closest friend." Here it seems obvious that the psalmist reaches the end of his prayer without receiving any answer, without so much as a crumb of comfort. Yet for this very reason, there can be a strange comfort in the reading of this psalm in times of deep trouble. It is good to be reminded that such a black outpouring really is Scriptural, that prayer need not be upbeat and optimistic. The true believer does not always rise from his knees full of encouragement and fresh hope. There are times when one may remain down in the dumps and yet still have prayed well. For what God wants from us is not the observance of religious protocol, but just that we be real with Him. What He wants is our heart.

The Dark Side

"May the day of my birth perish,
and the night it was said, 'A boy is born!'
That day—may it turn to darkness;
may God above not care about it." (3:3-4)

However we may try to sympathize with and rationalize Job's black moods, from the moment he opens his mouth in Chapter 3 the reaction of the normal Christian reader is to squirm with distaste and to turn away from him in contempt. The thing we find particularly abhorrent is all this gloom-and-doom death-talk of his, this expressed longing not just for death but for total annihilation, this ache not merely to cease existing but never to have existed at all. Good Christians do not want to listen to this. We just feel that Job is wrong—terribly wrong—to "curse the day of his birth," and we do not want to acknowledge that such ghastly and despairing words could ever actually be uttered by a believer in God, let alone by someone with a reputation for exemplary sanctity.

So it is not just Job's wife and friends who pass judgment on him; we too, as readers, are inclined at this point to dismiss and reject him, or else to block our ears and pretend that he does not know what he is saying. Perhaps he is not such a great and holy saint after all, we think. For as soon as things get bad enough he takes to whining and cursing and crying in his cup, just like any old drunk in a bar. Apparently the Devil was right about him, and when the pressure gets too great he caves in and loses his faith.

In all honesty, however, as black and turbulent as Job's thoughts are, is it really the case that they are essentially any different from the innermost thoughts of other believers? Or might the real difference simply be that Job speaks his thoughts aloud? Certainly he gives utterance to things which, we feel, ought not to be uttered—things which many people would not even admit to having inside them. But are they not there nonetheless, nightmarishly gnawing away in the subliminal murmurings of each and every mind? In *Job* such thoughts come out into the open and appear, shockingly, on the lips of a decent and upright man.

Being a believer in God necessarily implies grappling with the dark side of one's nature. Many of us, however, seem to be so afraid of our dark side that far from dealing with it realistically, we repress and deny it. If we do so chronically, we need to ask ourselves whether we really believe in the healing power of Christ's forgiveness and in His victory over our evil natures. Perhaps we have never frankly come to grips with the fact that we ourselves are evil. If we have not, then we are ill prepared for those times when believing in God is like being awake during open heart surgery. For our Creator is not yet finished with us; He is still creating us, still making us, just as He has been all along from the beginning of the universe. But for the short span of our life here on earth we have the strange privilege of actually being wide awake as He continues to fashion us, to watch wide-eyed as His very own fingers work within our hearts. Of course this can be a painful process, and there is no anesthetic for it. At least, the only anesthetic is trust—trust in the Surgeon. But trust is not a passive, soporific thing. When there is stabbing pain, trust cries out. It is only mistrust, fear, and suspicion that keep silent.

We must not blame Job, therefore, for giving verbal expression to feelings that in most civilized people emerge in other ways. He says out loud that he rues the day of his birth, and while most of us might never consciously think such a thought, let alone voice it, do we not often live as though it were true? Whenever we grumble, whenever we do anything unwillingly, whenever we say a bad word against someone else—are we not, in effect, rueing the day of our birth? Are we not being openly and rebelliously critical of God's gracious gift of life? Even in the face of the tiniest frustrations, our reactions may betray the presence of a lingering resentment over the fact that we were ever created and brought into such a hard world in the first place.

Only the person who maintains an attitude of pure and unwavering thankfulness for every precious moment that the Lord has given, has any right to say a word of censure against Job in Chapter 3.

Depression

"Why is light given to those in misery,
and life to the bitter of soul?" (3:20)

Many commentators on *Job* have felt that the sweeping change that comes over the man in Chapter 3, from radiant saintliness to unseemly despair, is not quite believable. Yet by this stage it should be clear that an entirely new trial has now overtaken Job: the trial of depression, of deep mental and spiritual trauma. The terrible disasters of the Prologue Job managed to weather admirably, with piety intact. But now the battle front has shifted, subtly but calamitously, from outside to inside. Now it is Job's inner psychic life, his very soul, that is under direct satanic attack. In the words of Proverbs 18:14, "A man's spirit sustains him in sickness, but a crushed spirit who can bear?"

Is it really true that God would allow Satan direct access to the very soul of a believer for the purpose of untrammeled oppression? Listen to what John of the Cross says about this: "In proportion as God is guiding the soul and communicating with it, He gives the Devil leave to act with it after the same manner." Elsewhere John states that God certainly does "permit the Devil to deal with the soul in the same measure and mode in which He conducts and deals with it Himself. . . . Thus the Devil cannot protest his rights, claiming that he is not given the opportunity to conquer the soul, as was his complaint in the story of Job."

It is important to realize that nowhere in this book are we given reason to believe that Job's depression, in and of itself, is ever viewed by the Lord as being his own "fault." On the contrary, in view of the clear mandate for unlimited harassment (short of death) given to Satan in the Prologue, we are constrained to see Job's psychic trauma as part and parcel with his other trials, just one more of the Devil's assaults upon his faith. In fact the message that begins to unfold in Chapter 3 is that depression in a believer, far from being unforgivable, is one of the things that the Lord is most ready and eager to forgive. It may even be something that does not call for forgiveness at all, and far from being a sign of loss of faith it may actually demonstrate the presence of the sort of genuine and deeply searching faith that God always honors.

Job teaches us that there are times (as paradoxical as this may sound) when spiritual hope can take the form of despair. As someone has said, "Only the desperate are truly hopeful." To be sure, there are varieties of despair and depression that are without hope at all, that are full of godless self-pity and destructiveness. But there is also a kind of despair that is the only authentic response that a truly godly temperament can make when confronted by certain situations. There is a kind of despair that is realistic, courageous, and persevering in the highest degree. This is the despair that a person will have when he knows that things are wrong—that they are all wrong—and that they absolutely must get better or else he will die. The reason he despairs, then, is that he knows in his heart that there is a better way, and he has made up his mind that he will not rest until he finds it. He will not settle for anything less. Such a person reaches a point of staggering abandonment, being prepared to live with an inconceivable weight of sensual and psychological deprivation for the sake of holding out for deep spiritual truth.

This is not despair; this is hope. It is like a spiritual hunger strike, an all-consuming protest staged against the world's complacency. A lazy and self-satisfied person will never despair in this manner. Only a person who believes ardently in God will have the courage to endure such despair. Only a person who hopes with all his heart, and whose soul therefore cries out day and night to the living God for help, can live with spiritual famine. Wrote the great Catholic painter Georges Rouault, "I believe in suffering; it is not feigned in me. This is my only merit. I was not made to be so terrible."

What sort of hope do most churchgoers have today? Is it anything more than a grim stoicism, the ability to keep a stiff upper lip in the midst of life's fray? Is it the sort of hope that hides from reality? If the average Christian fell into despair, would he even know it?

Hedge of Thorns

"Why is life given to a man
whose way is hidden,
whom God has hedged in?" (3:23)

At the beginning of the story Satan had accused the Lord of overprotecting Job by putting "a hedge around him and his household and everything he has" (1:10). Now Job uses this same metaphor of being "hedged" or "fenced in" to describe his feeling of separation from God, of being shielded not from evil but from good. So there is a good deal of irony in the repetition of this image, in that where Satan sees unfair protection, Job sees unfair obstruction.

The moral here should be evident: God's surest protection can sometimes take the form of apparent obstruction, of darkness and difficulty and pain. Indeed there are times when the very safest place for a believer to be is in the midst of obscurity and suffering, to all appearances cut off from God. If what is happening is by permission of the Lord (and when is it not?), then no matter what the situation may be, it is the very safest situation in the world.

In the book of *Acts*, for example, the entire penultimate chapter is taken up with the story of a violent storm at sea that raged for over two weeks and ended in shipwreck. Things grew so desperate that at one point the narrator, Luke, admits that "we finally gave up all hope of being saved" (Acts 27:20). Presumably the "we" here includes not just the unbelievers on board, but the believers as well. (Yes, even for the great Apostle Paul there came a point in his life where he "gave up all hope of being saved"!) Nevertheless, could anyone doubt that Luke and Paul were just as secure in God's hands at the very height of the storm as they were when they finally set foot safe and sound on the island of Malta?

The fact is, a storm can be the safest place of all. For when you are feeling strong and good and happy and are accomplishing great things for God, then Satan can still get at you, and this may even be the time when you are most vulnerable to temptation. But when you are hedged in, when your arms and legs are pinned and you are bearing your cross with Christ, then Satan cannot touch you, and the reason he cannot touch you there is that by this point you have penetrated so far into his own kingdom that he does not worry about you anymore. On the contrary, he now does something that the Lord never does: he forgets all about you. Why? Because he thinks he has already defeated you and won you over to his side! He thinks he has destroyed you and assumed you into his own realm, and he thinks this because he is such a miserable and agonized creature himself that he cannot stand to see anyone else happy, and so as long as you are happy he will look for ways to attack you, but when you are suffering he will do what every other loveless being does, and he will cease to take you seriously. He will dismiss you and reject you. For Satan cannot tolerate joy; it tortures him. But suffering he tolerates very well. He tolerates it so well, in fact, that he does not even notice it. He does not have an ounce or a crumb of awareness of the evil of pain or death, let alone of compassion for it, and so the Christian who is in the grip of great suffering is entirely hidden from his eyes. On the other hand, the Christian who is brimming over with happiness and fulfillment will almost certainly be infuriatingly visible to him. At such a time people often feel as though they understand everything; and yet, this may be precisely the time when they understand nothing. That is why in the last analysis the only way to escape Satan is to die—to die to oneself by being crucified with Christ, and so to be "hidden with Christ in God" (Col. 3:3). Hidden from what? Why, from the world, from our own sinful flesh, and from the Devil.

To be surrounded by God's hedge, therefore, does not always mean to be protected from evil and from all the shocks of life. The hedge may be a hedge of thorns, and often enough the loving protection of the Lord involves being thrust into the very midst of evil, and being asked to carry this burden up the hill to Calvary. Whatever our circumstances, the safest place to be is always in the Lord's will. The safest place is the hollow of His hand—even (and especially) when that hollow takes the form of a bleeding nailprint.

Loss of Peace

"What I feared has come upon me;
what I dreaded has happened to me.
I have no peace, no quietness;
I have no rest, but only turmoil." (3:25-26)

What causes a person to suffer is one of the surest indications of what it is that he or she believes in. "Where your treasure is," said Jesus, "there will your heart be also" (Matt. 6:21), and it is the heart that suffers most sorely. Amidst all the bitterness of Job's complaints, what is odd is that we seldom hear him complaining about the sort of things we might expect him to complain about. A lesser person than he would have been taken up with the pain of bereavement, with the excruciating agony of physical disease, and with the overwhelming personal losses he had sustained. Mysteriously, however, throughout the dialogue with his friends Job touches upon these very obvious and weighty sorrows only in passing. Never does he whine and wail that the Lord has taken away his children, his servants, his camels, and his buildings. No, in his eyes such worldly effects all belong to a transient estate, and while he deeply mourns the loss of this estate, he never begrudges it.

What Job does begrudge, however, is what he feels to be the loss of his *spiritual* estate. "I have no peace, no quietness, no rest," he cries, and what he is really bemoaning is the loss of his peace with God—the loss of unbroken fellowship with his Creator, the loss of any felt sense of the Lord's friendship and approval, the loss of the spiritual peace that passes all understanding. Here was something that was worth complaining about, and Job freely confesses his dread of this condition.

Loss of the heart's peace is indeed something that all believers may legitimately dread. Jesus said, "Do not be afraid," and in the same breath He promised, "My peace I give you" (John 14:27). The two are so inseparably linked that when peace vanishes, it is inevitable that fear will take its place. For the true believer in God this is the one crisis, the one great calamity. Let anything else happen, but not this. What does it matter if my life falls apart, so long as I have peace? Yet peace is precisely what was taken from Job, and it is this that he identifies as the greatest of his tragedies and the real nub of his anguish.

As Christians we would do well to ask ourselves what sort of things we complain about, and what causes us the greatest pain and fear. When we suffer, do we truly know the fellowship of Christ's sufferings? Or is our suffering only that which all the rest of the world experiences: the physical woes of a decaying body, the neurotic fears of a fallen mind, and the infinite gnawing *angst* brought on by selfishness and sin? Novelist Walker Percy, on the opening page of *The Second Coming*, writes of his protagonist: "For some time he had been feeling depressed without knowing why. In fact, he didn't even realize he was depressed. Rather was it the world and life around him which seemed to grow more senseless and farcical with each passing day." In this character Percy has captured something of the essence of contemporary civilization. If only more people would complain and protest bitterly against the absence of peace with God! But unfortunately, even many Christians do not seem to hold peace of heart in very high esteem. Instead we make our peace with the gods of overwork, anxiety, and quiet desperation. Too often a peaceful life is sacrificed for the sake of other goals: career, worldly accomplishments, entertainment, people-pleasing, the satisfaction of frantic activity, and other frivolities. We get used to living with chronic restlessness, even to the point of mistaking it for peace.

Job was a man who had a firm and intuitive grasp of the principle set out in Isaiah 32:17: "The fruit of righteousness will be peace; the effect of righteousness will be quietness and confidence forever." Since Job knew he was a righteous man, where then were the peace and confidence that were his due? Throughout the debate with his friends Job will repeatedly claim these clear terms of his covenant with the Lord, and yet at the same time he wastes no breath trying to claim anything that the Lord has not promised him. He insists on spiritual rights, not worldly rights, and it is this very insistence that makes of him a great man of faith. He holds God to His word, and no more.

Eliphaz

Then Eliphaz the Temanite replied: . . .
"As I have observed . . . those who sow
trouble reap it." (4:1, 8)

What sort of man was Eliphaz the Temanite? Many attempts have been made to read between the lines of the speeches of Job's friends and to draw character sketches of them. Eliphaz usually emerges as the most mature member of the group, a kindly and articulate older man. Words such as *balanced* and *diplomatic* may spring to mind. We might almost picture this elder statesman with a fine head of snowy-white hair and full matching beard, together with an ample paunch and a twinkle in his lively gray eyes, all reflecting a keen intellect and a dignified presence.

Yet when all is said and done, Eliphaz's noble bearing, his fatherly sincerity, and his adroit theologizing are not quite enough to cover up the underlying coldness of his heart. Certainly he presents a fine appearance—well-dressed, well-fed, and well-spoken—but eventually the book forces us to the conclusion that there is much of the pompous windbag about him. For Job sits before him stripped of everything, his heart torn and exposed, his words desperate, his eyes wild and probing and pleading for comfort, and what does the gentle Eliphaz have to offer? Amidst all his smoothly eloquent talk, perhaps the gist of his entire message may be summed up by the stinging yet almost hidden little comment in 4:8: "As I have observed," he observes smugly, "those who sow trouble reap it."

Surely under the circumstances these are words that drip with priggishness and, in fact, with contempt. "Like a lame man's legs that hang limp," says Proverbs 26:7, "is a proverb in the mouth of a fool." Whatever comfort Eliphaz may have meant to convey to his suffering friend, the actual effect of his ministry might best be summed up in the words of another proverb: "Like one who takes away a garment on a cold day . . . is one who sings songs to a heavy heart" (Prov. 25:20).

It is one of the supreme ironies of this book that only after the arrival of these three bosom friends of his does Job really lose a grip on himself and fall off the edge into despair. Their pedantic theology, their reforming zeal, and their subtle slights are more than the poor man can take, and undoubtedly this backhanded betrayal by his friends is Job's final and most severe trial. It is their utter failure to love him that hurts the most, and while this is not ostensibly the stated theme of the next thirty-five chapters of arduous dialoguing, it is the one that swims constantly and monstrously, like leviathan itself, just below the surface, so that in the long run the great questions of "theodicy" or the "problem of pain" very rightly take a backseat to the much more disturbing problem of correct but merciless theology, of the sort of religion that in its zeal to glorify God gives short shrift to the suffering of man.

Perhaps the New Testament figure whom Eliphaz most closely resembles is Nicodemus, as we first meet him in John 3. For Nicodemus too was a well-respected man, wise and courteous and with impeccable religious credentials. And yet Jesus told him straightforwardly that he was unregenerate, dead in his sins, and that until he was "born again" he could not know the first thing about the Kingdom of God. "How can this be?" asked Nicodemus, the wise man suddenly dull as an ox, and with gentle but firm irony Jesus rebuked him, saying, "You are Israel's teacher, and you do not understand these things?" (John 3:9-10).

Depending upon our own spiritual temperament, we may not want to go so far as to condemn Eliphaz outright as a total and godless hypocrite, a man "separate from Christ . . . without hope and without God in the world" (Eph. 2:12). Yet at least it must be admitted that his growth in God fell far short of the towering maturity of Job, and that he stood very much in need of the sort of correctional challenge to his faith that might only come through realistic grappling with the problem of suffering. Jesus told Nicodemus that in order for men such as himself to be brought to saving faith, "the Son of Man must be lifted up" (John 3:14-15)—that is, glorified through the unspeakable suffering of crucifixion. In many ways the story of Job is the story of how, at the horrendous cost of the suffering of a righteous man, even a self-satisfied traditionalist such as Eliphaz could eventually be brought to see the light of the gospel, and to embrace from afar the wondrous mystery of the redemptive power of the cross.

A Play for Voices

"If someone ventures a word with you, will you be impatient? But who can keep from speaking?" (4:2)

All the characters in this book seem impatient to get a word in edgewise, and all are quick to criticize one another for talking too much. From every quarter (including Job's) the air is thick with charges of "blustering wind" (8:2), "idle talk" (11:3), and "long-winded speeches" (16:3). How true to life it is to see passionate debaters continually brushing off the arguments of their opponents like so much lint from their sleeves, even while stabbing their own fingers into the table and yelling, "Now just listen to this!"

Such lively dramatic detail reminds us that the book of *Job* consists almost entirely of talk. Talk, talk, talk. The lives of five busy, important men grind to a complete halt, and the bulk of the story takes place in an immense and stultifying stasis in which hardly anything at all actually happens apart from the flapping of jaws. By the end of Chapter 31, when young Elihu appears on the scene with a fresh wind, one has the impression that the four other fellows have literally talked themselves hoarse.

The unusually sustained oral emphasis of *Job* points to the fact that in its literary form this book is essentially a drama. It is, first and foremost, neither a story nor a history nor an epic poem, but rather a play—not a stage play, to be sure, but a *play for voices*. If this is true, then it makes this work the only example of drama (or the closest thing to it) in the entire canon of Scripture. Moreover, this in turn may be an important clue suggesting that the book did not arise directly out of Israelite culture (in which a deep-seated taboo against theater prevailed) but rather was a product of the Gentile world. Such a theory would place the book in the curious category of being the only Gentile-authored composition in the Old Testament.

In any case, the intensely verbal character of *Job* has an enormous impact on the way the reader must approach and interpret this work. For by and large the writing in the Bible addresses its audience directly, whereas the genre of drama, like that of fiction, by its very nature speaks with considerable indirectness and artistic subtlety. Granted, the history books of the Old Testament have a style of narration that tends toward magnificent understatement; often events are related baldly, with very little by way of editorial comment. In the case of bizarre characters such as Balaam or Samson we are left to judge pretty much for ourselves the quality of their godliness and the rightness or wrongness of their actions. In *Job*, however, this hermeneutic complexity is compounded further still, for apart from some scraps of information in the brief prose sections, and a smattering of stage directions embedded in the text itself, the only standards we have for evaluating these people and their opinions are what they say about themselves and about one another. In the rest of Scripture this is unheard of. For humanity alone to occupy the stage is a mark of secularism. In other parts of the Bible is not God Himself a prominent speaker on nearly every page? But in *Job* the Lord is ominously silent (at least for the great majority of the book), and for thirty-five chapters the curtain goes up on human speech alone.

This is the trait that places *Job* in the category of drama, and that makes it impossible to understand this work through a straightforward reading of the words alone. Here is a book that requires uniquely to be read not just as a book, but as a script. Throughout the long Dialogue section we must read between the lines, carefully weighing such theatrical factors as characterization, set, tone of voice, mood, and even gesture or body language. For in drama as in real life, what happens on the surface of conversation, what is actually said, matters little in comparison with the underlying drama of attitudes and actions, the script behind the script. As Job himself puts it, "Does not the ear test words as the tongue tastes food?" (12:11). Ideally this entire book needs to be read aloud, or at least taken in at a single sitting, so as to be grasped whole in a kind of *gestalt*. This is the only way to appreciate fully what is essentially a work of drama, a living art form so finely wrought as to be just one step removed from the delicate intricacies of real life itself.

Faith and Works

"Should not your piety be your confidence,
and your blameless ways your hope?" (4:6)

Just six verses into his opening harangue, Eliphaz inadvertently broaches an issue that happens to be of signal importance to Christians: the debate between faith and works. Tipping his hand as to which side of this age-old question he is on, Eliphaz blithely advises Job to place confidence in his own "piety" and "blameless ways." But this is exactly where Job's confidence is not, and anyone whose life has fallen to pieces will understand why. To put any stock in one's own virtuous conduct, whether past or present, is like trying to use a sieve as a bucket. We humans cannot contain anything good; we can only channel what is good. Even the matchless Son of God confessed, "Why do you call me good? No one is good—except God alone" (Mark 10:18). Christ knew that in His human nature He was a conduit for the goodness that is inherent in God alone.

Whenever faith tries to base itself on good living, whether the focus be on external morality or on inner spiritual purity, the result is the most sophisticated of all pagan religions. Though it claims belief in God, in practice such religion places no trust in the Lord Himself but only in its own theology. As thoroughly orthodox and Biblical as this theology may be, it does not represent faith in the living God but in faith itself. Heaven help this religion of good works when it falls on hard times. For according to this view, hard things can only be explained as the chastisement of an angry God, and therefore good works must be done with the subliminal motive of appeasing God's wrath. By the same token, when all in life is going well such theology shows itself more pitiful than ever, for subtly and insidiously it takes all the credit to itself.

True faith depends not at all upon itself, nor upon its own system of piety, but rather upon the Lord alone and His faithfulness. It knows that our faith in God is only a reflection of God's faith in us. For our Father does believe in us; He *faithed* us into existence in the first place, and He continues day by day "sustaining all things by his powerful word" (Heb. 1:3). To have faith is to have trust in the faithfulness of our God, knowing that faithfulness is first and foremost not a human but a divine attribute. All we human beings can do is to become empty, in order that God's character of perfect faithfulness may flow into us. Genuine faith is not the faith to *do* anything at all, except to fall to the ground and die.

To be sure, as James famously contends in his epistle, true faith necessarily issues in good works. But the focus of the believer is not to be on the work itself, but rather on the One who in fact does the work. As Jesus testified, "It is the Father, living in me, who is doing his work" (John 14:10). When teaching about almsgiving and other charitable activities Jesus declared, "Do not let your left hand know what your right hand is doing" (Matt. 6:3). The left hand of faith, in other words, must not be distracted by what the right hand of work is doing. For the moment this happens, the work in question falls short of being fully a work of faith. And "everything that does not come from faith is sin" (Rom. 14:23).

Consider the roots of a plant. Do the roots worry, or think at all, about producing flowers or fruit? No; they never see what happens above the ground. They never even see the sun or the sky. All they see is the dark womb of the earth, and their only job is to soak up moisture and nourishment from it, to feed in the dark underground of faith.

The essential error of Eliphaz, and of Job's other friends, is in trying to shift Job's focus away from the roots of faith and onto its flowers and fruit. Even as they talk loftily of God, what they are really doing is distracting Job's full attention from the Lord and tempting him to concentrate instead on himself and his sin. Without realizing it, they number themselves among those whom Paul describes as "taking pride in what is seen rather than in what is in the heart" (2 Cor. 5:12). Assuming that the opposite of sin is virtue, they conclude that a righteous life is one that will always be producing the visible fruit that is its own reward. Yet in the vocabulary of the gospel, the opposite of sin is not simply virtue but grace. As Paul puts it in Romans 5:20-21, "Where sin increased, grace increased all the more, so that, just as sin reigned in death, so also grace might reign through righteousness to bring eternal life through Jesus Christ our Lord."

A Lying Spirit

"Amid disquieting dreams in the night,
when deep sleep falls on men,
fear and trembling seized me
and made all my bones shake.
A spirit glided past my face,
and the hair on my body stood on end." (4:13-15)

What a chilling passage this is! Just to read it is enough to send shivers down the spine. Eliphaz may present the appearance of a conservative, mild-mannered intellectual, but just get him talking about his mystical experiences and there opens up a whole new side to the man.

He tells of being visited in the night by a spirit that filled him with terror. In his hair-raising account one can sense the tone of mounting excitement in his voice. One even gets the feeling that, as frightening as this experience was, Eliphaz would not have missed it for anything, nor would he have minded having it repeated. He leaves no doubt that despite his terror he considered the visitation a good thing, and one that brought him a genuine spiritual insight, "a word *from the Lord*" (4:12). He is telling, he thinks, of an authentic encounter with a spiritual being sent directly from God, and he repeats the angelic message verbatim for Job's edification.

How different is Eliphaz's mystical fear from the sort of fear expressed by Job back in 3:25 when he said, "What I feared has come upon me; what I dreaded has happened to me." Job's dread, by contrast, was a feeling that he wanted nothing to do with, for in it he intuitively sensed the grip of something evil. Far from taking any secret delight in such a thing, Job recoiled from it in horror, and in his deepest instincts he was quite certain that there was nothing of God in it. In fact, it seems clear that without having any direct knowledge of Satan, without even knowing Satan's name, Job nevertheless must have sensed at some level the real and personal presence of the great enemy of his soul.

The difference between night and day could not be greater than the difference between the reactions of these two men to the movement of fear in their hearts. Eliphaz indulged it; Job shrank from it. Job saw it frankly as something evil, while Eliphaz, like a child at a horror movie, seemed almost to exult in the emotion itself. Careful reflection on these marked contrasts suggests that Eliphaz very probably committed the heinous—yet unfortunately all too common—error of mistaking an evil spirit for the Spirit of the Lord, and moreover of repeating the words of a demon as if they were those of God Himself.

Certainly it is true throughout the Bible that meetings with God are normally accompanied by an initial, overwhelming dread. When Isaiah saw the Lord his immediate response was, "Woe to me! I am ruined!" (Isa. 6:5), and when the glory of the Lord shone around the Bethlehem shepherds, "they were terrified" (Luke 2:9). Yet always in such cases the Lord's first word is one of peace to the trembling heart, for He knows that only in peace can we see and hear Him as He really is—the God of love, in whom "there is no darkness at all" (1 John 1:5). Gideon was so struck by this truth that, after first being terrified that he would die because he had "seen the angel of the Lord face to face," he ended by building an altar and calling it "The Lord is Peace" (Judges 6:22-24). From that day forth Gideon determined (though admittedly he pushed his conviction to the point of superstition) not to take a single step without having the felt assurance of the Lord's peace in his heart.

How tragic it is that so many religious people accustom themselves to hearing and obeying the voice of fear rather than the voice of peace. In doing so, they unwittingly pay heed to the Devil, even while fooling themselves that they are trying to follow Christ. This issue of correctly identifying the Lord's voice may appear at times very subtle and complex, and so it is for the chronic doubter. But for faith it is a simple enough matter. As Jesus promised in John 10:2-5, "[The shepherd] calls his own sheep by name and leads them out . . . his sheep follow him because they know his voice. But they will never follow a stranger; in fact, they will run away from him because they do not recognize a stranger's voice."

Inferiority Complex

"Can a mortal be more righteous than God?
Can a man be more pure than his Maker?"" (4:17)

Lest we have any doubt as to the questionable nature of the mystical communiqué received by Eliphaz, we need only examine its actual content. Like everything originating with the Devil, his words here have a good deal of truth to them. What other material has Satan to work with except the truth? Having no real creative power of his own, there is nothing the least bit original about him. Thus his normal method of working is simply to give the truth a subtle twist, a slight bend, refashioning and redirecting it for his own purposes. Essentially he is a sort of cosmic junk dealer, a recycler of truth. Often enough his wares are still shiny and eminently usable, with plenty of practical wisdom left in them. Indeed the more closely lies and perversions resemble the truth itself, the more likely they are to find a clientele, so that for those who shrink from paying the high cost of unadulterated truth, the Devil's second-hand garbage serves very well.

In 4:17-19 we see Eliphaz falling for two of Satan's classic methods of perverting truth: exaggeration and put-down. As to the first, apparently what Eliphaz picked up from Job's first speech was an undertone of spiritual hubris. He was alarmed that Job's primary concern was, rather than the faltering of his own faith, the apparent faltering of the Lord's faithfulness towards him. When Job openly accused God of deliberately hedging him in (3:23), he seemed to be setting himself up as a judge of God's ways. And so Eliphaz asks, through the intimidating words of his nocturnal spiritual visitant, "Can a mortal be more righteous than God?" As with the rhetorical question of a demagogue seeking to sway a crowd, the implied answer to this *reductio ad absurdum* is both entirely obvious and entirely irrelevant. Of course a human being cannot be "more righteous" or "more pure" than God—but no one is claiming that. All Job will ever claim in this book is that a human being *can* be righteous and *can* be pure, and indeed must be if he is to have any dealings with God at all. Yet even this view Eliphaz debunks in a later speech when he asks, "What is man, that he could be pure, or one born of woman, that he could be righteous?" (15:14). This is one of Satan's favorite strategies against believers—to undermine the very grounds and possibility of righteousness itself by rubbing our noses in the dirt of our own weakness and sin. This is exactly what Eliphaz proceeds to do in the following verses as, continuing to quote the words of the lying spirit, he challenges, "If God . . . charges his angels with error, how much more those who live in houses of clay, whose foundations are in the dust" (4:18-19). Eliphaz's real problem, as with all those who buy a mean-spirited theology, is that he has an inferiority complex regarding his humanity. He has a dismally low view of man, and therefore a dismally low view of God and of His grace.

True enough, the Bible itself paints man in the lowest possible terms as a creature not only frail and ephemeral, but utterly corrupt. Yet at the same time Scripture has an incredibly high view—indeed a most amazingly exalted view—of man's rightful status in creation, both of his original pristine nature and of his ultimate destiny. Thus whenever the Apostle Paul speaks to the people of God, his tone is very different from that of the friends of Job. Never do we catch him placing undue emphasis on what a worthless, abject, and degraded lot we are, fit only to crawl on our bellies in the dust. Instead he reminds us that we are the "dearly loved children of God," and he continually balances his teaching about sin with words of staggeringly lofty encouragement, such as those that open the epistle to the Ephesians: "Praise be to the God and Father of our Lord Jesus Christ, who has blessed us in the heavenly realms with every spiritual blessing in Christ. For he chose us in him before the creation of the world to be holy and blameless in his sight. In love he predestined us to be adopted as his sons" (Eph. 1:3-5).

Naturally we are utterly unworthy of such high privileges. But as George Müller wrote, "Do not let the consciousness of your unworthiness keep you from believing what God has said concerning you. If you are a believer in the Lord Jesus, then the precious privilege of being in partnership with the Father and the Son is yours."

The Holy One of God

"Call if you will, but who will answer you?
To which of the holy ones will you turn?" (5:1)

What words of encouragement and inspiration these are! Eliphaz as much as says, "You might as well give up praying, Job. You're too much of a hypocrite to get through to God. And if *He* won't listen to you, who will?"

There is particularly heavy irony in Eliphaz's unfortunate use of the term "holy ones." Though he appears to be speaking of the angels, the "Holy One of God" also happens to be a principal Biblical title for the Messiah (see John 6:69, etc.). Therefore in implying that there exists no such "holy one" upon whom Job may call in his distress—no intermediary between God and humanity—Eliphaz might almost be said to be denying Jesus Christ. All unwittingly he makes the clear disclosure that his religion lacks any inclination toward messianic hope, the hope of a mediator both compassionate and powerful. It is at points such as this that we may legitimately wonder whether the faith of Eliphaz, for all his talk of God, is genuine saving faith. As John spells out plainly, "No one who denies the Son has the Father; whoever acknowledges the Son has the Father also" (1 John 2:23). Or as Peter states even more simply, it is "through [Christ] you believe in God" (1 Peter 1:21).

Denial of Christ may seem a bizarrely extreme charge to bring against an Old Testament figure, far in advance of the full revelation of the gospel. But the fact is that every page of the Old Testament speaks of the coming of the Messiah, and the life of every true Old Testament believer in some way foreshadows, prepares for, or welcomes Christ's advent. Many even prophesy directly about Him. As Jesus noted in John 8:56, even Abraham "rejoiced at the thought of seeing my day," while of Moses it is written, "He regarded disgrace for the sake of Christ as of greater value than the treasures of Egypt, because he was looking ahead to his reward" (Heb. 11:26). Simply put, the God of the Old Testament *is* Jesus Christ, and throughout the Bible the quintessence of true faith is the joyous embracing of the promise of Christ, however dimly perceived, and of the righteousness that only He can impart.

This obscure longing for the Messiah is, as we shall see, one of the chief characteristics of the faith of Job, who seemed intuitively to sense, to know in his bones, that his whole predicament not only implied but demanded the involvement of a mediator between himself and his estranged God. This fantastic, visionary groping—this grasping at messianic straws—was something to which Job gave pointed expression on numerous occasions, not least of which was his famous prophetic utterance, "I know that my Redeemer lives!" (19:25; see also 9:33-34; 16:19-21; etc.) How different are such buoyantly optimistic words from the cynical and (by comparison) virtually atheistic views of Eliphaz. Without actually knowing Christ, Job nevertheless spoke about Him with startling clarity. At one point he even used the messianic title when he said, "I *have not* denied the words of the Holy One" (6:10). What words were these? Since Job almost certainly had no Scripture, he must have been referring to the sort of Scripture that Abraham had, written nowhere but on the wind. Job was one of those Old Testament prophets who, in the words of 1 Peter 1:10-11, "searched intently and with the greatest care, trying to find out the time and circumstances to which the Spirit of Christ in them was pointing when he predicted the sufferings of Christ and the glories that would follow."

Eliphaz, by contrast, unconsciously revealed himself to be someone whose religion was as yet too narrow to embrace any hint of the Holy One of God. In fact from the way he and the other friends prattle on and on about God's logical, airtight system of rewards for good and punishments for evil, one has the distinct impression that they would have been quite satisfied to remain forever under the old covenant of the law. But Job, meanwhile, was holding out for what Hebrews 7:19 calls "a better hope," a hope that would encompass not just obvious moral platitudes but the deepest mysteries of God, a hope that would be capable of sustaining the heart through every conceivable circumstance in this bewildering life—through the downs as well as the ups, through times of inexplicable suffering as well as of blessing. Like Abraham, Job was committed to finding a city not built by human hands, "the city with foundations, whose architect and builder is God" (Heb. 11:10). Job was looking for what could only be found in a manger, on a cross, in an empty tomb.

The Two Sons

"But if it were I, I would appeal to God;
I would lay my cause before him.
He performs wonders that cannot be fathomed,
miracles that cannot be counted." (5:8-9)

The story of Job may be compared to Jesus' parable of the two sons in Matthew 21. One son says to his father, "I will not obey you," but in the end he changes his mind and does his father's bidding. By contrast the other son says, "I will obey," and then promptly forgets all about it and does what he wants. The words these two young men pronounce with their lips, it turns out, are not at all an accurate reflection of what is in their hearts. In fact in each case what they say is exactly the opposite of what they believe. The real nature of their convictions shows up only in their actions. And so at the outset of the parable Jesus asks us, "What do you think?" We are invited to judge discerningly between the two.

In the same way, the friends of Job all represent themselves as being upright and godly men, and over and over in various ways what they say is that they believe in a God who is good and merciful, and they exhort Job to believe the same. Yet we cannot help wondering: if they really believed that God is merciful, could they not be expected to show that same mercy to others, and particularly to a dear friend in time of crisis? But this they fail to do. Instead of mercy they bring condemnation, and in place of compassion they exhibit doctrinaire rigidity. Do not the actions of such men speak louder than their words? Obviously they believe that people should be good; but do they really believe in a good God? As G. K. Chesterton astutely observed, perhaps what they really believe is "not that God is good but that God is so strong that it is much more judicious to call Him good."

Job, for his part, from Chapter 3 on has very little good to say about God, but instead rants and raves against His cruel silence and injustice, repeatedly calling God his "foe." In the long run, however, when the Lord finally breaks His silence and speaks to him, Job immediately softens and repents. So at the end he turns out to be very much like the first son in Jesus' parable, who initially dug in his heels and cried, "I won't!" and yet who, when it came down to brass tacks, submitted. Like the prostitutes and tax-collectors Jesus was highlighting in this story, Job's character under extreme pressure does not conform to the popular image of saintliness. But the Lord knows what is in his heart, and Jesus' question at the end of the parable is not, "Which of the two sons had the more correct theology?" but, "Which of the two did what his father wanted?" (Matt. 21:31).

Much of the theme of *Job* revolves around the perplexing reality that what people say they believe is often not the same as what they really do believe. Why is this so? It is because people do not know themselves. Our intellectual *impression* of our own creed can be a far cry from the *expression* of that faith in our daily lives. Accordingly, it was said of Jesus that "He did not need man's testimony about man, for he knew what was in a man" (John 2:25). To know what people really believe, we have to look much further than simply at what they say about themselves. As Jesus instructed the Pharisees, "Stop judging by mere appearances, and make a right judgment" (John 7:24).

Ultimately the little-known parable of the two sons has much in common with the more famous story of the prodigal son. In either case Jesus used two brothers to draw a distinction not just between two different kinds or degrees of faith, but rather between belief and unbelief, between living faith and dead legalism. In both parables the son who initially rebels is the one who, deep down, is being intensely honest with his father, while the other son, though he makes an outward show of toeing the line, is being fundamentally dishonest. In each story the point is that straightforward dealing with God leads, however circuitously, to eventual obedience and right action, while an insincere compliance with God—no matter how well-meaning or well-seeming—results in alienation.

Carnal Christianity

"Blessed is the man whom God corrects;
so do not despise the discipline of the Almighty.
For he wounds, but he also binds up;
he injures, but his hands also heal." (5:17-18)

Aspirin is a good and effective medicine. But it is useless against cancer. Similarly, so much of the advice that Eliphaz and the other friends dole out is, in its own right, correct and good and true. But because it is wrongly applied it becomes useless. More than useless, it is a lie. Eliphaz's basic assumption that Job is being divinely "corrected" and "disciplined" sounds good, but it is simply wrong, for God's primary intention in allowing Job's suffering is not to rehabilitate him, but practically the opposite: to honor him and to glorify his faith.

Yes, what Eliphaz says is true enough. But even the truth, when spoken at the wrong time or in the wrong circumstances—that is, when spoken without love—is a lie. "If the wrong man uses the right means," goes an old Chinese proverb, "then the right means works in the wrong way." Or as Paul put it in one of the most familiar passages in the Bible, "If I speak in the tongues of men and of angels, but have not love, I am only a resounding gong or a clanging cymbal" (1 Cor. 13:1). Elsewhere Paul wrote, "What you heard from me, keep as the pattern of sound teaching, with faith and love in Christ Jesus" (2 Tim. 1:13). Why would Paul bother to add the words "with faith and love" unless it were possible to "keep the pattern of sound teaching" without them? In the long run it may be that the mishandling of truth will be shown up to be an even greater travesty, in the eyes of God, than blatant sin. When truth lies it becomes a wolf in sheep's clothing, and though it dresses up in the clothes of the Spirit, underneath it is thoroughly carnal.

When Paul wrote, "If you live according to the *flesh*, you will die" (Rom. 8:13), he was not warning primarily against gross sins such as drunkenness or stealing or sexual immorality, nor even against the more genteel iniquities such as gossiping and dissension (which, incidentally, the New Testament brands as being equally serious: see

Galatians 5:19-21, where "envy" and "orgies," "selfish ambition" and "witchcraft" appear side by side in a list of what are termed "obvious" sins). No, Paul's warning was against Christians giving themselves to *any* behavior that had its origin in the flesh rather than in the Spirit. He was talking, in other words, about the misapplication of truth, and about insensitive and judgmental counseling of others. He was talking about hypocrisy and phoniness, about insincere love, and about conformity to peer pressure. He was talking about singsong evangelism, about the sterile, robotic mouthing of the gospel of Christ. He was talking about pasteboard smiles, vacuous laughter, and good deeds motivated by guilt or by the need to impress others. He was talking about settling for a lack of reality in the Christian faith.

If you practice such ways habitually, Paul says bluntly, and if you insist on continuing to live in this manner, then you will die in your sins. It does not matter if you call yourself a "Christian": if your inner attitudes and your lifestyle are primarily those of conformity to the world and the flesh, when in your heart you know better and have been given grace to follow the Spirit, then your life will be no real life at all, but a living death. And you will die a little more every day, and you will hate yourself (and God too) a little more every time you choose to settle complacently into the world's rut rather than obeying the life-giving promptings of the Spirit. As Jesus warned, "The Spirit gives life; the flesh counts for nothing" (John 6:63).

If we continually disregard the gentle, loving voice of the Lord deep within us, what else can we expect but that our hearts will grow cold and hard? Every time we shut out Christ's words, we make it that much harder to hear Him the next time, until the day may well dawn when we will be literally incapable of ever hearing His wonderful voice again.

Successful Living

"We have examined this, and it is true.
So hear it and apply it to yourself." (5:27)

The remainder of Eliphaz's opening speech trails off in a string of spiritual banalities, each one as patently true as it is monstrously callow. In the light of Job's present circumstances, for example, it is plainly ludicrous to promise that if he trusts in the Lord, "You will take stock of your property and find nothing missing" (5:24). And how cruel to croon comfortingly, "You will know that your children will be many" (5:25). When Eliphaz further assures Job, "You will be protected from the lash of the tongue" (5:21), surely there are few words in the entire book more larded with the sharp irony of inadvertent self-condemnation.

This rosy picture of the life of faith that Eliphaz paints for Job adds up to what is nowadays called the "health-and-wealth gospel." In this twisted theology, material and physical well-being are viewed more as rewards for faith than as wholly unmerited blessings, more as promised entitlements than as gracious gifts which, like all the gifts of God, are "distributed according to his will" (Heb. 2:4). As followers of a Lord who was whipped, pierced, destitute, and crucified, it is astonishing how hard of hearing we Christians can be when it comes to the necessity of suffering. We do not really want to be healed (with all that process entails); we just want to be well right now, period, thank You very much. It seems we are interested in every kind of health except spiritual health. Not many of us could address our sufferings in the way that Alexander Solzhenitsyn did in his famous apostrophe to the Gulag: "Bless you, prison . . . for it was in you that I discovered that the meaning of earthly existence lies, not as we have grown used to thinking, in prospering, but in the development of the soul."

Where the health-and-wealth gospel does its deepest damage is not so much in convincing us that we should be materially and physically well off, but in luring us into thinking that we should also be well in every other respect, including emotionally and psychologically. How the world admires the "well-adjusted" personality!

Unfortunately, what has been adjusted to in most cases is simply the fallen, evil nature of humanity. That can be adjusted to amazingly well, and in such a personality complacency becomes the prime strategy for living. Strong, competent, resilient individuals can grow so well-insulated to the normal shocks of life that they are barely aware of their own pain, let alone compassionate towards the struggles of others. Jesus issued a stern challenge to this illusion of the well-rounded, holistic Christian life when He preached, "If your hand or your foot causes you to sin, cut it off and throw it away. It is better for you to enter life maimed or crippled than to have two hands or two feet and be thrown into eternal fire" (Matt. 18:8). The gist of this teaching is that the person who is manifestly impaired (whether physically, emotionally, or mentally) may be the one who is truly alive, while the person who appears from a worldly point of view to have it all together may be bound for destruction.

As the Dialogue section of *Job* unfolds, it will be important to see how the highly reasonable theology of Eliphaz, Bildad, and Zophar is gradually exposed as little more than a private coping mechanism, a kind of protective armor against the harshest realities of life. Their religion is one that provides good insulation for themselves, but no consolation for others. In arguing with Job, their understandable concern is that in the depths of this man's despair his thoughts seem to be irreverently taken up with the collapse of God's good favor towards him, rather than with the collapse of his own faith. The supreme irony of this judgment is that really it is they who, by clinging to their theology of successful living or else, show themselves to be lacking faith in God, while Job, by honestly and passionately facing the shambles that his life has become, proves that in the pit of his heart he trusts his Lord.

John Calvin wrote, "While it is true that we are saved by faith alone, the faith that saves is never alone." As a general principle the point is a fair one. Nevertheless, in the story of Job we do see faith utterly alone. For so precious to God is the mystery of simple, naked faith that there are times when it is within His purposes to isolate it drastically, so as clearly to demonstrate that faith certainly can stand all by itself, cut off from every visible authentication of its worth.

The Weight of Suffering

"If only my anguish could be weighed
and all my misery be placed on the scales!
It would surely outweigh the sand of the seas!" (6:2-3)

Job's immediate response to his friend's callous words is a heartrending plea for mercy as he groans, "If only my anguish could be weighed!" His point is that Eliphaz seems to be arguing for a kind of balance-scales theology, a tit-for-tat religion in which we do things for God and then He does things for us in return. Just as virtuous deeds can, according to this view, be traded with God for tangible benefits, so all of Job's misfortune should be able to be set right by a proper, formal repentance. Thus everything about the spiritual life can be computed, totaled up, and kept straight and tidy.

But suffering is not like that; it is not tidy and mathematical. And neither is grace. And neither are any of the great mysteries of the Kingdom of Heaven. By their very nature spiritual realities are untidy. Think of how shocked Jesus' disciples were when He first began teaching them about the necessity of drinking His blood! "This is a hard teaching," they complained. "Who can accept it?" (John 6:60). The mysteries of eternal life are untidy because they are infinite and immeasurable. The blood of Jesus could not be kept neatly inside His body; it had to be spilled out. What was meant to cover the whole earth could not be contained for long in an earthen vessel. As Peter wrote, "You know that it was not with perishable things such as silver or gold that you were redeemed . . . but with the precious blood of Christ, a lamb without blemish or defect" (1 Peter 1:18-19). Things that are perfect and eternal overflow the world's containers; they upset the world's apple carts; they invalidate the world's balance scales. After all, it is not as though the atoning sacrifice of Jesus merely *outweighed* the sin of the world; much more than that, the cross of Christ canceled sin entirely.

No balance-scales view of God's judgment can ever account for such a wonder. Similarly, no human effort of will—even the will to repent in dust and ashes—can ever conciliate God or take even the tiniest step towards Him. As Paul wrote in Romans 11:35 (para-phrasing, in fact, the Lord's own words to Job in 41:11), "Who has ever given to God, that God should repay him?" The love of God is not a matter of calculation and accountancy. The trouble with Eliphaz and the other friends is that their thinking leaves no room for unmerited suffering, and therefore no room for unmerited grace, or for unmerited anything. Not only is the cross not at the center of their theology—it is not there at all. While Job holds to faith alone in the midst of his suffering, his friends seem to spend their energies doing the very opposite, seeking to avoid suffering altogether and doing so in the name of faith. As Job summarizes their attitude later in this chapter, "You see something dreadful and are afraid" (6:21).

We might as well face it: it is Job's suffering, and his suffering alone, which turns his friends against him, and which so often turns us away also from those who desperately need our love. In the words of Flannery O'Connor, who from her own battle with the grim disease of lupus had reason to know about such things, "Sickness is a place . . . where there's no company, where nobody can follow." How easily we distance ourselves from other people's pain! We are so good at rationalizing and accounting for suffering, so poor at doing anything about it, and so devastated when it is our own turn to suffer. Anyone who has wrestled with serious illness in a hospital room, and received visitors there, will know that between the sick and the well, between the paralyzed life of the sufferer and the full, energetic outer world of the visitor, there exists a vast and nearly uncrossable chasm.

But is the word "uncrossable" really a word in the Christian vocabulary? No, it need not be. Because of the cross of Christ, every chasm has already been crossed, every alienation bridged. If Eliphaz, Bildad, and Zophar were alive today and could read about them-selves and their suffering friend in the Bible, they would realize that this book is the Calvary of the Old Testament. They would see that the key to the sufferings of Job, and indeed to life itself, is the cross. They would realize that suffering, far from being something avoid-able, is the very heartbeat of life, and the door to Heaven.

The Yeast of the Pharisees

"Is tasteless food eaten without salt,
or is there flavor in the white of an egg?
I refuse to touch it;
such food makes me ill." (6:6-7)

What would you think of a friend who invited you to dinner and then put absolutely nothing on the table? Suppose you were to sit down to gleaming silverware, the best china, a lace tablecloth and candles, but no food? And what if your host even toasted you with an empty goblet, then picked up his knife and fork and began digging in on a bare plate, clearly inviting you to do the same? What would you do? Would you go along with this preposterous ruse, smacking your lips and complimenting your friend on his marvelous culinary skills? Or would you be angry with him for trying to make a fool of you, and would you tell him so in no uncertain terms?

Job is angry with Eliphaz for having pretended to feed him, when in fact he has deprived him of solid spiritual food. No doubt Job would feel the same way today if he were to visit many a contemporary church. The altar is set with linen, candles are lit, guests assemble, and there is even a plate passed around—but where is the food? There is an afterdinner speaker but no dinner. At least, whatever passes for dinner is about as tasty (as Job puts it in 6:6) as a bowl of egg whites. The meaning of the Hebrew here is obscure, and so we do not know exactly what food it is that Job says "makes me ill." But we can easily fill in this blank ourselves the next time we are subjected to a nauseatingly bland sermon. Job's metaphor may remind us of one of Jesus' comments in the Sermon on the Mount: "You are the salt of the earth. But if the salt loses its saltiness, how can it be made salty again? It is no longer good for anything, except to be thrown out and trampled by men" (Matt. 5:13).

After two chapters of Eliphaz's double-talk, there may still be some question in our minds as to what exactly he has said. But how-ever kind and wise Eliphaz's tone of voice may have been, Job has picked up on the real message: all his problems are his own fault and he had better clean up his act. It is the polite imputation of guilt in this counsel that repulses Job. He knows that wherever religion is founded upon and motivated by guilt, the result can only be evil. Evil spirits are drawn by guilt like moths to a light bulb.

Granted, guilt has its proper work to do, and many believers do not pay nearly enough attention to the call to live clean and godly lives. But many others, erring on the opposite extreme, are virtuous to a fault. They are punctilious about peccadilloes. By being overly scrupulous about selected issues of piety and morality, they unwit-tingly turn the gospel and its glorious freedom into just one more religion, just one more system of humanly-powered spiritual prin-ciples, with guilt at the core. It is not hard to spot such guilt-ridden faith, for it is full of anxiety, full of nagging worries about "finding God's will," "loving one's neighbor," "grieving the Spirit," or "tak-ing the gospel to the ends of the earth." This faith is endlessly and neurotically preoccupied with its own performance, with its own power and holiness or lack thereof. Always it has an eye on the heavenly box office, the celestial ratings. A bad rating will cause it not to love more, but to try harder; not to fix its eyes on Jesus, but to examine itself more feverishly. Worst of all, such hypersensitive egocentricity always spills over into an authoritative, judgmental attitude toward others.

This is the hypocrisy that Jesus called the "yeast of the Pharisees" (Luke 12:1). Whether He found it in the Jews who were plotting to kill Him, or in His own disciples, it is something He always angrily exposed and denounced. Paul too used the yeast metaphor when warning the Galatians to resist the powerful legalists in their midst, for "that kind of persuasion does not come from the one who calls you. 'A little yeast works through the whole batch of dough'" (5:8-9). The real root of religious hypocrisy is unresolved guilt, and this is the active agent in all legalism.

There is so much about morality and good living in the New Testament that it can be difficult to see that this is not really the point of Christianity (at least, it is neither the starting point nor the focal point), and it can be even more difficult for a disciple who started off well to detect in himself the gradual, poisonous growth of the yeast of the Pharisees.

An Unanswerable Question

"A despairing man should have the devotion of his friends. . . .
But my brothers are as undependable as intermittent streams . . .
that cease to flow in the dry season." (6:14-17)

In many ways the mystery of Job's friends is as deep and enigmatic as that of Job himself. What sort of faith, exactly, do these fellows have? Are they true believers whose minds have been temporarily darkened by the atmosphere of spiritual oppression surrounding Job? Are they solid, mature people whose wise counsel, in ninety-nine cases out of a hundred, would have been perfectly acceptable? Or are they the sort of folks we so often run into in churches today—sincere and knowledgeable but also rather arrogant and insensitive, doctrinally sound but lacking in compassion? Are these *bona fide* believers who just have a lot of growing to do? Or are they, perhaps, rank unbelievers, "having a form of godliness but denying its power" (2 Tim. 3:5)? Are they like the Pharisees of the New Testament whom Jesus flatly called "sons of hell" (Matt. 23:15)? Or would it be better to soften this judgment somewhat by suggesting they are "not far from the kingdom of God" (Mark 12:34)—that is, their religion, though on the right track, has not quite ripened into genuine saving faith?

These questions are immensely complicated by the fact that we meet Job's friends only in extenuating circumstances. They have, after all, taken an indefinite leave of absence from their own families, jobs, and comfortable routines in order to hold the hand of a sick and hurting brother who, far from being thankful for their help, lashes out at them in anger. Might not even mature believers, under stress, lose control of themselves and be bereft of their customary wisdom? Moreover, if Job himself, even while criticizing his friends, calls them "brothers" (as he does in 6:15), who are we to exclude them from the family of God? On the other hand, when we reach the Epilogue it begins to appear that God Himself may have excluded them, for only through the prayer of the righteous Job does their sin become forgivable (see 42:8). How is it that Job has direct access to the throne of grace, while his friends do not? Again, there are large sections of the speeches of Job's friends which, in any other setting, could hold their own as glorious hymns extolling the majesty of the one true God. And yet, if these men really are righteous before this God, could they not be expected to recognize righteousness in another? Is it not the guilty heart that is compelled to find guilt in others as well?

At least Job's friends did not physically abandon him, as Paul's friends apparently did when late in his life he complained, "Everyone . . . has deserted me" (2 Tim. 1:15). One wonders what can be said about all those Christians who deserted the great apostle in his time of need. Can any excuse be made for them? Or what are we ourselves to make of fellow believers who, however indirectly or with however good intentions, stab us in the back when the chips are down? What are we to do about professed Christians who consistently cloud and undermine the faith of others—and who do so, moreover, in a manner that may appear on the surface to be full of help, kindness, even wisdom? If we condemn such people outright as false believers, do we not run the risk of contracting their disease? And if we condemn the friends of Job as hypocrites, are we perhaps in danger of showing the same lack of compassion and discernment towards them that they do towards Job? Are not these men too mere human beings, just hurting and insecure people in need of love, people in process just as you and I are? When Jesus said to Peter, "*Get behind me*, Satan" (Matt. 16:23), He did not on that account treat Peter as an unbeliever. On the other hand, if Peter had persisted unrepentantly in his stubborn blindness, would not the other disciples have been compelled eventually to follow Jesus' instructions in Matthew 18:17—"Treat him as you would a pagan"?

Jesus said, "Do not judge" (Matt. 7:1). But to judge means not only to condemn; absolving others of guilt is also a judgment. Probably it is a mistake to try and pigeonhole Job's friends too narrowly in regard to the condition of their souls. Yet if we cannot condemn the sinner, we must still condemn the sin. One of the major themes of *Job* is the righteousness of one man as pitted against the religious hypocrisy of his peers. If we water down the starkness of this contrast, then we end up with a weak view of the sin of pharisaism—a view that will touch not only upon the lives of three characters in a book, but upon our own lives as well. There is a sense in which the glory of the gospel can only become clear in bold relief against this subtlest of all evils, hypocrisy.

Guilt Trips

"Teach me, and I will be quiet;
show me where I have been wrong." (6:24)

When it comes to isolating and naming the actual sin they believe to have led to Job's downfall, his friends beat about the bush. Throughout the dialogue they make veiled accusations, deliver general moral pronouncements, hum and haw, and equivocate. But all their insinuations are entirely without substance, and by way of actually identifying and getting at the root of Job's problem (which is, after all, the real goal of counseling), the best they can do is to suggest that his "attitude" is all wrong. It is a bit like telling a man with acute appendicitis that he should try not to feel so much pain.

The hurling of veiled insults and unsubstantiated charges is a favorite tactic of Satan's, and it is why he is called "the accuser of *the brethren*" (Rev. 12:10). If he can stir up clouds of guilt in our minds and unsettle us with nebulous worries, then the Devil is in his element. He loves to lay guilt trips, and this is such a familiar obstacle in the Christian life that it is something like the common cold, a condition with symptoms so stereotyped as to be drearily predictable. Whenever we find ourselves plagued by an obscure, uneasy sense of condemnation—a free-floating anxiety unattached to any clear course of remedial action—then the chances are that this is the work of the Devil and not of the Lord. It is the voice of accusation, not of conviction.

The conviction of the Holy Spirit is always precise: He identifies root causes of sin, and He moves the heart to specific acts of repentance and obedience. All those who trust God sufficiently to desire to obey Him, and who are patient in waiting upon Him, will find unfailingly that He gives clear guidance. "In all your ways acknowledge him, and he will *direct your paths*," promises Proverbs 3:6. For those who love God everything is aboveboard. To know Him is to know what He requires, and more than that, it is to have the power to carry it out. In fact these two—enlightenment and empowering—go hand in hand, and where they do not, then the Lord is not in it.

Undoubtedly God's ways are full of mystery, and there is much about His work in our lives that we cannot understand. But wherever His work does call for our active participation, in these areas we may be assured of full and precise guidance and enabling.

With the Devil it is exactly the opposite: far from giving clear insight and power to change, he robs us of these, engulfing us instead in clouds of doubt and indecision. True, Satan can be exceedingly clear in his promptings to sin. And he can also be distressingly specific in his accusations, putting his finger on obvious areas of sin and then sending us off on the most preposterous of self-righteous crusades. But such guilt trips end only in a miasma of *angst.* They are wild-goose chases through which Satan seeks ultimately to bring us to a complete standstill, rendering us incapable of any positive action at all. If he cannot make us wallow in guilt over something we have done, then he will gladly make us wallow in guilt over all that we have not done. He loves to get us dwelling on the myriad ways in which we have utterly failed, whether in our conduct towards God or towards our neighbor.

Yet what the Devil will not do, and can never do, is the very thing that the Holy Spirit always does—which is to kindle in our hearts a joyous willingness to perform some specific act of devotion to the Lord or of love for our neighbor. For the sphere of the Lord is the real world, the world of clear thinking and of decisive moral action. But the sphere of the Devil is that of the endless dimly-lit corridors and twisting staircases of morbid imagination. He is always nudging us toward insanity, and doing so through a complex system of eminently plausible, yet thoroughly paranoid, logic.

The friends of Job, by seeking to arouse murky qualms of compunction in him, and so coax him towards the verge of a reasonable but trumped-up repentance, play this neurotically logical game of Satan's. The very vagueness of their accusations gives them away.

Honest Words

"How painful are honest words!
But what do your arguments prove?" (6:25)

W here Eliphaz has been evasive in his accusations, Job is forthright, and Chapter 6 ends with a blunt, staccato summary—as plainly stated as a court indictment—of Job's precise complaints against the attitude and arguments of his friends.

First of all, he accuses them of "treating the words of a despairing man as wind" (6:26). What a terrible sin those commit who turn a deaf ear to the dejected, and who even dare to heap scorn on legitimate suffering. This is what the crowd did to blind Bartimaeus as he crouched by the roadside crying out, "Jesus, Son of David, have mercy on me!" (Mark 10:47-48). People told Bartimaeus to shut up, and the same thing happens today in many a church, where for one of a thousand expedient and doctrinally-justified reasons, the brokenhearted are silenced.

Job's next criticism of his friends goes so far as to hint prophetically at the most heinous of all the sins recorded in the Bible—the betrayal of Christ by Judas Iscariot. For Job says, "You would even . . . barter away your friend!" (6:27). Job's friends are his church, his community of faith; they are the people who should be supporting him and holding him up in prayer. But instead, Job says, they are betraying him. How often does it happen today that the earnest Christian finds his deepest struggle to be less with the world than it is with his own church? This is not a situation to be lightly or easily diagnosed. But sometimes it can be vital for a victim of institutionalized religion to grasp that his problems may not be his own fault, that he is not just an ornery and paranoid shadow-boxer. No, as in Job's case the issues that divide him from his own spiritual community may be quite valid and real, and like Job he may be fighting for his life against the very people with whom he is supposed to be in fellowship.

Having delivered this searing rebuke, Job's tone suddenly softens to a gentler plea as he says simply, "Now be so kind as to look at me" (6:28). In this play for voices it is fascinating to note the stage directions latent in the script. Here it appears that throughout Job's speech the friends have been hanging their heads and refusing to meet his gaze, while in an odd reversal of roles the sick man now holds his head high and looks his sleek and healthy inquisitors straight in the eye. Is this not just the sort of poignant moment that can occur in a real argument? Suddenly the one who is in the wrong feels compelled to avert the eyes, while the one who is right has the freedom to regard the other fearlessly.

Next, Job pleads with his friends to "reconsider, for my integrity is at stake" (6:29). Does Eliphaz really understand the seriousness of the insinuations he has been making? In Job's vocabulary the word "integrity" is almost interchangeable with "righteousness" (see 27:5). So Job's point is that Eliphaz has impugned not only his character but, by implication, the very genuineness of his faith. In today's terms it is as though one Christian were to say to another Christian in difficulty, "Friend, the reason for all of your problems must be that you are not really a Christian." While Eliphaz might not dare (at least at this early stage in the dialogue) to express himself quite so bluntly, Job is suggesting that this is what his charges actually amount to.

Accordingly, in the last verse of the chapter Job submits his faith to a virtual lie detector test when he challenges, "Is there any wickedness on my lips? Can my mouth not discern malice?" (6:30). These rhetorical questions have all the force of swearing on a stack of Bibles. Job is arguing that the mere word of a righteous man is fully admissible as evidence of his innocence because, as Jesus taught, "Out of the overflow of his heart his mouth speaks" (Luke 6:45). Granted, the last word of all belongs to God, but if a person really is righteous, then God stands wholly behind him.

With this line of defense Job pinpoints and clarifies the nub of the debate. Either he is a righteous man, with God on his side, or he is not. Either his faith is the real thing or it is not.

Mere Humanity

"Does not man have hard service on earth?
Are not his days like those of a hired man?
Like a slave longing for the evening shadows . . ." (7:1-2)

Like so many passages of great lyric poetry in this book, these stanzas have an uncanny power to evoke in just a few pen-strokes all the bewildering and homely reality of the human condition. The farmer in his cornfield; the stockbroker in his glass-and-steel tower; the President in his Oval Office; the Christian writer at his word processor: all of us know exactly what it is to be "a slave longing for the evening shadows." Job's questions at the beginning of Chapter 7 may appear to bring a complete shift in subject; but really they are a continuation of his primary line of self-defense, as he points out quite simply that it is the lot of humanity to suffer and that he, Job, is in this respect no different from any other person.

As we shall see so often throughout this story, Job's faith draws its strength not just from his knowledge of the Lord but from the profound awareness he has of his own mere humanity. In the previous chapter, for example, he had piteously lamented, "Do I have the strength of stone? Is my flesh bronze? Do I have any power to help myself, now that success has been driven from me?" (6:12-13). Job is keenly aware that he is not a man of stone or of bronze but of flesh and bone, and he knows also that flesh and bone are but dust. Here is a man steeped in the consciousness of his mortality and human weakness. He knows well his frailty; yet beyond this he knows that the Lord knows it too. In the words of Psalm 103:14, "[The Lord] knows how we are formed, he remembers that we are dust." Accordingly, in one of those odd paradoxes that serve like alternating current to animate the beating heart of faith, it is Job's intimate knowledge of his own utter helplessness that becomes the very ground upon which he stands as he reaches out boldly to shake the throne of God. "Give me a place to stand and I will move the world," boasted Archimedes. But Job was a still greater engineer, for he knew where to stand to move the heart of God.

Job's language in the opening verses of Chapter 7 may remind us of those New Testament passages in which the people of God are called "aliens and strangers on earth" (Heb. 11:13; 1 Peter 2:11). If we are aliens here, then it stands to reason that we will encounter many difficulties. As believers we will continue to suffer—that is, to experience evil firsthand—since in worldly terms we are no better off than anyone else. Indeed we are worse off, for does it not follow that those who love their Creator will feel the brunt of the fallen creation even more painfully than those who do not love Him? Becoming a Christian, far from reducing the normal hardships of life or the demands made upon us as human beings, actually increases them. God's gift of grace does not in this sense make life easier.

True, the Christian life is not without its privileges, even in worldly terms. But essentially our growth in Christ happens not by being lifted above the level of the world but rather by being immersed more and more deeply in it. What we are involved in is a process not of divinization, but of increasing humanization, for the way we become like God is by becoming more human—more of what He created us to be. Any theology that either demeans our humanness, or else tends in any way toward elitism (whether intellectual, social, or spiritual) is a twisted theology. Any spirituality that tries to rob people of their day-to-day creatureliness, or that lures them away from the ordinary struggles and duties of life in the real world, is a false spirituality. On the contrary, the more saintly a person becomes, the more closely he or she will be identified with the common lot of suffering humanity. Job is a great saint not because he is in any way superhuman, but because he is himself. There is no sham or deceit in him, no artificiality or posturing—and even if there is, it is only what is to be expected from dust and ashes.

Milan Kundera, Czech author of the novel with the haunting title *The Unbearable Lightness of Being*, once confessed, "My lifetime ambition has been to unite the utmost seriousness of question with the utmost lightness of form." Was this perhaps what God had up His sleeve when He created human beings—and even more, when He became one Himself?

Sleeplessness

"When I lie down I think, 'How long before I get up?'
The night drags on, and I toss till dawn." (7:4)

There are some aspects to the suffering of Jesus on the cross that are less obvious than others. To cite one example: He had not slept the night before. In fact He probably had very little sleep at all throughout the entire momentous week prior to His death. Certainly His disciples, by the time of that final evening in Gethsemane, were completely spent, not just overtired but "exhausted from sorrow" (Luke 22:45).

It is one thing to face the difficulties of life when well rested. But without sleep, even small problems can get blown out of all proportion. Most of us can survive one sleepless night without too much difficulty; we make up for it the next night by sleeping longer or more deeply. But two such nights in a row, or three or four, can be enough to cause even the healthiest, happiest, most resilient individual to come apart at the seams. Under pressure of prolonged sleep deprivation it is almost as though something in the very mind or character snaps, resulting in a temporary loss of sanity.

It is consoling to read in Psalm 127:2 that God "grants sleep to those he loves." But perhaps such a verse needs to be set against Proverbs 10:5: "He who sleeps during harvest is a disgraceful son." Paul mentions "sleepless nights" (2 Cor. 6:5) in his catalog of the normal hardships to be expected in the service of God. For him, we know, such wakefulness would have been occasioned by everything from beatings to storms at sea, from prayer vigils to late-night ministry, from prison discomforts to the demands of constant travel, from physical illness to plain old anxiety and "the pressure of my concern for all the churches" (2 Cor. 11:28).

For Job too, sleeplessness would have been one of his most severe trials. Not only would the festering boils all over his body have made rest virtually impossible, but there was the added torment of the monstrous fears and lurid imaginings that must have come over him in the middle of the night. Any suffering tends to be worse in the darkness, and so Job complains, "When I think my bed will comfort me and my couch will ease my complaint, even then you frighten me with dreams and terrify me with visions" (7:13-14).

Is it any wonder if the same man who at the outset of his ordeal responded so nobly with the words, "Shall we accept good from God, and not trouble?" (2:10) by Chapter 3 seems to have lost all perspective and to be unable to get a grip on himself? It is wonderful to read stories of the gloriously serene deaths of some of the great heroes of faith. But not every Christian dies that way. Many die like dogs. Many waste away in slums or in prisons or are butchered in back alleys. Thousands are killed in the womb. Many more go senile or insane; they become paralyzed, incontinent, comatose. Under conditions of grave illness or impending death, countless Christians are rendered incapable of glorifying God in any obviously meaningful fashion. They will never be written about in any *Lives of the Saints* or *Foxe's Book of Martyrs*.

Nevertheless, are their names not written in the only book that counts, the Book of Life? Are they not heroes in the eyes of God? Can He not save and exalt even those who die without any inspired confession upon their lips, and perhaps without even a rationally coherent thought of Him in their heads? As Jonah prayed from the belly of the whale:

> You hurled me into the deep,
>   into the very heart of the seas,
> and the currents swirled about me.
>   All your waves and billows swept over me. . . .
> To the roots of the mountains I sank down;
>   the earth beneath barred me in forever.
> But you brought my life up from the pit,
>   O Lord my God. (2:3, 6)

Jars of Clay

"My body is clothed with worms and scabs,
my skin is broken and festering." (7:5)

It is easy to see how Job's friends put two and two together. If a man's body were visibly rotting away, then what must his soul be like? Throughout both Old and New Testament times the uncleanness of the skin (including not just leprosy but every other kind of skin disease) was taken to be clear evidence of spiritual uncleanness. It was a vivid picture of living condemnation, of walking, breathing corruption. At one point Bildad actually has the temerity to speak this judgment aloud to Job's face, telling him that the fate of the wicked is to have their "skin . . . eaten away" and their "limbs . . . devoured" (18:13).

Amazingly, Job does not succumb to these terrorizing tactics, but rather holds fast to his spiritual integrity in spite of the decay of his flesh. Is this not one of the ultimate challenges of faith? For Christians today who are struggling with cancer or with any other consuming disease, the real hope lies not with radiation or with chemotherapy, or even with faith-healing (though all of these might bring healing), but rather with the simple conviction that those who trust in Christ are already as pure as the driven snow, regardless of outward appearance. Whatever our flesh might look like now (and the term "flesh" must be taken to include not just the body, but all the ugly thoughts and emotions to which the sick are inevitably subjected), the fact is that God has promised resurrection and glorification to this same flesh, and He will pay us back eternally for all our present indignity and pain.

Miraculous healing, to be sure, is as vital a part of Christian ministry today as it was in the first century. Without it the church limps along, lame and leprous. Nevertheless, it is possible to place so much emphasis on a miraculous cure that one completely loses sight of the inestimable worth of patient, faithful endurance of disease. We like to talk about "having the faith to be healed," but what about having the faith to be sick? Jesus did not heal Lazarus; He let him die, saying, "This sickness . . . is for God's glory" (John 11:4). Similarly when Paul first met the Lord, far from being healed he was struck blind! Even his subsequent healing was accompanied by the prophecy, "I will show him how much he must suffer for my name" (Acts 9:16).

In his second letter to the Corinthians Paul makes it clear that we have the treasure of the gospel in "jars of clay," and that "though outwardly we are wasting away, yet inwardly we are being renewed day by day" (4:7, 16). He goes on to say that "while we are in this tent, we groan and are burdened," and gently warns that "as long as we are at home in the body we are away from the Lord." Thus he encourages Christians to "live by faith, not by sight," and he condemns "those who take pride in what is seen rather than in what is in the heart" (5:4, 6, 7, 12). How rich and deep these chapters are for the sick and suffering believer! Perhaps the crux of the whole matter is to be found in 2 Corinthians 4:10-11: "We always carry around in our body the death of Jesus, so that the life of Jesus may also be revealed in our body. For we who are alive are always being given over to death for Jesus' sake, so that his life may be revealed in our mortal body." What do these words mean, if not that the Lord is doing with us exactly as He did with Job—that is, giving us over (according to the measure of our faith) into the hands of the Devil and his kingdom of mortality, together with all its accompanying tortures, in order that something far more glorious than worldly health and prosperity might be pressed out of us like wine out of grapes?

If we are to be true witnesses of Christ, we must witness to His death as well as to His resurrection. After all, we Christians have died already—we have died to sin. Already our flesh has been undone and our old nature is decaying amidst our new one. Why should we strive, as the unbelieving world does, to conceal such an obvious fact? We are like windblown fruit, sitting on the ground and rotting. But only in this way can the brand-new seed that lives within us be uncovered and planted. "I tell you the truth, unless a kernel of wheat falls to the ground and dies, it remains only a single seed. But if it dies, it produces many seeds. The man who loves his life will lose it, while the man who hates his life in this world will keep it for eternal life" (John 12:24-25).

Pouring out the Heart

"Remember, O God, that my life is but a breath." (7:7)

This may well be the most significant verse in the entire book. Why? Because this is where we first hear Job break into prayer. Even his great professions of faith in the Prologue were more in the form of meditations than prayers; for example, speaking of God in the third person he had reflected, *"The Lord gives, the Lord takes away,"* and, "Shall we accept good from God, and not trouble?" Here in Chapter 7, however, it is the direct, intimate vocative of true prayer that Job employs as he cries out, "O God!" And from this point on we frequently hear him slip into and out of this intensely personal form of language, as spontaneously as if a visible, incarnate God were sitting right there beside him, just one more participant in the discussion. Granted, Job's prayers are more often concerned with God's apparent absence than with His nearness. But the radiant proof of Job's genuineness of faith is that he prays *at all*—especially in view of the fact that prayer is conspicuously missing from all the talk of his friends. Nowhere in the book does one word of prayer pass any of their lips.

Surely this is the crucial, telling difference between the speeches of Job and those of everyone else. Job regularly talks *to* God; his friends talk only *about* Him. Like Christ on the cross, Job even in his agony continues to speak—now to himself, now to others, now to God. Thus his language is a rich and compelling blend of meditation, conversation, and heartfelt prayer, with the three elements so closely interwoven as to make it impossible at times to separate them. By contrast, the speeches of Eliphaz, Bildad, and Zophar are addressed only to Job himself, and we shall listen to them in vain for any demonstration of real intimacy with the Lord they so loudly proclaim. We can only presume that they must have felt terribly threatened by their friend's habit of constantly intruding his messy, private prayer life into their intellectual debate.

It is worth reflecting on how unusual it is for anyone to speak openly to God while other, non-praying people are present, and how hurtful to Job must have been this coldly objective attitude of his friends. What would you think of fellow Christians who came to console you by telling you all they thought you needed to know about God, yet who declined to pray with you because they were not much in the habit of it themselves, and moreover because they looked on you as a person full of sin and warped theology with whom it might be dangerous to enter into spiritual communion?

The point should be clear: Job is the only person in the book (with the possible exception, as we shall see later, of Elihu) who has any direct communication with God. Quite obviously he knew the secret of Psalm 62:8: "Pour out your hearts to him, for God is our refuge." Human hearts are full of many things: joy, anger, peace, weariness, anxiety, strength, bitterness, trust. To pour out the heart means to pour out not just some but all of these contents before the Lord, the bad along with the good. Would we try to conceal our bitterness from God? Or conversely, would we cling greedily to our joy? In either case we cannot really pray. In one sense joy is no better a thing than bitterness, because either can pass away in a moment. Yesterday's joy will not do for today. A flower is beautiful, but in drought it withers just like a weed. Therefore in prayer everything in the heart must be poured out to the Lord like a drink offering, so that the heart is kept empty for Him. God only fills hearts that have been prepared for His residence like a clean, swept house with all the windows thrown open to the sun.

This is what Job is doing when he prays. He is sweeping out all that is in his heart, even to the point of groaning, "I despise my life; I would not live forever. Let me alone; my days have no meaning" (7:16). Are these good Christian sentiments? It does not matter. What matters is that Job is not afraid of true prayer. He knows it consists not in flowery language, nor in false humility, nor in pretending to possess any greater faith than we really have, but rather in simply trusting God enough to spill our guts to Him. Because Job does this, because he speaks his heart to the Lord as frankly, as familiarly, as crudely as any hapless drunk to his bartender on a lonely Saturday night, the Lord in His time speaks back.

Job the Sinner

"I have sinned, [but] what have I done to you,
O watcher of men?
Why have you made me your target?" (7:20)

Was Job a sinner? Do the righteous continue to sin? All such questions should be clearly resolved by this verse, in which Job frankly confesses, "I have sinned." (The NIV translation reads "*if* I have sinned," but the word "if" is not present in the original Hebrew.) What Job is saying, in effect, is this: "I know I am a sinner, Lord. But what sort of sin could possibly have turned a forgiving God so violently against me?" This sense carries over into the next verse as Job asks, "Why do you not pardon my offenses and forgive my sins?" He is not pretending to have committed no sins or offenses. But as a believer in a merciful God he is accustomed to having his sins forgiven, not held against him. He cannot understand why his God seems suddenly to have changed the rules and to be withholding forgiveness.

Job's friends are anxious to persuade him not simply that he is sinful (that much is perfectly obvious), but rather that his present misfortune must be the result of willfully repressed or concealed sin. This charge Job vehemently denies. He does not need to be told to repent, for he is the sort of man in whom repentance is already a deeply ingrained habit of soul. Repentance is second nature to him; he knows he has kept strict accounts with God. In fact if it were possible for Job to find some grave, hidden, unconfessed sin in himself, this would no doubt come as a tremendous relief to him. It would shed light on his present suffering and give some meaning to it. As it is, he knows his conscience is clear, and paradoxically it is this very fact that troubles him, since it casts aspersions on the forgiving character of his God. In Job's mind the issue has nothing to do with whether or not he has sinned, but everything to do with whether God will pardon. His turmoil is centered not upon his own failure, but upon the Lord's apparent failure to forgive him. Writes Francis Andersen, "Job's faith does not relieve his agony; it causes it."

Has God ever promised people a surefire system that would keep us from sinning? No. His promise, rather, is that He will be with us in the midst of our inevitable failure, and we can trust Him to "redeem [our] life from the pit" (Ps. 103:4). The faithful, wrote John Murray, "are not perfect in holiness. But they have been translated from the realm of sin and death to that of righteousness and life. Sin is now their burden and plague. Why? Because it is not their realm, they are not at home with it. It is foreign country to them. They are in the world, but not of it." This is the notion Job clings to throughout the book—not that he is sinless, but that he is righteous. He is bold to believe that by faith such a blameless status in the eyes of God must be possible and achievable for a sinner even in the midst of his sin, and that if it is not, then all religion is a tragic joke and life is totally without hope.

Job's conviction is fundamentally Christian. Part and parcel of believing in Christ is believing in our own blamelessness before Him. How can we "gain access by faith into . . . grace" (Rom. 5:2) if we do not believe, first of all, that such grace is truly available, and secondly, that through simple faith in Jesus Christ it is ours? To believe this is to believe the gospel, to accept the good news. It can hardly be called good news if for some reason we think that we ourselves may be excluded from it. To believe we might be excluded is to believe bad news. To be afraid that Jesus does not or will not accept us, is actually to refuse to accept Him. For He Himself said, "Whoever comes to me I will never *reject*" (John 6:37). To trust God is to trust that He is good, and to trust that He is good is to trust that He is and always will be good *to me*, and cannot be otherwise.

This is the faith that saves. However, is such faith to be equated with what is popularly called "assurance of salvation"? No, it is not. Job has faith, but in his present circumstances he seems not to have assurance, and that is a topic for the next chapter.

Assurance

"Why do you not pardon my offenses
and forgive my sins?" (7:21)

Job believes and knows that his God is a forgiving God. His problem is that right now he does not *feel* forgiven. The very crux of the trial he goes through is that while he continues to have faith in God, he has no sense of peace or assurance that his faith will be rewarded. How much easier it would be if only he could have a deep inner confidence that God is on his side. But he has no such confidence. He may have had it before, but now it has vanished; or else what he had before seems curiously impotent to comfort him in his present plight. His beliefs have not changed, but now there is no feeling of certainty in his soul as to whether God is his friend or his foe, his loving Father or his executioner. As we have seen, Job knows full well that he is a sinner. But at this point in his life he cannot find any relief from the burden of his sin, and that is the real nub of his suffering. What good is all his faith if it does not take the weight of sin off his back?

Can a person who feels this way truly be said to have great faith? There are some people who, like the friends of Job, would condemn him on this score alone. If he does not have assurance of salvation, they would say, then his salvation itself remains in question. He may not have any real faith at all. How often have we ourselves let this thought cast its long shadow over our hearts? But it is a lie of Satan. The fact is, much of the purpose of the New Testament epistles is to help Christians—people who have already placed their faith in the Lord Jesus Christ—gain assurance and thus to enter fully into the joy of their salvation. If we assume that our faith cannot be the real thing if we do not have assurance, then we have fallen for a hoax that effectively stops the gospel in its tracks. Did Jesus have assurance when He cried from the cross, "My God, my God, why have you forsaken me?" (Matt. 27:46). The true gospel is much too important to rest simply on a settled feeling of security. While assurance is a product of faith—and a product greatly to be desired—in the final analysis it is not the foundation of faith. Listen to what Richard Baxter wrote about this:

> I do not ask whether thou be assured of salvation, nor whether thou canst believe that thy sins are pardoned, and that thou art beloved of God in Christ. These are no parts of justifying faith, but excellent fruits of it, and they that receive them are comforted by them; but perhaps thou mayest never receive them while thou livest, and mayest yet be a true heir of rest. Do not say then, "I cannot believe that my sins are pardoned, or that I am in God's favor; and therefore I am no true believer." This is a most mistaken conclusion.

Job's point, as he argues with his friends and even with God Himself, is precisely the same. He will not allow his faith to be disqualified on the ground of subjective feeling. He will "seek peace and pursue it" (Ps. 34:14), but the proof of his faith will be in the seeking itself and not necessarily in the finding. Job instinctively grasps one of the great keys to faith: our relationship with God is neither predicated upon nor authenticated by our feelings. Having the right sort of feelings toward God is something greatly to be prized, but it is not the bottom line of faith.

Having said this, it is important to state also that any believer who does not have assurance of salvation, along with all the accompanying spiritual affections of joy and peace, should earnestly seek these rewards with all his heart. He should "hunger and thirst for righteousness" (Matt. 5:6), petitioning God day and night and refusing to give up until his hunger is satisfied. For this is what Job did. He was prepared to hang on to nothing if he had to, but only because he knew instinctively that "all things are *ours*" in Christ (1 Cor. 3:21). His faith was such that he was able to hold these two contradictory positions in tension. Not having assurance or heart's peace, he did not waver in his faith, but neither would he settle for a religion without assurance. His faith consisted in the fact that he would not rest until he had secured the promises of God.

Bildad

Then Bildad the Shuhite replied:
"How long will you say such things?
Your words are a blustering wind." (8:1-2)

The cumulative weight of Job's arguments in Chapter 7 ought to have been enough to drive the final coffin nails into his friends' "health-and-wealth gospel." Anyone who counts on having tangible blessings as a reward or validation for faith will in the long run be disappointed. Such blessings may be thoroughly enjoyed in this life, but not insisted upon as prerogatives of righteousness. Being a believer in the Lord is no guarantee against any sort of failure or disaster, including sickness, family breakdown, or complete mental collapse. All God guarantees is that He will be with us and that ultimately we will be saved—and there are bound to come times when even on these promises He will appear to be reneging.

Job's views on this subject are full of depth and passion. As soon as Bildad gets a chance to speak, however, it is obvious that all of Job's unsettling eloquence has been wasted on him. If Eliphaz strikes us as the most refined member of this group, comparatively flexible and sophisticated, then Bildad the Shuhite comes across as the staunch, ramrod traditionalist, the one who sees all issues in black and white and who prides himself on his straightforward, no-nonsense approach. He is the kind of person whose mind is already made up—not only on every important question but on many unimportant ones as well—and whose faith is a simple matter of sticking doggedly to the old catechism of tried-and-true answers. As he himself puts it, "Ask the former generations and find out what their fathers learned, for we were born only yesterday and know nothing" (8:8-9).

People who place such heavy reliance on tradition show that they have little in the way of a personal relationship with the Lord. Bildad implies that Job's faith is like "relying on a spider's web. He leans on his web, but it gives way" (8:14-15). Yet Job is not leaning on a spider's web at all but upon the living God. The real question is:

What is Bildad leaning on? Is it anything more than a carefully-constructed little cairn of precious nuggets that he picked up in "Sunday school" years before? A man like Bildad has no stomach for the sort of dubious spiritual battle in which Job is embroiled. To him Job's complex ruminations are nothing but a load of double-talk and he tells him so outright: "Your words are a blustering wind." But Bildad's own bluster and rhetoric give him the lie.

Having painted such a negative portrait of Bildad, we should hasten to add that there is a danger in being too condemning of Job's friends. Pharisee-bashing can be such entertaining sport. There is something eminently satisfying about rooting out hypocrites and throwing them to the lions; it makes the rest of us feel like such shining saints. Yet how many have gone on witch hunts only to be tainted by witchcraft themselves? And are we really so confident that we can distinguish the diehard legalist who is a dangerous enemy of true faith from the immature believer who is our brother in Christ? This is the riddle that constantly confronts us in the friends of Job and, more importantly, in the people we know who may be like them. Indeed it is the riddle that confronts us in the depths of our own souls. We step over a line into the Kingdom of God, but there is no line we can step over and suddenly be transformed into mature, loving people.

In reading *Job*, just as in reading any complex work of literature, the most profit is to be gained not so much from identifying ourselves strongly with one character or another, but from seeing the different characters as aspects of ourselves, as windows into our own psyches. By depicting a highly subtle form of religious hypocrisy in the friends of Job, the book helps us identify pharisaism and see it for what it is—not only in others, but in ourselves. Surely this is how Jesus' stern warnings against the Pharisees are to be received by Christians. Not only did the Master instruct His disciples, "Leave them; they are blind guides" (Matt. 15:14), but He also told us to "be on your guard against the yeast of the Pharisees" (Luke 12:1)—that is, to be on guard against our own legalistic tendencies. If we cannot see the yeast of the Pharisees in ourselves, it may be because we are up to our eyeballs in it.

The Sins of the Children

"When your children sinned against him,
he gave them over to the penalty of their sin." (8:4)

Bildad strikes a low blow indeed when he tries to drag Job's children into the argument. Whether or not the latter may have been involved in serious sin is, perhaps, not the main issue. The main issue is that before God Job's own conscience is clear on this matter, and now Bildad is trying to muddy the waters. He is prying into a naturally sensitive area and seeking to stir up fresh pangs of guilt. Back in the Prologue, we were told that Job's children were in the habit of throwing big parties, and it is no secret that young people can get carried away on such occasions. This very problem seems to have preyed on Job's peace of mind, and hence his regular custom after his children's shindigs was to "send and have them purified" and to "sacrifice a burnt offering for each of them" (1:5). Just as Christians today view their sacraments as outward and visible signs of an inward and spiritual grace, Job would have believed implicitly in the effectiveness of his purificatory rites to secure divine forgiveness. At the very least, his own heart would have been set at ease that he had done everything in his own limited power to safeguard his family's sanctity. Without the availability of such assurance, what God-fearing father or mother could survive the ravages of parenthood?

Bildad, in rehashing the issue of family sin, throws all of this into question. In effect he casts doubt on the very foundation of the gospel, which is the reality of God's forgiveness. As we have already seen, this is one of Satan's favorite ploys against believers. If he cannot burden us with our own sins, then he will gladly get at us through the sins of our children. Satan loves to persuade people that real, heartfelt forgiveness of sins is unobtainable, and that there is no such thing as a clear conscience.

What then is Bildad's advice? Ironically, all he can suggest is the enactment of yet another religious ritual, but this time a specious one: "If you will look to God and plead with the Almighty, if you are pure and upright, even now he will rouse himself on your behalf" (8:5-6). Your first sacrifices, Bildad implies, obviously did not work; therefore go and dig up the cold ashes and burnt carcasses and haul them back onto the altar; maybe God will hear you this time—that is, provided you are "pure and upright"! Significantly, Bildad makes the cardinal blunder of thinking that one must be pure *before* he can approach God. Jesus exposed the folly of this when He taught, "It is not the healthy who need a doctor, but the sick" (Matt. 9:12).

Bildad's counsel may appear harmless enough. But essentially he is tempting Job to repent for things of which he has already repented—or, more subtle still, to produce a confession for crimes of which he is not guilty. Seen in this light, Bildad's innocent little promptings take on the proportions of a blackmailer's threats, or the strong-arm tactics of a secret police squad.

But Job is not to be taken in by the alluring yet false comfort of an extorted confession. Like any vigorous believer, he already lives and breathes repentance and he does not need to be exhorted to it. Unlike his pious friends it does not occur to him to dwell morbidly on his past sins, and therefore he cannot be coerced into bringing back to God's altar what he has already left there. What good is faith if it does not free us from carrying by ourselves the impossible load of sin and guilt? Job believes heartily in such freedom. Even in the absence of inner peace or assurance, still he believes robustly in the reality of forgiveness.

Do we think repentance means only being sorry for our sins? But that is not repentance; that is remorse. Remorse can lead to repentance, but it is also possible to get stuck in remorse and never move on. Full repentance means facing the fact that we cannot carry our own sins, that we cannot carry the guilt and the sorrow for them, and so turning everything over to God. If a wealthy friend were to invite me out to dinner, when I had not a penny in my pocket, would I fight with him over the bill? Even if the waiter made the mistake of presenting the bill to me, the only gracious (to say nothing of practical!) thing to do would be to slide it over to my host, saying quietly, "I believe this belongs to you."

Faith is the knowledge that whenever we try to foot the bill for our own sin, we are crushed, but that nothing can crush the Lord. It is humility, not pride, which lets God pay the whole shot.

The Way of the Cross

"Surely God does not reject a blameless man
or strengthen the hands of evildoers." (8:20)

Bildad is perfectly correct. Far from rejecting the blameless God says, "Never will I leave you; never will I forsake you" (Heb. 13:5). And as for "strengthening the hands of evildoers," the Lord does the very opposite: "He frustrates the ways of the wicked" (Ps. 146:9).

So in general terms Bildad is right. However, when this general truth is applied to the particular case of Job—and even more conspicuously, when it is applied to the case of Jesus Christ—Bildad turns out to be profoundly, egregiously wrong. For on Calvary it was God's explicit plan to "reject a blameless man" and to "strengthen the hands" of those who crucified Him. And so it was with Job. In *Job* we see what happens when the Lord places more weight on a man's shoulders than he can gracefully bear, and when He then abandons that righteous man to carry the weight by himself. Is this not what a cross is? It is abandonment (or at least the felt experience of abandonment) by God.

This strange experience is one from which no believer is exempt. All of us must share in the maddening paradox of knowing in our hearts that we are the loved and redeemed children of God, and freer than the wind, and yet still being compelled to experience firsthand the cruelty and injustice of a world in which the righteous are unwelcome intruders, and in which all too often the strength of evildoers goes wildly unchecked.

Naturally as Christians we suffer many woes simply on account of our own sin. As Eliphaz argued so glibly in 4:8, "Those who sow trouble reap it"—a saying which even the New Testament quotes as a warning to believers (see Gal. 6:7). But to endure the normal consequences of our own folly is not what it means to take up our cross and share in the sufferings of Christ. No, to suffer with Christ means to suffer undeservedly, as Jesus and His apostles did, and as Job also did. When Paul spoke of "filling up in my flesh what is still lacking in regard to Christ's afflictions" (Col. 1:24), he did not mean that he expected to add anything to the finished work of Christ's atonement. Rather, he was stating the heartfelt aspiration of all mature disciples to be like Jesus in every way, including having "the sufferings of Christ flow over into our lives" (2 Cor. 1:5).

The lot of God's children on this earth is something like being buried alive. First we are raised with Christ and made into entirely new creatures, pure and blameless, washed and redeemed and lifted up to Heaven. All of this happens by faith—which is to say, not in some imaginary way, but in a way more gloriously real than this present world can bear to behold. Yet no sooner has this spiritual transaction taken place, no sooner have we been veritably seated with Christ in the heavenly realms, than immediately we are sent down to earth again, just as Jesus was, and entrusted with a mission: "As the Father sent me, so I am sending you" (John 20:21). The moment we are born again we are sent right back into the world of sin and death. In fact we are set back down into exactly the same circumstances in which we found ourselves before we were saved, and there we are told to take up the work of the Son of God in that situation, however painful it might be. And this is a lot we are to accept with increasing graciousness.

Religion would be well deserving of the title Marx gave it—"the opiate of the masses"—were it not for the fact that in practical terms no such opiate exists. For no matter what system of beliefs people inject into their veins it is still impossible for them to escape pain. As T. S. Eliot wrote, "We only live, only suspire / Consumed by either fire or fire." Bildad, like many believers today, seems to be more interested in religiously avoiding pain at all costs, than in enduring it for Christ's sake. Obviously there is some place in his thinking for the stoical acceptance of suffering as a kind of "penance"; but there is clearly no place for the redemptive bearing of unjust, undeserved suffering. "Does God pervert justice?" (8:3) he asks Job sarcastically at the outset of his speech. He seems to think of faith as a way of getting out from under one's cross, rather than of taking it up.

Delighting the Father's Heart

Then Job replied: "Indeed, I know that this is true.
But how can a mortal be righteous before God?" (9:1-2)

Job now launches into the very heart of his argument as he poses the central riddle of this book: "How can a mortal be righteous before God?" It seems odd to hear this question from Job, whose entire case against his friends rests upon his confidence in his own righteousness. But while the friends ask this question ironically, not believing there can be any answer (see 4:17; 15:14), Job asks it in deadly earnest, implying not just that there must be an answer, but that without an answer all is lost. In taking this position Job commits himself to doing exactly what the gospel does—that is, he sets about to redefine the very meaning of the word "righteous."

In essence Job's reply to Bildad might be paraphrased as follows: "What you say is true, Bildad, but it is not helpful, because it does not go far enough. The exacting God you describe is a God whom no human being could ever satisfy. How could a mere mortal even begin to be righteous before such a God? No, there must be more to Him than that. There must be something more to the mystery of godliness than cold, mathematical justice. There are more things in Heaven and earth, Bildad, than are dreamt of in your philosophy."

In some ways "philosophy" really is a better term than "theology" for the friends' relentlessly logical way of thinking. The God whose ways can be neatly comprehended by human reason, Job argues, is not the same God who "overturns mountains in his anger" (v. 5). It is easy enough to sit in an armchair and make true statements about "God"—but what are you going to do when the living God "shakes the earth from its place" (v. 6) and your armchair with it? Trying to defend oneself or argue against such a God, says Job, is more hopeless than trying to win a game of chess against the most sophisticated of computers: "Though one wished to dispute with him, he could not answer him one time out of a thousand"

(v. 3). Later in the chapter Job expresses the same truth in exquisite paradoxes: "Though I were innocent, I could not answer him" (v. 15); "Even if I were *blameless*, my mouth would condemn me" (v. 20).

Job is valiantly seeking to expand his friends' vision of God (and his own too) so that together they can stop clinging to pat answers. Without really foreseeing the full implications of his own line of argument, Job is proceeding exactly as any preacher of the gospel must proceed. That is, he is establishing the fact that the chasm between man's sin and God's holiness is so impossibly wide that all human attempts to bridge it are exposed as utterly useless. All efforts at philosophy, spirituality, or good moral living become meaningless before the all-surpassing holiness of such an awesome God. Yet for this very reason, Job contends, there must exist something else, something besides virtue or sacrifice or even correct theology, that will be acceptable to this God as righteousness. Job's faith, in fact, consists precisely in this—that as unapproachable and enigmatic as this Deity is, he knows there must be *some* way to approach Him and to stand before Him. Just because He is so great and wonderful, there must be *some* means of gaining His approval and of having Him say to us, "Well done, good and faithful servant! . . . Come and share your master's happiness!" (Matt. 25:21).

Job is right. There *is* a way to delight our Father's heart—but it is not through bending over backwards to be good. In his prophetic soul Job knows that is it not our business to try to make ourselves perfect, as the Buddhists do, but rather to have faith in the perfection of the Son of Man, who alone is "full of grace and truth" (John 1:14). God's delight is not in a life lived in undeviating virtue, but rather in seeing the most twisted and chaotic life turned in humble expectation towards Him. The truly righteous person, it turns out, is the one who places no expectations upon himself. From God he expects everything, but from himself he expects nothing, because he knows he is but dust. The freedom of the gospel is the freedom to make no demands upon oneself. This is the freedom Job has, and it is this that so perplexes his friends. The friends are like those whom Paul warns of who "spy on the freedom we have in Christ" (Gal. 2:4). Nothing is more maddening to such people than to pour all of their energy into doing all the right things, only to end up hopelessly entangled in them, and then to be confronted by someone who is doing it all wrong, yet who is free.

Incarnation

"His wisdom is profound, his power is vast. . . .
He treads on the waves of the sea. . . .
He performs wonders that cannot be fathomed. . . .
Who can say to him, 'What are you doing?'" (9:4, 8, 10, 12)

I n verse after verse in the first part of this chapter, Job does something surpassingly marvelous: he lauds the transcendent,
untouchable power and holiness of the Almighty God, and yet
in doing so he uses language that for any Christian reader is richly
suggestive of the deeds and character of a man who walked this
earth: namely, Jesus of Nazareth. Listen:

If God alone "treads on the waves of the sea" (v. 8), what must
we conclude from the fact that Jesus did the same?

If God is "the Maker of the Bear and Orion [and] the Pleiades"
(v. 9), what could be more fitting than that a brand-new star should
be created to announce the birth of His Son?

If God "performs wonders that cannot be fathomed" and "miracles that cannot be numbered" (v. 10), then of course this description fits also the ministry of Jesus.

If it is true of God that "when he goes by, I cannot perceive him"
(v. 11), then it follows that Jesus too would have the power to make
Himself invisible in a crowd (as He does, for example, in John 8:59).

If no one can say to God, "What are you doing?" (v. 12), then in
the life of Jesus too it would come to pass that "no one dared ask
him any more questions" (Mark 12:34).

If "God does not restrain his anger" (v. 13a), then Jesus too might
be expected to show anger.

Finally, if "the cohorts of Rahab [i.e., the powers of darkness]
cower at [God's] feet" (v. 13b), then for Jesus too it would happen
that "whenever the evil spirits saw him, they fell down before him
and cried out" (Mark 3:11).

What wonderful irony there is in seeing Job set out to describe
the immortal and invisible God, and in the process paint a stun-
ningly accurate portrait of the earthly Jesus! Or was it the other way
around? That is, did Jesus Christ, having been born into this world,

set out deliberately to spend His life painting a visible and tangible portrait of His unseen Father as described in the Old Testament? For that is certainly just what Jesus came to do: to fulfill the Scriptures, making the transcendent God immanent. The staggering wonder of the Incarnation is that the same God who by definition stands absolutely above and outside the universe, perfect and uncreated and inscrutable, in the historical person of Jesus entered His own creation and so made Himself visible, understandable, available. As John testifies in his first epistle, "That which was from the beginning . . . we have heard . . . we have seen with our eyes, we have looked at and our hands have touched" (1:1).

Reading through this passage in *Job*, such a clear portrait of Jesus Christ begins to emerge that one can almost envision Father and Son sitting down together prior to the Incarnation and deciding how best these very verses might be enacted and fulfilled in the flesh-and-blood life of a human being. Do we find it strange that Job should have had such uncanny insight into the mystery of Christ? But all the great Old Testament people, after their own fashion, knew Christ, followed Him, and spoke about Him. Naturally in any study of the Old Testament it is well for us to keep in mind the basic exegetical questions, "What did the original author mean?" and "How would the original audience have understood this passage?" Yet we must also bear in mind that such questions do not seem to have been nearly so important to the first Christian exegetes, the apostles, as they set about to reinterpret the Old Testament Scriptures in the light of Jesus Christ. These men had no doubt that the prophets before them had spoken far more than they knew, and far more than their audiences could possibly have understood. In the same way, to people today who have walked and talked with Jesus, it is perfectly obvious that every word of the Old Testament points in some way directly to Him who is the Word of God incarnate.

The Song of Skepticism

"My days are swifter than a runner;
they fly away without a glimpse of joy.
They skim past like boats of papyrus,
like eagles swooping down on their prey." (9:25-26)

Some of the most beautiful poetry in *Job* expresses some of the bleakest thoughts. How plangently lovely is Job's picture of his days skimming by like papyrus boats! One image like this can carry such a freight of feeling, nostalgia, suggestion. One cannot help wondering, for instance, where on earth Job would have seen the papyrus-reed boats of the Ethiopians. Had he perhaps traveled in his youth? Had he visited the land of the "tall and *bronze-skinned* people" and watched at dusk their light craft plying the Nile's glassy current like tiny water-spiders (see Isa. 18:2)? Wherever it originated, this image of the swift little boats now comes back to Job to express for him both the ephemerality and the fragility of his life, along with something of the one-dimensional, surface quality of an existence from which the very roots have been torn out. If we were to read these lines in a modern poem, they might evoke for us a scene of carefree boys making paper boats and setting them adrift on a stream. This is actually not far from Job's thought, for he feels that God is treating his life lightly, even toying with him. The tone of the entire middle section of this chapter might almost be summed up in Shakespeare's familiar line, "As flies to wanton boys are we to the gods; they kill us for their sport." Job virtually says as much in 9:23: "When a scourge brings sudden death, [God] mocks the despair of the innocent."

We can imagine how pagan and nihilistic such thoughts must have sounded to Job's friends, especially when he states baldly, "*I care nothing for my life; it is all the same to me*; that is why I say, '[God] destroys both the blameless and the wicked'" (9:21-22). Job seems to have concluded that it does not matter what one believes, since God just goes ahead and does what He wants anyway.

If we think that as Christians we are exempt from this feeling, then we may have some living to do. When the cold hand of the scourge touches our own life, suddenly it might not matter how well we have known the Lord in the past; very likely we will feel that now we hardly know Him at all. We will feel afraid of Him, alienated, even unclean before Him, and we will not be able to figure out what in the world is going on. "Why is it," asked the German poet Heinrich Heine, "that the just must endure such suffering on earth? The book of *Job* does not solve this perplexing question. On the contrary, this very book is the Song of Songs of skepticism."

It is a very strange thing to be a Christian and yet to feel alienated from God. Yet in all honesty, is this not a real dimension of every Christian's experience? What is strange is that all our theology tells us just the opposite—that we are His dearly loved children and He will never forsake us. But there is a level of spiritual experience that theology cannot touch. Just as there are black holes in space that no telescope can ever probe, so there are depths to reality that theology tries to plumb but never can. Our creed may be ever so orthodox, but how shall we fare when God Himself begins doing the unorthodox? "I will strike the shepherd," quotes Jesus in Mark 14:27, "and the sheep will be scattered." Oddly enough, if our faith makes no practical allowance for confusion, alienation, and oppression, then Christianity becomes a pollyanna religion in which the very possibility of the Lord's direct and supernatural intervention has been leached away.

As believers we need to remember that profound disillusionment is one of the essential stages in the training of the disciple. Without three days of despair, there could not have been the wide-eyed, astonished disbelief of resurrection morning. Matthew tells us that even in the very presence of the risen Lord, "some doubted" (28:17). How could they? How dare they! Yet without this skepticism, there could never have been the greater comfort and the sealed conviction that came only with the gift of the indwelling Holy Spirit at Pentecost. Unless our faith has a healthy component of skepticism, there will be no surprises for us in Heaven. As spiritual adolescence must precede maturity, so a book like *Ecclesiastes* is the necessary preface to the *Song of Songs*.

A Man Like Me

"[God] is not a man like me that I might answer him,
that we might confront each other in court." (9:32)

For any Christian reader the splendid irony of this verse jumps right off the page. For we know that in Jesus Christ the Almighty God *has* become "a man like me," and moreover a man who by standing before Pontius Pilate and the Sanhedrin has confronted every one of us in court—and yet not, as we may have expected, in His rightful capacity as Judge, but rather as the accused, the prisoner in the dock. Through this reversal of roles He meant to show us that it is mankind who first condemned God, not the other way around, and that only by faith in Jesus can this condemnation be lifted so that we can be set free. We are desperate for God to accept us; but have we accepted His Son?

For Job, unaware of the prophetic irony in his language, the above words simply expressed with great poignancy the most profound of human longings: the desire to see God face to face and to hear Him speak. Job's speeches are full of the universal yearning to have "God with us," to be able to relate to Him easily and naturally as one human being relates to another, rather than as to a maddeningly elusive ghost. Of course, in reality human relationships are not so easy and natural as we may imagine them. And it is not God who stands in the way of having normal relationships with people, but rather it is people who, by sin, mar their intimacy with God. God has no desire to conceal Himself; on the contrary His desire is for full self-disclosure. The real problem is that people hide themselves from God, and God has to go looking for them (see Gen. 3:8-10). So it is not God who is the ghost, but man.

Job knows this, and yet still he wonders: is there not some way for man to shed his sick, ghostly unreality and to come into the light and deal with God directly? Does not much of the problem of suffering have to do with the sheer invisibility of God? "When he passes me, I cannot see him," sighs Job in 9:11, and later his lament intensifies: "If only I knew where to find him; if only I could go to his dwelling. . . . But if I go to the east, he is not there; if I go to the west, I do not find him" (23:3, 8). Strangely, the disciples of Jesus made the same complaint: "Lord, show us the Father and that will be enough for us." Imagine Philip saying this when God incarnate was standing right before his eyes! Hence Jesus' reply: "Don't you know me, Philip, even after I have been among you such a long time? Anyone who has seen me has seen the Father" (John 14:8-9).

The message of the gospel is that in Jesus, and only in Jesus, are all our yearnings to see and to hear God fulfilled. Granted, short of Heaven this fulfillment is only by faith—faith in the Son's co-equality with the Father and in His full authority to take away every spot of sin in the world, everything that spoils our intimacy with God. A fulfillment by faith is not quite the same as the literal fulfillment that will take place at the end of time; but it is, to borrow Philip's expression, "enough for us." So it is with a curious mixture of caution and celebration that John writes at the beginning of his *Gospel*, "No one has ever seen God, but *the Only Begotten*, who is at the Father's side, has made him known" (John 1:18).

Job's faith is the sort that gropes with an unerring instinct toward the knowledge of this mystery of mysteries. Even as he complains, "God is not a man like me," he knows in his spirit that in some sense God *must* be a man like himself, else how could human beings have any real communion with Him at all? That the Almighty God is not just some colossal and inaccessible computer in the sky—this is precisely the miracle of the Incarnation. God did not rest His case on His omnipotence alone, but rather He "so loved the world that he gave his one and only Son, that whoever believes in him shall not perish but have eternal life" (John 3:16). Truth alone is worthless; truth must be mediated by love. Just as Christ's judgment is tempered by His mercy, so His Deity is tempered by His humanity. Job's friends, though they wax eloquent on the topic of God's sovereign transcendence, seem to have no inkling of His human side.

Binding Arbitration

"If only there were someone to arbitrate between us,
to lay his hand upon us both,
someone to remove God's rod from me,
so that his terror would frighten me no more." (9:33-34)

In the context of the Old Testament, what daring and revolutionary words these are! Job wishes so passionately for his suffering to be relieved and his faith vindicated that he goes so far as to challenge and bend orthodox doctrine by introducing the strange notion of an "arbitrator" or mediator between himself and God—someone to "lay his hand upon us both." Many a Christian who knows the New Testament backwards and forwards would be hard pressed to put the gospel of Christ into terms any clearer than this.

To Job's friends, however, such a notion must have sounded at best fanciful, at worst heretical, as it would have seemed to mollify or to water down divine justice by placing man on an equal footing with God. Yet oddly enough, the Lord Himself turns out to be a bit of a heretic. For God too wishes so passionately to bring about peace between Himself and humanity—peace at any price—that He becomes willing to bend. He bends, in fact, all the way down from His lofty throne in Heaven to a lowly stable in Bethlehem, in order to provide mankind with the very mediator for whom Job here prays. If there is really no other way for God and man to agree, says the Lord, then I Myself will sit down at the bargaining table and negotiate. I—even I, the awesome and glorious Lord of all—am prepared to bind Myself to arbitration.

In truth—and this is the central secret of the Bible—it was the Lord's own idea all along that both He and mankind should submit themselves to binding arbitration: in other words, to *covenant*. It has always been His plan to make peace with the human race through a mediator, through someone who could "lay his hand upon us both" by being at one and the same time the Son of God and the Son of Man, a perfectly fair and impartial representative of each party. From our point of view, we may tend to presume that because this mediator, Jesus Christ, is Himself God, He must be biased in God's favor. But this is surprisingly not the case. For Christ is not only God but man, and so He is just as much on man's side as on God's. Indeed the cross is the great evidence of the fact that He is essentially on no side at all, for He did not come to take sides but to make peace. "God did not send his Son into the world to condemn the world, but to save the world through him" (John 3:17).

Job, of course, has no clue as to how exactly his preposterous wish for a mediator will in the fullness of time come true. Yet even by the end of the book there is a sense in which his prayer is already answered and fulfilled. For in dreaming of a mediator for his own case, the irony is that Job himself ends up being given a mediatorial role—not on his own behalf, but on behalf of Eliphaz, Bildad, and Zophar. As the Lord says to these three in the Epilogue, "My servant Job will pray for you, and I will accept his prayer and not deal with you according to your folly" (42:8).

Sadly, the business of standing between God and humanity and mediating between the two is a dirty job. For essentially it means becoming the enemy of both sides. God will never give up His holiness, and man will not and cannot give up his sin. So there is an impasse. And whoever dares to step into this impasse and negotiate a peace must inevitably become the target of both man and of God, the whipping boy for both sides. This is how it was for Moses and for all the prophets, this is how it was for Job, and this is how it would be for Christ Himself and for His followers. The fact is that God is looking for people just like this, people who by faith are so radically convinced of their own ultimate vindication by the Lord that they become willing to suffer any amount of divine wrath in this world, and along with it the wrath of their fellowmen, for the sake of making peace. God is looking for people who are ready to stand in the gap between sin and holiness, people who, by abandoning themselves to the bearing of the unbearable tension between flesh and spirit, between time and eternity, between necessity and possibility, become living signs of the reconciling of earth and Heaven.

A Look of Agony

"I loathe my very life;
therefore I will give free rein to my complaint
and speak out in the bitterness of my soul." (10:1)

Most of the complaining that people do is petty and sinful, arising in one way or another from the fear of losing something to which they are neurotically attached. But when a person is in the situation of having literally nothing left to lose, the result may be a different kind of complaint altogether.

Job has already admitted that it would be nice if he could just pull himself up by the bootstraps and stop being an old sourpuss. But he cannot, for "if I say, 'I will forget my complaint, I will change my expression, and smile,' I still dread all my sufferings" (9:27-28). Under such circumstances the wearing of a smile would be the wearing of a mask; it would not be a true smile at all but a simper, a pasteboard lie. We should not be surprised to learn that references to smiling are rare in the book of *Job.* What is more surprising is to consult a concordance and discover that the word "smile" occurs hardly at all anywhere in the Bible!

In short, Scripture never suggests (unlike many churchgoers) that the wearing of a cheerful countenance is a good tonic for the soul. On the contrary in *Ecclesiastes* we read, "Sorrow is better than laughter, because a sad face is good for the heart" (7:3). How is it we have bought the lie that a Christian's face is only publicly presentable when the corners of the mouth are pushed up? The Apostle James actually exhorts us to "grieve, mourn and wail. Change your laughter to mourning and your joy to gloom" (4:9). It is not that James has anything against joy and laughter; but he wants them to be genuine. As the poet Emily Dickinson put it in her trenchant style, "I like a look of Agony, because I know it's true."

Undoubtedly Scripture exhorts us to "rejoice in the Lord" and to "be of good cheer." Yet nowhere are we commanded to "put on a happy face." Nowhere are we told that it is all right to complain in the heart while outwardly appearing bright and jovial. How much damage has the feigning of happiness done to the cause of Christ! If we look at the character of Jesus, can we escape seeing a streak of morbidity broad enough to make us uncomfortable? While we never read of our Lord laughing, we do know for certain that "Jesus wept" (John 11:35), and that in the Garden of Gethsemane He said, "My soul is overwhelmed with sorrow to the point of death" (Mark 14:34). How would we react today to hearing a fellow believer speak so gloomily? Would we upbraid him for grumbling? Would we immediately try to cheer him up? The very presence in Scripture of writings as dark as *Job* and *Ecclesiastes* should set God's people free to confess their disillusionment, to frown and complain when appropriate, to be fed up with life, or to "speak out in bitterness of soul." For the view of the Bible is that it is far better to be sincerely discouraged and world-weary than to pretend enthusiasm, better to be authentically sad than artificially happy, better to have honest doubt than phony faith.

It has been said that the primary task of the preacher of the gospel is to get his people lost—for only then can he begin to get them saved. Before people can be introduced to Christ, they need to be introduced to the unconscious complaints that inhabit their souls beneath all the painful smiles, and before they can grow in Christ they must learn to distinguish between petty, selfish complaints and the legitimate kind. The end of faith, after all, is not religiosity but reality, and reality is something that cannot be painted on but that must well up irrepressibly from within. According to Proverbs 15:13, "A happy heart makes the face cheerful"; but the process will not work in reverse. If anything, the excruciating effort of insincere smiling will make a sad heart even sadder and will drive a wandering soul farther than ever from the truth.

Letting God Be God

"Did you not pour me out like milk
and curdle me like cheese,
clothe me with skin and flesh
and knit me together with bones and sinews?" (10:10-11)

Are these the words of a doubting and rebellious man? Definitely not. On the contrary, how tenderly Job talks of the way he has been formed by the hand of his God! That he should speak this way even as his body is covered with open sores, in the midst of his torment paying such gracious homage to the intricate and loving handiwork of his Creator—surely this is an eloquent testimony to his faith. In tone and imagery, and for sheer beauty and intimacy of expression, these verses cannot help but remind us of Psalm 139:

> You created my inmost being;
> > you knit me together in my mother's womb.
> I praise you because I am
> > fearfully and wonderfully made! . . .
> My frame was not hidden from you
> > when I was made in the secret place.
> When I was woven together in the depths of the earth,
> > your eyes saw my unformed body. (vv. 13-16)

Reading these lines of David and of Job, we can almost picture these men tracing with wonder the imprint of the Lord's fingers still fresh upon their bodies, and feeling even now the soft pressure of the heel of His hand still molding and shaping them. Particularly striking is Job's comparison of the formation of the body in the womb to the curdling of cheese. Such a homely image this is, and yet there is something wonderful about it too, something that perfectly captures the mysterious texture and consistency of human tissue—at once so solid and so giving, so soft and yet as glossy as polished marble, and with its strange blending of the opaque and the translucent, the earthy and the numinous. In many ways there is nothing more ordinary than the human body, much like a hunk of cheese. What makes the body extraordinary is that it is so obviously something *made*—and more than that, something *made by hand*. A fine piece of lace might carry a label reading "Handmade In Italy," but on our bodies we bear a label far more exotic: "Handmade by the Lord." Just think what a piece of furniture from the hand of Jesus the carpenter might sell for today! But are we ourselves not infinitely more precious and exquisite?

What Job reveals in these verses is how profoundly aware he is of his own creatureliness. He is not his own; he belongs to Another. Therefore he can say to this Other, "Your hands shaped me and made me. Will you now turn and destroy me?" (10:8). In such words there is challenge and pluck, there is life and vigor—and this in spite of the fact of Job's physical and emotional trauma, his frailty and his exhaustion. Is this a man speaking up on his own behalf? No, it is not himself Job is defending with such robust and vibrant poetry; rather, he is defending the private property of Another. If Job has a creature's humility, he also has a creature's pride. Even while he says, "I despise my own life" (9:21; 10:1), his faith compels him to maintain an underlying admiration for himself as a masterpiece of divine creation. Is this, one wonders, why Job's despair never takes the form of a suicide wish? True, back in Chapter 3 he wished he had never been born; but once alive the thought of destroying himself seems, surprisingly, never to have occurred to him (or if it did he never spoke it aloud). That is how acutely conscious this man is of belonging wholly to Someone Else.

It is precisely because Job has such a realistic sense of his proper place in the scheme of things that he can depend so heavily on the One who put him there in the first place. When people subtly and insidiously usurp the place of God by taking upon themselves responsibilities that rightly belong to Him alone, the result is legalistic and idolatrous religion. But the sign of true faith is people simply letting themselves be people, and letting God be God. Over and over in Scripture the Lord promises, "You will be My people, and I will be your God." Job is bold enough to take God up on this deal. It is just as though he were to say, "God, I'm doing my part—why aren't You doing Yours? I'm being the person—why aren't You being the God?" One mistake Job never makes is to play God. He plays the man part, and he fully expects God to play the God part. In short, he adheres perfectly to the terms of the Lord's own covenant.

Hesed

*"You gave me life and showed me kindness,
and in your providence watched over my spirit." (10:12)*

The word translated here as "kindness" is the great Hebrew word *hesed*—a word so rich in its connotations as to be virtually untranslatable. Usually it is rendered by such double-barreled expressions as "lovingkindness" or "steadfast love." But probably the best translation of all, preserving the greatest range of the word's deep resonances, is simply the good old Anglo-Saxon word *love*. How strange it is that in this long book, containing so much suffering and so much mystery and so much strenuous grappling with the deep things of God, this little word *love*—surely the key word not only in the Bible but in all of human language—occurs only twice. (The other occurrence of *hesed* comes in 37:13, in the speech of Elihu.)

Yet here is something even stranger: people who are going through the deep waters of suffering can grow to hate this word. They can arrive at the point where they cannot even stand to hear it anymore, without feeling an actual physical revulsion in their gut. Why? Raymond Carver hinted at the reason when he titled one of his books, awkwardly but arrestingly, *What We Talk About When We Talk About Love*. What, indeed, do we think we are doing as we bandy about this four-letter word so glibly and cavalierly? Does it ever dawn on us that just to speak it is like speaking the whole world into existence all over again? That it is like speaking the most sacred of all mysteries, that of all the names of God it is the most holy and awesome? Yet it is such an easy and gratifying little word to say, and it is particularly easy and gratifying when everything is going well for us. When life feels good and we have the world (or even just our own small corner of it) by the tail, then it is no great thing to love. It is nothing to love God under such circumstances, and nothing at all to love the whole of humanity with an expansive radiance. As long as we are getting our own way in life, love sits well in our stomachs and rolls fluently off our tongues, and that is why people who are suffering may grow to hate it so much. For it makes it sound as though the secret of life were a much commoner, cheaper thing than it is.

But love in the midst of suffering is something dreadful. To love, and to keep on loving when all human reserves for it have been exhausted, is a more fearsome thing than hate. Such love is a furnace, a fire hotter even than Hell. The one who loves in this way— long and honestly and without restraint—will love alone, and will inevitably be punished for it most severely by the world. Such love, like prayer, is something we must do in the sight of God and of God alone, or else not at all.

Some Christians treat love as though it were an evangelistic strategy, a kind of gospel-bait. Love is seen as a useful tool for attracting or luring people into the Kingdom. Naturally, once the fish has been hauled into the boat, the lure is cut from its mouth. But love is not a silver spoon or a jitterbug. Love is not bait for the gospel; love *is* the gospel. Love is not a means towards some other end; love is means and end together. The moment love is used as a tool, it ceases to be love. When people try to use love in this way, what they are really doing is using God. Instead of being used by God, they try to turn the tables and use Him. Religion becomes an instrument for the expansion of one's own personal power. Love becomes a weapon of aggression. Little wonder that the person who is suffering comes to hate it. For true love is not aggression; true love is not concerned with gaining power over others. Rather, love is the humility in which self becomes subservient to relationship.

In the Kingdom of God nothing moves, nothing happens, without love. In churches many things happen because of human goals, programs, bureaucratic necessity, idealism, private fantasy, or neurosis. But it is not so with God. God has no plan, no program, no agenda except love. That is why He had no other recourse but to send us His only Son Jesus Christ, who on the one hand loved God His Father with a perfect love, and who on the other hand loved mankind no less. These were the two hands that were stretched wide on Calvary. Christ's two great loves struggled like mighty wrestlers within His breast, until finally love itself tore Him apart on the cross.

This is the dreadful, fearsome love of God, the love that will never let us go. This is the Love who made us and remade us for no other purpose except that of His own great *hesed*.

Doubt

"If I am guilty—woe to me!
Even if I am innocent, I cannot lift my head,
for I am full of shame and drowned in
my affliction." (10:15)

The relationship between faith and doubt is often miscon-
strued. We tend to think of doubt as an intellectual problem,
when really it has more to do with the emotions and the will.
Many people who have no intellectual doubts about their creed are
nevertheless wracked by a different kind of doubt, by something
that is closer to shame. This sort of doubt does not question the
basic truth of such doctrines as the virgin birth, the authority of
Scripture, the deity of Christ, or the physical resurrection. Where
such questions are persistently present, they usually have less to do
with doubt than with plain unbelief. To stand apart from these great
and glorious realities and to try to evaluate them with the human
mind is not doubt but a kind of trust: trust in oneself.

With real doubt it is different. Real doubt begins with such a profound distrust of self that one is driven into the arms of God,
because there is literally nowhere else to go. To be cast upon God in
such a way that it is like being adrift on the wide open ocean in a
tiny raft without rudder or sail or oars—this is doubt.

The person who doubts, in other words, is not the agnostic, not
the person who questions whether or not God exists. That is just
unbelief. No, the person who doubts is the one who has already
come under the profound conviction of the Holy Spirit and is therefore convinced of the absolute truth of all the basic tenets of the
Christian faith. Intellectually there may still be many questions
about the various doctrines and their exact nature and application.
But such questions are not the real focus of doubt. For the heart of
this doubter knows full well that what it is up against is the Truth,
and so the real question is no longer whether Christianity is believable but rather, What am I going to do about it? Knowing already
that the Kingdom of Heaven is real, what the doubter actually struggles with is how to respond to this staggering reality.

So the problem of doubt is less a cognitive one than a personal one. Even the sort of doubter who, like the disciple Thomas, seems to be mulling over the case for and against the resurrection may not really be asking, "Did Christ literally rise from the dead?" but rather, "If my good friend Jesus *did* conquer the grave, why am I still so afraid of death?" The issue is not, "Is the gospel true?" but, "*Since* the gospel is true, why hasn't the world been more obviously turned upside-down by it? And why do I myself, having whole-heartedly embraced Christ, still experience boredom and fatigue in my life? Why can I not conquer certain sins? Or why am I not working miracles? Am I doing something wrong? Despite all my praying and churchgoing and Bible reading and good works, is my faith, in the final analysis, phony?"

These are the real questions of doubt. Real doubt is not doubt of God but of self. In self-doubt there is no longer any serious doubt of God. If anything, God is too real. He is far more immense than our puny little selves can cope with. Sometimes we would like to turn Him off, like the television set, but we cannot. Instead we are wholly alive to God; He is more present to us than we are to ourselves. It is not God's reality we doubt, but our own. We look at the life of Jesus and it petrifies us. We doubt very much whether we can follow Him or obey Him or in any way please Him, let alone glorify Him and be like Him.

This is the struggle of doubt, and it is the fundamental struggle in the book of *Job*. Between the lines of every verse we hear Job asking, "With my life in such a terrible mess, is it possible to believe that even now I might be pleasing to God?" What the Christian sufferer so often forgets, of course, is that it is precisely this deep personal insecurity that is directly addressed by the gospel. This same overwhelming self-doubt is finally and gloriously resolved by the very God whose holiness so overwhelms us. For so simple is His gospel that it asks nothing else of us but this: having believed in His Son, we take hold of the hope that, however messed up our lives may be, we are in fact more pleasing to the Father than we can possibly comprehend.

Four Darknesses

"Turn away from me so I can have a moment's joy
before I go to the place of no return,
to the land of murk, of deep shadow,
to the land of deepest night,
of deep gloom and disorder,
where even the light is like darkness." (10:20-22)

For the second time in the book Job's mood plunges to a nadir as his language dons the same black sackcloth as in Chapter 3. It is difficult to translate (let alone to talk about) this passage without sounding trite and redundant, for even English with all its somber shading and its Anglo-Saxon crudity seems not to contain enough darkness to express such deep despair. One senses here that Job himself is nearly at a loss for words, and the wonder is that he is able to speak at all. Finally he resorts to using no less than four different Hebrew words for "darkness," translated variously as "midnight black," "the shadow of death," "the land of murk and chaos," "where confusion reigns," "where light itself is like the dead of night," and so on. Job masses these words together, piling one on top of another for a cumulative effect as solemn and impressive as anything in Shakespeare. The author of *Job* makes language toll like a bell.

Yet once again the question must be asked: does such despair, as artistically sublime as it may be, really have anything to do with faith in God? Perhaps the book of *Ecclesiastes*, so replete with pessimism, provides a necessary perspective when it reflects, "There is a time for everything, and a season for every activity under heaven"—including "dying," "uprooting," "killing," "mourning," and even "hating" (3:1-8). The Preacher is not so much advocating these negative extremes, as soberly allowing for their inevitability. Even Jesus, remember, made allowances for darkness. Night figured in His plans, as when He stated, "Night is coming, when no one can work" (John 9:4), or when He warned, "Walk while you have the light, before darkness overtakes you" (John 12:35). And during those appalling days while He waited for His friend Lazarus to die before going to him, He explained His delay by saying, "Are there not twelve hours of daylight? A man who walks by day will not stumble, for he sees by this world's light. It is when he walks by night that he stumbles, for he has no light" (John 11:9-10).

Darkness, let us face it, is a fact of life, and the message of *Job* (and ultimately of the cross of Christ) is that we zealous and competent Christians must make way for the inevitable incursions of evil into our pleasantly unrealistic worldview. Even so valiant a saint as Paul had to confess to one of his churches, "We wanted to come to you . . . again and again—but Satan stopped us" (1 Thess. 2:18). Since when is an apostle of Christ stopped in his tracks by Satan— and not just once, notice, but "again and again"? Perhaps it is these very experiences of defeat and constraint that teach us how very different are the Lord's ways from our own, and that therefore lay the foundation for worship. Certainly we would never worship the Lord if He had not drawn near to us and freed us from darkness; but neither would we worship a god whose light and power were so accessible that he became for us a kind of divine bellhop, always at our beck and call.

Do we Christians leave sufficient room in our lives for chaos, for meaninglessness, for the awful "waste" of long seasons of sorrow and temptation? Or are we too intent on always being cheerful, capable, and energetic? Do we know how to lie low? Or do we keep on pushing ourselves round the clock and thus defy Jesus' clear admonition to walk only in the light? Have we got time in our busy week's schedule for a bad day or two? Or are we too busy living victoriously?

One thing is certain: we *will* have bad days. We will have horrible days (whether or not we fully acknowledge to ourselves just how wretched they are). And something else is certain too: if we do not have time in our life for bad days, we will never have time to minister truly and deeply to others when they are having bad days, or when they are having bad lives. We may not even see that darkness can be precisely where the Lord is most gloriously at work. In the words of Francis Bacon, "The pencil of the Holy Ghost hath laboured more in describing the afflictions of Job than the felicities of Solomon."

Zophar

Then Zophar the Naamathite replied:
"Are all these words to go unanswered?
Is this talker to be vindicated?" (11:1-2)

Zophar has obviously been chomping at the bit for a chance
to put in his two cents' worth, and right off the bat he shows
himself to be the sort of fellow who shoots first and asks
questions later. In his criticism of Job he is not just blunt but insulting, calling his friend a scoffer and a windbag (v. 3) and broadly
accusing him of arrogant self-righteousness (v. 4). Clearly the discussion is heating up. It may be in Zophar's nature to be caustic and
abrupt, or it may just be that things have reached such an impasse
that all the friends are now prepared to level direct accusations at
Job. In any case, from this point on the dialogue assumes more the
character of a full-blown argument than a civil discussion. Mud-
slinging becomes the order of the day, and Zophar's openly scornful attitude certainly contributes to this.

It is worth noting, however, that none of Job's friends is a mere
two-dimensional strawman. All are complex characters in their own
right, with lively and interesting minds. Granted, Zophar is probably the least sophisticated of the three, the one who wastes the least
breath on tact and diplomacy. Yet this very trait can be both a
strength and a weakness, and it may even have been Zophar's
rough-and-ready bluffness that drew him to Job as a friend in the
first place. For is not Job this way too? Like many people, Zophar
is probably as genuinely likable a person in good times as he is nasty
in bad.

Zophar's real fault, as with all Job's friends, lies in his forcing of
the issue—that is, in the injury he does to the freedom and inviolability of Job's will by trying to press him into accepting simplistic
answers. It is the essence of hypocrisy to cling to easy answers in the
face of difficult realities. But with *Job* easy answers are not possible. Implicit in the book is the lesson that theology must not try to
be any clearer about God than God is about Himself. This is where
so much fundamentalist religion goes astray, as it seeks to pin things

down that are unpinnable, to systematize truths that by nature are unsystematic. Pharisees theologize the life out of truth. They are so wrapped up in expounding the Word of God that they forget it is the Word of God which expounds us.

Probably the characteristic sin of evangelicals is this bull-in-a-china-shop approach to the consciences of other people. How often have we met buttonholers like Zophar in the church foyer? More to the point: how often have we been like him ourselves? The prime danger of fundamentalism is that a good firm grip on fundamental doctrines can be accompanied by a fundamental lack of respect (to say nothing of love) for other people. Orthodox theology is a good servant but a poor master. If our faith is not "faith expressing itself through love" (Gal. 5:6), then it is dead. And here is a strange fact about love: genuine love would rather see other people go to Hell than have them in any way coerced, cajoled, tricked, or trapped into the Kingdom of Heaven. Isn't this what the love of God is like? He would sooner see us damned to Hell than railroaded into Heaven.

One of the main weakness in Zophar's argument shows up glaringly in 11:6, where he tries to mollify his hardline position somewhat by telling Job, "Know this: God has even forgotten some of your sin." In this apparently harmless little comment there lurks a monstrous implication—namely, that Job has gotten off lightly by receiving a smaller dose of suffering than he really deserves! Zophar's words actually contain a serious theological flaw. For does God ever forgive only some of our sin? Is partial forgiveness even possible? No, it is not. There is no such thing as selective forgiveness, whether in the divine or the human sphere. To be genuine forgiveness it must be extended to the whole person. Strictly speaking God does not forgive sin at all; He forgives people. This truth is wonderfully expressed in H. G. Spafford's classic old hymn "It Is Well with My Soul":

> *My sin—oh, the bliss of this glorious thought—*
> *My sin—not in part, but the whole—*
> *Is nailed to the cross and I bear it no more,*
> *Praise the Lord, praise the Lord, O my soul!*

Divine Contradiction

"Can you fathom the mysteries of God?
Can you probe the limits of the Almighty?
They are higher than the heavens—what can you do?
They are deeper than the depths of the grave—what can
you know?" (11:7-8)

After his opening gibes Zophar does manage to voice some
impressive thoughts on the majesty and mystery of God. Yet
his point here seems to be that the divine ways are so totally
foreign to human ways as to render God essentially unknowable.
While there is truth in this premise, it is truth of which Job is already
well aware. In the first half of Chapter 9 we heard him speak more
profoundly than any of his friends ever will on this same topic of
the Lord as, to borrow the German phrase of Karl Barth, *totaliter
aliter*—Wholly Other. Indeed one of the main purposes of Job's
speeches is to awaken in his friends (and in us) a sense of the sheer
mystery of God.

Job is less concerned with tying up all the loose ends of faith than
he is with taking a good hard look at the loose ends themselves. If
it is systematic theology we want, we will not get it from him. On
the contrary the systematic approach is represented by Job's friends,
and ultimately by Satan who systematically tortures Job. But the
ways of the Lord (even in the end) remain largely inscrutable. For
mystery belongs to the Lord—it is one of His attributes. But there
is nothing really mysterious (in the truest sense of that word) about
Satan. When the Devil is exposed he is shown up to be a cosmic
bore, whereas when the Lord shows Himself He becomes more mysterious than ever. Those who do not really know the Lord take
exception to His riddles and paradoxes. But to know Him is to
know continual, exponential growth in one's capacity to live with
contradiction.

Divine contradiction is like an exotic food or music: one must
acquire a taste for it. Many people, even the very religious, have no
real stomach for *mysterium tremendum*. They are fine when gazing

up into a starry sky, but when they encounter the infinite abyss of Christ on the human level, it turns their stomachs. This was apparently the case with one of the great writers of the twentieth century, Franz Kafka, who when asked his opinion of Christ answered, "He is an abyss filled with light; one must close one's eyes if one is not to fall in." Often people perform the most astounding mental gymnastics in order to keep from falling into the mysteries of God. Such paradoxes as predestination and free will are endlessly debated, when if only we would submit our minds to the bright unyielding enigmas of Scripture, we would see that the New Testament plainly teaches both. Often even mature Christians have, in some areas, a monaural theology; the richness of stereo sounds like noise to their ears.

The greatest test of genuine faith comes in situations where God seems to us to be contradicting Himself or playing games. When the Lord told Abraham to sacrifice Isaac, wasn't He grossly flouting His own moral law? Since when did the Lord take pleasure in human sacrifice, and moreover in the sacrifice of one whom He Himself had promised to bless with as many descendants as the stars? Abraham's situation as he stood that day on Mount Moriah was inherently, outrageously unthinkable. Yet it is right here, in the turbulent waters of divine contradiction, that faith must perform its strange navigation. By steering a course between the Scylla and Charybdis of two utterly contradictory words from the Lord, Abraham was established as the father of faith.

This is exactly what we see in the character of Job. What distinguishes him from his friends is his ability to live with the awful untenableness of his situation. He does not like it; he does not understand it. But somehow in the midst of it he manages to hold himself together like the driver of a team of wild horses. He confronts head-on the implicit contradiction in the problem of righteous suffering, without ever denying it or rationalizing it away as his friends do. Perhaps the essential lesson here has to do with control, with spiritual rigidity versus spiritual dependency. Job's systematizing friends seek vainly to keep control of the wild horses, while Job is out of control and knows it, and so calls desperately upon the Lord to take the reins.

Cheap Guilt

"If you put away the sin that is in your hand
and allow no evil to dwell in your tent,
then you will lift up your face without shame;
you will stand firm and without fear.
You will surely forget your trouble;
it will be like water under the bridge." (11:14-16)

Once again Job is exhorted by his friends to repent. Zophar's message is essentially the same as that of the others: your problem is sin, and the one cure is repentance. The friends make it sound as though confession is the only sure-fire strategy available to the believer for dealing with all of life's rough spots.

Job does eventually repent (see 42:6), but only after refusing to repent throughout the majority of the book. This reversal may strike the reader as puzzling, until we realize that one of the mainstays of Job's righteousness is his repudiation of all false, shallow, or premature repentance—in other words, his adamant refusal to accept inappropriate guilt. It is of the utmost importance that when Job does repent, he does so not because of the pressure of adverse circumstances, nor in response to the coercion of his counselors. Rather, Job repents at the word of the Lord, and for no other reason. Here is a man who knows intimately the voice of his God and whose heart remains impervious to any other stimulus.

Yet is this not precisely Job's problem? What is such a believer, whose very life depends upon the daily bread of the living Word of God, supposed to do when God is silent? His friends urge him to focus on his own guilt as the reason for this silence, and to "put away the sin that is in your hand." But Job knows that genuine repentance cannot be motivated by fear or doubt, or extorted under duress from an anxious soul. He knows nothing of the rote confession of sin as a tranquilizer for the troubled heart. No, while true repentance certainly includes a confession of guilt, it can never be initiated in response to guilt but only in response to the voice of the Lord, which in turn is always accompanied by a revelation of His overwhelming mercy and love. As Francois Fénélon described it,

"We hear this voice which carries a tender reproach to the bottom of our hearts, and our hearts are torn by it. This is true and pure contrition."

To whom the believer offers repentance, then, and under what circumstances, are issues of the weightiest consequence. For the offering of repentance is tantamount to the offering of worship, and a fear-induced repentance is essentially the worship of a false god. To bow down in abject humility before any other promptings or convictions than those of the Holy Spirit is to offer a kind of worship to Satan. Was this not one of the temptations of Christ in the wilderness—to grovel and demean Himself before the Prince of Darkness? The fact is that the Devil, in his own way, is just as eager to induce repentance as the Lord is, for he knows it to be a secret to gaining power over troubled souls.

Dietrich Bonhoeffer warned about "cheap grace." But guilt too can come cheap. Cheap guilt enervates and paralyzes. Like a giant leech it latches onto the conscience and saps all the dignity and vitality out of it. True contrition, on the other hand, purifies the conscience, bathing it as in tears even while energizing it with the vision and the power for positive change. How tragic it is when God's children waste precious time and strength bowed low in the grip of cheap guilt's endless accusations. We can be so busy repenting that we fail to hear the glorious and forgiving voice of Christ who alone is to be obeyed. "If I worship God from fear or superstition, then I am wrong," wrote Oswald Chambers. "Job's point of view is that if I do anything in order to appease God, I am committing iniquity." Certainly there is a proper place for repentance, and "unless you repent, you too will all perish" (Luke 13:3). But genuine repentance is something so beautiful that, like a kind of chastity of the soul, it must not be tossed away upon every passing shadow of shame, but carefully guarded and saved for the Lord alone.

THE DIALOGUE:
ROUND 2
(Job 12–20)

"You are smearing me with lies! You are quack physicians, all of you!"

—JOB 13:4

If anyone is preaching to you a gospel other than the one you accepted, let him be eternally condemned!

—GAL. 1:9

Authority

Then Job replied:
"Doubtless you are the people,
and wisdom will die with you!
But I have a mind as well as you;
I am not inferior to you.
Who does not know all these things?" (12:1-3)

I t is not always the case that Job flatly disagrees with his friends. More often it is just that his thinking is so far ahead of theirs as to leave them in the dust. Few situations are more exasperating than that of trying to communicate with people who insist on answering everything you say with the obvious, conventional wisdom that you have already considered and digested. Long ago Job had covered the traditional ground to which his would-be counselors are trying to recall him, and the issues that confront him now are beyond their sphere of competence.

Nevertheless, we do not hear Job suggesting to his friends that he himself is any wiser, better, or more spiritually mature than they are. On the contrary he limits himself to saying simply (both in 12:2 and again in 13:2), "I am not inferior to you." Here his attitude is like that of the Apostle Paul, whose ultimate trump card in matters of theological disagreement was not his God-given authority as an apostle, but rather a humble statement such as, "I think that I too have the Spirit of God" (1 Cor. 7:40).

Granted, when forced to defend the integrity of his ministry Paul frequently cited his apostolic authority. But when his back was really against the wall and this authority was seriously in question (as it was at the Jerusalem Council of Acts 15, and at many points in the epistles), Paul knew that he had only one thing to fall back on, which was the simple fact that he too was a Christian, and that in him the Spirit of Christ was authentically and undeniably alive. Hence he could say, "If anyone is confident that he belongs to Christ, he should consider again that we belong to Christ just as much as he" (2 Cor. 10:7). What would have been the point of an apostle "pulling rank" when it was that very rank that was in dispute? Besides, Paul did not think of himself as holding rank but as representing someone else who did hold rank—the highest-ranking One of all. When he pleaded with the churches to acknowledge his authority, he did so not out of neurotic insecurity but for their own good. It was like one pedestrian shouting to another, "Watch out! There's a truck coming!" Paul was authoritative, but he was not an authoritarian. Among believers more mature than the Corinthians he could say simply, "If on some point you think differently, this too God will make clear to you" (Phil. 3:15). That is how confident he was that the Spirit of Christ was "one Spirit" (Eph. 4:4) and could never be divided (1 Cor. 1:13).

Job and Paul were two men who, judging by their external behavior under stress, gave every appearance of being boastful and arrogant. Yet in reality this brashness arose not from pride but from humility, from a total absence of pious presumption. Their occasional flamboyance meant only that they had nothing whatsoever to hide. Moses too was a man often accused of arrogance, but in fact he was "more humble than anyone else on the face of the earth" (Num. 12:3). These were leaders who were always heedful of Christ's warning not to exult in spiritual power, but rather to "rejoice that your names are written in heaven" (Luke 10:20).

This is finally the one practical basis upon which differences between Christians can be settled—the basis of our common salvation in Christ. Of course the Bible is authoritative—but try and get two different churches to agree on all the major doctrines it presents! At the foot of the cross, however, there can be fellowship, for here there is no rank or favoritism, no superior intelligence or higher spirituality, and in a sense this is true even for Jesus Himself. The ultimate basis for Christ's authority over mankind resides in His Deity, but His appeal to authority comes more from His humanity, and especially from the simple fact that He died for us. Because "he humbled himself and became obedient to death—even death on a cross—therefore God exalted him to the highest place" (Phil. 2:8-9). The cross is God's glorious throne on earth. It is as one lowly human being among billions of others that the Lord clinches the case for His divine sovereignty.

Powerlessness

"Men at ease have contempt for misfortune
as the fate of those whose feet are slipping." (12:5)

M uch of the dialogue in *Job* illustrates the exasperating paradox that when life is good we tend to have no questions, but when life is bad we have no answers. "Men at ease have contempt for misfortune" because the secret of successful living seems, in happy times, so perfectly obvious, so clear and easy, that anyone who happens to be struggling with life appears ignorant and foolish. "Poor wretch!" we think secretly. "Why can't he see the stupid mistakes he is making? If only he would do this or that, things would turn out well for him." No matter how wise and good a person may have been in the past, when misfortune strikes we tend to see it as exposing the victim's hidden foibles. If a man has a heart attack, then perhaps he was working too hard. If our neighbor goes bankrupt, then probably he had it coming to him. Whatever our theology might be, in any tragedy there is just something in our finite minds that gravitates immediately toward the theory of human causes.

Job's purpose in Chapter 12 is to expose the utter godlessness of such thinking. For if human beings bear direct responsibility for everything bad that happens to them, then the plain corollary of this thesis is that we also have the power to effect our own good. Such a thoroughly watertight system of cause and effect, Job correctly sees, leaves no room for dependent faith, no room for the gospel. Error supplants sin, and divine mercy is represented as human virtue. In 12:6 Job provides a classic definition of this humanistic idolatry when he speaks of "those who carry their god in their hands." The god of such people is only as strong as their own strength, only as wise as their own conscious or subconscious minds, only as good as the tangible blessings which accrue to them.

Job's argument throughout this chapter is that there is nothing he can do about his suffering because it is the Lord's will. Like any mature believer in trouble, in his heart he knows he can neither reason his way out of it (though he may realize how irrational are his negative thoughts), nor pray his way out (though he continues to pray, automatically), nor run away (though he might be sorely tempted to try), nor do anything whatsoever to ameliorate his circumstances. He knows he is powerless to help himself, and so it is up to God to help him. To adopt such a stance under conditions of trauma is the highest kind of faith.

Obviously such a passive strategy can be abused, for it is also necessary to "put on the full armor of God" (Eph. 6:13). But the point is that no amount of spiritual discipline, positive thinking, or holy worry can in itself add a single hour to a life or an ounce of happiness to a heart. The admission of personal powerlessness is absolutely fundamental to faith, and herein lies the great difference between Job and his friends. The latter assume not merely that Job is able to help himself, but that they too can help him, and here they fall prey to the basic flaw in much of what goes by the name of "counseling" in our society. In the words of Psalm 60:11-12, "The help of man is worthless. With God we will gain the victory." Or as Job puts it in 12:13, "To God belong wisdom and power; counsel and understanding are his."

Whatever power we human beings may appear to exercise, it is only for a season and within a very limited sphere. The President of the country is President only for a term, and in his own home he may have no authority at all. The general who commands thousands of troops might be totally powerless to command enough discipline to reduce his waistline, and he might end his days in a hospital bed being ordered around by women in white. The author of the book you are reading may have a way with words, but when it comes to dealing with people he could be quite inept. As Thomas Millar writes, "Man has a will to power, but he has no real power. Any one of us could get leukemia tomorrow. How's that for being captain of your fate? We're all just children trying to grow up. We think that means getting power. What it really means is learning to accept the powerless nature of the human condition."

The First Gospel

"Ask the animals, and they will teach you,
or the birds of the air, and they will tell you;
or speak to the earth, and it will teach you,
or let the fish of the sea inform you.
Which of all these does not know
that the hand of the Lord has done this?" (12:7-9)

How refreshing it is to see Job turning the discussion away, however briefly, from the claustrophobic abstractions of the last ten chapters and pointing vividly to the animals, the birds, the fish, the very earth itself as conspicuous and trustworthy beacons of wisdom. In its focus upon nature this passage contains a hint of the Lord's own answer to Job at the end of the book. Could this be the reason why verse 9 contains the only example in the entire dialogue of the use of the Hebrew name "Yahweh"? Some commentators like to point to this as evidence of the verse's doubtful authenticity, but is it not more satisfying to see in it a poetic foreshadowing of the theophany? When God finally speaks in Chapters 38—41, He does not advance any abstract arguments, nor does He make a single reference to any of the events of Old Testament history (no doubt for the simple reason that most of those events had not yet occurred). Instead the Lord's entire appeal is to the wonders of nature, and the effect of this is to move the whole stuffy convoluted debate between Job and his friends outside, out into the fresh air of the real world.

Job's speech in Chapter 12 holds a foretaste of this. His primary argument for the soundness of his theology is that it corresponds to the real world. Job's faith encompasses all the strangeness and wildness of reality itself, while the faith of his friends does not. If you want to know the ways of the Lord, says Job, just look around you. You can theologize all you want, but if your theories do not mesh with the nature of things as they are, then what good are such theories? Even a dog has more knowledge of God than you do!

Sadly, this comment is all too true of the great majority of thinking and theorizing that people do about God. Often it does not even square with natural law, with the observable created order of things, let alone pierce through to the supernatural reality of the transcendent Creator. Even at its best, theology is like a jigsaw puzzle of the sky, in which human beings take all the available bits of evidence about sky and carefully piece them together into a complete picture. Yet somehow the picture is not complete: everyone's picture turns out to be different, and all the pictures have pieces missing, and there are always a few extra pieces lying around that seem to have been left over from some other puzzle. Even a finished puzzle-picture of the sky would still have all the lines and cracks showing, and would be a far cry from the living reality that anyone can see simply by looking out the window.

Hence Paul writes, "Since the creation of the world God's invisible qualities—his eternal power and divine nature—have been clearly seen, being understood from what has been made, so that men are without excuse" (Rom. 1:20). Nature, Paul implies, was God's original word to man, His original revelation. It was only when people rejected this perfectly obvious and adequate display of His glory that the Lord was obliged to change tactics, so to speak, and to deal with sin through the special revelations of Scripture, and ultimately through the message of the cross. Nevertheless, nature still stands as His first and sufficient revelation, His first gospel. Mother nature is theology's subconscious. She is our Father's mother tongue.

This can be a difficult concept for Christians, among whom the revelatory role of the creation tends to be greatly undervalued. But while it is important that the Christian faith be book-centered, it is just as important that it not be bookish. What Job does in this passage is to urge his friends to get their noses out of their books, out of their scholarly religious treatises (for they probably had no Scripture as such), and to take a good look around them at the real world. As David wrote in Psalm 19:1, "The heavens declare the glory of God; the skies proclaim the work of his hands."

Appearances

"He leads priests away stripped
and overthrows men long established.
He silences the lips of trusted advisers
and takes away the discernment of elders." (12:19-20)

Job knows from personal experience that the Lord "overthrows
men long established." This is exactly what has happened to
him. As for his other comment here about befuddled "advisers"
and "elders," is this perhaps a thinly-veiled gibe at his friends? In
their view, the fact that Job has lost everything is evidence that he is
being judged by God. But would it not be just as reasonable, Job
wryly suggests, to draw the conclusion that they too are under judgment, since they seem to have been bereft of their senses?

Job's point is the same as it was in 1:21: *"The Lord gives and the
Lord takes away."* It is the Lord who exalts people and the Lord
who humbles them. Exaltation does not stem from human virtue
any more than debasement stems necessarily from sin. And the same
is true of wisdom: it is the Lord who gives light and the Lord who
withholds it. "What he opens, no one can shut; and what he shuts,
no one can open" (Rev. 3:7). What reader of the Bible has not had
the experience of seeing a passage virtually leap off the page as if the
words were written in fire? Yet at other times these same words can
appear as ordinary as the daily newspaper, and at still other times
they swim unintelligibly before our eyes, as if the Devil himself had
scrambled them. "I wept and wept," writes John, "because no one
was found who was worthy to open the scroll or look inside" (Rev.
5:4). The Word of God is for Him to open and for Him to close.
Apart from His will it is impossible for anyone even to take a Bible
off the shelf, let alone to understand it. And is it not exactly the same
with the book of life? Sometimes the Lord will cast a rosy glow over
the whole of creation so that it is very easy for us to feel close to Him
and to understand the secrets of living. But at other times the world
appears drab and colorless, and at still other times everything is
blackness and confusion. Such changing appearances, Job maintains, have little to do with our personal sanctity. We are not "more

holy" when we feel good or "less holy" when we feel bad. All that can be said is that the Lord opens and the Lord closes, He lifts up and He casts down.

Job's contention is not that worldly appearances have nothing to do with spirituality, but rather that the deep connections between the two are largely beyond rational comprehension. The meaning of our lives, or of life in general, is far broader than can be determined simply by taking stock of our immediate feelings and circumstances. This is where Job's friends miss the boat. Their theology is essentially subjective, contingent upon present personal experience. But Job's theology is objective, rooted instead in extrinsic authority. That is why Job constantly appeals outside of himself, beyond the narrow limitations of his own bewildering private circumstances, to the external authority of a God who is bound by His very nature to be just, and whose eternal justice overrides all earthly appearances. The unbelieving mind cannot make this leap. Having no extrinsic reference point, it cannot see past its immediate situation. No matter how broad its perspective may seem, the unregenerate mind is literally trapped inside itself. As Ambrose Bierce lamented concerning human reason, "Its chief activity consists in the endeavor to ascertain its own nature, the futility of the attempt being due to the fact that it has nothing but itself to know itself with."

There is only one way out of this vicious circle, and that is faith. Only faith has the mysterious power to lift a person outside of himself, yet without leaving himself—to give a vantage point outside of the world, yet without leaving the world. Faith is the ability to see in the dark, to pierce beyond all that is visible, tangible, sensible, or even conceivable, and yet still to connect with something solid. This spiritual landfall is what frees us from the prison of ourselves and of the world's passing show. If our gospel is not one that, like Job's, will stand up to the prolonged test of having absolutely no circumstantial evidence of worldly success, then it is a gospel of straw. It is a gospel founded on appearances, not on the cross of Christ.

The Squeaky Wheel

*"I desire to speak to the Almighty
and to argue my case with God." (13:3)*

Job really believes that if he summons God, God will appear and answer him. This is astounding. He seems obstinately determined to talk with God face to face and to hear answers from God's own lips, and he will not settle for anything less. Indeed the very essence of Job's faith is this insistence upon having a personal encounter—more than that, a personal relationship—with the Lord God Almighty. It is as if he knew and took absolutely literally the promise of Jesus Christ, "Ask and it will be given to you; seek and you will find; knock and the door will be opened to you" (Luke 11:9).

Significantly, this verse from Luke follows immediately upon the parable of a man who needed bread in the middle of the night and so went pounding on the door of his sleeping friend. "I tell you," Jesus concludes the story, "though he will not get up and give him the bread because he is his friend, yet because of the man's *boldness* he will get up and give him as much as he needs." Is it wrong to be stubbornly determined in pursuing a speaking-terms relationship with God? No; on the contrary it is wrong not to be determined enough. To give up too easily is catastrophic. "Make every effort to enter through the narrow door," Jesus warned, "because many, I tell you, will try to enter and will not be able to. Once the owner of the house gets up and closes the door, you will stand outside knocking and pleading, 'Sir, open the door for us.' But he will answer, 'I don't know you or where you come from'" (Luke 13:24-25). The time to stand at the door of Heaven and knock and plead for entry is not later, but now.

A similar moral lies behind the parable of the persistent widow in Luke 18. Job's case is strikingly parallel to this woman's, for he too seeks justice from an apparently unjust Judge, and he does so in the stubborn hope that somehow, in the final analysis, true justice must prevail. Astonishingly, this very stubbornness God accepts as faith. To cite yet another example, Job could be compared to the prophet Habakkuk whose book begins, "How long, O Lord, must

I call for help, but you do not listen?" (Hab. 1:2). The fact that God appears to be turning a deaf ear to this prayer does not deter the prophet from continuing to call. No, Habakkuk is resolved to "stand at my watch and station myself on the ramparts; I will look to see what he will say to me, and what answer I am to give to this complaint" (2:1). How long the prophet had to wait for his answer we are not told, but apparently the wait was well worth his while, for the very next verse in the book declares, "Then the Lord replied," and two verses later appear the famous words, "The righteous will live by his faith"—a statement so much admired by the New Testament apostles that they quote it no less than three times (see Rom. 1:17; Gal. 3:11; Heb. 10:38).

Many people, of course, have questions for God. But hardly anyone is willing to hold out and wait (let alone to wheedle and pester the Lord) for an answer. Most people will not wait on God even for one minute. Why not? Surely it is because we do not really expect any answer. Job's friends are scandalized (as many religious people would be today) by the very thought of bringing God directly and personally into their affairs. "Just imagine!" they must have thought; "What kind of a kook does this Job think he is, calling on God as though He were a person like you or I, and actually expecting an answer? No, this is a serious theological discussion we're having; let's not drag any charismatic nonsense into it!" But the message of *Job*, of *Habakkuk*, and of Jesus' parables on prayer is all the same: the word of the Lord comes without fail to those whose faith takes a peculiar form—the form of despair honestly and passionately expressed, combined with stubborn persistence in holding out for consolation. If just a few people in a dead church would get down on their knees and rattle the gates of Heaven, refusing to be comforted until the Lord had brought revival, then would not God respond to such prayer and "rend the heavens and come down" (Isa. 64:1)? In the economy of the Holy Spirit, the squeaky wheel gets the grease.

Job's Comforters

"You are worthless physicians, all of you!" (13:4)

Job called them "worthless physicians." Today we call such people "Job's comforters"—a scathing little phrase which by dint of
its sheer utility has found a ready niche in our vocabulary. Job's
comforters are those who think that the way to minister to others
in need is by straightening them out. Job's comforters may be full of
boundless reserves of patience and sincerity and hard work and
cheerfulness and self-sacrifice, and over all of these virtues they may
put on something they take great relish in thinking of as "love." Yet
somehow the result of all their effort, for those unfortunate enough
to be on the receiving end, is that a bad situation is made worse.
Job's comforters succeed only in twisting the knife in the wound,
and if you try to tell them that this is what they are doing to you,
they will tactfully remind you that you are the one with the problem.

Job's unmitigated scorn for his friends' virtuous posturing is
nowhere more evident than in this chapter. Much more on the
offense than the defense here, he openly denounces his friends as
liars (v. 4), blabbermouths (v. 5), heretics (v. 7), and hypocrites (v.
9). These men are representatives of all the twisted and damaging
"ministry" that is carried on in the name of the Lord, yet apart from
love, apart from the Holy Spirit. Their basic problem, Job suggests,
is that they have no real fear of God (v. 11), no overwhelming sense
of the majesty of His reality, and so their theology is reduced to
"proverbs of ashes" (v. 12). Three chapters later Job is still blasting
them: "Miserable comforters are you all! Will your long-winded
speeches never end?" (16:2-3). It would be easy to see Job as need-
lessly fanning the flames when he taunts, "Come on, all of you, try
again! I will not find a wise man among you" (17:10). Yet in passages like these it is not so much that Job is being deliberately inflam-
matory, as that he is challenging his friends to bare their true souls
and to speak their minds as plainly as he is doing. This takes
tremendous courage, and it also demonstrates yet another aspect of
Job's faith: his faith in people. If Job eggs people on, it is ultimately
because he trusts the quality of the human soul and the resilience of

relationships. He believes in people enough to probe and to test them—ironically, just as God is doing with him. As the Lord bets His own honor on Job's faithfulness, so Job is not afraid to put the quality of his human friendships on the line. If his friends fail their test, it is the sort of failure that eventually opens the way for healing and reconciliation, and so Job's trust proves well-founded in the end.

The bravery of such a stance is not to be underestimated. What strength of character Job must have had—this sick, tortured, exhausted man—to keep sticking to his guns even when it meant alienating the only people who were in a position to comfort him, the ones whose presence (cold as it might have been) was nonetheless the only human companionship he had. How much easier it would have been for Job simply to have tagged along with his friends, nodding agreeably to everything they said, going to any lengths just to hang on to their friendship. Is this not precisely the strategy adopted by many sufferers? Suffering attracts sympathy, and it is only human nature to try to exploit and manipulate this sympathy, to milk the attention of others for all it is worth. But not so with Job. Far from using his suffering to evoke pity, he actually rejected pity in favor of probing the motives behind it. "Any port in a storm" was not his motto. The only port he sought was that of God, and his refusal to kowtow to the shallow counsel of his friends was in effect a refusal to have his storm calmed by anyone but the Lord.

Job was wise to the fact that sympathizers can be just as manipulative as the sufferers to whom they minister, attaching subtle but powerful strings to their proffers of help. In this case the strings were theological, for as long as Job's theology failed to line up with that of his friends', their hearts would remain fundamentally closed to him. How many Christians are like this, making soundness of doctrine their yardstick for measuring out mercy? Does our compassion suddenly run dry once others make it crystal-clear that they do not buy our brand of theology? Do we realize that if God had followed this policy in regard to the human race, there would be no gospel?

Falling to Pieces

"Why do I put myself in jeopardy
and take my life in my hands?" (13:14)

"hy am I doing this?" cries Job. "Why am I spilling out my
guts to you fellows and making a complete fool of myself
in front of you?" Consider how easy it would have been
for Job to have handled his friends' criticisms in a different way, by
simply turning his face to the wall and groaning, "Go away and
leave me alone." Silent sulking is one of the most alluring strategies
open to sufferers for wresting at least some meager satisfaction out
of their misery. Job, however, chose a much harder course in deciding to stand his ground and argue the issue through with his friends.
Why was he prepared to do this? Why put himself through all the
added stress and unpleasantness of a heated discussion? Surely it
was because Job deeply cared for these men, and he took their
friendship seriously.

The more intimate we are with people, the more likely we are to
voice our displeasure freely. With strangers we put on a bright and
confident face; but among our own family we have the liberty to
gripe, moan, and weep, and if we do not, then we are probably not
a very close family. Among loved ones the stoical maintenance of a
saintly exterior, at the expense of honest and meaningful sharing, is
nothing short of sinful. To hide one's struggles from another is to
withhold the gift of oneself.

By talking openly and at length about his inner trials, then, Job
is actually paying his three friends a great compliment. It is the compliment of trust, of deep faith in the quality of their friendship.
"Greater love has no one than this," said Jesus, "that one lay down
his life for his friends" (John 15:13). There are many ways, short of
shedding one's blood, of laying down a life. Shedding lies, shedding
masks, shedding dead traditions, shedding inhumanity in any form:
these also can be convulsive and revolutionary acts of sacrificial
love.

Job was like Paul who wrote to his Corinthian congregation, "I
am afraid that when I come I may not find you as I want you to be,

and you may not find me as you want me to be. I fear that there may be quarreling, jealousy, outbursts of anger . . ." (2 Cor. 12:20). Paul was afraid that he as well as the Corinthians would become embroiled in argument. He was afraid of outbursts of anger on both sides. What is so painful about this letter is the way Paul has to plead so pitifully for the Corinthians' affections, begging them to "make room for us in your hearts" (7:2). The whole of the epistle is, in a way, a defense of Christian passion, of the frantic, yearning, desperate side of genuine love. Paul goes so far as to say, "If we are out of our mind, it is for the sake of God" (5:13).

Job could have made the same claim. Paradoxically, it is not those who somehow manage to stay on top of their problems who are necessarily the most mature believers. Often it is the ones who come apart at the seams who exhibit the greatest faith of all. Just to fall apart is nothing. But to fall apart in the hands of God is to lay down one's life for others. It is to show the world what it means to depend on God and on nothing else, what it means to stand on a rock even when that rock feels like quicksand.

Job's daringness in relating to his friends grows directly out of the daringness of his relationship with God. The friends say that they believe in a powerful and gracious God. But does not their rigid, uptight behavior speak louder than all their words? In Job, however, we have someone who is disarmingly frank, who says and does outrageous things, who even goes so far as to pray intensely personal prayers in front of others. Here we have a man who weeps publicly, who squirms, groans, shouts, and beats his breast, a man in crippling pain who nevertheless summons the presence of mind to engage in serious conversation. Just think for a moment about this sort of behavior, and then consider the question, What sort of faith does such a man have? Regardless of what he says, regardless of all the doubts and confusion and anger that he gives vent to in words, what is it that his actions indicate? Do not the actions show that, in his heart of hearts, here is someone who believes? Is not this the conduct of one who has come to trust implicitly in a God of love, and who therefore is utterly distressed and perplexed when his Heavenly Father should apparently leave him in the lurch? A child who has grown up in a loving home reacts with shock and horror when plunged into a loveless environment. But a child who has never known love, never expects love. For that one, lovelessness becomes the norm.

Yes!

"Though he slay me, yet will I hope in him;
I will surely defend my ways to his face." (13:15)

With these words, God has just won His wager with Satan. On earth Job and his friends will continue to slug it out for a while longer. But in Heaven everything is now settled, and it is settled on the basis of Job's clear and stunning declaration, "Though he slay me, yet will I hope in him."

Remember the Devil's initial taunt, "Does Job fear God for nothing?" (1:9). Without at all realizing what he is doing, Job now delivers a direct answer to that taunt, and his answer is a resounding yes! YES!—Job's trust in God is unconditional. YES!—this man is not just out for himself. YES!—there is such a thing as faith that carries absolutely no ulterior motive—in other words, there is such a thing as love! And YES!—Job possesses this entirely disinterested faith and love towards God. Even if God Himself should strike him dead, Job declares, he will not cease to trust Him.

Did we catch the weird but unmistakable implication in these words? It is that even a dead person can exercise faith in God. If this were not the case, then why did Christ descend into Hell in order to "preach even to those who are now dead" (1 Peter 4:6)? Or how could dead Lazarus have heard the voice of Christ and come out of his tomb, except by faith? Indeed, is it not true that every one of us was stone-cold dead in our sins at the time when we first heard the gospel, and believed, and so were saved?

But note that Job does not say merely, "Even if I die, yet will I hope in him." No, the thought is infinitely stronger than that. For even if this same God of love in whom he trusts should Himself be the agent who hounds and harries and hates him into the grave— even then, Job testifies, he will continue to cry out to this God in the faith that He must and will hear him, and must finally reverse His judgment and vindicate him. Here is a kind of faith against which the Devil has nothing to say. Here is the faith of a man upon whom neither death nor Hell has any hold. Perhaps there are only two other places in the Bible in which such faith is so purely and intensely expressed: in the willingness of Abraham to sacrifice his only son Isaac, and ultimately in the willing death of the Son of God on a cross.

What is the secret of such faith? Perhaps the secret lies in the second part of Job's statement: "I will surely defend my ways to his face." It is the first half of the verse that is the famous part, but the second half is, on reflection, equally arresting. In fact the second half is almost a commentary on the first, for it tells me that the way to hope in God is to accept unwaveringly His gift of personal righteousness, even (and especially) when the reality of that righteousness seems most in question, even when all earthly appearances suggest that God Himself is against me and is bent on blotting me out. The time when I feel most overwhelmed and defeated by the onslaughts of the Devil, by the pressures of the world, by the weight of my own sin, and by the threat of death itself—this is the very time when I am to cling most vigorously to the promised and inalienable truth of my righteousness, which is the hope of the gospel. This is the time when I shall not fail to defend my way to God's face. For what is my way? My way is Jesus Christ.

Job's testimony is all the more remarkable for having come long before the historical advent of Christ, at a time when death held not the slightest promise of spiritual enlightenment for the orthodox believer. We today find this state of affairs almost impossible to grasp, but the fact is that in the Old Testament the place of the dead, Sheol, was the realm not of eternal life but of eternal murk and shadow, featuring at best cessation from worldly striving. The Old Testament contains hardly a hint that those who died would end up any closer to God than those who remained alive; on the contrary, the clear implication was that at death one lost touch with some vital dimension of real existence. Not only the physical but the spiritual pilgrimage came to an abrupt and inelegant end. How could it be otherwise, at a time before Jesus Christ had arrived in person to burst the gates of Sheol and free the dead along with the living? The fact that Job had a faith which he assumed would be operative even in Sheol stands as powerful evidence that he was fundamentally a believer in the gospel of Christ. Like Paul he as much as said, "I am convinced that neither death nor life . . . nor anything else in all creation, will be able to separate us from the love of God that is in Christ Jesus our Lord" (Rom. 8:38-39).

The Legal Metaphor

"Now that I have prepared my case,
I know I will be vindicated.
Can anyone bring charges against me?" (13:18-19)

There is a striking similarity between this passage in *Job* and a portion of one of the "Servant Songs" in *Isaiah*: "He who vindicates me is near. Who then will bring charges against me?" (50:8). Apparently Isaiah was here quoting the words of Job, just as Paul cites both Job and Isaiah in an even more familiar passage in *Romans*: "Who will bring any charge against those whom God has chosen? It is God who justifies. Who is he that condemns?" (8:33-34).

Job's confidence in his innocence and his yearning to have his name cleared take the form, increasingly, of an earnest plea to have his case tried in court—and not just in any court, but before the judgment-seat of God Himself. Just as Paul often employs legal terminology to underscore the objective, factual basis of Christian faith, Job too makes ample use of words such as "case," "plead," "defend," "judge," "justice," "summon," "hearing," "guilty," "innocent," "charges," "appeal." (See, for example, 9:15-20; 23:4-7; etc.) This constellation of images in *Job* is known by commentators as the "legal metaphor," and it reflects Job's implicit trust that the God of the universe must ultimately be a God of justice, and that if only Job's case can be tried before the highest of courts his innocence will be resoundingly affirmed.

In the *Gospels* we often hear Jesus speak to the Pharisees as though He were giving formal testimony in a court of law. Frequently He prefaced statements with the formal idiom, "I tell you the truth" (or, in the more sonorous phrasing of the *King James Version*, "Verily, verily, I say unto you")—just as though He were swearing on a stack of Bibles. This approach unnerved the Pharisees, who would have preferred to keep things on the level of a straightforward theological debate. But Jesus could see what to their eyes was invisible: the heavenly courtroom, with God the Father presiding on the bench. Aware of this other dimension, Christ conducted

Himself accordingly and gave bold testimony. The Pharisees tried to discredit this stance, saying, "Here you are, appearing as your own witness; your testimony is not valid" (John 8:13). But Christ persisted, making it clear that whether the Pharisees liked it or not the highest of all courts was already in session, and even now the weightiest of evidence was being heard, evidence that would lead to certain conviction for all who refused to acknowledge the truth.

Job conducts himself similarly. While he has never actually seen the supreme court of God, as Jesus had, nevertheless he assumes its existence and calls upon it to convene. He even addresses himself to it in advance, filing what today we might call a formal deposition. Thus Job prefaces his strong statement at the head of this chapter with the phrase, "Listen carefully to my words" (13:17)—a solemn idiom which, like Jesus' "Verily, verily," signals that a most serious and authoritative disclosure of truth is to follow, a declaration whose probity is absolutely beyond question. This is the context in which Job with unshakable conviction asserts, "Now that I have prepared my case, I know I will be vindicated."

In a sense, to be a Christian is to spend one's life preparing one's case for Judgment Day—carefully and patiently amassing evidence to parade before the Devil whenever he accuses us, and before the Lord when He comes to judge the earth. It behooves us, therefore, to be as certain as we possibly can of the strength of our defense. And the only way to do this is to make very sure that our stand is squarely on the work of the Lord Jesus Christ, and not on any merits of our own. Jesus is the divine defense counsel appointed to all who believe, and He does not lose His cases. For those He defends there is really only one question, and that is whether we are prepared to accept and to trust in the divine fiat of our righteousness in Christ. This righteousness is a *carte blanche*, a final and unappealable verdict of Not Guilty which places us once and for all beyond the law. It is a condition entirely uncomplicated by fine print, loopholes, liens, riders, or codicils. "If God is for us," declares Paul, "who can be against us?" (Rom. 8:31). So to be against our own regenerate selves is to be against God.

God Is My Witness

"Only grant me these two things, O God,
and then I will not hide from you:
Withdraw your hand far from me,
and stop frightening me with your terrors." (13:20-21)

These two prayer requests of Job's happen to be the very conditions that God in fact grants to human beings through the grace of the gospel—the gospel that Job already believes in his heart, even though it has not yet been revealed to the world. For by faith in Jesus Christ believers are, first of all, "saved from God's wrath" (Rom. 5:9), and secondly we are "enabled to serve Him without fear, in holiness and righteousness before him all our days" (Luke 1:74-75).

As we saw in the last chapter, Job understands that spiritual truth is like legal truth. In both areas a case may appear hopelessly complicated on the surface, and yet underneath the confusion there is always a hard kernel of truth. Either the defendant is guilty as charged or he is not; either the sinner is saved or he is not. This present life may be clouded with gray, but the job of the legal system, whether temporal or spiritual, is to make everything black and white, bringing all the facts out into the open to weigh them and pass judgment. While human law accomplishes this goal imperfectly, God's law will in the end accomplish it perfectly. In either case, however, the process of making things clear takes time—often a very long time—and in the interim objective reality is obscured by subjective illusion. The solid legal truth that remains all along at the heart of the issue is temporarily overshadowed by an apparent, circumstantial "truth" that is really a pack of lies. This happens in human law, and it happens also in regard to God's law. Just as outlaws of society can get off scot-free, so blatant offenders against God can go on living as though they are innocent, when the fact is that they are guilty as sin. By the same token, righteous believers who have been acquitted of their sins can, through the unrelenting pressures of the world and the flesh and the Devil, turn around and live their daily lives just as though they are still under condemnation.

This is the very corner that Job's friends are trying to back him into, but he will have none of it. For Job knows in his heart that his God is a God of love and forgiveness. He seems intuitively to understand the message of 1 John 4:10: "This is love: not that we loved God, but that he loved us and sent his Son as an atoning sacrifice for our sins." Job is well aware that he himself does not love God as he should; but he also knows that his love for God is not the basis of his faith. The basis, rather, is God's love for him. Therefore the fact that at present he is not feeling a peaceful, joyful trust and love towards his God is not what is uppermost in his mind. What is uppermost is the fact that God loves him, with a love that is rooted in objective, judicial reality, and that something must have gone terribly wrong for all the tangible evidences of that love to have been torn away from him. In beseeching God to bring his case to court, Job is not being unduly demanding; he is simply seeking his legal rights from a just God. While law and gospel may sometimes appear to be at odds, in reality they are in perfect harmony, so that the person who trusts in God's love trusts also in His justice, and vice versa.

The Apostle Paul, at times when his probity was in question, went so far as to say, "I call God as my witness" (2 Cor. 1:23). Job too is so bold as to believe that God Himself will ultimately testify on his behalf. As preposterous as this may sound, surely it is the very essence of the gospel. For our God is one who has sworn to take our part and to defend us eternally against all accusation, and to believe in Him is to take Him at His word and gratefully to accept His protection. It is on this very basis that we in turn become witnesses for Him, taking the stand to declare His faithfulness to a lost world. Such faith is not a religion but a relationship. In other words, it is not one-sided but two-sided, being comprised not merely of our faith in God but of His in us. It is our faith that behind all the fear and pain of life in a fallen world lies a loving and all-sufficient God, and it is God's faith that behind our corrupt nature lies a being with a capacity for perfection and everlasting life.

The Place of the Dead

"At least there is hope for a tree:
If it is cut down, it will sprout again . . .
at the scent of water it will bud . . .
but man lies down and does not rise;
till the heavens are no more, men will not awake
or be roused from their sleep." (14:7-12)

Sooner or later in this book we must grapple with the complex question of Job's attitude (and that of the Old Testament in general) towards death and the afterlife. Throughout Chapter 14 Job is preoccupied with this issue, and if we were to translate the above passage into modern parlance his blunt conclusion would seem to be, "When you're dead, you're dead." Is this the position of great faith?

Significantly, Job chooses the image of a tree to represent the possibility of new life. Though a tree be cut down and destroyed, he says, "at the scent of water" it is capable of budding again. From a Christian perspective this imagery is splendidly rich. Yet ironically it was not so for Job, who knew nothing of the "shoot" that would arise from the "stump of Jesse" (Isa. 11:1), nor of the dead tree on Calvary that would spring up to eternal life.

Similarly, Job's statement that the dead "will not awake" may appear to be softened by the qualifying phrase "till the heavens are no more." Again to the Christian this language is replete with meaning, as it conjures up that awesome occasion when "the heavens will disappear with a roar" and the Lord will usher in "a new heaven and a new earth" (2 Peter 3:10-13). For Job himself, however, who had no such knowledge of Christian eschatology, the phrase "till the heavens are no more" did not carry any deep prophetic overtones. For him it was simply a figure of speech describing something impossible, unthinkable. He meant that it was as unlikely that human beings would ever rise from the dead as that the stars would fall out of the sky.

In expressing this view Job was, surprisingly, representing accurately the standard Yahwist teaching that would have prevailed in his own era in regard to the afterlife. Indeed it is important to realize that throughout the Old Testament there was no equivalent to the Christian concept of "Heaven." Heaven was the place where God dwelt, but there was never any suggestion that the faithful might go there when they died. Rather, the Hebrew word for the abode of the dead was "Sheol," and Sheol was a murky limbo of a place, cold and forbidding. As David described it in Psalm 88:10-12, it was a region of "darkness" and "oblivion": "Do you show your wonders to the dead? . . . Is your love declared in Sheol? . . . Are your wonders known in the place of darkness, or your righteous deeds in the land of oblivion?" Clearly, it was far better to be alive on earth than to be in Sheol!

Strange as it may seem, it appears that when Old Testament believers died they did not go to Heaven but to someplace rather nearer to (though not the same as) the Christian concept of Hell. Instead of going to be "with the Lord," they were merely (and rather nebulously) "gathered to their people" (see Gen. 25:8, etc.). Granted, when Moses and Elijah appeared with Jesus on the Mount of Transfiguration it was in a glorified state, for the God of Abraham, Isaac, and Jacob "is not the God of the dead but of the living" (Matt. 22:32). On the other hand, what are we to make of the great prophet Samuel who, when he was called up from the grave, appeared back on earth not as a radiant and glorified being but as a perturbed spirit, a ghostly old man whose comings and goings were at the mercy of a pagan spiritualist (see 1 Sam. 28)? As Jesus taught, "No one has ever gone into heaven except the one who came from heaven" (John 3:13). Again, when Jesus told His disciples that He was going to His "Father's house" in order "to prepare a place for you" (John 14:2), the clear implication was that prior to this no such place had been prepared. Even in the case of King David, Peter thought it important to declare in his Pentecost sermon, "Brothers, I can tell you confidently that the patriarch David died and was buried, and his tomb is here to this day," and he "did not ascend to heaven" (Acts 2:29, 34). In the words of Thomas à Kempis, "Under the Old Law the gates of Heaven were shut and the way to Heaven dark."

This may seem a bleak and muddled conclusion. But what else was there to say on this grim matter of death before Jesus Christ had come to break the bonds of the grave and to set all its captives free?

Death Without Frills

*"If only you would hide me in the grave
and conceal me till your anger has passed!
If only you would set me a time
and then remember me!" (14:13)*

Job finds himself in an impossible situation. His agony is so great that one of the few thoughts that brings him any significant measure of comfort is the thought of death. Yet at the same time, even death holds no real comfort for him, since he knows full well that it will only leave him worse off than before. Is it any wonder if his feelings about death swing back and forth in wild ambivalence? On the one hand, there are times when he passionately longs for the grave, extolling it as a realm of comparative "peace" where "the weary are at rest" (3:13, 17). But on the other hand, he knows in his heart of hearts that the grave is the one thing to be feared more than anything else, for it is the "place of no return . . . of deep shadow and disorder" (10:21-22).

What a grim realist Job is! He knows there must be some way out of this impasse, and yet he knows too that whatever the answer is, it is something dark and obscure, not yet revealed in the orthodox doctrines of his day. As we have seen, even in conventional Israelite theology there was no reason to look forward to anything good after death. Enoch and Elijah, it is true, somehow escaped the fate of Sheol (see Gen. 5:24; 2 Kings 2:11)—but that was only because they had mysteriously been spared from dying. For everyone who died, however, there was but one common destiny. As David lamented to the Lord in Psalm 6:5, "No one remembers you when he is dead. Who praises you from the grave?" Or as the author of *Ecclesiastes* observed in his blunt manner, "All go to the same place; all come from dust, and to dust all return. Who knows if the spirit of man rises upward?" (3:20-21).

For those of us who live in the age of grace, it is very difficult to comprehend how Old Testament believers could ever have sustained their faith in God under such circumstances. What conceivable hope was there for the dying? We can sidestep this thorny question by dismissing pre-Christian views of the afterlife as simply vague and indistinct. But if anything, the Old Testament writers saw into this matter only too clearly, and what they saw was totally different from what any of the other, pagan cultures all around them saw. What they saw in death was the great, gaping, terrifying antithesis of everything that was good in this present life. No wonder one of the most curious features of ancient Israelite religion was its attitude of profound reserve, indeed of near-total silence, on this crucial religious question of the nature of the hereafter. For what was there to say? Unlike the Egyptians, for example, pious Jews had no interest in spiritualism or the occult or in any esoteric knowledge of Heaven or the underworld, and neither would they have anything to do with elaborate funeral rituals designed to expedite the soul on its "final journey." On the contrary, their death was a death without frills, and it is one of the great distinguishing marks of the Hebrew Bible that it refuses either to idealize or to mythologize death, showing absolute scorn for any attempt to fill in the intolerable blank of the grave with man-made fantasies.

As the Lord Himself admonished Job in His great speech out of the whirlwind, "Have the gates of death been shown to you? Have you seen the gates of *deep shadows*?" (38:17). If the Old Testament prophets had little to say on this burning issue, it was for the simple reason that little had been revealed by God. They said what they had been authorized to say, and no more, and so like Job himself they saw death for exactly what it was—a "land of gloom and deep shadow" (10:21) where "the dead are in deep anguish" (26:5).

Unless we can think our way back into this eerily primitive eschatological position, we will not be able to comprehend the sheer boldness and originality of Job's proposed solution to the dark riddle of death in 14:13—that he might be "hidden in the grave" until God's "anger has passed" and then, at a set time, be "remembered." Isn't this the very plan of resurrection which began to be fulfilled on Easter morning?

Resurrection

"If a man dies, will he live again?
All the days of my hard service
I will wait for my renewal to come." (14:14)

Job now poses the ultimate question: "If a man dies, will he live again?" It is worth noting that the question is not, "If a man dies, will he go to Heaven?" or, "Will death turn out to be the doorway into something wonderful?" No, Job's question is a more unusual one than that, for it concerns whether or not a human being, once dead and doomed to Sheol, might possibly live again. What is remarkable in this approach (and that of the Bible as a whole) is that it neither sidesteps nor soft-pedals the harsh reality of death. Instead, making no attempt to belittle death's undoubted finality, Job looks its horror straight in the face. He accepts this dark destiny as his necessary due and so becomes, like Jesus Himself, "obedient to death" (Phil. 2:8).

In the face of such absolute gloom Job's prophetic eye nevertheless discerns a quickening ray, in the form of the strange hypothesis that even those long dead in the grave might one day be brought back to life. It is important to grasp that this notion had no place whatsoever in the orthodox theological doctrine of Job's day. Later Old Testament writers, from David on, were to deliver startling prophecies of bodily resurrection (see, for example, Ps. 16:10; Isa. 26:19; Dan. 12:2). But in the more primitive Biblical literature there is no such teaching. As commentator Norman Habel writes, "The resurrection terminology employed in Job's speech seems to reflect a popular tradition *against which* standard Israelite teaching was directed" (italics added). To the ears of Job's friends, in other words, all his fine eschatological conjectures would have been heresy, and Eliphaz says as much in his ensuing rebuttal (see Chapter 15).

There is a funny thing about heresy, however, which is that in the odd case where the heretic turns out to be right, he is no longer a heretic but a prophet. And Job's solution to the intolerable question mark of death just happens to be God's own solution, as proclaimed by Jesus in John 5:25: "I tell you the truth, a time is coming and has now come when the dead will hear the voice of the Son of God and those who hear will live." With what heartrending tenderness Job pictures the enactment of this very event when he predicts, "You will call and I will answer you; you will long for the creature your hands have made" (14:15). Moreover he declares that however long it might take, "I will wait for my renewal to come" (v. 14). Surely Job's attitude is the very epitome of New Testament faith, as Christians too "wait eagerly for our adoption as sons, the redemption of our bodies. For in this hope we were saved" (Rom. 8:23-24). Having posed the question, "If a man dies, will he live again?" Job places so much weight on an affirmative answer that he as much as states with Paul, "If the dead are not raised . . . your faith is futile; you are still in your sins" (1 Cor. 15:16-17).

In the light of all this, Job must certainly be seen as a very early (and perhaps the earliest) Christian prophet of the resurrection. In Chapter 14 his thinking on this subject is still groping and tentative. But in subsequent speeches, as he continues to probe the open wound of death, his statements grow increasingly bold to the point where in 19:25-26 he will attain to the great climactic confession, "I know that my Redeemer lives. . . . And after my skin has been destroyed, yet in my flesh I will see God." Surely this is the essential Christian hope and promise, so much so that the earthly life of the Christian may be said to consist in practicing for this moment of resurrection: "Wake up, O sleeper, rise from the dead, and Christ will shine on you" (Eph. 5:14). Other religions may be quite happy to let the old body rot in the ground, so long as the soul journeys onward or is reincarnated. But to the Christian this is a horrifying evasion of reality—as it is to all those who have grappled hard and honestly with this issue (including, oddly enough, many a pagan culture like that of the ancient Egyptians, who could not conceive of the hereafter except in bodily terms, and so loaded their tombs with hordes of worldly effects). In the final analysis it is not so much the salvation of our souls that we human creatures are primarily concerned about, as the salvaging of our poor, dear, bedraggled hides. For we do not just *have* bodies—we *are* bodies. And so what we really long for is not to become pure disembodied souls, but rather to have our souls harmoniously reunited with our bodies in order that our bodies can work the way they are meant to without ever wearing out. And lo!—this very dream turns out to be exactly what our Savior Jesus Christ has for us up His amazing sleeve.

Sin and Death

"Surely then you will count my steps
but not keep track of my sin.
My offenses will be sealed up in a bag;
you will cover over my sin." (14:16-17)

It should not surprise us that in the midst of his meditations on death Job meditates also on sin, for in his mind these two brutal realities are so inextricably entwined as to be virtually one and the same. The very reason human beings die is that they are sinners. "Death came to all men," wrote Paul, "because all sinned" (Rom. 5:12). Thus death is not only the consequence but the evidence of sin, stripping people of every last layer of disguise that might have camouflaged the ugly truth of their innate wickedness. How true it is that "the sting of death is sin" (1 Cor. 15:56)! When the body dies, all that is left is sin; all that is left is the naked fact of total corruption, plain now for all to see. Hence the old warning, "Your sin will find you out."

Is this not the very nub of Job's present problem? Because he finds his body "wasting away like something rotten, like a garment eaten by moths" (13:28), he can only conclude that the Lord is refusing to forgive him, refusing to release him from his sin, and this knowledge stings him to the quick. As far as Job is concerned, so long as sickness and death remain at large in the world, sin remains unconquered. His friends seem to believe that righteousness consists in living without any taint of moral corruption. Yet if this were really possible, it should be equally possible to avoid physical corruption. Then the righteous would go on living forever, while only the godless died. Clearly this is not the case, reasons Job, and so for him the physical death of the righteous was an immense and immovable obstacle against which the theology of his friends was helplessly naive. Moreover, any religion that could not literally free the faithful from the curse of death had also not dealt adequately with the problem of sin.

The contrast between Job and his friends is nowhere more evident than in their two vastly different approaches to the double-barreled problem of sin and death. The friends, like most people, have struck a kind of compromise or bargain with death, whereby they agree just not to think about it very much. It is to such people that the Lord addressed the words of Isaiah 28:18: "Your covenant with death will be annulled; your agreement with the grave will not stand." Job, however, has no such covert agreement, and that is why he is free to protest loudly to his God about the outrageous insult of death: "As torrents wash away the soil, so you destroy man's hope. You overpower him once for all, and he is gone" (14:19-20). Similarly in the case of sin, where the friends imply that it is possible to "put away sin" (11:14) and lead an impeccable life, Job's sole hope is that the time will come when his sin will no longer be "kept track of" by God but will be "sealed up in a bag." He seems to know the truth of 1 John 1:8—"If we claim to be without sin, we deceive ourselves and the truth is not in us." Thus he freely admits he is a sinner, and yet still he clings to an obscure hope that somehow the Lord will "cover over" his sin, and by this he means nothing less than that his God must save him from the curse of death. For Job, liberation from death would be the only acceptable sign and proof that his sin had indeed been forgiven. Conversely, freedom from sin would be the sole and necessary sign that death had verily been conquered.

Is this not a peculiarly modern issue with which Job was wrestling? What Christian has not struggled with the text of 1 John 3:9—"No one who is born of God will continue to sin"? Or what Christian has not wondered at Jesus' promise in John 8:51—"If *anyone* keeps my word, he will never see death"? What Job so presciently understood was that sin and death are but two heads of the same monster, different in visage but in substance identical. This is why the Son of God had to die in order to take away sin. In the same way, Christ rose from death to guarantee us righteousness, for the righteousness of Christ is true life. Job, by drawing a direct equation between righteousness and life itself, proposed a solution to the problem of sin and death that turned out to be the solution of the gospel itself: the gospel of a divine forgiveness so radical that it would not only cancel all sin but, by that very act, raise the dead to eternal life.

Today in Paradise

"He feels but the pain of his own body
and mourns only for himself." (14:22)

In the last verses of this chapter Job returns to his gloomy but profoundly realistic ruminations on what existence in Sheol must be like. The lot of a dead man, in the words of the *King James* translation of 14:22, is that "his flesh upon him shall have pain, and his soul within him shall mourn." This prospect bears little resemblance to the fond notions many people have of what the next world might be like. Yet this is the Bible's consistent teaching on the fate of everyone who dies apart from faith in the resurrected Christ. Significantly, even Jesus Himself, when He died, did not go to Heaven but rather descended into Hell, where His passion continued until "God raised him from the dead, freeing him from the agony of death" (Acts 2:24).

As we saw in the last chapter, Job took the problem of physical death so seriously that to him it greatly detracted from any hope or comfort proffered by orthodox faith. In this he turns out to be in surprising harmony with the New Testament. Listen to Paul: "While we are in this tent, we groan and are burdened, because we do not wish to be unclothed but to be clothed with our heavenly dwelling, so that what is mortal may be swallowed up by life" (2 Cor. 5:4-5). We may find it strange that Job continues to groan about death even after he has clearly stated his faith in a future resurrection. Yet do we not do the same? Have not all believers done the same ever since that eerie, cosmically disillusioning moment in the first century when the utterly unexpected happened, and for the first time in history a born-again Christian did not "die" but (to use the New Testament's conspicuous yet opaque euphemism) "fell asleep"?

Remarkably, Job's thinking has already begun to shift from the hope of resurrection to an idea more radical still: eternal life. The fact is, future resurrection is not enough for us. What we really want (and what Job wanted) is life now. What we want is not just to be raised from the dead but to bypass death altogether. After all, why should the righteous have to die at all? How can eternal life truly be called eternal if it does not begin now, here in this world, the moment we believe? What sort of eternity would it be that would exclude the present moment and that would have to be interrupted, however temporarily, by a state of limbo? At this point, even the towering faith of Job runs up against a brick wall. He could believe in the future resurrection of the body, but could he, in all practicality, believe that he would not first have to face death just like everybody else?

And where do Christians stand in this dilemma? Is the situation any different for us? Jesus declared, "I am the bread of life. Your forefathers ate the manna in the desert, yet they died. But here is the bread that comes down from heaven, which a man may eat and not die" (John 6:48-50). Do we believe this? If we do, then the difference between the Old Covenant and the New Covenant becomes the difference between night and day. According to the gospel, to believe in Christ is to have died already; it is to have "crossed over from death to life" (John 5:24), so that for the Christian death is no longer a future event to be feared but something already over and done with.

Yet our carnal minds protest, How can this be, when Christians appear to go on dying just as regularly as everybody else? The only answer must lie in the brand-new approach to righteousness that was being hammered out even in the soul of Job—the approach which states that true life is not a matter of outward appearances but of the condition of the soul. Nowhere does the Bible promise that our external selves will ever be perfect in this world, but it does testify to "the spirits of righteous men made perfect" (Heb. 12:23). Christ is "the perfecter of our faith" (Heb. 12:2)—not of our visible selves, notice, but of our faith in Him. Since eternal life is not yet a manifest reality in the world but one which all the evidence of our senses contradicts, it can only be laid hold of by faith, and it is on this basis that Jesus promises, "If *anyone* keeps my word, he will never see death" (John 8:51).

Will we take the Son of God at His word? We say so glibly that "Jesus died for me"—but do we really believe it? Do we understand that Jesus died in our place, so that we will not have to die at all? For the believer in Christ there will be no imprisonment in Sheol, no time of being "hidden in the grave" until God's "anger has passed" (14:13), because for the Christian God's anger has already passed, and death with it, and "today you will be with me in paradise" (Luke 23:43).

Cancer of the Heart

Then Eliphaz the Temanite replied:
"Would a wise man answer with empty notions. . . .
Would he argue with useless words?" (15:1-3)

E mpty notions" and "useless words": this is how Eliphaz sums
up all of Job's profound and beautiful meditations in the previous three chapters—all the precious thoughts on righteousness and forgiveness, all the prophetic insights into the hope of
resurrection, all the honest wrestlings and doubts. What sort of man
is it whose ears are deaf to such wisdom and whose heart is closed
to such agonized searching?

The first speech of Eliphaz was courteous and cautious. But now
he rolls up his sleeves and proceeds to level one serious charge after
another against Job, from deliberate deceitfulness (v. 5) to the corruption of true religion (v. 4). Eventually he just throws up his hands
and says, "Your own mouth condemns you, not mine" (v. 6). If prior
to this the discussion had centered around whether or not Job had
sinned in the past, that question is now dropped. The real point,
stresses Eliphaz, is that he is sinning right now, by his haughty and
unrepentant attitude.

As the discussion deepens we see all three of the friends growing
more and more convinced that Job is his own worst enemy and that
his trials are entirely of his own making. From their point of view
this is the whole problem in a nutshell, and that is the end of the
matter. What can be done with someone who obstinately refuses to
repent? In the eyes of these spiritual doctors, Job is like a patient
who has lung cancer because he has smoked too much. And now,
they say, just look at the old fool—in spite of all the radiation and
surgery and chemotherapy, he's still puffing away like a human
smokestack. In such a case, conclude the doctors, it is useless to
waste even an ounce of pity. The fact that they themselves might
have contracted a far worse disease—a cancer of the heart brought
on by the failure to love—is conveniently overlooked in their medical textbooks.

Nevertheless, as much as Job's doctors would like to wash their hands of him and absolve themselves of personal responsibility, they cannot. For the fact is that these men are not only being deeply affected by their friend's pain, but (without daring to admit this to themselves) they are feeling implicated in his apparent sin and guilt. Subconsciously they fear that if he does not soon snap out of his slump, they themselves could be dragged down into the morass. That is why these would-be comforters, at first sincerely moved and perplexed by their friend's trauma, turn gradually cool and condescending, then hot and bothered, and finally angry and even abusive over the man's stubborn refusal to listen to reason and, in particular, over their own inability to console him. While their involvement in their friend's tragedy may have arisen initially out of an altruistic desire to help, it is now being fueled by neurotic compulsion. In a twist consummately ironic, they begin to exhibit some of the very same emotional excesses as the sick man himself does, although totally without due cause, and so they prove the truth of that scathing yet little understood text of Romans 2:1: "You, therefore, have no excuse, you who pass judgment on someone else, for at whatever point you judge the other, you are condemning yourself, because you who pass judgment do the same things."

How often do Christian acts of mercy that began in a spirit of genuine love and compassion end up going sour as the element of judgment enters in? Real suffering is such an ugly business, such a messy and draining and thankless and long, drawn-out affair that all the soundest theology in the world, powered by the most heartfelt sympathy and the loftiest motives and all the grandest resources, simply crumbles to dust in the face of it. Therefore the Apostle Peter warns, "If anyone serves, he should do it with the strength God provides" (1 Peter 4:11). Any charitable venture that does not find its source in the tireless energy and the inexhaustible compassion of the Lord Himself is doomed to failure. Only the Holy Spirit has a strong enough stomach to take on the extremities of suffering.

Translation Problems

*"Would a wise man . . . fill his belly with
the hot east wind?" (15:2)*

Besides making little sense in English, the above translation
from the *New International Version* fails to convey the full
force of Eliphaz's tone. To have Job "spouting hot air" might
be more idiomatic—and yet even that phrase does not quite capture
the full sense, since what Eliphaz is really suggesting is that Job's theology is about as edifying as a belch. Thus a more accurate rendering of the verse might be something like, "Does a wise man go
around belching hot air?" A good translation should reflect the significant fact that at this point the very proper Eliphaz has turned vul-
gar and vituperative.

This is just one example of the manifold translation problems for
which the text of Job is infamous. Consider some other cases:

In 19:27 the final line reads literally, "My kidneys have ended in
my chest." The *Jerusalem Bible* translates this, "My heart within me
sinks," but in the context the thought is obviously just the opposite:
"I'm so excited my heart could burst!" Or as the NIV puts it, "How
my heart yearns within me!"

In 7:19 Job says to God, "Can't you leave me alone long enough
for me to swallow my spit?" The NIV translation of this text is ane-
mic: "Will you never look away from me, or let me alone even for
an instant?" Both the *Jerusalem Bible* and the *King James Version*
are better, but still they opt unfortunately for the more polite word
"spittle," rather than the common "spit" which Job himself would
surely have used.

Job's plainspokenness is something that in most translations is
shamefully watered down. In 31:9-10 Job says bluntly, "If my heart
has ever been enticed by a woman . . . then may my wife grind for
another." The NIV translates this, "May my wife grind another
man's grain," but the word "grain" is not present in the original,
and its addition all but obliterates the clearly-intended sexual pun.
Similarly, in 27:5 the NIV reads, "I will never admit you are in the
right," but since the Hebrew has the force not simply of a strong

statement but of an oath, the line could better be rendered, "I'll be damned if I ever give in to you!" (Job would have used the word "damned" not for cheap slang effect, but literally, and so the charge of profanity would not apply.)

One special difficulty in translating ancient Hebrew is the fact that the language contains no purely concrete or purely abstract nouns, but instead every noun has both a concrete and an abstract connotation. A familiar example of this is the word *ruah*, which does double duty as "wind" and "spirit." The poetry of Job exploits this concrete/abstract phenomenon through frequent use of the literary device of *double entendre*. In 7:6, for example, Job complains that his days are drawing to an end "without hope." The Hebrew word translated "hope" is "*tiqwa*," which also means "thread" or "cord." Most translators feel compelled to employ the abstract noun and thus sacrifice the metaphor. But consider Norman Habel's version: "My days are swifter than a weaver's shuttle; they end when the thread runs out." (Interestingly, this same word "tiqwa" is the one used in Joshua 2:21, where Rahab ties a scarlet cord of hope in her window.)

All in all, the language of Job is so brilliantly rich and convoluted that it must be read in some respects like modern poetry. In places the mode of expression is so highly compressed that the sense is all but unintelligible and can only be grasped intuitively, impressionistically. As with surrealist or symbolist images, the gist must be "caught" the way one catches sight fleetingly of an exotic bird in a tropical forest. Is it any wonder if some of the loftiest and most celebrated verses in the book are among the most difficult to interpret? One notorious instance is 19:25-27, the passage beginning "I know that my Redeemer lives." If translators cannot agree on the meaning of such a text, isn't it partly because Job is expressing thoughts that boggle the mind? As with any great poet or prophet, Job's words are like new wine in old skins, full of raw, crude, explosive power. Probably it was the author's deliberate intent that in this hero's wildest rantings the Hebrew tongue should come close to being murdered. To write off such passages as being hopelessly "garbled" (as so many modern scholars seem to do)—to say nothing of omitting or shifting around whole blocks of text in order to force the lines to "make sense"—this is simply to take the lazy, prosaic man's approach to reading poetry.

Fix-it Counseling

"Are God's consolations not enough for you,
words spoken gently to you?" (15:11)

If the text of Job were to be translated into colloquial English, we might at this point catch Eliphaz saying, "Enough of this kid-glove treatment! What you need, Job, is a good tongue-lashing." Job's friends cannot get past the notion that there ought to be something he can do to straighten out his life and get back on track. Theirs is a medical, remedial approach to religion, in which whatever tribulations cannot be overcome by faith must either be ignored or else chalked up to sin.

Many Christians pride themselves on denying the modern-day gift of miraculous physical healing. And yet, when it comes to emotional or psychological healing, these same conservatives seem to have a double standard. For subtly but clearly they convey the message that every believer should exhibit a certain level of emotional well-being (or at least show steady progress in that direction), and if anyone does not yield to their ministry, then that victim's faith becomes suspect. But is the healing of the soul any easier than the healing of the body? In either case the message "only have faith and you will get better" is simplistic and cruel.

Whatever form it may take, the theology of hyper-faith causes Christian compassion to deteriorate into an obsessive fix-it mentality. People and their problems can no longer be tolerated, but must be instantly remedied. Why? Because the self-esteem and the emotional equilibrium of the supposed helper are at stake. In the hands of such "care-givers," the one being cared for cannot be allowed simply to work through a problem in his own way and at his own speed. No, there is no room for that. Instead the thing has to be fixed immediately. Right now practical steps must be taken to bring the uncontrollable under control. Whenever any counseling situation takes this turn, what is happening is that the real problem and the real suffering have been swept under the rug, and an entirely new problem has assumed center-stage. This new problem is the unresolved guilt and insecurity of the counselor. In the case of Job's friends, over the course of the dialogue we see their well-intentioned solicitude degenerating into paranoid, even hysterical self-defensiveness. Rather than helping Job, what they are really doing now is struggling frantically to maintain and justify their status as counselors.

In the face of such mounting pressure, we must continue to marvel that Job's focus is not at all on escaping his suffering or getting his problems "fixed." Rather, his whole focus is on securing his (and his God's) moral vindication. Job would have put little stock in the prayer, "Lord, get me out of this!" He knew that in most situations we are better off to stick with the problems we have and to see them through. For life is full of problems, and as soon as we get rid of one there is another (and maybe a worse one) ready to crowd in and take its place.

What Job realized, in his own way, is that there is no progress in the spiritual life except through the cross. Naturally we are forever trying to avoid the cross, either fleeing from it or else searching for some way around it. But with the cross there is no way around and no going back. We must go through. In fact, every step we take forward as believers must be through the cross. There is simply no other way of advancing. That is why we must learn never to leave the cross, never to take our eyes off it. Daily we must pick up our cross and die to ourselves in order that the power of Christ might rest upon us. For the truth is that we do not die all at once but little by little, and every time a little part of us is nailed to the cross and dies, immediately the grace of the Lord Jesus flows into that dead part and renews it. This is how we live by grace. The power of grace is activated through the cross.

Too many Christians are looking for graceless, fix-it solutions to their problems, and to the problems of others as well. We forget that one of the great mysteries of the gospel is that God did not fix us when He saved us. By grace He simply saved us, warts and all.

The Primal Scream

"Why has your heart carried you away,
and why do your eyes flash,
so that you vent your rage against God?" (15:12-13)

D ialogue" is a very polite term for what happens in Job. Really it is an argument, and a hot one at that. Not only does Job argue with his friends, but he also argues with God. As for the friends, they too are engaged in a heated dispute with God, but like many people they do not care to admit this, and so their anger is directed instead against Job. A man like Eliphaz thinks that if he gets mad at God, God in turn will get mad at him and condemn him. So Eliphaz suppresses his anger and lives in continual, subconscious fear of divine wrath. He is like a hermit who prides himself on having no interpersonal hassles to upset his tranquil and ordered lifestyle. But anyone who lives in a family, in close fellowship with others, lives with tensions, complaints, disputes. Different families cope with these stresses in different ways—some quietly and some noisily, some effectively and some pathologically—but no family survives for long without some form of argument, and the family of God is no exception.

Is not the whole human race engaged in one long argument with God that is called "history"? The difference between believers and unbelievers is that while the former argue on speaking terms with the Lord, the latter do so by turning their backs and giving Him the silent treatment. Those who choose to live outside the family circle end up with no proper forum for expressing their hurts and resentments against their Heavenly Father. But those who gather around the Father's table know that such problems must be regularly aired, for if they are not, they will poison intimacy.

In our culture anger is generally frowned upon as being disruptive. But there are different ways of being disruptive. A chronically angry, loud, critical person is certainly disruptive. But a polite, well-behaved person may also be disruptive, and in a church such a person may be using their friendly and unassuming ways to obstruct the purposes of God. A cult of niceness is as effective as heresy for destroying the spiritual life of a church. Anger, on the other hand, may be used by God to break up a spirit of complacency. Consider Ezekiel, who when the Lord first called him to a prophetic ministry reacted "in bitterness and in the anger of my spirit" (3:14). In this case the Lord used anger and bitterness to inflame Ezekiel's heart with passion for Him. If Ezekiel had insisted on remaining a quiet, mild-mannered priest (which he probably was by nature), he would have thwarted God's purposes.

Little wonder that the great believers of the Bible have also been great arguers with God—from Jacob, who actually came to blows with the angel of the Lord, to Peter who in Acts 10 answered a divine command three times with the words, "Surely not, Lord!" Clearly, anger at God can be a sign of spiritual growth. It can mean we are outgrowing a concept of God that is no longer adequate for us. It could even be said that our anger is directed not at the living God Himself but at our own idolatrous concept of Him. While we ourselves may not understand this, nevertheless our anger functions to move us closer to God as He really is. Religious phonies will go to almost any lengths to hide the fact that their relationship with God is not real or satisfying. But people who truly love the Lord have a consuming hunger for reality. Freedom, truth, peace, joy: such things have a taste and a feel all their own, and we know them when we see them. If the people of God are deprived of these fruits of the Lord's real presence, naturally they grow angry and disconsolate. Is it their fault that they cannot live without God?

There are times when the Lord is actually honored and glorified by our anger at Him, in ways that He may not be by an attitude of unruffled "trust." Job provides a healthy balance to the traditional picture of the bloodless, gutless, cheerfully suffering saint. At the very least, anger means that we are taking God seriously and treating Him as a real person—real enough to arouse our passions. Angry prayer is not to be recommended as a steady diet, perhaps, but it is certainly preferable to lip-service prayer. Doesn't artificiality in relationships belie a far greater hostility than the honest expression of deep emotion? In the prim and proper prayer lives of many devout folk, a good old-fashioned temper tantrum might be one of the best things that could happen. In the courts of Heaven there is a place for the primal scream.

The Time Is Coming
and Has Now Come

"All his days the wicked man suffers torment. . . .
Before his time he will be paid in full." (15:20, 32)

W e have examined some of Job's thoughts on immortality. But how did his friends approach this delicate subject? What Eliphaz says here about the wicked applies also, from his point of view, to the good—"Before his time he will be paid in full"—and this emphasis on the present world as the sphere of all punishment and all reward is the constant theme of the friends' speeches. Admittedly, in the latter part of Chapter 15 Eliphaz does point to death itself as the ultimate punishment for the wicked. Yet why the righteous must also die is a question that seems, oddly, never to occur to him. In an earlier chapter Eliphaz had promised that if Job mended his ways he would "come to the grave in full vigor, like sheaves gathered in season" (5:26). But what happens to the sheaves in the grave he would not venture to say. Somehow the friends manage to steer clear entirely of the issue of what happens after death, making it seem as if all of Job's intimations of immortality are completely irrelevant to his present crisis.

It must be remembered that for the Old Testament believer, the proper focus of faith was not Heaven but earth. The Lord never promised Abraham a place in Heaven, but rather that his descendants would become a great nation on earth, and for that reason his name would always be remembered and blessed. Later on the symbol of the "promised land" would come to be spiritualized, but to Abraham himself, and to generations of Israelites after him, the promises of God applied very much to this world rather than to another. Thus David declared in Psalm 27:13, "I am still confident of this: I will see the goodness of the Lord in the land of the living," and in Psalm 115:17-18, "It is not the dead who praise the Lord, those who go down to silence; it is we who extol the Lord, both now and forevermore."

What is striking in this latter passage is that the word "forevermore," taken in context, has nothing to do with Heaven. Instead the picture presented is that of a nation of faithful people being continuously maintained upon the earth, generation after generation. Apparently the principal hope of ancient believers was that their name after death would live on through their progeny, and in this way their life's work and reputation would be firmly established forever. What a long way we have come from the time when the most important item in the national economy was children, and when the most significant work that people could do was the godly rearing of the next generation! While it is true that both Abraham and David had glimmerings of the resurrection of the dead (see Heb. 11:19; Acts 2:31), even this phenomenon, strange to say, by definition had to take place not in some "other" world but in this one.

To our ears the Old Testament emphasis on salvation in this world may sound bizarre. And yet there is a sense in which even today this focus continues to be the proper one for Christians. For "now is the time of God's favor, now is the day of salvation" (2 Cor. 6:2). Now is the point at which time meets eternity, or not at all. This present world is the place in which God and man are reconciled, or not at all. Jesus expressed this paradox whenever He employed that peculiar expression, "A time is coming and has now come . . ." (John 4:23; etc.). As believers we are looking forward to the coming Kingdom of Heaven, but we also believe that this Kingdom "has now come"—it is already here!

In either event, it may surprise us to learn that the main goal of our faith is not to "go to Heaven." Instead, Heaven is coming here. Heaven is the background to our faith, but earth is our proper foreground. Earth is our main stage; Heaven waits in the wings. The problem with Job's friends was that they missed seeing the wings completely, and therefore their stage loomed far too large and became wholly secular. Job, by contrast, managed to struggle his way toward a healthier balance between the two, and this remains the challenge for contemporary Christianity. Today as then, too much emphasis on the here-and-now will produce the triumphalist, health-and-wealth theology of the friends. Yet if we err on the opposite extreme and place too much stress on heavenly reward, the result is that life in this world is devalued, and a gnostic schizophrenia sets in between flesh and spirit. The beauty (and also the agony) of Job's faith was that he managed to straddle the seemingly impossible chasm between this world and the next.

Mercy

"I also could speak like you,
if you were in my place. . . .
But my mouth would encourage you;
comfort from my lips would bring you relief." (16:4-5)

It is easy to kick a man when he is down, points out Job. But any theology that does not bring comfort and encouragement to the hearts of the downtrodden is bad theology. For the sign of true faith is mercy toward others. The test of true piety is its power to unburden the weary, to bring light into darkness, to love the unlovable. In the words of a hymn by Samuel Crossman, the fruit of the gospel is "love to the loveless shown, that they might lovely be." Or as Charles Wesley wrote, "Jesus, Thou art all compassion; pure unbounded love Thou art." In many ways this is the central message of Paul's epistle to the Romans: "Let no debt remain outstanding, except the continuing debt to love" (13:8). Normally this letter is taught from a doctrinal standpoint, with heavy emphasis on the message of "justification by faith." But Paul's underlying burden is not so much doctrinal as pastoral. He was not writing an abstract treatise on theology, but a word of exhortation to a church that he felt was harboring seeds of strife. The strife (as so often happens in the New Testament) was between Jews and Gentiles, both of whom seemed to be using their newfound faith as an occasion for one-upmanship. Paul's purpose in writing was to cut the ground from under all those whose so-called faith issued in pride and presumption and the judging of others, rather than in mercy and charity. That is why the main thrust of the epistle comes not so much in the dense theological argument of the early chapters, but rather in the later chapters with their sustained appeal to love and unity in the Body of Christ: "Be devoted to one another in brotherly love. Honor one another above yourselves" (12:10); "Let us stop passing judgment on one other. Instead, make up your mind not to put any stumbling block or obstacle in your brother's way" (14:13); "Accept one another, then, just as Christ accepted you" (15:7).

Paul's message boils down to this: do not become conceited in your faith (11:20, 25), because the moment you do, it shows that you have no real faith at all. As soon as you start looking down on your brother and being scornful and critical of him, your behavior gives you away, proving that you have fundamentally failed to grasp the astounding breadth of God's mercy as it has been shown to you. For if you had really grasped it, then that same mercy would automatically flow out of you to others. If it does not, that can only mean you have not actually received God's mercy yourself. So the refusal to extend mercy is the same as the refusal to receive it, and to withhold mercy from others is to withhold it from oneself. Mercilessness is the equivalent of faithlessness, because faith means trusting God fully for deliverance, and not just for oneself but for others. In fact, mercy might almost be defined as faith on behalf of others. Paul did not waste time writing letters to people in whom he had no faith! No, to believe in God is to believe also in His people. If we cannot believe in God's people—even when they may seem to us most unlovable—then perhaps we do not really believe in God either.

The chief reason for being suspicious of the theology of Job's friends is that it is so obviously lacking in mercy. Even if they did not possess sufficient resources of faith to pierce through the oppressive atmosphere surrounding Job's trials and to find words of comfort to speak to him, they ought at least to have practiced the wisdom of Romans 12:15—to "mourn with those who mourn." Was it not for merciless religion that Jesus consistently reserved His harshest words of censure? In Matthew 9 Christ had mercy on a paralytic when He said, even before healing him, "Take heart, son; your sins are forgiven." When the judgmental Pharisees objected, Jesus condemned them for their "evil thoughts," and a few verses later He told them, "Go *away* and learn what this means: 'I desire mercy, not sacrifice.'"

Who but a godless person would want it any other way? Is it so hard to show mercy? Is mercy a heavy and burdensome task? No, it is just the opposite. As Shakespeare wrote, "The quality of mercy is not strained, but falleth as the gentle rain from heaven." Why should we shun something so pleasant and delightful, and choose instead to nurse hearts that are pinched and wan with judgment?

The Suffering Servant

"Men open their mouths to jeer at me;
they strike my cheek in scorn
and unite together against me.
God has turned me over to evil men
and thrown me into the clutches of the wicked." (16:10-11)

Normally *Isaiah* is thought of as the Old Testament book in which the theme of the Messiah as a suffering servant is most clearly prophesied. But the further we delve into the speeches of Job, the more we begin to see that this book too is steeped in the riddle of righteous, redemptive suffering. Indeed it is tempting to speculate that Job, this most primitive passion story of all, may actually have been Isaiah's own gospel, the book that first fired that prophet's spiritual imagination with the visions that would subsequently fill his Servant Songs. What must Isaiah have felt when he read a passage such as the one quoted above? Or consider the strange words immediately preceding it: "Surely, O God . . . You have bound me—and it has become a witness" (16:7-8). Or look at these lines from the following chapter: "My days are cut short. . . . Surely mockers surround me. . . . God has made me a byword to everyone, a man in whose face people spit" (17:1, 2, 6). Such language is redolent with the peculiar perfume of Good Friday, the scent of darkness mixed with the pungent, sweet odor of righteous blood.

This is the central mystery of the gospel, this mystery of the love of God poured out upon the world not primarily in the form of supernatural wonders, but rather in the form of His own shed blood, His own humiliation unto death, together with the suffering and humiliation of all His righteous children. Warm feelings, excitement, miracles, peace, success, material prosperity, health and wholeness—all those things that the friends of Job hold so dear—these are but the crowning of the life of faith, not its foundation. The sole foundation is the gospel itself, firmly rooted in the cross.

What picture of Christ do you hold at the center of your faith? What aspect of His character drives you most profoundly? Is it

Christ the great teacher? The healer and wonder-worker? Is it Christ the social radical? Christ the evangelist? Is it the risen Christ? Is it the ascended Christ, sitting in glory at the right hand of the Father? All of these archetypes of Christ are true and real and immensely significant. But there is only one Christ who deserves to be kept as the very center and animating focus of our faith, at the deep heart's core, and that is Christ the suffering servant, Christ on the cross. Other slants on the gospel, other emphases, will work (or will seem to work) temporarily. But only the cross-centered gospel will lead the disciple forward with perfect trustworthiness and consistency through every conceivable situation of life, through thick and thin, through darkness and light, through valleys and up mountains and then down the other side.

When the people of Israel were wandering in the wilderness, questions of spiritual authority frequently arose. During one such dispute the Lord directed that twelve staffs be set aside, one from each of the leaders of the twelve tribes. Overnight the staff belonging to Aaron miraculously budded and blossomed and even bore fruit, thus confirming the unique priestly authority of the tribe of Levi (see Num. 17). But "Aaron's rod," as it came to be called, was also a symbol and prototype of something much greater: the cross of Christ, the dead branch that springs up to eternal life. There are other rods of authority available to the Church, other vital doctrines and guiding principles, other staffs on which various members of the Body may legitimately lean. But the cross of Christ rules, and overrules, them all. Where any other theological focal point is allowed to take precedence over the cross, it is the authority of Christ Himself that is being challenged, with the inevitable result that division and heresy can creep ever so subtly into the Church. There is so much that can divide believers, and so precious little that can unite us. The ground upon which true Christian fellowship can take place is so very, very narrow—as narrow as the base of the cross.

Surely what is so compelling about the figure of Job is the way he takes his stand indomitably upon this narrow, narrow ground, within the very shadow of the Crucified One, and insists upon this single naked and desperately unlikely hope as the one sure foundation for faith.

No Guts, No Glory

"[God] has made me his target;
his archers surround me.
Without pity, he pierces my kidneys
and spills my gall on the ground." (16:12-13)

In Renaissance art one of the most commonly portrayed martyrdoms was that of St. Sebastian. The sight of this great lover of God with his body riddled with bloodied arrows is a shocking one, as the artists intended it to be. Yet how much more shocking it is to state, as Job does here, that God Himself is the cruel archer who so tortures His own saints to death.

What are we to make of Job's seeming sacrilege? Have some of us, perchance, had these same feelings about God but without daring to put them into words? Job's faith is that of a champion, a marathon runner, an Olympic wrestler. But it is precisely because his faith is so mighty that it is capable of withstanding such great storms of doubt, confusion, and rage. This man has an inner confidence that faith in God is not some puny fragile thing that needs to be neurotically coddled and nursed along lest at any moment it slip out of one's fingers. No, real faith is powerful, energetic, elastic, and durable—in short, a fit vessel for containing the entire gamut of human passions. Nothing else on earth, in fact, is stronger or more lasting than faith in the Lord. As the only force in the universe that can conquer death, it must be potent indeed!

The sort of faith that eats death for breakfast is not going to be piously preoccupied with the maintenance of a saintly exterior. Rather, it works from the inside out. It follows Jesus' advice to "first clean the inside of the cup and dish, and then the outside also will be clean" (Matt. 23:26). Patience, gentleness, and self-control are wonderful qualities to have, the very fruit of the Holy Spirit. But they are only virtues when they are truly authentic—that is, when they emanate irrepressibly from deep within the heart. When, on the other hand, they are laid on as a veneer over top of insincerity, then there is nothing in the world more ugly. When virtue is faked, it is a sickening thing, and doubly sinful.

How much better it is for a believer in God to exhibit a rough exterior than to bottle things up inside under a tawdry, saccharine layer of Christian "goodness." As Richard Sibbes wrote, "Some infirmities discover more good than some seeming beautiful actions. Excess of passion in opposing evil, though not to be justified, yet sheweth a better spirit than a calm temper, where there is just cause of being moved. Better it is that the water should run something muddily, than not at all. Job had more grace in his distempers, than his friends in their seeming wise carriage."

Self-control is a vital quality in Christians—but not to the point where it completely eviscerates our passions. Is not God Himself an intensely passionate being? He loves passionately, He hates passionately, and there is absolutely nothing about which He is dispassionate. He is capable of passionate jealousy and passionate anger, and more than that there was a time (if we are to believe Genesis 6:6) when He grew so despairingly furious with mankind that He actually regretted having created us at all.

Because God's feelings toward us are so strongly emotional, He respects strong emotion in a human being. He respects a person who, in pursuit of truth, can simply open his mouth and express the way he honestly feels inside. Yet how sad it is that so many who claim to believe in this God have also a fundamental suspicion of their own deepest feelings and instincts, an innate distrust of the very way in which they were made. Rather than living spontaneously according to the impulses of their hearts, such people end up conforming slavishly to external, pietistic images of expected behavior. With mature disciples of Jesus it is just the opposite. They are the ones who have learned to trust their own gut reactions, who know that it is all right (and at times essential) for what is in the gut to come out—not because there is anything fundamentally good or trustworthy about a human soul, but rather because, quite simply, in a true Christian that is where the Lord Himself has taken up residence: in the gut.

The Sanity of Tears

"My face is red with weeping . . .
as my eyes pour out tears to God." (16:16, 20)

We must constantly remind ourselves that not only is Job's frame of mind not detached and logical, like that of his friends, but that he does not really have a frame of mind at all. His mind has been rocked right out of its customary framework, and he is in the grip of powerful and unruly passions. Like anyone stricken with grief he is subject to uncontrollable bouts of weeping; he can burst into tears at the drop of a hat. The emotional instability of such a person might almost be likened to that of a newborn baby. That is how labile and vulnerable Job is, and perhaps this is exactly what his role in the Bible is meant to be. He is the distressed, disoriented infant who cannot be comforted and whose wailing goes on and on and on.

If Job can be compared to a crying baby, then perhaps his friends fit the role of the beleaguered parents. It is the middle of the night, 3 A.M., and hour after hour they sit up with their child and try every trick in the book to get him settled down. They walk the floor, rock, coo softly and sing, and even (though they must know better) try to talk sense into the kid. Outwardly they are mustering all the calmness and patience and rationality they can manage. But inside are they not seething with rage? Nearly insane at having their precious schedules interrupted and their sensible strategies shot to smithereens, all they want is for this kid to shut up. All they want is to climb into their nice warm beds and drift back to sleep.

All babies cry (even the baby Jesus was surely no exception), and most young children devote considerable energy to fussing and fuming. In one respect, such behavior can be attributed simply to hormones and to a lack of self-control and maturity. Yet at the same time it must be said that the outbursts of children are not always without real provocation, and that often enough they issue from justifiable outrage at the intolerable conventions of the cruel adult world into which they have been thrust. The storms of childhood spring from a natural heart of innocence (or better, call it ignorance) which simply cannot grasp the sheer enormity of evil that is at loose in the world (nor, admittedly, in itself), and which therefore reacts with instinctual pain and horror.

Why is the crying of babies so upsetting to mature adults? It is upsetting because it reminds us that the world in which we live is an evil place filled with inconceivable terror. Who wants to be reminded of this? When children cry, we adults do not feel so mature anymore. In fact, subconsciously we begin to wonder whether all our precious maturity might really be little more than an adaptation to wickedness, a learned set of skills for dealing in a civilized way with the evil in our lives. When toddlers throw tantrums, all our delicate coping mechanisms come unglued. Chaos wriggles out of its cage. Crying children testify, all unwittingly, to the untamed presence of darkness in our world.

From this point of view, howling one's head off may actually be a more mature and realistic response to reality than the elaborate social skills of many adults. With the latter so frightfully focused on grinning and bearing their way through life, perhaps babies are the ones to whom God has entrusted the important work of doing the crying for the whole world. Have we ever stopped to think how desperately we need this service from our children? Without it, we might die. Though kids themselves may not know exactly why they cry, nevertheless their message rings out loud and clear: "Give us more love! Give us more and more and more of the thing we were made for!" Without this high-pitched reminder that the purpose of life is nothing less than love, our mature, smiling, devil-may-care society might politely smile its way right off the edge of all goodness and plunge forever into total barbarity.

Grievous weeping, whether in a child or an adult, turns our eyes to the cross. For our cry, at its deepest level, is for the love of a Savior.

The Mediator

"Even now my witness is in heaven;
my advocate is on high." (16:19)

Job has a fundamental grasp of the most important of all religious concepts: since God is too holy for sinful man to have anything to do with Him without being destroyed, if there is to be any contact at all (let alone friendship) between God and man it can only come through an "advocate" or mediator, through someone who is qualified to be on good terms with both parties. Who this someone is, Job does not know. But somehow he knows that this is the only hope, and it is his tenacious faith in this odd and unlikely solution that marks him as a believer in Christ.

Therefore in the midst of the despairing darkness of Chapter 16, with its shadowy hints of crucifixion, Job rises suddenly to a point of ecstatic vision, remarkably like that of the martyr Stephen who, just before his death, cried out, "Look! I see heaven open and the Son of Man standing at the right hand of God!" (Acts 7:56). When Christ is "sitting" at God's right hand, He is resting in His glory, but when He is "standing" He is interceding for humanity. The image suggests a defense counsel standing before the judge's bench and pleading for his client, and this is the picture that inspired Stephen to pray for his murderers: "Lord, do not hold this sin against them" (Acts 7:60). When we believe in a heavenly mediator, then we ourselves become mediators on earth. We become peacemakers, and the seventh beatitude applies to us: "Blessed are the peacemakers, for they will be called sons of God" (Matt. 5:9). The sons of God are those who, through faith in the Son of Man, share His work of intercession.

Of course the role of the divine mediator is more complex than simply that of a glorified lawyer. For God made Christ "to be sin for us, so that in him we might become the righteousness of God" (2 Cor. 5:21). What does this mean? Perhaps we can picture it this way: God and man are sitting at either end of a long table, arguing, while Jesus the mediator sits between them trying to negotiate a peace. But the argument drags on and on, and no compromise is in sight. Finally Jesus gets up from His place, walks down to man's end of the table, and places His hand on man's shoulder in a quiet gesture of approval and identification. "Father, forgive him," Jesus says, "for he does not know what he is doing." It is as if Christ is looking down the long table and pleading, "Father, I can't help it; I love mankind too much. I'm taking his side." At this, God the Father loudly denounces His Son and pronounces Him cursed. What else can He do? Jesus has become sin; God's only Son has identified Himself with everything that God Himself hates. As the Father storms out of the room, the Son collapses in a heap on the floor; there is an earthquake and the sun turns black, and then the curtain rings down.

It is wonderful to know that there is a divine mediator willing to place His faith in man. But is man willing to place faith in the mediator, even after the curtain falls? Job does—first by prophetically foreseeing the necessity of having an "advocate on high," and then by consistently adopting the perspective of this advocate as his own. Throughout his ordeal Job refuses to condemn himself but rather dares to take his own part, man's part, even against God. And strangely enough, when the curtain rises again on resurrection day it will be shown that this is exactly the sort of faith God was looking for.

Job's vision of a heavenly advocate foreshadows the truth that Paul expresses more fully in 1 Timothy 2:5-6: "There is one God and one mediator between God and men, the man Christ Jesus, who gave himself as a ransom for all men." There are many people who believe in one God. But as James warned, "You believe that there is one God. Good! Even the demons believe that—and shudder" (2:19). It is too easy for people to claim faith in God. The real test of faith is whether or not we acknowledge and bow before His Son. The real test is whether we are willing to place all of our hope in utmost confidence not merely upon "God," but upon the "one mediator between God and men, the man Christ Jesus." For "everyone who loves the father loves his child as well" (1 John 5:1). As Jesus Himself put it, "If you knew me, you would know my Father also" (John 8:19).

The Spirit of Christ

"My intercessor is my friend
as my eyes pour out tears to God;
on behalf of a man he pleads with God
as a man pleads for his friend." (16:20-21)

Wºhat a beautiful description this is of the intercessory work of Christ before the throne of Heaven as He defends the cause of all His followers on earth. How could Job utter such words if he himself were not a friend of Jesus? Surely he was one of those to whom the Apostle Peter referred when he wrote:

> Though you have not seen him, you love him . . . for you are receiving the goal of your faith, the salvation of your souls. Concerning this salvation, the prophets, who spoke of the grace that was to come to you, searched intently and with the greatest care, trying to find out the time and circumstances to which the Spirit of Christ in them was pointing. . . . (1 Peter 1:8-11)

In saying that the "Spirit of Christ" was in the prophets, Peter was really declaring, quite simply, that these early Old Testament believers were Christians. They were disciples of Christ in the deepest sense, people who had embraced what Paul called "a righteousness from God, apart from law, to which the Law and the Prophets testify" (Rom. 3:21). Not all the Israelites embraced this righteousness; but it was certainly made available to them. Paul notes that even as the children of Israel wandered in the wilderness, they "drank from the spiritual rock that accompanied them, and that rock was Christ" (1 Cor. 10:4). The author of Hebrews actually speaks of this first generation under Moses as "those who formerly had the gospel preached to them," although in their case "the message they heard was of no value to them, because those who heard did not combine it with faith" (4:6, 2).

In Job we get a thrilling insight into the mind of one of those Old Testament figures who did manage to hear and to accept the living Word of God. We see the way faith operated in the pre-Christian heart, and still operates today among those who have not had the privilege of having Christ clearly presented to them. Such a heart knows when something is missing, knows when things are not right, and in its own way it cries out to God day and night for His Kingdom to come. By contrast, how much more common is the other kind of heart, the kind that may be exceedingly religious but that nevertheless hides and represses its deepest God-given yearnings, stoically adapting itself to life as it is while struggling to pretend that nothing is amiss—or at least, that things are not as drastically, satanically amiss as the Bible makes them out to be.

Job was a man whose "eyes poured out tears to God" as the Spirit of Christ in him groaned for grace and understanding. Even as New Testament Christians we have much to learn from such an example. For oddly enough, as much as we have had the message of the gospel drummed into us, still we face situations in which the reality of God's forgiveness in Christ is not a felt reality, but one we must hold on to by sheer grit, almost as though we were in Job's own shoes and beholding the messianic mystery from afar, through a thick fog, searching intently in the present for something that is yet to be revealed. Even for believers on the threshold of the third millennium of our Lord, still there are times when we seem to be incapable of seeing Jesus any more clearly than Job did. Then it is once again the God of the Old Testament with whom we have to deal, the God of the whirlwind. At such times we must be able, by grace, to reinvent the wheel; we must discover the gospel for ourselves all over again. In the midst of the darkness we must put our hand into the hand of our divine mediator, the God-Man Jesus Christ, and so exclaim as Job did, "Even now I have an advocate on high, a heavenly intercessor who is my friend!"

It's Your Move, God

"Give me, O God, the pledge you demand.
Who else will put up security for me?" (17:3)

At the beginning of *Paradise Lost* Milton announces that his aim in writing is to "justify the ways of God to men." This would appear also to be the aim of Job's friends. Job's concern, however, is a deeper one, and one more closely attuned to that of the New Testament: namely, to have God justify man. Most people, rather than waiting on the Lord in times of trouble, squander what little energy they have in endless conjecture, self-analysis, and rationalization. But Job actually refrains from any attempt either to justify himself or to fathom the reasons for his downfall. Instead his sole recourse is to look to God to clean up the mess. It is God's problem, not his. Job's eyes are so totally and scandalously on the Lord alone for deliverance that it is as if he were to say, "Look, God— You got me into this fix, now You can get me out of it!" Or: "Okay, God, the ball's in Your court now. It's Your move."

Job's friends seem to believe that when something goes wrong in our relationship with God, the onus is on us to put it right. But Job insists that the onus is squarely on God to put things right. This is the sort of God Job believes in—One who, although He has absolutely no obligation to sinners, nevertheless takes upon Himself the primary responsibility for reconciliation. This is the God of the New Covenant, not of the Old. The sole purpose of the Old Covenant with all its human obligations was to lead us to the God of the New Covenant, the God who is Himself the sacrifice who takes away the sin of the world. Job shows that he knows this God already when he prays, "Give me, O God, the pledge you demand. Who else will put up security for me?"

This new, revolutionary method of negotiations between God and humanity does not, of course, eliminate the need for repentance and obedience. Yet what is it, primarily, that we humans need to repent of? And how are we to obey? What we need to repent of is precisely our propensity to take matters into our own hands, to atone for our own sins, to provide our own sacrifices. We need to repent of our reliance on religion rather than on the gospel of grace. We need to repent, in a sense, of repentance itself. In other words, we need a whole new vision of what repentance is. As for obedience, the way we obey is by sticking to this one vision, come what may. In the Old Testament there were dozens of different sacrifices, or acts of repentance, prescribed for dozens of different sins. But in the New Testament there is only one sacrifice, a final and perfect one, and there is only one repentance, a repentance actually supplied by Christ Himself as stated in Acts 5:31: "God exalted him to his own right hand as Prince and Savior that he might give repentance and forgiveness of sins to Israel."

So helpless are we that even our repentance must come from God. This helplessness is well illustrated in the paralytic of Matthew 9, who could not even come to Jesus by himself but had to be carried. Once there, he did not so much as open his mouth before Jesus looked at him and said, "Take heart, son; your sins are forgiven." And they were! Then to prove it (not that forgiveness requires any proof), Jesus told the man to get up and walk—and he did! For this man, repentance consisted simply in letting himself be carried, sinful as he was, into the presence of Christ. The Lord did all the rest. The Lord did everything.

Interestingly, the story immediately following this one is that of the calling of Matthew—a person who, "sitting at the tax collector's booth," was in his own way totally paralyzed when Jesus found him and told him to get up on his feet and follow Him. Again, in Matthew 19 we read the account of a young man who asked exactly the wrong question of Jesus: "Teacher, what good thing must I do to get eternal life?" No wonder this fellow, so intent on what he was going to do for God, in the end "went away sad." By contrast Simon Peter, when he first began to glimpse the glory of Christ, saw in that same moment how utterly incapable he was of doing anything good, and so cried out, "Go away from me, Lord; I am a sinful man!" (Luke 5:8). With this confession Peter entered into the Master's inner circle.

In the final analysis, the only way to approach Jesus Christ is by sinning—that is, by acknowledging our sinfulness. If we try to approach Him innocently, happily, energetically, piously, or purely, then we will never get near Him. He only forgives sinners. He only saves the lost. He only causes to walk those who are totally paralyzed. He only gives life to the dead.

Betrayal

*"If a man denounces his friends for reward,
the eyes of his children will fail." (17:5)*

You would even barter away your friend!" Job had complained following Eliphaz's first speech (6:27). Here again he suggests in no uncertain terms that these "friends" of his are no true friends at all, but betrayers. "Surely mockers surround me," he laments; "my eyes must dwell on their hostility" (17:2). There is a starkly ironic contrast between Job's heavenly friend who pleads with God on his behalf (16:21) and his earthly friends who are busy doing just the opposite—rebuking and maligning him. Compare David's words in Psalm 55:12-14:

> If an enemy were insulting me, I could endure it;
>   if a foe were raising himself against me,
> I could hide from him.
>   But it is you, a man like myself,
> my companion, my close friend,
>   with whom I once enjoyed sweet fellowship
> as we walked with the throng at the house of God.

A central ingredient of the humiliation of Christ was His betrayal by a human friend. So significant was this act that Jesus made a point of including it in His own prophecies of His death: "The Son of Man will be betrayed" (Matt. 20:18), or "will be handed over" (Luke 18:32). It was not enemies who eventually overthrew Jesus; He was betrayed by a friend. After all, what are human enemies to the Almighty God? Had not Jesus often slipped out of the hands of His enemies with ease? But to a friend, even God becomes vulnerable. Somehow it was necessary for Christ's ministry on earth to be undone in this sordid fashion—not primarily by the open opposition of people whose minds had never been enlightened by the gospel, but rather in a backroom deal involving the premeditated decision of one of His own disciples. Judas did something more complex and deliberate than either opposing or deserting his

Master: he double-crossed Him. The crucifiers faced Jesus and drove their nails forthrightly; but Judas stabbed Him in the back.

The word *double-cross* says it all, for betrayal is a kind of double crucifixion. Perhaps it is the shadow of Judas' deed that lies behind that terrible warning recorded in Hebrews 6:4-6: "It is impossible for those who have once been enlightened, who have tasted the heavenly gift, who have shared in the Holy Spirit, who have tasted the goodness of the word of God and the powers of the coming age, if they fall away, to be brought back to repentance, because to their loss they are crucifying the Son of God all over again and subjecting him to public disgrace." It can be very difficult for a modern mind to comprehend the heinousness of this deed of the betrayal of Christ by Judas Iscariot. But Jesus' own verdict was this: "It would be better for him if he had not been born" (Matt. 26:24). Of Hell it is sometimes said that while we can be sure it exists, we cannot be sure of the name of anyone who is there. But this is false. We do know the name of Judas Iscariot, "the one doomed to destruction" (John 17:12), and because of this one name the reality of Hell takes on a more shuddering enormity.

How strange it is to think of Judas and to realize that here was a man with a keen theological mind, who just like the other disciples would have enjoyed talking for hours on end about all the glories of the coming Kingdom of God, and more than that would have preached many a rousing sermon and must even have healed people and cast out demons (see Matt. 10:1). Yet in the final analysis, the basis of his discipleship turned out to be an empty ideology rather than a personal commitment, for when it came to facing the hard reality of the cross that is at the heart of the gospel, Judas turned coat. Peter denied his Lord, but Judas betrayed Him. In the Garden of Gethsemane Peter briefly took up the sword; but Judas took up a weapon far more ugly: the kiss. With a kiss he drove in the first nail.

In the case of Job's friends, happily, the implicit comparison with Judas breaks down in the end, for they did not go out and hang themselves. Rather, they repented of their mean-spiritedness and were finally reconciled both with Job and with God (see 42:7-9). Yet the fact remains that throughout the main body of the story these men played the part of betrayers, and if they had persisted in their stubborn resistance to the will of God as it was being worked out in the life of Job, we can only presume that they, like Judas, would have gone down to destruction.

Hold On

*"Nevertheless, the righteous will hold to their ways,
and those with clean hands will grow stronger." (17:9)*

It is hard to resist comparing Job with Martin Luther—not so
much in the degree of the two men's suffering (though Luther
certainly had his share of it), as in the radical, tenacious hold they
both had on the simple truth of the gospel, and in the uncompro-
mising stand this caused them to take against establishment religion.
Job's great assertion that "the righteous will hold to their ways" is
like Luther's famous words, "Here I stand, I can do no other." These
are the statements of men who did not merely believe the truth, but
who knew it in their bones. They had the sort of faith that the author
of Hebrews defines as "being sure of what we hope for and certain
of what we do not see" (11:1) and that led the psalmist to encourage us not simply to "believe" but rather to "*know* that the Lord is
God" (100:3). To such believers faith is not a fond hope but a superior form of knowledge. Knowing what they know, they can no
more alter their creed than add a cubit to their stature. They hold
to the truth exactly the way a shipwrecked sailor clutches a life pre-
server, because there is literally nothing else to hang on to. Like Peter
they say, "Lord, to whom shall we go? You have the words of eternal life" (John 6:68).

This is the faith that the New Testament continually exhorts us
to have and to hold to. Even when we seem to have lost sight of it,
we are told to hold on anyway, to "hold on to what you have" (Rev.
2:25; 3:11). What is it we are to hold to so tightly? We are to hold
on to whatever it was that first saved us, that first washed away our
sins and ushered us clean and new into the Kingdom of God. We are
to hold on to our very first experience of the gospel, to the word of
truth as it first came to us in all its grace and power. After all, if this
simple message was good enough to set us free in the first place, then
surely it is good enough to continue setting us free. Therefore we are
to keep going back to it. We are to keep on returning to this one,
initial, earth-shattering event of our salvation, when Jesus first took

all of our burdens and rolled them into the sea, and to this we are to cling for dear life.

For the Christian in time of trial, this is the one all-pervasive message of the New Testament epistles: *hold on!* The writer of Hebrews says: "Let us hold unswervingly to the hope we profess" (4:14; 10:23). John says: "See that what you have heard from the beginning remains in you" (1 John 2:24). Paul says: "Hold firmly to the trustworthy message as it has been taught" (Titus 1:9). Of course, hand in hand with this message to "hold on" goes the message to "remember," for we cannot safeguard what we have forgotten. Christ Himself admonishes: "Remember what you have received and heard; obey it, and repent" (Rev. 3:3). And again: "You have forsaken your first love. Remember the height from which you have fallen! Repent and do the things you did at first" (Rev. 2:4-5). Paul summarizes all of this at a crucial point in his first letter to the Corinthians: "Now, brothers, I want to remind you of the gospel I preached to you, which you received and on which you have taken your stand. By this gospel you are saved, if you hold firmly to the word I preached to you. Otherwise, you have believed in vain" (15:1-2).

Elsewhere Paul writes, "Just as you received Christ Jesus as Lord, continue to live in him" (Col. 2:6). In other words, the way to grow in Christ is to keep going back to our initial experience of salvation, and to keep on taking that very same step we took when we first believed. For the last step is the same as the first, since we have "a righteousness that is by faith from first to last" (Rom. 1:17). Therefore we are never to tire of returning to first principles, to what it was that we saw when we first saw the light. All the writers of the New Testament were utterly convinced that the simple gospel of justification by faith in Jesus Christ was the only gospel that had to be preached. This one message was the only one the world needed, and it was not a message that had to be qualified, enhanced, packaged, or apologized for. All that was needed was to preach it, to insist upon it, and to hold to it through thick and thin. As Paul wrote with such clarion urgency to the Galatians, "Stand firm, then, and do not let yourselves be burdened again by a yoke of slavery" (5:1).

Wishful Thinking

*"If the only home I hope for is the grave. . . .
where then is my hope?" (17:13-15)*

As in Chapter 14, Job now returns to his dark musings on the
impenetrable enigma of death. Being a man of deep faith did
not protect Job from maintaining a proper fear and loathing
of the grave. The fact was, he had no peace about death, for he did
not see it as something natural but as wildly unnatural. It would not
bring him nearer to God but further away. He harbored no vague
hope that somehow he might survive death or that it might prove,
after all, to be merely a transition to some "better place." No, if it
were not for the extreme pain of his present circumstances, the
thought of an afterlife would have held no interest whatsoever for
Job. For normally he would have held to the very curious Old
Testament notion (curious, that is, from a post-Easter perspective)
that this present life was, for all practical purposes, *all there was.*
An "other world" existed, certainly, but only the way shadows exist,
bearing no comparison with the richness of present reality.

How strangely secular this thinking sounds. These Old Testament
believers were such dreadful literalists: to them the sight of a dead
body constituted ironclad evidence that life came to an ignoble end.
Whatever happened after that, there was nothing glorious or even
mystical about it. What was glorious and mystical was incarnation—the miracle of soul and body united and walking around in
the sunshine. But for the body to rot in a tomb, with the living soul
ripped out of it and dispersed somehow into thin air—no! This was
preposterous and unthinkable. This was decidedly not what human
beings were made for.

As it turns out, the Old Testament literalist was right. Death really
is an undeniable tragedy. Jude 9 describes an eerie scene in which
"the archangel Michael . . . was disputing with the devil about the
body of Moses." Why else would spiritual powers argue over an old
corpse if the human body were not vitally important, if it were not
fully involved in eternal life? The wonderful news announced in the
New Testament is that our mortal bodies are not meant to be aban-

doned or cast aside at all, but rather will be raised up to put on immortality like a new suit: "When the perishable has been clothed with the imperishable, and the mortal with immortality, then the saying that is written will come true: 'Death has been swallowed up in victory'" (1 Cor. 15:54). According to this text, even the perishable will not perish, but will be enshrined in eternity like a living museum case. Consider, by analogy, the bodies we had when we were children. Were they cast aside or destroyed? Are they rotting in the ground? Not at all. Instead they have been mysteriously incorporated into our adult bodies. The child is, in a manner of speaking, "swallowed up" by the adult. In the economy of God nothing is wasted, nothing is lost. Just as Jesus promised, "Not a hair of your head will perish" (Luke 21:18).

This truth about our physical bodies applies also to the entire physical creation. Christianity has nothing to do with the odd idea that we might one day leave behind us once and for all this beautiful blue-green jewel of a planet and go sailing off into some pristine spiritual Heaven. No, our God knows that what we truly and deeply yearn for (if we would only admit it) is something entirely different. What we really want, so much that we can taste it, is to have the best of both worlds: somehow to scrape through into eternity, yet at the same time to keep our two feet solidly planted on good old *terra firma*. And lo!—is this not the very miracle our God has in store for us? For He has promised to create not just a new Heaven but "a new earth, the home of righteousness" (2 Peter 3:13).

As Job seeks to give voice to his obscure yet urgent longings for physical regeneration, his friends assume that he is only indulging in a bit of wishful thinking. But in a righteous person wishful thinking is serious business, and because Job really is a righteous man and is therefore in tune with God's deepest thoughts, his wishes will turn out to be the Lord's commands. "Ask," Jesus promised, "and it will be given to you." Why? Because the profoundest desires, wishes, dreams and hopes of a child of God turn out to be the very stuff of the Lord's own will. If He promises to "give you the desires of your heart" (Ps. 37:4), it is because He is the one who has planted those desires in the first place. Wishing may seem to be the province of magic and fairy tales, and hence dangerous ground for the Christian. But really the opposite is true: in a real believer wishing is the very essence of childlike faith.

Unspiritual Leadership

Then Bildad replied: . . . "Be sensible, and then we can talk. Why are we regarded as stupid cattle in your sight?" (18:1-3)

There is no record of Job having actually called Bildad a "stupid ox"—but perhaps the designation is an apt one for this lumbering, dogged dogmatist whose power of rhetoric outweighs his spiritual maturity. The whole of Bildad's second speech is a classic fire-and-brimstone sermon: "Fire resides in [the wicked's] tent," he rants; "burning sulfur is scattered over his dwelling" (18:15). If only Bildad realized that by terrorizing his friend with these dire warnings of damnation, he is actually treating him just the way Satan is, applying all his considerable skill to undermining Job's intimacy with God.

Bildad is the epitome of the clever, articulate, authoritative, and virtually loveless Christian leader of today. Crowds of people may hang on every word of a man like this, thinking they are being mightily fed, and then go away with their spirits parched as dust. Such pastors do not necessarily preach hellfire; more often these days they serve up pabulum. But either way, a preacher like this can appear ever so competent and sincere, he can be full of good spiritual advice, he can even be theologically correct—but the end result of his speaking is that all his fine words fall to the ground. On Sunday morning he sounds good, but by Sunday afternoon there is nothing left of his message to nourish the soul. Why? Because the Holy Spirit was not in it. A sermon may be so sound that no one point in it can be singled out and faulted. But if it is unspiritual, no hearts will be touched.

This is a very delicate matter, but in the church of Christ it is also very deadly. A church blessed with a healthy number of godly and mature Christians, and yet cursed with a pastor like Eliphaz, or with teachers and elders like Bildad and Zophar, may carry on for years in a pitifully lethargic fashion and be almost totally ineffectual. Though for a season such a church may experience numerical growth, spiritual growth is nil and genuine ministry grinds to a halt.

On the surface the leadership seems strong and capable, but underneath it is cold and self-serving. How does this happen? Unfortunately it happens because there is real power and prestige to be gained through a career in Christian ministry. Such work naturally attracts the power-hungry, those same strong personalities who in the secular sphere might be drawn to politics, show business, counseling, public relations, or other professions involving the influencing of large numbers of people. With this type of character in the pulpit, categories such as liberal or evangelical, charismatic or conservative become meaningless. One must resort to simpler words: godly or ungodly, loving or unloving. As Paul wrote, "Such people are not serving our Lord Christ, but their own appetites" (Rom. 16:18), "having a form of godliness but denying its power" (2 Tim. 3:5).

Everything that unspiritual people touch in the church withers. Prayer meetings die, or else carry on hideously in a spirit of frozen and tedious eloquence. Music becomes a matter of performance rather than worship. Committees and programs proliferate, among them the ubiquitous "building program." Cliques form, and within these cliques there is a lively social life; but the fellowship is not in Christ. And so on and so on.

In these situations everyone is unhappy, yet few are able to admit their misery. Even those discerning enough to recognize the problem will find that they are unable to do anything about it. It will be as though their hands are tied—as indeed they are, for the only real answer to this plight is prayer, and yet under the circumstances effective prayer becomes nearly impossible. So massive and dense is the fog created by unspiritual leadership that it surrounds and beclouds every member of the church, making it exceedingly difficult for anyone even to believe that the situation is really as serious as it is. This is Job's problem with his friends. He knows there is something terribly wrong in what they are saying; he knows their spirit is all wrong. But they are such slippery, damnably orthodox characters that it is well nigh impossible to pin them down. In such a stifling atmosphere, it is all the more to Job's credit that he does manage to pin these men down and to call them to account, and that he persists in exposing and rejecting their alluringly respectable dogmatism.

Torn

"You who tear yourself to pieces in your anger,
must the whole world be rearranged to suit you?" (18:4)

Bildad accuses Job of tearing himself to pieces. Job himself had used this same figure of speech back in 16:9, but there he named God as the perpetrator: "God assails me and tears me in his anger." As Christians we know that both Job and Bildad are wrong, and that if anyone is guilty of tearing Job apart it is the Devil. Yet perhaps more important than the question of who is to blame for this tearing is simply the fact of the tearing itself, the condition of being torn. Paul uses the expression "I am torn between the two" (Phil. 1:23) to describe the tension he feels between the desire to go on living in this world (so as to spread the gospel) and the opposite pull to depart and be with Christ. Yet in more general terms, isn't the word "torn" an apt description of what the Christian life is all about? Because the people of God are necessarily a people of dual citizenship, citizens simultaneously of Heaven and of earth, we are therefore obliged to function honorably in both realms, conducting ourselves in a responsible manner both towards God and towards humanity. Yet since God and humanity are at odds, what else can the godly person be but torn between the two? As Christ was racked on the cross, so His followers are people whose essential vocation is to be torn apart by tensions of cosmic proportions.

This is exactly what is so compelling about the figure of Job. He is a man of God who is being torn to pieces. And for that reason he speaks powerfully to other believers who are being torn, to other faithful disciples who cannot understand why, rather than enjoying the life of peace and blessing that ought to be the fruit of loving the Lord their God, they find themselves instead being buffeted by incredible storms. When Daniel was lowered into the lions' den, the Lord shut the lions' mouths so they could not harm him. But in the case of Job it must be admitted that the Lord allowed the lions' mouths to open, so that this man (at least for a time) was torn apart.

Granted, Job was not thrown to the lions quite so literally as were countless Christians in a later age. For God's deal with Satan was that the latter "must spare [Job's] life" (2:6). Still, is there not something horrifyingly chilling about the thought of a person being given over wholly into the hands of Satan—wholly, that is, except for his very life? It is like an order in wartime for an enemy to be "taken alive"—not because anyone wants to spare his life, but rather that it might be taken as slowly, as painfully, and as publicly as possible. This is the fate that has befallen Job, not only in terms of his worldly life but of his spiritual life. The whole point of this story is that it is not Job's body and estate alone but his faith, his very heart, that has been thrown to the Devil's lions.

Without a deep appreciation of this fact, there is simply no way to understand the struggle that some Christians go through. We tend to tell ourselves that, no matter what happens, we should always be able by faith to "rise above" our circumstances. But is this really so? Did Paul rise above the trials he alludes to in the opening chapter of 2 Corinthians? No; at the time he was utterly crushed by them. Listen: "We do not want you to be uninformed, brothers, about the hardships we suffered in the province of Asia. We were under great pressure, far beyond our ability to endure, so that we despaired even of life. Indeed, in our hearts we felt the sentence of death" (1:8-9). How was it that the great apostle, who believed that "to die is gain" (Phil. 1:21), suddenly seemed to be afraid of dying? Or was it, even more mysteriously, the fear of spiritual death that had somehow gripped Paul? Can we imagine this man so oppressed that he actually despaired of being saved? There is a third possibility, however, which is that Paul at this stage had not yet come to terms with the idea that he himself might not remain alive until the coming of Christ—a thought that, as it began to dawn, must have been incredibly painful and disorienting for him. Whatever the case, at this point in Paul's life his distress was so great that it broke him and he could no longer cope. Yet as he goes on to say, "This happened that we might not rely on ourselves but on God, who raises the dead" (1:9).

What great care must be exercised by secure, happy believers that they not act the part of Job's comforters toward brothers and sisters in Christ who are in spiritual crisis, and particularly toward those who, in any of a variety of ways, may be experiencing "the sentence of death" in their hearts.

The King of Terrors

"[The wicked man] is torn from the security of his tent
and marched off to the king of terrors." (18:14)

It is true that Job has been "marched off to the king of terrors"—
but not for the reason Bildad supposes. Job is in the hands of
Satan, not to be punished, but in order that his "faith . . . may
be proved genuine and may result in praise, glory and honor when
Jesus Christ is revealed" (1 Peter 1:7). It is not Job's wickedness but
his faithfulness that the Lord is disclosing through this ordeal. In fact
there may be nothing our God wants more than to bring each one
of us to the point where He can do with us exactly what He did with
Job: hand us over with perfect confidence into the clutches of Satan,
knowing that even then our faith will hold. For God loves to see
human beings standing up to Satan, answering him on his own turf,
and finally defeating him with a word. The Lord is looking for people who can, by faith alone, stand in the midst of the fray, resisting
not only the Devil but the world and their own flesh, and come out
winning. Though the cost of this victory, like the cost of the cross,
may from a worldly point of view be appalling, God wants people
who know that by grace they are rich enough to afford such a cost.

We have all wondered at the strangeness of that sentence in the
Lord's Prayer, "Lead us not into temptation." Why should a loving
God lead us into situations in which our faith may be compromised?
Alternatively, if He does have His reasons for doing this, why
should we ask Him not to? At the outset of the temptation of Christ
we are told that "Jesus was led by the Spirit into the desert to be
tempted by the devil" (Matt. 4:1). Yet as the temptation proceeds
we read the even more remarkable statement, "The devil led
him . . ." (Luke 4:5). What could it mean that the Son of God
allowed Himself to be "led" by Satan? Did Satan perchance take the
Lord by the hand as they made their way up to that pinnacle of the
temple, and did the two of them stand arm in arm on that lofty
mountain peak to survey all the kingdoms of the world and their
splendor? However it transpired, it is clear that Jesus *went with* the

Devil, that the two of them spent time together there in the wilderness. They spent time, one might say, getting to know each other.

And so it was with Job: he was led into temptation, which is to say, he was ushered into the presence of Satan. The Devil took him by the hand and showed him his kingdom. Unlike Jesus, Job was not taken to a high place but to a deep valley. Yet to a lover of God, are these two not much the same? Mountains or valleys, the Devil's territory is all a wasteland. There is nothing scenic or thrilling about it. To the regenerate soul there is nothing even interesting about being in the personal presence of evil. On the contrary it is precisely the horror, the turmoil, the barrenness, and the torment that prove this is the Devil with whom one has to do.

The story of Job is an insider's view of an intimate meeting with "the king of terrors." It is an account of what temptation feels like on the inside, and this is an experience which every one of us must taste. We will all spend time with Satan in his kingdom, we will listen to him talk, we will inspect his wares, and often enough we will feel our feet caught in his machinations. "*God does not tempt anyone*" (James 1:13), but He does "seek an occasion to confront" His enemies (Judg. 14:4), and so we can expect that the Lord in His own time and way will schedule for us appointments with evil. Ever since the Fall it has been a necessity of man's condition that he "know both good and evil" (Gen. 3:22), and temptation means knowing evil. It means going with, being with, the Devil. It means spending time with him wherever he may be, and considering his arguments. It means looking at things through his eyes and so becoming familiar with all his ways.

Obviously this is not a path that we can choose for ourselves, and that is why we must pray, "Lord, lead us not into temptation." The Devil is so subtle that the only way we can possibly be successful in combating him is by praying continually that we might be spared the pleasure of his company. Are we not mighty adept at finding our own way into temptation and then glamorizing the spiritual struggles that inevitably ensue? Remarkably, this is a trap that Job never fell into. He never sensationalized his battles; he only fought them.

Get Behind Me, Satan

"How long will you torment me
and crush me with words?
Ten times now you have reproached me;
shamelessly you attack me." (19:2-3)

If we think of Job as a temptation story prefiguring the temptation of Christ, where do Job's friends fit in? What part do they
play? The answer to this question is linked to the curious fact
that after the Prologue the figure of Satan seems to disappear completely from the story. What becomes of him we do not know, but
we do know this: Job's friends are there to rush in and take his place.
Just as Satan will not believe in the purity of Job's faith, neither will
Job's friends, and they too become bent on discrediting him. Herein
lies the great, terrible, beautiful secret of the book's unity, as we see
Satan attacking Job not only through disaster and disease and
depression, but through the faithlessness of his friends. We need not
go so far as to class these men as deliberate accomplices of Satan,
but they are certainly his pawns, and for us the sobering lesson is
that Christians are not above being used as instruments of the Devil.
If the Devil himself were to appear on Job's doorstep and attack him
verbally, would his accusations be any more subtle and stinging than
those of the friends? With friends like these, one is tempted to ask,
who needs enemies?

Structurally the book of *Job* is built upon the paralleling of these
two major conflicts: first of all the clash between God and Satan that
opens the story, and secondly the clash between Job and his friends
that monopolizes the balance of the book. The latter conflict mirrors the former one; the earthly mirrors the celestial. Since there is
not a lot that we as humans can know about God's dealings with
Satan in the heavenlies, the book concentrates on the down-to-earth,
visible dimension of this war, which is the battle between people
with conflicting theologies. So Satan does not really disappear following the Prologue; he just goes underground.

Most wars, after all, are not won primarily by troops and tanks

and bombs, but by propaganda and espionage. There must be infil-
tration behind enemy lines, and the successful spy must learn to
speak the enemy's language without a trace of accent and to melt
into the alien culture like butter on toast. This was the essence of
Satan's tactics with Christ in the wilderness. He sought to camou-
flage his voice as the voice of God, quoting Scripture as though it
were his native tongue, and even going so far as to solicit personal
worship. In *Job* we see a similar strategy at work, only this time
administered through Job's friends. As the two sides in the dialogue
trade perfectly plausible theological arguments, it is almost as
though the Devil were whispering, "It is written . . ." while Job vehemently responds, "It is also written . . ."

Theology, it turns out, is Satan's favorite game. Material destruction, sickness, death—these are child's play to him. But if he can
insinuate himself into our thoughts and feelings, if he can worm his
way into our very soul, if he can (even as God Himself seeks to do)
fill us with his spirit—this is exactly what the Devil most longs to
do. And who is better qualified to invade the heart of a righteous
believer than a friend? A friend can go where the Devil cannot. And
so there is nothing Satan wants more than to poison friendships,
deploying friends against one another to accomplish his ends.

In the *Gospels*, just as in *Job*, after the initial temptation scene we
never again catch a glimpse of Satan personally harassing Jesus.
Instead the Lord's subsequent trials all tend to come through human
agents—and not only through the Pharisees, but through Jesus' own
friends and family. Perhaps Job's friends could be likened to the disciple Peter on the occasion when the Lord rebuked him with the
words, "*Get behind me*, Satan!" (Matt. 16:23). At that moment,
was not Peter engaged in an activity identical to that of Job's comforters? He was negating the spiritual worth of suffering. He was
trying to persuade his friend to take the triumphalist highway rather
than the narrow path of the cross.

Whoa!

"[God] has blocked my way so I cannot pass;
he has shrouded my paths in darkness." (19:8)

In the book of *Numbers* there is a well-known scene in which the prophet Balaam tries to make his way along a road, while the angel of the Lord repeatedly blocks his path. Balaam cannot see the angel, but Balaam's donkey sees him, and three times the donkey balks and refuses to go any further. Finally, we read, "the Lord opened Balaam's eyes, and he saw the angel of the Lord standing in the road with his sword drawn. So he bowed low and fell face-down" (22:31).

Most people do not know it when the Lord is blocking their path. But Job knew it, and so did David when he wrote in Psalm 139:5, "You hem me in, behind and before; you have laid your hand upon me."

Soren Kierkegaard tells the following parable:

> If you were to ask a peasant, a cabman, a postilion, a liveryman, "What does the coachman use the whip for?" you would get the same reply from them all: "Of course it is to make the horse go." But ask the King's coachman, "What does a coachman use the whip for?" and you shall hear him reply, "Principally, it is used to make the horse stand still." This is the distinction between being a simple driver and a good driver.

Kierkegaard goes on to explain why it is that the horses of the king stand still at the touch of the lash. It is not primarily because of the stinging pain; rather, it is because these horses understand who it is who wields the whip.

Surely one of the darkest of spiritual riddles is the fact that even Satan, despite having almost unlimited power in this evil world, is nevertheless but a whip in the hands of the Lord. And for what does the Lord use this terrible whip? Principally it is used to make the world stand still. The horse driver cries, "Whoa!" But the Lord cries, "Woe!" Four consecutive chapters in Isaiah, for example, begin with this little word "Woe!" (28–31). It is a way of saying sharply, "Stand still and listen!" For what the disobedient hear as condemnation, the obedient hear as an irresistible stimulus to draw nearer to the Lord. "Be still, and know that I am God," invites Psalm 46:10 in the midst of turbulence. And at a crucial juncture in Israel's history the prophet Samuel commands, "Stand still and see this great thing that the Lord is about to do before your eyes" (1 Sam. 12:16).

Sadly, many Christians misinterpret the lash of woe to mean, "Get going! Pull up your bootstraps!" It is taken as a signal to try harder, to master or suppress one's personal pain and to keep on moving. But when we do this again and again, do we not begin to resent our God as a hard driver, a taskmaster? Hence the seasoned Christian, at merely a touch of the whip, learns to stand still. "Are there not twelve hours of daylight?" asked Jesus at a time of great woe in His own life. "A man who walks by day will not stumble. . . . It is when he walks by night that he stumbles, for he has no light" (John 11:9-10). At this very moment Lazarus was lying mortally sick; yet even Jesus could not go to him right away but had to wait out the spiritual night. His lesson was that the children of God must learn to accept the constraints placed upon them. They must do their work during daylight hours, and at night they must stand still.

This is exactly what Job does, and so the majority of his story takes place in one long, immense stasis. As in the book of *Exodus*, after the fast-paced events of the opening chapters all action grinds to a halt in the wilderness, and for months on end there is nothing to do but sit tight and wait upon the Lord. Job's friends are extremely uneasy about all this waiting; they want to see action. But Job waits, and his waiting is not to be confused with inaction. On the contrary, such waiting is a highly intense and concentrated form of action, a truth well captured in the title of a book by Henry Miller: *Stand Still Like the Hummingbird*. When the hummingbird stands still, it is to extract the nectar.

Crucifixion

*"God has stripped me of my honor
and removed the crown from my head." (19:9)*

Job's language in Chapter 19 is full of haunting premonitions of
Christ's crucifixion: "[God's] anger burns against me; he counts
me among his enemies" (v. 11); "My friends have forgotten me"
(v. 14); "I am loathsome to my own brothers" (v. 17); "Those I love
have turned against me" (v. 19); "I am nothing but skin and bones"
(v. 20).

Not until fairly late in His ministry did Jesus begin to impart to
His disciples the hard message of His impending death. Even then
they could not grasp it. While Christians today have little trouble
accepting the fact of their Lord's death on a cross, it remains a tall
order for us to let the full impact of that death be felt in our daily
lives. This part of the good news we really do not want to hear. In
fact we do everything we can to shut our minds against it, and of all
our sophisticated defenses, probably the subtlest and most effective
is the pretense that we already know all about the cross, when really
we have barely glimpsed it.

How else to explain the appalling casualness with which the cross
of Christ is treated today? Theologies of all shapes and sizes file rev-
erently before the cross, tipping their hats and paying it lip-service,
only to go running on ahead to deal with what they claim to be the
"real" issues. Paul wrote, "As I have often told you before and now
say again even with tears, many live as enemies of the cross of
Christ" (Phil. 3:18). Here he was speaking not of blatant unbelievers but of church people. He was warning the church against the
very real danger of "the cross of Christ being emptied of its power"
(1 Cor. 1:17).

Paul knew that in the church's zeal to be relevant and exciting,
the cross can get shouldered aside. We can get too accustomed to
this frozen icon; we grow anesthetized to it. However, perhaps it is
not so easy to shoulder our way past the towering, inscrutable agony
of a figure like Job. That the Son of God should be tortured to death
as a ransom for all mankind—well, maybe that is God's business.

But that the divine will might also ordain excruciating suffering for a common person such as Job, or for you or for me—this thought is not so easy to theologize our way around.

Naturally it is not wrong to expect faith in Christ to bring us untold blessings and a sense of well-being. But it is wrong to think there can ever be a shortcut to these treasures—that is, that there is any way to fulfillment other than the way of the cross. If we make a concerted effort to avoid all unpleasantness in our lives, it is possible that we might, for a little while, fool ourselves into thinking that we have gained the upper hand over suffering. But really all that has happened is that our pain has gone underground, and it is bound to crop up again in some other form. For the sole route to Heaven is the cross, and if we think we know a shortcut we will only find ourselves going the long way around in the end. Jesus' parable of the "narrow gate" is really a parable of the "narrow gate and narrow road": not only is there a gate to be entered, but a road to travel—"*the narrow road* that leads to life" (Matt. 7:13-14). This narrow road is the *via dolorosa*, the path of the cross. Jesus did not rise above suffering; He went right through it.

At the onset of his ordeal Job said, "*The Lord gives, and the Lord takes away.*" His entire ensuing struggle centers around the question of what happens to a person's faith when the Lord takes away. So: take away material prosperity; take away emotional highs; take away miracles and healing; take away fellowship with other believers; take away church; take away all opportunity for service; take away assurance of salvation; take away the peace and joy of the Holy Spirit . . . Yes! Take it all, all, far, far away. And what is left?

Tragically, for many believers there would be nothing left. For does our faith really go that deep? Or do we, in the final analysis, have a cross-less Christianity? Unless the simple gospel has centerplace in our faith, it has no place at all. Unless the cross is everything, it is nothing.

V.I.P.

"Have pity on me, my friends, have pity,
for the hand of God has struck me." (19:21)

Who is the most important person in a church?
Is it the head of the denomination? Is it the local pastor?
Is it the person who is most filled with the Holy Spirit? Or how
about one of those hard-working deacons, the one who somehow
has a hand in everything and without whose tireless service the
whole church would (or so it seems) collapse? Or perhaps the most
important person is that unassuming angel of mercy whose humble
but towering faith is known to the Lord alone? Or what about the
prayer-warrior? Isn't there always one saint who seems more
ardently and joyfully committed to prayer than all the rest of the
church combined? Is he or she the most important?

But no. Oddly enough the answer is none of the above. Rather
the answer is this: the most important person in the church is the
one who is suffering.

Consider the analogy of the human body. If I injure my foot and
cannot walk, then all of a sudden the most important part of my
body becomes my foot. Immediately all the rest of my body (including my wonderfully sophisticated brain) must be put at the service
of my foot (or maybe it's my toe, or even my toenail) in order to care
for the injured member until it gets well and I can walk again. For
as long as my foot cannot walk, neither can the rest of me. In fact,
if the injury is serious and there is great pain, I will not even be able
to think clearly until the problem is attended to. I might even lose
consciousness from shock or loss of blood and be totally unable to
look after myself.

In such a situation, what would we think of a brain that, rather
than bending all its energies and intellect towards the care of the
injured foot, decided to amuse itself with mathematical puzzles?
What if our brain took the attitude that there was really nothing
wrong with our foot, that it was probably just pretending to be
injured in order to get attention, or that in any case it ought to be

able to look after itself and do its own healing? As ludicrous as this may sound, are there not people who function just like this, people who live their whole lives in denial of the very health problems (whether physical, psychological, or spiritual) that are destroying them? In the same way, are there not Christian congregations which refuse to deal with the suffering in their midst? For all their talk of ministering to the needy, when faced with real suffering they have a highly developed facility for passing by on the other side.

In *Job* we see five men (counting Elihu) whose lives are inconvenienced by the suffering of one. Four of these men are, subconsciously, so deeply resentful of this interruption that they cannot see that the problem is really theirs just as much as it is Job's. Frantically they try to theologize their way out of any personal implication in their friend's pain. Their behavior is like that of a stubborn man who insists on walking around on a broken foot—or even going skiing or roller-skating! But it is no use: Job's friends are involved in his trials, whether they like it or not, and everything would go a whole lot more smoothly if they would simply accept their share of the responsibility, and get on with learning the compassionate arts of understanding, comfort, healing, and restoration.

Here is what Paul says about these things in 1 Corinthians 12:22-26:

> Those parts of the body that seem to be weaker are indispensable, and the parts that we think are less honorable we treat with special honor. And the parts that are unpresentable are treated with special modesty, while our presentable parts need no special treatment. But God has combined the members of the body and has given greater honor to the parts that lacked it, so that there should be no division in the body, but that its parts should have equal concern for each other. If one part suffers, every part suffers with it; if one part is honored, every part rejoices with it.

Lovelessness

"Why do you pursue me as God does?
Will you never get enough of my flesh?" (19:22)

P eople are fond of posing the dual questions, "Why is there so much suffering in the world?" and, "Why doesn't God do something about it?" Strangely, however, we seldom think to ask the deeper and more pertinent questions, "Why is there so little love in human hearts?" and, "Why don't we do something about it?"

The greatest mystery in the book of *Job* is not why Job suffers, but why a man crippled by suffering is forced to fight a long, drawn-out theological battle with people who are supposed to be his friends. Or, to pose the same puzzle in contemporary terms, why is it that in most churches people who are in deep need find so little real help? Why doesn't the church of Christ, whose beliefs are supposedly grounded in love, have more love in it? Paul wrote that believers should be taught to be "sound in faith, in love, and in *patience*" (Titus 2:2). Yet as D. L. Moody commented on this verse, "The church has been very jealous about men being unsound in the faith. If a man becomes unsound in the faith, they draw their ecclesiastical swords and cut at him. But he may be ever so unsound in love, and they don't say anything." Why is this so? Why is the commandment of Jesus to "love one another" so watered-down and ignored? Why do Christians waste precious time and energy wrangling over a whole host of other less important issues?

In all fairness, it must be admitted that before real love can actually happen between Christians, the other great doctrines of the faith must be firmly in place. No doubt this is what much of the wrangling is about, and it may be that some of it is constructive wrangling. But as Alexander Whyte wrote, "Rather let the truth of God suffer, than that love suffer." When Christ said to the Church of Ephesus, "You have forsaken your first love" (Rev. 2:4), He was speaking to Christians who had worked hard for the Lord and whose doctrine was impeccable. As Paul warned, "The entire law is

summed up in a single command: 'Love your neighbor as yourself.'
If you keep on biting and devouring each other, watch out or you
will be destroyed by each other" (Gal. 5:14-15).

As we saw in the last chapter, it is not the strong, happy, hard-
working people, but rather the suffering ones who are the soul of a
church. For, in the words of Martin Luther, the message of faith in
Christ "has a good savor for all who are afflicted, downcast, troubled, and tempted, and these are the ones who understand the
gospel." Hence the Lord says, "I will bind up the injured and
strengthen the weak, but the sleek and the strong I will destroy"
(Ezek. 34:16). Unfortunately, the political control of a church is
commonly in the hands of the sleek and the strong, and often it is
the case that these strong people have very little meaningful contact
with the weak. Even if the strong must be involved with the weak
face-to-face, in their hearts it is easy enough for them to pass by on
the other side. It is hard for them really to be concerned about those
who suffer with the same all-consuming concern that they have for
themselves. Besides, for all their strength, the strong cannot actually
help the weak at all. Only Jesus can help them. Only Jesus Himself
can help both the weak and the strong together. Only Jesus can
strengthen the weak and save the strong from the oblivion of their
self-confident lovelessness.

Even if we are people who have known real suffering ourselves
(and who has not?), once we bounce back we so easily forget what
it was like to be miserable and sick. We forget that all of us are constantly, chronically sick, sick unto death. We forget that being
"wretched, pitiful, poor, blind and naked" (Rev. 3:17) is the
unchanging condition of every human being in this world, a condition from which even the greatest saint does not graduate this side
of Heaven. Is not the purest soul still infested with countless faults,
weaknesses, and old hurts from which it will never be delivered in
this life? This is precisely why we all need to receive and to give the
only truly healing medicine, which is love. The most precious service we can perform for another person is not to free him from a
problem, but to love him in it, for "love covers over a multitude of
sins" (1 Peter 4:8). No matter how much we may specialize in holiness, or no matter how saintly and spiritual we become, we are
bound to miss a few sins here and there. But to love is to cover them
all.

Go'el

"I know that my Redeemer lives." (19:25)

Towards the end of Chapter 19, in a pattern that is now becoming familiar, Job once more is momentarily lifted out of his despair and rocketed into a kind of prophetic ecstasy where he "utters mysteries with his spirit" (1 Cor. 14:2). The entire book rises to an amazing climax here, a climax centering on this mysterious, thrilling word "Redeemer." Where did Job get this word, and what did it mean to him?

In Hebrew the word is *go'el*, and it had two general applications. In daily usage its primary meaning was "one who restores," or "one who puts something back into its original or pristine condition." For Christians who know the Lord not only as their Creator but as their re-Creator, this primary meaning of the word *go'el* is rich in connotation.

But the word also had a secondary, specialized sense that for the Christian is even more richly resonant. This other use of the word was within the family or tribal unit where, as Norman Habel explains in his commentary on the above verse, *"go'el* referred to the next of kin who intervened to maintain the rights or preserve the continuity of the family. . . . The responsibility of a *go'el* could involve avenging the blood of a murdered member of the clan or family; redeeming someone from bondage; regaining family property to keep it within the family inheritance; or marrying a widow to provide an heir for her deceased husband."

Probably the best example of this latter usage comes in the book of *Ruth*, where Boaz is the next-of-kin *go'el* who, by marrying the foreigner Ruth, not only keeps her family line from dying out but literally saves her and her family from hopeless poverty. The story is a beautiful parable of the way our Lord redeems His people, not merely "renewing our lives" (Ruth 4:15), but actually taking us to Himself as a husband takes a bride. While the book of *Ruth* is very explicit about the sweeping legal implications of Boaz's action, its real focus is more subtle; its real focus is on the amazing fortuitousness of the fact that Boaz—this elder, avuncular, bourgeois landowner who, though related to Ruth, has no more reason to take notice of her than to fly to the moon—this man actually falls head over heels in love with a poor and alien peasant girl! He does not marry Ruth out of a sense of social duty, but rather because he passionately loves her and desires her for his wife.

The moral of the story is that this is exactly how our Lord feels toward us. Although there is no reason on earth why the great King of the Universe should look twice at this petty, filthy breed of grasshoppers called mankind, nevertheless He says to us, "You have stolen my heart, my sister, my bride; you have stolen my heart with one glance of your eyes" (Song 4:9). Imagine—we have stolen the heart of God! And this same awesome, awestruck God turns out to be our very own next-of-kin, our long-lost rich relative, the one person who happens to be closer to us than anybody else and who is bound to us inextricably—not only by a blood covenant, but also, astoundingly, by the simple fact of His profoundly genuine love for us.

What great good fortune is ours! It is this same preposterously unlikely goodness that Job confesses faith in when he cries, "I know I have a *go'el*!" Which specific connotation of the expression he may have meant is perhaps not clear, but certainly he used the word because, within his own culture, it had an indescribably sweet and wild ring to it. It was a delicious word, a passionate word, a word that smacked of chains falling off, of finding buried treasure, of suddenly having more good fortune fall into one's lap than one had ever dreamed of or imagined. *Go'el* was a word something like "Zion": originally the name for the citadel or inner stronghold in old Jerusalem, Zion came to represent the ultimate hiding place, the final refuge for the believer. No earthly Masada that would one day crumble, this was a stronghold to last forever, and so to the ancient Jew (and to countless modern Jews as well) "Zion" came to mean what "Zen" means to Buddhists: the secret of secrets. Such a word packs a mystical, subterranean explosiveness impossible for any outsider to grasp. Perhaps it is no coincidence (who knows?) that *go'el*, the English transliteration of the Hebrew, happens to come remarkably close to another little word that has the power to ignite the hearts of believers: *gospel*.

Come, Lord Jesus

"I know that my Redeemer lives,
and that in the end he will stand upon the earth.
And after my skin has been destroyed,
yet in my flesh I will see God;
I myself will see him
with my own eyes—I, and not another.
How my heart yearns within me!" (19:25-27)

On July 20, 1969, the first man landed on the moon. One morning in spring about the year A.D. 33, the first New Man landed on the earth. His spaceship was a tomb, and He left His pressurized linen suit inside and walked out into a garden. He was the first human being with a glorified resurrection body ever to set foot upon the earth, and for forty days He walked around, talked, ate, passed through walls, disappeared and reappeared, and finally floated straight up into Heaven in order to demonstrate that He was in no way bound to the old order of things and that His visible presence among earthlings was a matter of pure grace. Because of those forty days of extraterrestrial visitation, this old world of ours has never been the same.

This is something of what Job prophetically foresees in the famous passage quoted above. But Job's vision goes on to encompass not just the first Easter but also his own personal Easter, his own participation by faith in the resurrected glory of his Redeemer. Notice how emphatically Job uses the first person pronoun—"in my flesh I will see God . . . I myself will see him with my own eyes—I, and not another." This is not the First Coming of Christ but the Second Coming. It is the time of 1 Thessalonians 4:16 when "the Lord himself will come down from heaven . . . and the dead in Christ will rise," and of 1 Corinthians 15:52, when "in a flash, in the twinkling of an eye . . . the trumpet will sound, the dead will be raised imperishable, and we will be changed."

The resurrection of the body is a much stranger notion than even many Christians may have supposed. For one thing, the Bible plainly teaches that resurrection is not a phenomenon that will transpire up in Heaven but rather—much more shockingly—right here on earth. Here is where death occurs; here is where the dead will rise. To dust our bodies were consigned; from dust they shall be reclaimed. Listen: the very graves will open their mouths, and the dead will spring out of them and begin walking around—just as Jesus did on Easter morning!

Yes, our God is so much more earthy than we give Him credit for. In fact for the Old Testament believer the entire focus was not on some mystical "Heaven" or "hereafter" but on the here-and-now. As David prayed in Psalm 39:13, "Look away from me, that I may rejoice again before I depart and am no more." Even the New Testament, surprisingly, turns out to be not quite so Heaven-centered as we may have thought. The great concluding prayer of the Bible is not "Take us to Heaven, Lord Jesus," but rather, "Come, Lord Jesus" (Rev. 22:20). Again, Jesus declared that "Heaven and earth will pass away" (Matt. 24:35)—and if even Heaven must pass away, then obviously the ultimate Christian hope must be focused on something other than Heaven.

What is this "something other"? It is what Job foresees in the verses quoted above, when he envisions his God-Redeemer "standing upon the earth" and himself beholding Him in a state "after my skin has been destroyed, yet in my flesh." The fullness of the gospel vision does not lie in the idea that the soul (or even the whole person, resurrected body and all) is to be transplanted out of the earthly realm and into the spiritual, but rather that the Kingdom of Heaven must descend right down into this present world, so that like some cosmically inconceivable sperm and egg the two spheres will merge together to form something stupendously new.

For now, Heaven remains a kind of government-in-exile, committed to staging a long and arduous coup upon the earth. But when this coup is finally complete and all earthly powers are overthrown—and "the last enemy to be destroyed is death" (1 Cor. 15:26)—then the "new Jerusalem will come down out of Heaven like a bride" and there will be "a new heaven and a new earth" (Rev. 21:1-2). Then Heaven and earth, spirit and flesh, will be married! And so we shall have exactly what Job's aching heart (and ours too) so crudely and ardently longs for: the best of both worlds. We shall have our pie-in-the-sky and eat it too.

The Comfort of Judgment

*"You that mutter, 'How we will hound him,
since the root of the trouble lies in him,'
you should fear the sword yourselves;
for wrath will bring punishment by the sword,
and then you will know that there is judgment."*
(19:28-29)

Jesus was crucified on Good Friday, but the moment He walked out of the tomb on that first Easter morning, it was the world's turn to be crucified. Henceforth even the dew-fresh lilies of the field would turn to ashes before the glory of His presence. For Christ not only inaugurated the Kingdom of Heaven on earth, He also gave the earth a new taste of Hell, in the sense that all those who refused to believe in Him would become literally the walking dead. For "we are convinced that one died for all, and therefore all died" (2 Cor. 5:14).

While Jesus "did not come to judge the world, but to save it" (John 12:47), nevertheless the wheels of divine justice were set in motion by His coming, since "whoever does not believe stands condemned already, because he has not believed in the name of God's one and only Son" (John 3:18). And when Christ comes the second time, it will be finally and irrevocably to "judge the living and the dead" (2 Tim. 4:1). This is why Job's thinking at the end of Chapter 19 moves so swiftly from the vision of the glorious Redeemer and the resurrection He will bring, to the prospect of wrath and judgment. In reality these two events are one, and so in Job's spirit his longing for the Messiah becomes one and the same as his longing for justice.

In the passage quoted above, Job is pleading with his friends not to continue attacking him but rather, in view of the certainty of impending judgment, to stick by him and defend his innocence, as his Redeemer certainly will. If they do not, then they stand to incur the wrath of this same Redeemer. For Job's Redeemer is not just gentle Jesus meek and mild, but the furious and unbendingly righteous Judge of all the earth. So Job is issuing a warning to his friends like that of James 5:9: "Don't grumble against each other, brothers, or you too will be judged. The Judge is standing at the door!" Or in the simpler words of Matthew 7:1, "Do not judge, or you too will be judged."

How intriguing it is that Job, even while his tragic circumstances have induced in him a fresh fear of God, never exhibits the least fear of God's judgment. On the contrary he clings more and more to the very thought of judgment, and is actually eager to see it through, being somehow fully persuaded of the shielding power of his faith. His friends, ironically, are so busy terrorizing him with threats of the judgment hanging over his head that they fail to see that this is precisely what Job yearns for. They cannot fathom that he does not see his Judge as being "judgmental" but rather as defending and upholding the rights of His people. Why should Job not look forward to that time when all the hidden facts of his case will be brought to light and when divine justice will take its course with him? As he himself admits, "No godless man would dare come before him" (13:16). Job's sole protection against the righteous wrath of God is his settled conviction that only the very unleashing of this wrath will ever bring him the vindication for which he longs.

Surely this is a hallmark of the highest faith. To the mature saint the inexorable judgment of the Almighty is not something to be dreaded or evaded, but rather to be eagerly and even jubilantly anticipated. Consider Psalm 96, which is a tremendous song of joy over the prospect of the Lord's judgment: "Let the sea resound, and all that is in it; let the fields be jubilant, and everything in them. Then all the trees of the forest will sing for joy; they will sing before the Lord, for he comes, he comes to judge the earth" (vv. 11-13).

Why is God's judgment an occasion for such delirious rejoicing? Because, as the final verse of the psalm states, "He will judge the world in righteousness and the peoples in his truth." Among the faithful, the great Day of the Lord is looked forward to as a time of triumphant celebration, for on that day—and not a moment sooner—everything that is wrong with the world will once and for all be set right.

No Obligation

Then Zophar the Naamathite replied: . . .
"Surely you know how it has been from of old,
ever since man was placed on the earth." (20:1, 4)

Here is the by-now familiar appeal of Job's friends to tradition, to the way things have always been. These men want Job's spiritual life to proceed along conventional, predictable lines. But Job feels no compulsion to adhere to any pattern or regimen of spiritual development. He is a free man who is no longer under any obligation to do things in the customary, worldly sort of way. His obligation is elsewhere, just as Paul says in Romans 8:12—"We have an obligation—but it is not to the sinful nature."

What good news this is—that we have no obligation whatsoever to the world or the flesh! For it is the habit of our sinful nature continually to hound and berate us like a shrew, striving at any cost to keep us enslaved to its endless demands. "Look here, my friend," it loves to say, "you have an obligation to do this or that. You are not free, you are obligated. You cannot just pick up and follow Jesus. Just because you are a Christian, does that mean you can suddenly base your whole life on joy and peace and make all your decisions accordingly? Oh no! It's not that simple, my friend, for you have obligations to fulfill. You have debts to pay to society, to your friends, to your family. And what about yourself? You cannot just kick over all your old habits. You are bound to them. They have you running in circles and you know it. No, if it's freedom you want, then maybe you can have a taste of it for ten minutes a day when you pray, but that's as far as it goes. You do not really think you can live that way, do you? Don't be a fool. Pray and read your Bible if you like, but the rest of your life is bound. You have obligations, and you cannot escape them."

This is the way our sinful nature speaks to us. We cannot live for Jesus because we have other obligations. The mortgage must be paid and the grass mowed. There is no end of meetings and social functions to attend. We have to keep up all our friendships. And then there is our career—we must maintain upward mobility there too.

And on and on it goes. These are the things Jesus called "the worries of this life, the deceitfulness of wealth and the desires for other things [that] come in and choke the word, making it unfruitful" (Mark 4:19). Meanwhile we completely miss the message of the gospel, which is that we who believe in Christ are under no compulsion whatsoever to keep on obeying the incessant promptings of the world and the flesh. If we feel such a compulsion, it has nothing to do with God. Rather, we have one godly compulsion and only one, which is the compulsion to comply with the gracious movement of the Holy Spirit as He pours His new life into our hearts. In fact, if we neglect this "one thing . . . needed" (Luke 10:42), striving instead to keep up with the interminable pressures of a worldly life, then we will lose the grace to follow Christ. "For if you live according to the sinful nature, you will die; but if by the Spirit you put to death the misdeeds of the body, you will live, because those who are led by the Spirit of God are sons of God" (Rom. 8:13-14). In a few words Paul gives a seldom-heard definition of the Christian: someone whose life is controlled by the Holy Spirit. We might almost say that a Christian is someone whose only obligation is to live without any obligations—or at least, with only one, which is the obligation to the One who says, "My yoke is easy and my burden is light" (Matt. 11:30). Which is easier, to live with a thousand responsibilities or with just one? As one writer expressed it, "Hold fast to Christ, and for the rest, be totally uncommitted."

To live this way is perfect freedom. Perfect freedom does not mean freedom from all responsibilities, but rather freedom from every inhuman responsibility. This lends a radically new, Christian dimension to the humanistic credo, "Man is the measure of all things." For did not God Himself become a man? Since God was pleased to express all the fullness of His being in human form, the only obligation of godly people is the obligation to human freedom and authenticity—that is, to be what He made us to be. Our only commitment is to be ourselves. "If you are led by the Spirit, you are not under law" (Gal. 5:18). You are not under any law except the law of your own unique being as conceived and created by God.

Conformity

"[The wicked] will perish forever, like his own dung." (20:7)

Z ophar's message in his second and last speech boils down to yet another tiresome tirade against the woes of the wicked. Even as Job's thinking grows more profound and inspired, that of his friends is increasingly exposed for its shallow redundancy and mean-spiritedness. These men all sound the same; as their speeches drag on there is less and less to distinguish them as individuals. Whatever personal uniqueness they may have shown at the outset is quickly broken down by their common scorn of Job. For that is exactly what scorn does: it erodes character. Love builds character by allowing for the growth of different gifts and traits in different personalities. But scorn attacks and tears down diversity and instead presses people into dreary molds.

"Knowledge puffs up," wrote Paul, "but love builds up" (1 Cor. 8:1). By "knowledge" he meant precisely the sort of conceited theologizing practiced by Job's friends, which takes what it knows about God and actually uses it to ruin others: "So this weak brother, for whom Christ died, is destroyed by your knowledge" (8:11). Paul's main concern is not whether the knowledge in question is true or false knowledge; his point is that even the truth can be used to bludgeon and stifle others. "We know that we all possess knowledge," he says; but the real issue is whether we possess love. Do we know how to use our knowledge to build people up rather than tearing them down? Do we know how to respect and encourage the fine distinctions in others' temperaments, however different they might be from ourselves, just as we would care for the various kinds of flowers in a garden? Listen to what Thomas Merton says about the sanctity of Christian individuality:

> There are no two saints alike: but all of them are like God, like Him in a different and special way. In fact, if Adam had never fallen, the whole human race would have been a series of magnificently different and splendid images of God, each one of all the millions of men showing forth His glories and perfections in an astonishing new way, and each one shining with his own particular sanctity.

Strangely, in many Christian circles it can be much harder to be an individual than it is in society-at-large. Often the world seems more accepting and even admiring of the virtue of nonconformity. But wasn't Jesus the most radical nonconformist who ever lived? And all the world respects Him for it. So it is tragic when His Church succeeds in enshrining the notion (usually more intrinsic than expressed) that the loss of individuality is the necessary cost of being "one in Christ." How often we see churches full of conformists, full of people who instead of discovering and releasing one another's unique identity in Christ have banded together like lemmings, squeezing themselves into a straightjacket of pet doctrines, narrow lifestyles, class values, and regimented ideas. This kind of church is no longer a crucible for saints but a club for cripples. Whenever this happens, whenever doctrinal and behavioral conformity is exalted above love as the central principle of unity, then human character grows cramped and stilted. "Gregariousness is the refuge of mediocrities," wrote Boris Pasternak. In the case of Job's friends it is the very sameness of their personalities and ideas, their stereotyped conventionality, that shows them up to be more dead than alive. Job, despite the fact that he is "nothing but skin and bones" (19:20), is the only full-blooded and three-dimensional character among them, the only true individual. He is the kind of person of whom one says, "When that fellow was born, they threw away the mold."

Why are more Christians not like this? Probably it is because we are so deathly afraid of one another. Most Christians are much more afraid of other Christians than they are of demons—and no doubt rightly so, since in Christ we are more powerful than demons! How wonderful it is to meet someone in whom these chains of fear have begun to be broken, someone who is out to obey God alone rather than other people, someone bent on being a God-pleaser rather than a people-pleaser. In the end, after all, isn't God the only one we *can* please? People can never be satisfied; they demand impossible standards. But God is easy to please, and this is the good news of the gospel in a nutshell. Only God asks for nothing but love.

Unity

"[The wicked man] will spit out the riches he swallowed;
God will make his stomach vomit them up." (20:15)

Because Job's spiritual experience does not line up with their rigid expectations, Job's friends brand him a "wicked man." This is fundamentalist religion at its worst—the sort of legalism that cuts itself off from the living, growing edge of the very faith it seeks to preserve.

One day when the American composer Charles Ives was a boy, he heard two marching bands approaching from different directions, converging on the same street corner. The two bands were playing different tunes, in different keys, and as they drew closer and closer these two wildly incongruous sounds began to swirl together into a single monumental mélange of musical noise. Ives later called it the most beautiful and exciting sound he had ever heard in his life! He went on to become the first composer in western culture to explore polytonality and polyrhythms.

Musical fundamentalists, of course, may question and even ridicule the value of Ives's artistic contributions. But the composer's childhood experience does provide a good metaphor for the meaning of unity in the Christian Church. Church unity does not happen because everyone is wearing the same uniform, marching in the same direction, and playing the same tune. That is the worldly concept of unity. But in the Church the sole basis for unity is that everything be done to the Lord and in mutual love. True, this sometimes results in grand communal projects in which everyone pulls together toward a common goal. But more often church unity has a different sound, a sound that only the ear of patient faith can resolve into anything but cacophonous dissonance. The sound of a vigorous church is like the sound of many waters, or like a great city at rush hour, or of a symphony orchestra tuning up, or of a multitude of angels speaking in many tongues.

The secret to Christian unity is conformity, yes—but not conformity to one another. If each musician played only what his neighbor was playing, it would be a very dull symphony. Rather, the conformity that is required is conformity to the maestro. This message comes through in one of the Bible's most familiar passages on unity, Jesus' prayer in John 17: "*I pray that all those who believe in me* may be one, Father, just as you are in me and I am in you. May they also be in us" (vv. 20-21). Unity will never come through human beings conforming to other human beings; that is not what Jesus prays for. Rather, He asks that our conformity will be with the Father and the Son, so that by being united with Christ just as He is with His Father, we might eventually be brought into perfect unity with one another. Jesus' emphasis is on vertical union as being the prerequisite for horizontal unity.

Paul wrote, "Do not conform any longer to the pattern of this world" (Rom. 12:2), but rather be the sort of person who "can take pride in himself, without comparing himself to somebody else" (Gal. 6:4). We are not to compare ourselves to others because each one of us is an incomparable individual. Not that individuality for its own sake is the goal; rather, the goal is Christlikeness. The motive for Christian nonconformity must never be rebellion against others, but rather conformity to Christ. Some oft-quoted words of Henry David Thoreau may be appropriate here: "If a man does not keep pace with his companions, perhaps it is because he hears a different drummer. Let him keep step to the music which he hears, however measured or far away. Why should he turn his spring into summer?"

Sometimes it seems as though God is asking the question, "How different can My children be from each other and still be one in Christ?" In the church there is a creative tension between the need for both unity and nonconformity, and this truth is well summed up in the saying of Jesus, "Have salt in yourselves, and be at peace with each other" (Mark 9:50). We are to preserve the uniqueness of our individuality, but not to the point of disrupting peace with other believers. But the rule works also in reverse: we are to keep the bond of peace, yet not to the point of watering down the saltiness of radical Christian character.

THE DIALOGUE:
ROUND 3
(Job 21–31)

"I will teach you about the power of God; the ways of the Almighty I will not conceal."

—JOB 27:11

The message of the cross is foolishness to those who are perishing, but to us who are being saved it is the power of God.

—1 COR. 1:18

Loneliness

"Listen carefully to my words;
let this be the consolation you give me." (21:2)

Ironically, Job's only consolation comes from himself. Like many a great preacher, he finds himself in that excruciatingly lonely position in which his own sermons are the only ones that really speak to him. Perhaps this is the very school in which great preachers are made. When a sermon has real power, and when it comes with fire and with tears, is it not because the preacher is first of all preaching to his own soul? The reason he preaches to his own soul is that he can find no one else who will preach to him the message he himself so desperately needs to hear.

A story is told of Charles Spurgeon, who was subject to black bouts of depression. One time he felt so crushed in spirit that he simply could not carry on with his commitments in his home church. Hurriedly he arranged for another pastor to fill in for him and then left town for the weekend. That Sunday he attended a tiny country church, where the sermon that was preached had such a dramatic effect upon him that immediately his depression lifted and he felt totally refreshed and eager to return to his ministry. At the door he introduced himself to the young, unknown preacher, thanking and praising him mightily. The poor man seemed dreadfully embarrassed, however, and finally he had to confess that the sermon he had just preached was in fact one of Spurgeon's own.

It is a wonderful thing to find someone else who, when we are low, can speak to us words of real encouragement. In the Church of Christ this ought to be more common than it is. Nevertheless, even in a good church people experience a certain measure of isolation, a certain poverty of human fellowship, and this is not without purpose. For this loneliness, this place in our hearts that no other human being can touch, is the place reserved for God alone, the place that only He can fill. No human being can love us as God does. No other person can speak to us from the bottom of our own hearts as the Holy Spirit does. No one else can plumb the mystery of our character and discern our peculiar needs and gifts as clearly as we ourselves can, by the Spirit's light. Accordingly, all of us must discover what it means to have no other comfort except the comfort that we ourselves can draw from our God in the lonely privacy of our own prayers. The Apostle John goes so far as to say, "The anointing you received from him remains in you, and you do not need anyone to teach you" (1 John 2:27).

Of course we have a need for teachers too, and for spiritual directors. But the even greater need is for every individual to cultivate a deep life of personal prayer and to hear and to heed the voice of the Lord. We need to take our problems to God first, before rushing out to spill them to others. How can we know which others to trust, unless our God shows us? When Paul was making his final journey to Jerusalem, his fellow Christians "urged him not to go," and there were even those who "through the Holy Spirit . . . pleaded with Paul not to go up to Jerusalem" (Acts 21:4, 11-12). Yet he went anyway, for he had set his face to follow Jesus even to the point of death. How was it that the Holy Spirit, speaking through others, seemed to contradict Paul's own innate sense of God's will for his life? This is a mystery. Yet what a testimony it is to the profound sanctity of each individual's unique relationship with the Lord. Before we are answerable to any other person, we are answerable directly to the Lord, and in His eyes there is nothing more precious, no higher authority, than this intimate personal bond in which "deep calls to deep" (Ps. 42:7).

However we theologize it, the experience of isolation is still one of the most distressing and disorienting of the Christian's trials. At least we may take comfort from the fact that we are not alone, so to speak, in our loneliness—for was anyone ever lonelier than our Jesus? Or consider John the Baptist, spending his last days languishing in Herod's dungeon. After this final ordeal, what a great grace it must have seemed to John to be relieved of the enormous weight of his head! And so the list of lonely Christians goes on. Perhaps in Heaven there will be a special part of the banquet hall set aside especially for the lonely, where the jubilant din of fellowship will be louder and more tumultuous than at any other table.

Chaos

"Why do the wicked live on,
growing old and increasing in power? . . .
Their homes are safe and free from fear;
the rod of God is not upon them." (21:7, 9)

Job's sermon of self-consolation in this chapter (see verse 2) takes a form exactly opposite to the sermons of his friends. Rather than harping on the emptiness and misery of the lives of the wicked, he instead ponders why the wicked are allowed to experience as many of the good things in life as they do. Why should people who say to God, "Leave us alone!" still be blessed with healthy children and thriving businesses and still have the ability to laugh and relax and even enjoy a certain measure of inner peace (vv. 7-18)?

What possible consolation could Job find in posing such questions? His thinking seems to run like this: if good things happen to the wicked in this world (and they do), then there is ample reason to suspect that bad things are also going to happen to the righteous. And all of these good things and bad things are going to be doled out without any apparent pattern to them, without any discernible method in the madness. People who think they see a pattern (as Job's friends do) are simply fooling themselves. In the words of *Ecclesiastes*, "No one can comprehend what goes on under the sun. Despite all his efforts to search it out, man cannot discover its meaning. Even if a wise man claims he knows, he cannot really comprehend it" (8:17).

What Job is saying is this: when it comes right down to it, life makes no sense. And by a strange twist of reverse rationality, Job actually finds comfort in this thought. He finds relief in simply throwing up his hands and saying, "I don't understand anything anymore! There's no rhyme or reason to it whatsoever!"

Oddly enough, Job is largely correct. Belief in God does not bring an ability to answer all questions or to account for everything that happens under the sun. On the contrary, mature faith accepts that there is a great deal which cannot be explained. Only in Heaven will we "know fully, even as [we] are fully known" (1 Cor. 13:12).

Meanwhile we must content ourselves with being "aliens and pilgrims in the world" (1 Peter 2:11), strangers in a strange land that has been profoundly infected and deranged by chaos. True, the face of the Creator still shines through His creation. But His image is no longer perfectly reflected in the nature of things. The waters of the world have been muddied by evil.

To Job's friends, theology is a lens through which to examine reality, and for this reason they tend to see only the way things *ought to be*. But Job refuses to surrender his instinctive grasp of the way things actually *are*, and so he emerges as the greater theologian. His view of life is, in Lenin's famous phrase, "as radical as reality itself." Job's immediate predicament is one that rips away all religious pretensions, forcing theology to come out of the clouds and down to earth where life is lived. By Job's standards any faith that cannot actually be lived, day in and day out, under all circumstances, is absolutely worthless. If it is the real thing, it must cover every conceivable eventuality. When any system of theology comes up against even one exception to its rules and theories, the system must be reevaluated. The scandalous suffering of the righteous Job is the Old Testament's grand exception to the rule of blessing for the faithful, the spectacular exception that ultimately guards against God (or Satan, for that matter) being turned into an abstraction. By persevering in faith under conditions of chaos, Job preserves faith from being reduced to fantasy.

Does all of this sound reasonable? Really it is not. The story of Job defeats reason. It is impossible to read or to think about this book without getting tangled up and stymied. It is all so messy, this business of suffering. It boggles the mind. It is so big, so monstrous, so untheological. Against the systematic tidiness that Job's friends try to impose upon this chaos, Job asserts a healthy belief in the present reign of anarchy.

The God of This Age

*"[The wicked] sing to the music of tambourine and harp;
they make merry to the sound of the flute." (21:12)*

Job continues to press his point about the irrational element, the bizarre uncertainty principle, that is at loose in the world. "Look," he cries, "at this very moment the wicked are having a high old time, and yet here am I, a righteous man, swamped in misery."

Without fully realizing what he is doing, Job is actually arguing the case for the existence of Satan. Why do the wicked prosper? On the one hand, it is because of God's patience and grace. But on the other hand, it is because for the time being He has chosen to withhold His justice and to surrender control of the world to someone else—someone whose laws and methods of governing make no sense whatsoever. Indirectly Job is postulating the existence of this alien usurper. He is feeling his way toward a belief in some personal, supernatural agent of chaos whose irrational activity makes it impossible to grasp the whole meaning of life in any orderly, reasonable fashion, and yet whose every action takes place within the superintendence of a sovereign God. Is this not exactly the picture of Satan that is presented in the Prologue?

Granted, since Job apparently has no conscious knowledge of Satan's existence, he cannot help but see the two powers of order and chaos as somehow being one and the same, and in this his theology is defective. Yet his instinct remains accurate—for there *is* a negative spiritual power whose jurisdiction in the universe is so awesome and sweeping as to be virtually indistinguishable from the jurisdiction of God Himself. Even Christians, after all, do not have perfect discernment in this area. Are we not prone to confuse the hand of the Lord with the hand of the Devil, just as Job did? But the real point is this: in the same way that Job knew nothing of Christ, and yet intuitively grasped the need for a Savior, so too he knew nothing of Satan and yet somehow saw the absolute necessity for Satan's role in the universe. He saw that the ultimate source of chaos and evil had to lie outside the realm of mere human beings, and that it had to be both supernatural and intelligent. Augustine described the mind of faith as one which looked at reality and discerned a "God-shaped vacuum." Of Job we might say that he correctly discerned the presence not only of a God-shaped vacuum, but of a Satan-shaped vacuum.

This is precisely the way genuine faith behaves. Somehow, mystically, it understands the true nature of things, even when it does not understand at all. Job did not understand his suffering and railed against it. Yet at the same time, deep within him was rooted the stubborn conviction, as enigmatic as it was unshakable, that the final cause of his suffering was not to be traced to his own sin, but rather to the fact that he lived in a world in which someone other than his God held the balance of power. In this conjecture he was perfectly right. There is indeed someone else who rules the world and who keeps justice from being done upon the earth. There is someone who stands in the way of the righteous receiving their just rewards immediately, and of the wicked receiving swift and unmitigated punishment. He is the one who has put a veil over the truth so that people cannot grasp the full implications of their actions. He is "the prince of this world" (John 14:30), "the god of this age" (2 Cor. 4:4), "the ruler of the kingdom of the air" (Eph. 2:2).

These facts about Satan need to be faced. His power is breathtaking. He can take the brightest mind and the most cheerful heart and fill them with thoughts of perversion and violence. He can turn faith into a pack of lies and nonsense. He can twist Scripture or make its words swim meaninglessly before the eyes. One touch from him, and the stoutest believer will barely be able to whisper a prayer. It is an evangelical lie that the Lord always preserves us from such things. By and large He does—hallelujah!—but He is not obliged to do so, and it is not always within His purposes to protect His children from an evil influence. Will not Satan in the last days be "given power to make war against the saints and to conquer them" (Rev. 13:7)?

True, it is the Lord Himself "who has created the destroyer to wreak havoc" (Isa. 54:16), and who assuredly holds final veto power over everything that Satan does. Yet for the time being God seems to exercise His veto erratically—as if to emphasize by His inscrutable ways the very majesty of His sovereign power, which by a mere word created the universe, and which by a mere word will at the end of time cast the Devil and all his demons into the lake of fire.

Delayed Reaction

"It is said, 'God stores up a man's punishment for his sons.'
Let him repay the man himself, so that he will know it!"
(21:19)

Having faith in God means living daily with the hard reality of delay—the delay of the full expression of His Kingdom. How much easier it would be to live a godly life if there were immediate rewards for good conduct and immediate punishments for wrongdoing. Being good would then be no more difficult than keeping our hands away from a hot stove. In such a world, however, there would of course be no real goodness at all. There would be no true morality, no need for the conscience, no place even for God. This present, visible world would constitute the be-all and the end-all, and the only god worth heeding would be a person's own natural savvy, his innate proclivity for pursuing whatever brings immediate pleasure and for avoiding whatever causes pain.

Accordingly, the Lord in His wisdom has built into the nature of things a principle of delayed reaction. In the moment of sinning we do not know how, when, or if we will be punished, just as in the moment of doing good we do not know how, when, or if any tangible rewards will follow. Indeed if we were to do our good works with a view to obtaining some personal benefit, they would no longer be good. Real goodness, which Jesus described as giving "without expecting to get anything back" (Luke 6:35), would become impossible. It takes time for good fruit to form and to ripen. In the same way, it takes time for the true nature of evil to rear its hoary head. The Lord did not immediately give the Promised Land to Abraham because "the sin of the Amorites had not yet reached its full measure" (Gen. 15:16). It takes time for sin to "become utterly sinful" (Rom. 7:13).

In moral terms, then, there is a delayed reaction between cause and effect in this world, and it is precisely this delayed reaction that makes real morality possible. The delayed reaction is the gap—the gap between act and consequence, between time and eternity—that can only be filled by spiritual attributes, those highest and most elusive of qualities. But there is a high price to pay for this gap, for this wildly unpredictable delay in both gratification and punishment, and that price is that through this gap are bound to enter, like poisonous insects through an open screen door, all the humiliation and suffering of the righteous. We can moan and groan that "life ain't fair." But that is precisely the point: life is *not* fair. It is grossly unfair. Why? Not because God is unfair, or nonexistent, but rather because in large measure He holds back His fairness, His justice, for a future dispensation.

What Job has been describing in Chapter 21 is the "fairness," as it were, of Satan. This, he argues, is how things work in Satan's kingdom. For Satan too, like God, is a ruler and legislator, who by means of his own system of laws (which Paul in Colossians 2:20 calls "the basic principles of this world") keeps all the earth in the dungeon of his darkness and in thrall to his evil illusions. How do these principles work? Largely, they work by fastening our focus on immediate pleasure and pain, and so confusing and finally annihilating the human conscience. This is not to say that present feelings are unimportant in the spiritual life. But the Devil loves to blur the vital distinction between emotional feelings, which are fickle and untrustworthy, and spiritual feelings, which are deep and foundational and which we ignore at our peril.

Yes, life would seem simpler without the troublesome complexities of conscience. It would seem so much easier to walk with the Lord if we could somehow see immediately the full results of our good and our bad behavior—if, in short, virtue always felt good and vice always felt bad. Then we would not need a conscience, for we would be like Pavlovian animals responding to direct stimuli. But for some reason, the delicate prize of a finely-tuned and discerning conscience is extremely important to the Lord, as painful as it is for human beings to acquire. Hence Jesus promises, "Blessed are you who hunger now, for you will be satisfied" (Luke 6:21); and by the same token He issues a warning to those who "will have no reward from [their] Father in heaven" because "they have *already* received their reward in full" (Matt. 6:1-2). Somehow the Lord wants us to learn to distinguish between good and evil by some other barometer than that of present gratification, and this is much of the reason behind Job's trials.

The Right Cross

"So how can you console me with your nonsense?
Nothing is left of your answers but falsehood!" (21:34)

How powerful are the opinions of other people! To denounce and reject the views of others to their faces can seem, in its own way, like a kind of blasphemy. For no matter how deeply held our own convictions might be, do we not still harbor shades of doubt? Is there not always some little corner of our hearts in which, from time to time, we find ourselves seriously questioning whether those who oppose us may, after all, be right? Surely such niggling doubts would have been part and parcel of Job's trials. If the question of his innocence were really entirely settled in his own mind, would he still be arguing the point so vehemently?

Doubt, whether of oneself or of God, is not necessarily contrary to faith. In *Job* doubt emerges not as the opposite to faith, but rather as the route to the deepest faith. If we really believe, we can doubt energetically; we can wonder, vacillate, challenge, dispute. Just to permit oneself to voice problems aloud is to imply a belief in solutions. *Job* is the answer to the kind of fearful faith that nails a lid on doubt, suppressing it.

Is there any suffering of which doubt is not a part? Since suffering can come alike to either the righteous or the sinful, the former must always face the haunting question, Is it right to be suffering like this? Is this the right kind of suffering? Is this the right cross I'm carrying? When Christians are maligned and persecuted, how do we know when it is appropriate to "rejoice and be glad, for great is your reward in heaven" (Matt. 5:12), or when we ought rather to be ashamed that we have not been a greater credit to our God? When we are troubled in heart, how do we know whether to call it lack of faith or satanic oppression? Or when we fall sick, is it "just one of those things," or have we ourselves done something to bring it on? Have we left ourselves open to attack? Who is to blame for all this unpleasantness—ourselves or the Devil?

It is easy to assume that if Job and his friends had consciously recognized the existence of Satan, they might have saved themselves a lot of breath. But then again, would it really have made much difference to blame everything on him? Blaming the Devil is a tricky business; blame will not stick to him—his hide is so damnably slippery. Christians who adopt an aggressive stance against Satan always run the risk of ignoring one crucial little fact, which is that the very evil we fight against has a foothold in our own flesh. Are we fully assured that the enemy is entirely outside of ourselves? Surely this is the hardest part of any suffering: trying to decide whether this is an undeserved attack that the Lord has allowed for the sake of His own glory, or whether it is something we have brought upon ourselves through sin and foolishness. If only we could know for certain which was which! But we do not always know, and this is exactly Job's predicament.

Job's problem is like the one Jesus wrestled with in the Garden of Gethsemane. Wasn't Jesus really asking His Father, Is this the right cross? Is this really the death You have planned for Me? Is this Your idea, or Mine? After all, there are so many ways to suffer and to die. Is this the right way?

A similar question faces every Christian, every day. For daily we must pick up our cross and follow Jesus. But there are so many crosses! What if I pick up the wrong one? What if I take a wrong turn somewhere and fool myself into thinking that the Lord is still with me? Having assurance of salvation is wonderful, but somehow it does not always keep me from laboring under a nagging suspicion that I may have missed some part of the will of God. A sense of condemnation, whether in whole or in part, still feels like condemnation. One can have full assurance about going to Heaven, and yet not rest at all assured about the quality of one's Christian life right here on earth.

So these problems that I have today—are they the right problems? Are they really the ones God has ordained for me? Am I sharing in the sufferings of Christ? Or is my anguish due largely to neurosis, which Carl Jung called "a substitute for legitimate suffering"? A song entitled "Hard Love" by Bob Franke expresses the problem this way: "The Lord's cross redeems us, but our own just wastes our time, and to tell the two apart is always hard love."

Telling the two apart is the gospel.

Bloody Love

"Can a man be of benefit to God? . . .
What pleasure would it give the Almighty if you were righteous?
What would he gain if your ways were blameless?" (22:2-3)

Eliphaz's point seems orthodox enough. Is he not simply arguing the case for the self-sufficiency of God? God needs nothing; God lacks nothing. Since God is already absolutely perfect, He did not create man out of any personal deficiency or compulsion, and therefore man cannot give anything to God. This is standard orthodox doctrine. "[God] is not served by human hands, as if he needed anything" (Acts 17:25).

The only problem with Eliphaz's brand of orthodoxy is that it removes God entirely from the sphere of compassionate involvement with humanity. It is as if he were to say, "Who do you think you are, Job, carrying on as though God actually *cares* about you? Do you think it's any skin off His nose whether you live or die?" Behind such thinking lies the image of a god who cannot love—a god for whom love would be too awkward, too demeaning, too sullying an activity. Such a god is beyond feeling altogether, whether it be feelings of gladness or of pain. This god is too abstractly pure to be involved in anything except his own perfection. Such a deity could not possibly take any real pleasure in his creation, nor could his heart ever be moved to grief by the petty problems of his creatures.

Even today the concept of a feeling, suffering God is almost impossible for most people to grasp. Particularly where the influence of Eastern religions has been felt, God is often seen to be beyond suffering, and consequently so is love itself. In this view the whole purpose of religion is to wean people from their messy emotional lives so as to lift them up onto the higher plane of divinely dispassionate existence. Such sterile stoicism has no divine Person behind it, no real God at all. Certainly it cannot begin to embrace the God who loved the world so much that He gave His only begotten Son to be murdered for its sake.

Contrary to what Eliphaz says, then, it is of the utmost importance to God whether or not people are righteous. That is why He died, and why He continues both to rejoice with us in our righteousness and to agonize with us in our sin. This is "how wide and long and high and deep is the love of Christ" (Eph. 3:18). Eliphaz apparently has no idea of what is really at stake here, not merely in Job's trial, but in the whole human project in the broadest sense. He seems to have no concept of how infinitely precious humanity is to God, and how much God's own honor is at risk in everything that happens on earth. Job's friends are so preoccupied with religious correctness that they turn God into a kind of moral mechanism, a faceless clockworks. To believe as they do in the idea that people get exactly what they deserve (a view we might call "Biblical karma") does not require any great faith. But to believe with Job that righteousness is a gift of God, whose gracious magnanimity is wholly disproportionate to our just deserts—this requires an experimental commitment of faith so daring and radical that most people shrink from it in fear. The very idea that God is love (or better, the idea of committing ourselves to act in all circumstances *just as though* God is love) fills us with a strange terror—so much so that mankind has literally put the God of love to death, both on Calvary and ever since, in a vain effort to stifle His consuming passion for us.

In our language the word *love* (unlike some of our other four-letter words) has a euphonious sound, and there is no taboo attached to its use. Nevertheless in polite company the real thing—the bloody love that gushes from the side of the Crucified—remains an obscenity. Whether we meet it in *Job* or in the *Gospels*, the cross of Christ has always been a scandal. God's answer to the world's suffering has never taken the form people wanted it to. He has not given us a closely-reasoned *apologia*, but rather His answer was to enter into the arena of suffering Himself in the person of the Son whom He loved more than any of us has ever loved anyone. "The Lord will lay bare his holy arm," prophesied Isaiah, "and all the ends of the earth will see the salvation of our God" (52:10). The image of God's bared arm points first to the Incarnation, and then beyond it to that day on Calvary when the Lord would solve all the problems of the world by rolling up His own sleeves and getting His own hands dirty and bloody.

As We Forgive Others

"Is not your wickedness great?
Are not your sins endless?" (22:5)

I f in the past Eliphaz has been at all guarded in his criticism of
Job, he is guarded no longer. In this chapter, his final speech, he
pours forth an incredible stream of invective, in which he directly
accuses Job of "stripping men of their clothing, leaving them naked"
(v. 6), "withholding food from the hungry" (v. 7), and "sending widows away empty-handed" (v. 9). Prior to this the only straightforward indictment Job's friends have dared to bring against him has
concerned his present insolent attitude (see 15:6). Apparently this
righteous man's conduct in the past has been so unimpeachable that
there has been nothing obvious to pin on him, and so we can only
presume that these new charges constitute pure slander. Even if there
is some grain of truth to them, surely there is more truth in the
words of Psalm 130:3—"If you, O Lord, kept a record of sins, O
Lord, who could stand?" Or in Zechariah 7:10—"In your hearts do
not think evil of each other."

How cautious we need to be about leveling even the smallest criticism against the loved and elect children of God. Do we really think
we can get away with grumbling against the friends of Jesus? If we
stopped to realize who it is we were attacking, wouldn't we bite out
our tongues? As Glenn Tinder writes, "The Christian universe is
peopled exclusively with royalty." Far from picking on the obvious
faults of others, we need to take note of their virtues. We need to see
the goodness in them that perhaps no one else (including even themselves) can see, and when this goodness does not seem to be present
we need to pray it into them. For this is when love is most loving,
most Godlike—when it "calls things that are not as though they
were" (Rom. 4:17). This is true Christianity, the faith that believes
not only in God but in other people. This is the faith Jesus had when
He called out to a dead man, whose body was already rotting,
"Lazarus, come out!" (John 11:43). If the Lord had not believed in

Lazarus (far more than poor Lazarus had ever believed in himself), He could not have loved him back to life.

If I as a believer am truly blameless in the eyes of God, then shouldn't I also treat other believers as being blameless? I need to find ways of making others' hearts lighter, not heavier. I need to say to myself, "This is a person whose sins are forgiven. If Christ has forgiven, who am I to condemn?" Many of us have struggled hard and long to gain assurance of salvation and the unspeakable comfort it brings. Should we not struggle just as hard to share this comfort, to lift the pall of condemnation that hangs over the souls of others? "I want you to know how much I am struggling for you," wrote Paul to the Colossians. "My purpose is that [you] may be encouraged in heart" (2:1-2).

In the Lord's Prayer we say, "Forgive us our sins, as we forgive those who sin against us." What this principle boils down to is that if we want to be allowed to be human, we must learn to accept the humanness of others too. Then we will find ourselves not only forgiving others, but actively ministering God's forgiveness to their spirits. Then we will begin to "carry each other's burdens, and in this way you will fulfill the law of Christ" (Gal. 6:2). Then we will start treating one another as Christ has treated us, even to the point of taking the brunt and burden of another's sin just as He has taken ours, and so participating in the cleansing and freeing and healing of one another, all in the name and power of our Savior.

To love one's neighbor is to minister the gospel to him. It is to give to him the same free gift of love and grace and full acceptance that the Lord has given to us. If Job's friends ever knew this secret, they have forgotten it. Job's faith is being tested in this story, but so is theirs, and they fail their test. They are "worthless physicians" (13:4) and "miserable comforters" (16:2) because their would-be consolation is really condescension. Instead of working to discover their friend's sin they should have worked at disclosing his saintliness. They should have let go of being saints themselves and concentrated instead on being plain old sinners. Then they might have told Job about the never-failing love of God, and they themselves might have embodied that love for him. But they missed their chance.

Law and Gospel

"Submit to God and be at peace with him;
in this way prosperity will come to you." (22:21)

We have all had conversations in which we knew that what the other person was saying was "right," and yet for some reason we could not go along with it. As much as we might have agreed with the words, somehow we felt we could not agree with the person. What was being said may have been all very well and good, but it did not change anything. It was not helpful.

This is basically the way Paul characterizes the law in Chapter 7 of *Romans*. In itself the law is good, even holy—and yet it does not keep anyone from sinning. Is the law irrelevant, then? No, of course not. But the simple fact is that it is of no practical use to a person who is struggling and suffering.

The subtlety of this point is lost on Job's friends. They think they are helping Job by reminding him of certain fundamental spiritual principles. There is nothing wrong with their maxims. What is wrong is for such pious rules of thumb to be set up as the basis, the central motivating factor, of life. For law cannot motivate at all; it can only expose and convict. "No one will be declared righteous in [God's] sight by observing the law; rather, through the law we become conscious of sin" (Rom. 3:20). Job's friends try to make law do what it was never meant to do, setting up moral exhortation in the place of grace. By twisting law into center position and riveting full attention upon it, they do something very similar to what Satan did to Eve in the Garden of Eden, turning her gaze upon the one tree from which she was commanded not to eat. This is what every human religion or system of morality has always done, effectively casting God in a harsh and negative light by stressing the "thou shalt not" of righteousness. Only the cross of Christ does the opposite. Only the cross puts the focus in the right place, on the tree of life rather than on the tree of moral knowledge—that is, on the never-failing love of God rather than on the always-failing moral conduct of man.

In addition to the libelous accusations Eliphaz brings against Job in this chapter, there are any number of criticisms we ourselves might make of Job's personal conduct and character. Even by normal standards of civility, he may strike us as an impatient, cantankerous, demanding person. Yet could not similar charges be brought against many other great saints in the Bible? Consider Abraham, who twice lied about his wife Sarah and gave her to other men, and who even bore an illegitimate son in defiance of the Lord's promise that he and Sarah would have a son of their own. Nevertheless, the writers of the New Testament do not dare to say one negative word against Abraham or his faith. On the contrary Paul assures us that the patriarch did not "weaken in his faith," that "he did not waver through unbelief regarding the promise of God," but rather he was "fully persuaded that God had power to do what he had promised" (Rom. 4:19-21). How is it that in Paul's view Abraham comes out so squeaky clean? What Paul correctly saw was that the man's external conduct was not the point at issue; rather, the point was his righteousness, his faith alone. This is the kind of faith that enables a person to glorify God even in the midst of moral failure. In the storms of life the feet of such a believer may repeatedly stumble and fall, and yet in his heart of faith he never falters. His confidence is not in works but in faith, not in holy living but in a holy God.

In the final analysis the proof of our holiness lies not in our conduct, but in the cross. It is the blood of Christ that redeems us, not our sinless lives. Dependence upon holy living will lead to frustration and ruin. Only dependence upon God pleases God and qualifies as righteousness. This is the gospel, and it is the only gospel by which sinners can be saved. This is the one loophole in the law, the one way (however illegitimate it may seem to strict legalists) to wriggle free of the law's condemnation. This is both the door and the road to life, both the narrow door of justification and the narrow road of sanctification. It is the two rolled into one, and no other door or road is necessary. To a Pharisee this sounds like cheating. And it is! It utterly cheats a person out of any possibility of being good, leaving that achievement and all its glory entirely to God.

Day in Court

"I would state my case before [God]
and fill my mouth with arguments. . . .
Would he oppose me with great power?
No, he would not press charges against me.
There an upright man could present his case before him,
and I would be delivered forever from my judge." (23:4, 6-7)

Unlike most people Job sees the judgment-seat of God as a place of refuge, not of condemnation. In fact what he longs for more than anything else is to be judged by God. Naturally there is also a part of Job that stands in fear of divine judgment; yet for him it would be a far more fearful prospect if God's judgment never fell, and such is the case with all true believers. Job is convinced that something about his case must be hidden, that somehow all the evidence has not yet come to light. He believes that if only the whole truth could be brought out into the open, and if only his case could be argued under circumstances of clear and unbiased justice, then his name would be resoundingly cleared. Therefore he longs for his day in court—that day when, in the words of Psalm 37:6, "the justice of [his] cause will shine like the noonday sun." As Jesus put it, "Everyone who does evil hates the light, and will not come into the light for fear that his deeds will be exposed. But whoever lives by the truth comes into the light, so that it may be seen plainly that what he has done has been done through God" (John 3:20-21).

Job's friends are scandalized (or should we say terrified?) by this suggestion that their abstract theological debate should be brought directly to the throne of God for adjudication. How, they must have wondered, did Job envision such a thing happening? Did he see Heaven opening and some grand hall of justice being literally lowered out of the clouds and plunked down before their very eyes? Or was it something more mystical he had in mind? This is perhaps an interesting question; but the real point is simply that Job believes in this divine court, in a way that his friends do not. He believes in its immanence, in its immediate relevance—which is to say that far ahead of his time he believed in exactly what Jesus Christ came to preach: "the kingdom of God is *at hand*" (Mark 1:15). To Job's friends God is not real enough to make such a prospect at all feasible. Their religion operates too much on the level of the rational and the pragmatic to allow for any breaking of the transcendent into the daily world. But Job, like the Apostle John who saw "the new Jerusalem, coming down out of heaven" (Rev. 21:2), looks for and intensely desires the invasion of earth by the Kingdom of Heaven. He actually believes that there must be some way for a human being to invoke the presence of this Kingdom *right now*. A. W. Tozer described the Christian as "a holy rebel loose in the world with access to the throne of God." Job believes in this access. He believes a mere man can gain a personal hearing before the Lord Almighty.

So impatient is Job for this process to begin that he dares to arraign the Lord in court. In effect, he wants to sue God for defamation of character! If this sounds shocking, then how much more shocking is the attitude of the unbelieving world, which seeks to defend itself against God by relegating Him to unapproachable nebulousness. Job, by contrast, is eager to have God come out into the open and clarify His purposes. By bringing the Lord to court, Job's ultimate aim is to see not only himself but his God vindicated. He wants the Lord's name cleared as much as his own. His faith is like that of Jeremiah who prayed, "You are always righteous, O Lord, when I bring a case before you. Yet I would speak with you about your justice" (Jer. 12:1). It is precisely because Jeremiah believed implicitly in the Lord's justice that he had the courage to question Him about it, and to hold out for an answer.

What Job does not fully realize at this point is that the great day in court for which he so ardently longs has already begun. What he cannot see is that his present "trial" (in the sense of "tribulation") is really a "trial" in the formal legal sense, and that he himself, far from being the defendant in this case, is in fact the star witness for the Crown Prosecution. To Job this entire proceeding seems nothing but an outrageous waste of time, as pointless as it is painful. Yet how precious this trial is to God! For this is the very thing God waits for throughout history—that moment when His faithful witness will take the stand and, against enormous odds and intense opposition, publicly place his trust in exactly the prospect from which the rest of the world flees in terror: the judgment of Almighty God.

Enlarging the Heart

"[The Lord] knows the way that I take;
when he has tested me, I will come forth as gold." (23:10)

There is an implied corollary to Job's statement, "[The Lord] knows the way that I take." The corollary is: "I do not." In the words of Proverbs 20:24, "A man's steps are directed by the Lord. How then can anyone understand his own way?" Or as a more familiar proverb puts it, "Trust in the Lord with all your heart and lean not on your own understanding" (3:5).

This is what Job is doing. This is "the way" he is following—the way of admitting that he has no understanding of what he is passing through. He cannot analyze and diagnose his spiritual condition and come up with practical remedies, as his friends seek to do. All he can do is describe his symptoms: pain, anger, bewilderment. His speeches are reports sent back from an alien and hostile land, a *terra incognita* of the heart. It is a place in which God is nowhere to be found: "If I go to the east, he is not there; if I go to the west, I do not find him" (23:8). Under such circumstances, it is the most natural thing in the world for a believer to begin to lean upon his own understanding. In the utter absence of God, what else are we to do? If the Lord declines to speak to us or to guide us, must we not by our own efforts puzzle things through and so force the perplexities of life to submit to order and reason? Yet this is exactly what the Bible warns us not to do. Instead, "Wait for the Lord; be strong and take heart and wait for the Lord" (Ps. 27:14).

By our own natural strength and understanding, we human beings cannot take one step on the road to Heaven. We cannot do our own growing. We cannot grow our spiritual lives any more than we can grow our bodies. True, we can eat and drink; but we eat and drink primarily because we are hungry and thirsty, not in order to grow. Of the two years he spent living alone at Walden Pond, Thoreau remarked, "I grew the way corn grows in the night." Growth is a phenomenon that takes place behind our backs, when we are not looking. It happens the way seeds sprout in the earth: "As the soil makes the sprout come up and a garden causes seeds to grow, so the Sovereign Lord will make righteousness and praise spring up" (Isa. 61:11). Jesus taught the same in a parable about the Kingdom of God: "A man scatters seed on the ground. Night and day, whether he sleeps or gets up, the seed sprouts and grows, though he does not know how. All by itself the soil produces grain" (Mark 4:27-28). Again He said, "See how the lilies of the field grow. They do not labor or spin" (Matt. 6:28).

In the life of faith one of the hardest things to do is to refrain from laboring and spinning (from spinning, one might say, in circles) and instead to see ourselves as being like flowers or grain, growing not by our own efforts but by the grace of God. Why is this so hard? It is hard because it means giving up all our own plans for ourselves, all our pet projects for making ourselves into something. It means surrendering our will. It means giving up on ever getting our own way, and choosing instead the way of the Lord, the way of growing by the darkness of His grace rather than by the light of conscious, self-determining effort.

During the night of grace, our faculty of reason could be likened to a house with sealed-off rooms. No matter how hard we try, we cannot get into the locked rooms. We cannot see clearly what is happening to us. Like Job, we may feel as though the Lord has abandoned our house altogether; we cannot seem to locate Him in any of the old haunts. But has He really deserted us? No, He is still there; but He is in the sealed rooms. And there He is preparing something for us: a brand-new addition. The Carpenter of Nazareth is busy adding a new wing to our mansion. He is enlarging our heart. Not until everything is ready in the new chambers will we be able to go in, for if we went in too soon we might fall through the floor. But when all is finished and we finally enter the new wing, how delighted and astounded we will be to see that everything—literally every last detail—has been custom-built and immaculately appointed for our personal accommodation.

When Joshua was leading the Israelites across the Jordan into the Promised Land, he gave them strict orders to stay behind the ark of the covenant and to follow it, for "then you will know which way to go, since you have never been this way before" (Josh. 3:4). Since we do not really know what eternity is like, how can we go there except by a way that we cannot imagine until we have already traversed it?

The Level Path

"My feet have closely followed his steps;
I have kept to his way without turning aside.
I have not departed from the commands
of his lips." (23:11-12)

We who see ourselves as often straying from the straight and narrow may be somewhat skeptical of Job's claim that he has kept all the Lord's commands and stayed on the right path "without turning aside." Surely Job must be exaggerating? Surely he must have made a few slip-ups somewhere along the line? If we find ourselves incredulous here, it may be because we are laboring under a false conception of what the path of righteousness really is.

In many religious traditions one of the central symbols of this path is a mountain, and the way to make spiritual progress is by climbing arduously to the top of the mountain along a route that is notoriously difficult, fantastically treacherous, all-but-impassable. This image is so pervasive in the world's mythologies that it has even been adopted by many Christians. But in fact it is not a Biblical image at all. In the Bible the way of righteousness is more commonly pictured as a smooth, level path. When the psalmist David is happy he sings, "My feet stand on level ground" (Ps. 26:12), and when he is troubled he prays, "May your good Spirit lead me on level ground" (Ps. 143:10). Similarly a proverb exhorts, "Make level paths for your feet" (4:26—a verse significant enough to be quoted in Hebrews 12:13). Again, Jeremiah promises that the Lord will lead His people "on a level path where they will not stumble" (31:9), and Isaiah declares, "The path of the righteous is level; O upright One, you make the way of the righteous smooth" (26:7). As one of the Old Testament's most famous prophecies of the gospel states, "Every valley shall be raised up, every mountain and hill made low; the rough ground shall become level, the rugged places a plain" (Isa. 40:4).

If the Bible had wanted to make mountain climbing the principal sport of the faithful, it would have placed its holy city on the snowy peak of Mount Hermon, the country's highest point of land, rather than at Jerusalem. As it is, the road to Mount Zion had such a gentle rise that pilgrims could sing as they traveled along it, which is why Psalms 120—134 are known as the "Songs of Ascent." So there is a wonderful irony in Micah's prophecy that "in the last days the mountain of the Lord's temple will be established as chief among the mountains" (4:1). The king of mountains, it turns out, is no towering Everest, but rather just a little molehill that any toddling child could easily navigate.

What a lovely metaphor this is for the fact that the Biblical way of ascent is not strenuous or backbreaking, but rather a way of gentleness, meekness, humility. The way up is really a way down. Hence the Lord can promise, "What I am commanding you today is not too difficult for you or beyond your reach" (Deut. 30:11). Climbing mountains is hard work and will wear you out. But Jesus says, "Come to me, all you who are weary and burdened, and I will give you rest" (Matt. 11:28). Moses went up on a mountain in order to receive God's law. But Jesus came down to ground level to preach the gospel. Anyone who has been to Israel will know that the so-called "Sermon on the Mount" was not preached from a mountain at all, but from a "mountainside" or a gently sloping hillside. In fact Luke tells us that when it came time to preach this sermon the Lord "went down and stood on a level place" (6:17). Didn't Jesus teach His disciples that if they had faith they would be able to move mountains? Why go to all the trouble of climbing a mountain if by faith you can have it thrown into the sea (see Mark 11:23)?

Far from scaling mountains in order to reach God, it is precisely from such tortuous paths that we must turn in order to accept the smooth and level highway of simple faith that Jesus has paved for us. Even He, when He ascended to Heaven, did not climb up but "was taken up" (Acts 1:9). In truth, to be saved is already to have reached the mountaintop—just as Noah in his ark, without raising any canvas or pulling at any oar, came to rest on the summit of Mount Ararat.

"I Am Who I Am"

"He stands alone, and who can oppose him?
He does whatever he pleases." (23:13)

In Exodus 3:14 God revealed His name to Moses as "I am who I am." This is a name as pellucid, as fathomless, as infinitely expressive as the sky, the sea, or a human eye. Its meaning cannot be explained any more than the name "God" or "Job" can be explained. A name is a name is a name. It is an elemental fact, something beyond even "meaning." Names do have meanings, but somehow the meaning carries less weight than the name itself. It is the name of Jesus, not only its meaning, that drives out demons and secures answers to prayer. Thus when the Preacher wails, "Everything is meaningless!" (Eccl. 1:2), what he is really saying, in a strange sort of way, is that everything simply is the way it is and that is all that can be said. When we read *Ecclesiastes* this way, we see that even in the midst of his existential despair the Preacher was actually praising God. How else to explain the beauty and the majesty of words such as these: "All streams flow into the sea, yet the sea is never full. To the place the streams come from, there they return again" (1:7). This book glorifies the hard, bright, intransigent fact of reality itself—or rather, of Reality Himself. For this writer has come to the end of his own understanding, to the end of all human resources, and now he is up against the sheer naked extremity of "I am who I am."

Whatever else we may say about God, we have to say that He is who He is. "'To whom will you compare me? Or who is my equal?' says the Holy One" (Isa. 40:25). There is a craggy individuality about the Lord, an unassailable actuality, an *otherness*, a *thereness*, an ontic and immutable aboriginality. God is not to be gainsaid; neither is there any going around Him. Rather He is to be wrestled with, reckoned with, and ultimately bowed to. "He is the Lord," confessed the broken old priest Eli; "let him do what is good in his eyes" (1 Sam. 3:18). God is who He is, and what He says goes. His word goes into every corner of the universe, and also into every nook of our own paltry little lives. "Our God is in heaven; he does whatever pleases him" (Ps. 115:3).

That a Being so awesomely inscrutable should have a name at all—let alone a name that a mere human being can know and call upon—this is the mystery of faith. And the mystery goes even deeper still, for this high and holy name also has a face, a human face like ours. There may be much that puzzles and disturbs us about the God-Man whose character is revealed in the pages of the New Testament. Words such as "blood," "demons," "hell," "obedience" and "authority" may, in this modern age, profoundly unsettle us. But in the end Jesus is who He is, and this is the language He speaks; this is the reality He lives and breathes. And since "there is no other name under heaven given to men by which we must be saved" (Acts 4:12), we are bound to accept this Christ as He is and to love Him for it. "In the evening of life, you will be examined in love," wrote John of the Cross. "Learn to love as God desires to be loved, and abandon your own ways."

But even this is just half of the gospel mystery. For the gospel is a relationship, a covenant, and therefore it has two halves or parts. The other half of the gospel is that this Jesus, who is as He is and whom we are bound to accept and love just as He is, this Jesus also does us the extraordinary honor of loving and accepting us *just as we are*. The moment we throw in our lot with the God whose name is "I am who I am," there is a sense in which our name too, our new and secret name, becomes "I am who I am." Perhaps Paul lets slip this tremendous secret when he writes, "By the grace of God I am what I am" (1 Cor. 15:10). How strange that the apostle should speak of himself in words that so jarringly echo the most holy name of the Lord Almighty! He might as well have said, "I live no longer, but 'I am who I am' lives in me."

Job's problem is that he knows (at least consciously) only half the gospel. He knows that God is who He is. He knows that "God stands alone and does whatever he pleases." But the greatness of Job's character is that he also senses intuitively the inherent dignity and inviolability of his own human self, created in God's image, and this other half of the gospel he fights for tooth and nail. He fights for the sanctity of his own name and identity, because he knows that to be a believer in the great "I Am" is to be able to stand before the throne of this gloriously intractable Deity and to declare to His face in all boldness, "I, too, am who I am, for this is how You have made me."

I Believed,
Therefore I Spoke

"God has made my heart faint;
the Almighty has terrified me.
Yet I am not silenced by the darkness,
by the thick darkness that covers my face." (23:16-17)

Job's strongest assertions of faith seem always to be coupled with equally strong assertions of fear and pain. In this chapter his confidence in his own righteousness is more unassailable than ever (see vv. 11-12), yet at the same time "thick darkness covers" his face and he is filled with dread. Somehow Job's faith is elastic enough to embrace simultaneously both terror and confidence, and any Christian who has done serious battle with the Devil will know exactly what Job means. One is confident, and yet one is terrified, and there is no contradiction. Terror is the very fabric of war. Only fools are unafraid in battle. Without fear, one does not take evil seriously. Yet without confidence, one cannot take a stand against it.

Human beings are bicameral creatures, having two of everything: arms, legs, eyes, ears, lips, nostrils, and sides of the brain. We seem especially designed for handling contradiction, for being pulled in two directions at once. There is no getting around this fundamental bifurcation of our lives, and of the Christian life in particular. If we are not torn apart by our faith, then it is not the real thing. Paul describes the struggle like this: "The sinful nature desires what is contrary to the Spirit, and the Spirit what is contrary to the sinful nature. They are in conflict with each other" (Gal. 5:17). Becoming a Christian does not eradicate the sinful nature; rather, it gives one a place to take a stand against it. To believe in Christ is to be a witness, not only for God, but against oneself: "You are witnesses against yourselves that you have chosen to serve the Lord" (Josh. 24:22). This is why a simple equation between righteousness and goodness can never be made. We are never good; but by faith we can be righteous.

Believers know that the real battleground between good and evil is the human heart. Faith acknowledges the inevitability of this interior war, and gives assent for it to be fought on one's own turf. To be a Christian is to be a little Korea or Viet Nam—a tiny country torn apart by superpowers. Day after day I must take heart, put on the armor of righteousness, and face the enemy. The enemy is all around me, but I cannot face him until I have first dealt with the enemy inside myself. So terror is never far away, and indeed it comes closer and closer, for the larger the territory Christ wins within me, the more I become conscious of my own depravity. Hence at all costs I must keep my eyes on Jesus, because to look away from Him for a moment and back at myself is to see a sight that becomes more and more horrifying as the Christian life progresses. For I live no longer, but Christ lives in me. I myself am dead, and so to look back at myself is to look at myself dead, fallen in battle, my mangled body lying in a pool of congealed blood and crawling with worms and maggots. No wonder I get scared!

And no wonder Job is scared. When the felt presence of God is removed from a believer's life, all that is left is the sight of his own moldering flesh. Paul sees this as an inescapable part of the Christian experience: "We who are alive are always being given over to death for Jesus' sake, so that his life may be revealed in our mortal body. So then, death is at work in us, but life is at work in you. It is written: 'I believed; therefore I have spoken.' With that same spirit of faith we also believe and therefore speak" (2 Cor. 4:11-13). The Old Testament Scripture Paul quotes here—"I believed; therefore I have spoken"—is from Psalm 116. What was it that the psalmist spoke out of his heart of faith? He said, "I am greatly afflicted" (v. 10). He said, "The cords of death entangled me. . . . I was overcome by trouble and sorrow" (v. 3). He said, "All men are liars" (v. 11). In short, the psalmist says what Job has been saying all along. He complains, he squirms, he rails, he craves death. Like Job, even though he is faint and terrified, he is "not silenced by the darkness." Because he believes, he speaks out. He speaks his agony, knowing that "precious in the sight of the Lord is the death of his saints" (v. 15)—and not just our final death, but the way we die a little every day.

The Face of Suffering

"Men move boundary stones . . .
and take the widow's ox in pledge.
They thrust the needy from the path
and force all the poor of the land into hiding." (24:2-4)

From focusing primarily on his own problems, Job now turns his gaze upon the sorrows of the whole world and pours out a litany of grief for the poor, the oppressed, the helpless, the dying. Why will God not do something about it all? Even Christians who are too "reverent" to voice this question aloud nevertheless feel it in their bones. And those who do not, have simply not looked, recently, into the face of a dying child, a tortured political prisoner, or an AIDS victim.

Whose faces are these? Who is it, really, we are looking at when we see something that revolts and sickens us? Isn't it the Devil? Isn't it the face of the enemy we peer into when we see human tissue eaten away by cancer, or bodies mutilated by terrorist bombs? What we are seeing is the Devil's unique seal and signature, the stamp of his authoritative rule over the earth. Suffering is the unmistakable evidence that Satan is here.

This is something that the book of *Job* never lets us forget. Although the name of Satan is not mentioned once outside the Prologue, his presence is pervasive. His signature is on every page. The name of God appears over 150 times in the book, and yet throughout the Dialogue section it is Satan who invisibly dominates. Why? As Jesus was preparing for the cross He told His disciples, "The prince of this world is coming. He has no hold on me, but the world must learn that I love the Father" (John 14:30-31). In Job's case, too, the world had to learn that here was a man who loved God. Long before the time of Christ, the world still had to be shown the strange spectacle of a righteous man leaning the entire weight of his flesh and spirit upon no other staff but a cross.

So there is another face besides Satan's that looks out at us from the world's suffering, and that is the face of the crucified one, the face of the God who groans and sorrows along with His creation.

On Calvary we see these two faces, the face of the Lord and the face of the Devil, brought together with brutal clarity. The Devil thought he had Christ; he thought he had won possession of the Son of God. And for three days and three nights it looked as though he might be right. During that time the two faces of darkness and of light came nose to nose in a showdown, and in this showdown the hearts of good and of evil were laid bare. Here the Lord confronted Satan on his own turf, physically took hold of Satan's own chosen weapons— violence, torture, irrationality, mob rule, desertion, desolation, hatred, death—and then once and for all Jesus destroyed those weapons, melting them down and reforging them into instruments of love.

Ever since then, suffering has meant something entirely different to Christians than it does to all the rest of the world. The Lord "turned the rock into a pool," sings Psalm 114:8, "the hard rock into springs of water." And so it happens that out of the least likely of sources—the granite of suffering—God brings the living water of life. To deny that suffering of all kinds has not only a legitimate but a central place in Christianity is to deny the gospel. "We must go through many hardships to enter the kingdom of God," teaches Paul in Acts 14:22. Or listen to Charles Spurgeon:

> Trials are a part of our lot, they were pre-destined for us in God's solemn decrees, and bequeathed to us in Christ's last legacy. So surely as the stars are fashioned by His hands and their orbits are fixed by Him, so surely are our trials allotted to us; He has ordained their season and place, their intensity and the effect they shall have on us. Good men or women must never expect to escape troubles; if they do they will be disappointed. . . . It is ordained of old that the cross of trouble should be engraven on every vessel of mercy as the royal mark whereby the King's vessels of honour are distinguished.

The crucifixion of the flesh of man is not a beautiful thing. It is not a sweet mystical phenomenon. Rather it is a face-off with the Prince of Darkness. It is seeing the holy face of Christ set against that other face. If we find this experience delightful and uplifting, then it is not really the cross of Christ we are experiencing. The cross was torture for Jesus, and it will be torture for us too. Jesus cried out upon it, and so will we. Jesus died upon it, and so must we.

The Mystery of Children

"The fatherless child is snatched from the breast;
the infant of the poor is seized for a debt." (24:9)

Job's litany of woe and injustice in the world encompasses one of the deepest of all mysteries to the mind of faith: the lot of children. Many people like to ask, "What kind of a God lets little children suffer?" Really they are asking, "What kind of a God lets children suffer before they are even old enough to know the comfort of faith?" In an early chapter Job drew attention to the case of the "stillborn child" who dies "*without ever seeing* the light of day" (3:16). While he never develops this issue at any length, clearly the underlying message to his friends is, "Here is something your theology cannot touch." And he is right. Theology cannot touch the mystery of faith as it pertains to a child—let alone to an unborn fetus. This is one area in which theologians are dumb, blind, foolish. Why? Because theology is for the adult mind. It is for the mature and the rational and the intelligent. Oswald Chambers put it this way:

> A scientist can explain the universe in which common-sense men live, but the scientific explanation is not first; life is first. The same with theology: theology is the systematizing of the intellectual expression of life from God; it is a mighty thing, but it is second, not first. . . . If we put it first, we will do what Job's friends did, refusing to look at facts and remaining consistent to certain ideas which pervert the character of God.

When it comes to the heart of a child, theology has nothing to say. Yet it has to say something (or thinks it does), and so it gets itself into some terrible predicaments. For example, some theologies allow children to die in Christ, but not to be baptized. Children are welcome to serve the Lord (in a church choir or pageant, let's say), or to suffer unspeakably for His name, but they might not be welcome to be served or succored in turn at the Lord's Table. And so it goes. Wherever it touches the lot of children, theology is a cripple, a lunatic, an undeveloped fetus of a thing. That is why Jesus said, "I praise you, Father, Lord of heaven and earth, because you have hidden these things from the wise and learned, and revealed them to little children" (Luke 10:21). What did He mean? He meant, of course, that a child may have a finer and a better-developed faith than an adult. Not only that, but "unless you change and become like little children, you will never enter the kingdom of heaven" (Matt. 18:3).

The Bible is full of babies, godly babies, who influenced the course of sacred history just as profoundly as any adult. Religious people may laugh at this notion, and that is why the first of these wondrous infants was named Isaac, a word meaning "laugh." Isaac was the original grace-child, the child of divine promise who simply by being born confounded all responsible, mature notions of religion and glorified the God of grace. And then there was Moses. Who can doubt that the Lord was just as mightily at work, for the salvation of His people, in the baby Moses as He was in the adult Moses? Hebrews 11:23 tells us that "by faith Moses' parents hid him for three months after he was born, because they saw he was no ordinary child." How did they know? What did they see in this tiny, mewling newborn? They must have seen something of what the shepherds saw when they entered the stable in Bethlehem, or of what Simeon and Anna saw in the temple when they broke into ecstatic prophecy before a tiny stranger, eight days old. Or consider the story of John the Baptist, whom Scripture records as being "filled with the Holy Spirit even from birth" (Luke 1:15). More remarkable still, when the Messiah was little more than a single cell inside the womb of a young virgin, at His first approach the baby John leapt in his mother's womb (Luke 1:41)—proving once and for all that even an unborn fetus can be a born-again Christian! God is sovereign! As Psalm 22:9 declares, "You made me trust in you even at my mother's breast."

There is more here than meets the rational, theological eye. The life of a child may seem a simpler life than that of an adult, but it is still a *moral* life. Children are fully moral creatures who, somehow, make choices of their own from the time of conception. If a baby can be born in sin, then a baby can also be saved. For faith is not a faculty of the reason, but of the spirit and the will. Jesus taught consistently that the way to know God is not merely by assenting to a creed, but by doing His will. Can a little child not fulfill the will of God? Is God's will so complicated that only adults can do it? Has not God ordained praise "*out of the mouths of babes and sucklings*" (Ps. 8:2)?

More Than
Conquerors

"The groans of the dying rise from the city,
and the souls of the wounded cry out for help.
But God charges no one with wrongdoing." (24:12)

It might be possible to read these words in a controlled tone of voice, as though Job were advancing arguments in an abstract debate. But to do so would be to miss the whole point of his speech. No, these are the words of a man who has just sworn that he "will not be silenced by the darkness" (23:17), and the way to read this speech is as a cry, almost a scream, wrung from the pit of Job's being. Such a cry does not come from someone who is confidently victorious in his faith, but rather from one who, whether he knows it or not, shares the depths of the heart of God.

In Christian spirituality there is an ancient distinction between *theologia crucis* (theology of the cross) and *theologia gloriae* (theology of glory). The spirituality of glory, explains Ruth Burrows, is essentially human-centered, serving its own ends under the guise of serving God. It "seeks a boost, wants proof, testimonies from within or without, excitement, feelings, miracles, success—all that flatters human pride." The spirituality of the cross, on the other hand, "seeks God and accepts having none of those things; if they are there it refuses to overvalue them or attach significance to them."

The *theologia gloriae* does, of course, hold a legitimate place in Christianity. But when it is allowed to overshadow the cross, then the gospel itself is overshadowed. Triumphalism can preempt the blunt, uncomplicated message of salvation. Certainly God is pleased by a victorious Christian life, but what pleases Him most of all is faith. Faith is the thing that really thrills Him. As C. S. Lewis observed in his droll fashion, "The cross comes before the crown." A believer who is intent on victorious, Spirit-filled living can end up being totally self-absorbed and useless to God. But the one who walks by simple faith will always be close to His heart.

One reason triumphalist teaching falls short of the whole truth is that it is true only for some Christians, some of the time. Clearly God gives to every believer a certain measure of victory, and there are some who so overcome the world that in and through them the Kingdom of God seems to explode into visible, tangible reality. Yet oddly enough, this is not every Christian's lot. Not everyone finds the power to win souls, heal the sick, cast out demons, preach stirring sermons, confound the world with wisdom, or even rise above personal difficulties. Instead it falls to some disciples to spend their entire lives with Christ in the wilderness, or to stay with Him in Gethsemane or on the cross, or perhaps to share His hidden life in Nazareth. Who is going to glorify the infant Jesus, or the adolescent? If the Church is truly to be the Body of Christ on earth, then it must embody *all* of Christ and not just the public and sensational aspects of His ministry.

Not all Christians, in short, are going to be blessed with healthy bodies, well-balanced characters, or obviously fruitful ministries. Many will find themselves entering into eternal life maimed and blind (see Matt. 18:8-9). Such believers may not be conquerors, but they are "more than conquerors" (Rom. 8:37)—that is, they are something better than conquerors, since they hold to their faith in the midst of apparent defeat. To require victorious lives of such saints would be tantamount to demanding that Jesus come down from the cross. For these people have their victory already, and yet it is not the sort of victory we (or even they) expect. It is not victory in any recognizable form, but rather it is a mystery wrought by God, and He will reveal its glory in His own good time.

As we saw in the last chapter, authentic Christian faith can be present even in the total darkness of the womb. Who knows how many saints die, or are murdered, without ever having seen the light of day? Where is the victory in that? No one even knows whether these nameless ones belong to Christ or not. They have never appeared before the church and given their testimony! Their entire ministry consists in the wordless proclamation of the mystery of the Incarnation.

The book of *Job* is a passionate defense of all these helpless ones, all these unborn and stillborn, all these handicapped, all these insane and comatose, all these defeated and victimized children of God. It is a defense of the sick against the well, of the misfit against the well-adjusted, of the incoherent against the articulate, of the utterly powerless against the religiously powerful.

The Dialogue
Breaks Down

"The womb forgets [the wicked],
the worm feasts on them;
evil men are no longer remembered
but are broken like a tree." (24:20)

About halfway through Chapter 24 a strange thing happens to the book of *Job*: it starts coming apart at the seams. In the verse above, for example, we hear Job spouting off about the fate of the wicked in a manner that reminds us suspiciously of the preachy sermonizing of his friends. Most modern commentators, refusing to believe that such words could possibly have been uttered by Job, assign them instead to Bildad or Zophar. But this issue will be dealt with more extensively in connection with Chapter 27, where the problem reoccurs.

For now, notice the other textual irregularities that arise at this point. Beginning at Chapter 25, the formal structure of the book would dictate two more chapter-long rebuttals, one from Bildad and one from Zophar, to complete the third round of the dialogue. But this is not what happens. Instead Zophar has no final speech at all, and Bildad's third speech is cut drastically short. So the formal debate never is finished. At Chapter 26 the dialogue grinds to a halt, and from there until the end of Chapter 31 Job holds forth alone in a long and loose-jointed peroration which, because it has many of the marks of being a patchwork affair, is often rearranged by scholars to make it more artistically satisfying. Finally in this list of textual problems, there is the odd case of Elihu, the brand-new character introduced near the end of the book, who delivers what many readers feel to be the most long-winded, boring, and irrelevant discourse of all.

It would be nice just to gloss over such blemishes, or else to apply to them the scissors-and-paste solution of modern scholarship. But isn't this a bit like trying to grow flowers without dirt? The textual problems of this book are embedded in it like nails in a crucifix. We can pry the nails out and prettify the artwork. But life is not all prettiness, and neither, in the final analysis, is the artistic form of *Job* an entirely pretty thing. The book breaks down, grows ponderous and unwieldy. Like an old man, it has warts and bumps. It is still God's Word, but in the very brokenness of its form it is as if the Lord is saying, "There are things here too weighty to be expressed, too deep to be contained." A mere book—even a book of holy Scripture—cannot finally encompass the whole mystery of suffering and the divine answer to it. The mystery and the answer come through, but in spite of human artistry, not because of it.

One can sense the author wrestling with this paradox even as he writes and edits his masterpiece. Reading between the lines, one can see him working and reworking his material under the powerful influence of the Holy Spirit, trying to get everything God is saying to fit neatly into the original scheme of a formal poetic dialogue. Yet it will not go. The poet cannot get it right. The enormity of the theme overwhelms him. At last he decides to let these middle chapters stand, disorganized though they be. Maybe he can get back to them at a later date and polish them off. But every time he tries, the same thing happens: the book falls apart in his hands. The material itself defeats him. Finally, in desperation, he remembers the young man Elihu and decides to include him as a way of gathering up some up some of the story's loose ends. Yet even this does not work. Not really . . .

And so time passes, and the author of *Job* grows more and more perplexed and disheartened. He grows old and frail. He cannot finish his great book . . .

A fanciful picture? Perhaps. But the point is, this is exactly what happens in the spiritual life when the ground is being prepared for an appearance of the Lord. The fabric of things breaks down; there is a failure of all human resources. But it is out of this very failure that the Lord speaks. Without such total breakdown, do we really think we could have the magnificent conclusion of *Job*?

Perhaps we can picture our poet very late in life, still pondering the big manuscript that sits unfinished in his drawer. Then suddenly one day the heavens open, and in a rush of inspiration there come to him the great divine speeches of Chapters 38—41. Furiously he writes it all down, and after that he lays aside his pen forever. After that, what need is there to go back and fit all his material into a nice tidy scheme? Better to leave it to future generations of clever academics to spend their best years trying to reassemble this Spirit-authored book into a more pleasing shape.

The Best of a Bad Job

*"If even the moon is not bright
and the stars are not pure in his eyes,
how much less man, who is but a maggot." (25:5-6)*

Chapter 25, Bildad's third and final appearance, is only six verses long, and for this reason many scholars feel that the remainder of his speech has either been lost or transposed. But a more likely explanation is simply that Job's friends are running out of steam. They are played out; they have no more fight left in them. It is not that they feel they have lost the debate; rather, what they have lost is all patience with Job. They have given up on Job as a bad job. From now on their only argument will be the argument of silence, of throwing up their hands in disgust. What can you do with a man who is so pig-headed and incorrigible? All of this can be read between the lines of this pitifully brief chapter. "Man is but a maggot," concludes Bildad, and it is a fair summation of the entire message of Job's friends. In passing, we may observe the irony that being maggots themselves has not in the least discouraged Bildad and his colleagues from presuming to pass judgment on their fellow maggot Job. But who are mere maggots to exercise judgment?

In all probability Job actually cuts Bildad off at this point, and with good reason, since the man obviously has nothing new to say. He begins promisingly enough—"Dominion and awe belong to God" (25:2)—but the conclusions he draws from the fact of God's sovereign majesty are exactly opposite to those of Job. To Bildad, the surpassing greatness of God is an argument for the utter insignificance and wretchedness of human beings. But for Job, the very grandeur of God is itself an argument for the grandeur of humans, who are made in their Creator's image.

Job and his friends would have been intimately familiar with the various pagan mythologies of the ancient Near East. In many of these mythologies (the Babylonian, for example), mankind was thought to have been created by the gods because they felt overworked. The gods wanted creatures who would be capable of performing their menial tasks for them, and so the human being was invented as a kind of robot, a slave of the gods. This account of things is dramatically antithetical to the Hebrew and Christian view. Jesus said, "I have come that they may have life, and have it to the full" (John 10:10). The God of the Bible created mankind not to work for Him, but to enjoy fellowship with Him and to share in His abundant life. As far as work goes, what Jesus said about the Sabbath might be equally well applied to work: work was made for man, not man for work. We are not slaves, but children and heirs. We are the children of the Father of Light, made in His image for the express purpose of doing the very work that He Himself does: loving, creating, judging, showing mercy, possessing and administering the universe, and radiating perfect holiness and righteousness forevermore.

This extraordinarily high view of humanity is nowhere evident in the speeches of Job's friends. They do not seem to care about their birthright, any more than Esau cared about his when he sold it to his brother Jacob for a bowl of soup. For this reason the Lord said, "I have loved Jacob, but Esau I have hated" (Mal. 1:2-3). It was not just that Esau lacked faith in God; he lacked faith in himself. By throwing away his birthright he degraded the loftiness of his own destiny, showing a profound disregard for the divine image in himself and therefore in all of mankind. He was like those Jews who, by rejecting the gospel, drew this surprising accusation from Paul: "You do not consider yourselves worthy of eternal life" (Acts 13:46).

It is always the case with unbelievers that their view of humanity is too low. They may be ever so full of humanistic ideals and hubristic fancies, and they may even like to claim that man is a "god." But essentially their view of man comes nowhere near the majesty and mystery of the Christian view, which is not that man is or is becoming a god, but, more amazing still, that God Himself became a man—and not many men at different times, but one single man who was born and died once only, just like everybody else, and so lived by the same excruciating rules as apply to every other child of flesh. No mysticism is more mystical than this. No humanism is more far-reaching than the humanism of God as expressed in Jesus Christ. The good news of the gospel is that faith in God implies faith in humanity. Why? Because there is a human being in the Trinity. In the words of Irenaeus, "The glory of God is man fully alive."

Discernment

*"Who has helped you utter these words?
And whose spirit spoke from your mouth?" (26:4)*

In his very first speech in Chapter 4, Eliphaz told of a mystical experience in which a spirit had imparted to him a message essentially the same as the one Bildad has just delivered in his final, aborted speech in Chapter 25. Just as Eliphaz started the whole argument by posing the wry question, "Can a mortal be more righteous than God?" (4:17), so Bildad now asks, "How then can a man be righteous before God?" (25:4). Like a broken record, the first words and the last words of Job's friends are exactly the same, and all their words in between have been but variations on this one theme.

Now Job directly confronts these men with a delicate but vital question: by whose spirit have you been speaking? Who is it who has been inspiring you? Job's implication is clear: behind the vehement sophistry of his friends lies the calculating intelligence and energy of some alien spirit, some spirit actually antagonistic to righteousness, a spirit other than the Spirit of God. Without any direct, revealed knowledge of personal evil, Job nevertheless smells a rat.

This is a most serious charge, and yet it is one that the entire book begs us to consider. As the discussion between Job and his friends has dragged on and on, far from reaching any point of agreement the result has been an increasing polarization. With each succeeding chapter the two sides have grown farther and farther apart. Since "God is not a God of disorder but of peace" (1 Cor. 14:33), we cannot help but wonder what is going on when believers gather together and cannot agree, and when no amount of talking can bring resolution or harmony. Under such circumstances, can we say that the Holy Spirit is present in one party but not in the other? Or do we conclude that He is absent altogether? Or is it possible that a spirit of evil is stirring up strife?

Such questions cry out for answers. Yet clear answers in this area are not always to be had, and meanwhile there are choices to be made and steps to be taken. Life never stands still for long. Every

moment presses for decisions, large and small, and to avoid deciding is itself a decision. Indecisiveness is an adopted stance. How
much easier it would seem if the Lord could simply tell us, plainly
and directly, exactly what to think and what to do in every situation. For some people, some of the time, He would seem to do just
that. But most of us encounter a good deal of fog in our spiritual
discernment, and while we might like to think of ourselves as always
flying with the Holy Spirit as our pilot, in practical terms don't we
fly a good deal by the seat of our pants? Often only later (if at all)
does the Lord show us exactly where our judgments were right and
where they were wrong.

For some reason, this element of uncertainty in spiritual matters
is vastly important to the Lord. If it were not, then He would clear
up all questions for us right now, and the practice of discernment
would be an obsolete art. Colored lights would go on in people's
souls so that we could tell instantly who is born again and who is
not, who speaks by the Holy Spirit and who does not. We would
know for certain when fellow Christians were being misled by some
outside spiritual influence, or when the strangers on our doorstep
were really angels. We would see, as Jesus did, just how it happens
that "the last shall be first and the first last," for when some little
old widow puts two cents in the church collection plate, the sound
of it would reverberate like thunder in our ears.

Yet by and large we do not see such things with any great clarity.
The discernment of spirits is a gift, and it is a gift that must be slowly
developed, severely tested, and refined like precious metal. The very
nature of this gift is such that it must be tried under the most arduous and bewildering of circumstances, and exercised at tremendous
personal risk. Indeed to risk making the sort of judgment that Job
makes concerning the counsel of his friends is to risk everything. It
is like that first great risk we ever took as believers, the risk of throwing ourselves into the arms of a God whom we could not see. Ever
since then, as baffling and painful as the work of discernment can
be, it is work that is immensely pleasing to our Lord, as we learn
again and again under every conceivable circumstance to recognize
His unique voice, and to pick out, as if from a crowd, the lovely, elusive presence of the one Spirit in all the universe who truly knows
and loves us.

Abaddon Uncovered

"Death is naked before God;
Destruction lies uncovered." (26:6)

Wherever Satan is, there is confusion, and for that very reason his presence can be difficult to discern. His ways are bewilderingly complex and, like bacteria, capable of endless mutation. His strategies keep pace with our level of cultural sophistication, on the one hand, and with our spiritual maturity on the other. Those who are very worldly will be tempted with worldly ways and things, while those who are spiritual will be spiritually tempted. Jesus, as we know, was tempted "in every way, just as we are" (Heb. 4:15). But has it ever occurred to us that for Him, just as for us, temptation consisted in the experience of confusion in the presence of Satan? For that is what temptation is (at least in its more advanced stages): it is a sense of uncertainty as to whether the spirit that is tugging at our hearts is a good spirit or a bad spirit. Should we give in to this influence, or resist it? That is the big question posed by temptation. This is why James is careful to note that God "*does not* tempt anyone" (1:13), for the Lord does not speak with the voice of confusion but rather with the voice of clarity and peace. "The wisdom that comes from heaven," James goes on to say, "is first of all pure" (3:17). When the Holy Spirit has His way, either with an individual or a group, there is no admixture of confusion. When confusion is present, we may take it for granted that Satan's influence is also present.

Simply knowing this, however, is not enough to overcome temptation. To overcome the enemy we must first penetrate the nature of his deception, and then find a way of answering him. We must expose the lie by countering it with the truth. It is significant that in the temptation of Christ it was not until the third and final test that the Lord actually called His adversary by name: "Away from me, Satan!" (Matt. 4:10). Is it possible that Jesus, up to this point, had not yet positively identified Satan, and that the whole reason for the struggle was that the Lord had to be absolutely certain that this powerful influence He was under was not that of His Father? After all, these were no ordinary temptations. These were not allurements to drinking and smoking and illicit sex. Rather, the prospects that Satan dangled in front of Christ were all things that might possibly be within God's will: the working of miracles, reckless abandonment to faith, and the exercise of political influence. Later on in His ministry, Jesus did in fact prove Himself in all these areas. But He did so in humble obedience to His Father's voice and timing, and not at the instigation of the Devil. This was the very point at issue in the wilderness temptations, and it seems that only after this crisis, in which the voice of Satan was once and for all distinguished from the voice of God, could Jesus begin His ministry in earnest.

Is it not the same for us? When we first begin as Christians, we are almost as much in the dark about Satan as Job was. Unlike Job, we do know Satan's name, and we know some facts about him. But we have not learned to recognize his voice and all his ways, nor have we acquired the boldness to address him by name and say, "Get away from me, Satan!" Even if we do say this, we find that he tends not to obey us. He still has his foot in the door of our lives, and he is not about to leave without a fight. He knows we are confused about who he is, and that very confusion is the secret of his power over us. He knows we are still afraid that he might be God. We are still afraid that this dark shadow that hangs over our lives is the shadow of God, and that this spirit of fear that controls us must be the Spirit of God, and so we are afraid to tell this shadow and this spirit to go away. Only as we grow in confidence that the Holy Spirit has nothing to do with fear and darkness but is a Spirit of perfect love and light and peace—only then can we begin to unmask Satan and to put our hands on the weapons of authority over him.

This is the struggle in which Job is engaged, and he shows the progress he is making when he declares, "Death is naked before God; Destruction lies uncovered." In Hebrew the word translated "Destruction" is actually a proper name. It is the name "Abaddon," the name that the book of *Revelation* attaches to "the angel of the Abyss" (9:11). Job is beginning to come to terms with the fact that, both in his own trials and in the arguments of his friends, he has been dealing with some other spirit than the Spirit of God. He is beginning to unmask Satan, and as he does so his declaration of faith, in this chapter and in the next, rises to a soaring climax.

The Fringe of
His Garment

"He spreads out the northern skies over empty space;
he suspends the earth over nothing. . . .
And these are but the outer fringe of his works;
how faint the whisper we hear of him!
Who then can understand the thunder of his power?"
(26:7, 14)

In this chapter Job momentarily pierces through the veil of his suffering to sing a sublime hymn to the power of God in creation. After touching on the beauty and mystery of such elemental phenomena as clouds, moon, light, darkness, sea, and sky, he sums up everything with the wonderful verse quoted above. This speech is one of the finest passages in the book, bearing comparison with the grandeur of God's own words at the end. Does Job upstage God, then? In a sense he does. Job anticipates much of what the Lord will finally say to him, just as any believer, however dull or slow of faith, may have grand moments of being caught up in visions of glory.

Do we wonder at the volatility of Job's moods—the way time and again he rises to great heights of inspired faith, only to sink down to the depths once more? But isn't this just what it is like to be in a storm? Trials come in billows, wave upon wave. From the crest of the waves one sees things one never saw before. And between the waves there are troughs, interludes of strange peace. There are lulls and respites in the midst of the fray. There is the unearthly tranquillity in the eye of the storm, where all at once one remembers things one never knew.

What is it Job suddenly remembers here? To this day orthodox Jews wear tassels on the corners of their garments as a conspicuous reminder of their devotion to the Lord (see Num. 15:38). In a similar vein, Job now suggests that all the marvels of creation are but a fringe on the robe of God, a visible and ever-present sign to people of the reality of the Lord. How great this God must be, if the enormous suspended globe of the earth is no more than a bauble on a bracelet around His wrist! He puts on the dawn the way a man puts on an old pair of pants to mow the lawn. The seven seas are but seven coins in His wallet—so much loose change. This is the message Job reads in the world's wonders: the grander they are, the higher their Creator towers above them.

In the New Testament sick people "begged [Jesus] to let them touch even the edge of his cloak, and all who touched him were healed" (Mark 6:56). It was not necessary to have a long series of private counseling sessions with Jesus; it was only necessary to touch the hem of His robe. In Job's case, he did not have the incarnate Christ to touch, but he did have the universe, "created by him and for him" (Col. 1:16), which is the fringe of Christ's royal garment. To this fringe Job latches on as to a healing hand. In the midst of all his confusion, just to touch the bright wonders of nature was to touch something solid and real. If he could not see God or any other evidence of Him, then at least he could see the tassels of His robe. In the same way, the Lord showed Jeremiah the branch of an almond tree as evidence that He was "watching to see that my word is fulfilled" (Jer. 1:12). A tree branch might not seem like much. But for the true believer, all of nature is an omnipresent witness to the power and justice of God. When a child is abused or a saint martyred, the sky and the trees and the very ground stand watch. "Listen!" cried the Lord to Cain after the murder of Abel; "your brother's blood cries out to me from the ground" (Gen. 4:10).

Throughout the Bible the things of nature are immensely significant as living signs of our Creator's glory. Yet more than that, they are signs of the inestimable worth of His highest creatures, human beings. Just to look into the eyes of the most miserable and repulsive person on earth is to be closer to God, in truth, than when gazing at a flowery meadow or a starry sky. Stars are finite things, but a human being goes on forever. A flower can develop only so much and be only so beautiful, but for people there are no such limits. In his *Divine Comedy* Dante wrote, "The more a thing is perfect, the more it feels of pleasure and of pain." How much pain does a sunset feel, or what pleasure does it take in its own beauty? The wonders of creation that Job praises in Chapter 26 are magnificent, but greater by far is the human eye that admires them, and especially the one that does so even in the midst of profound suffering.

Saint Job and
the Dragon

"By his power he quelled Yam;
by his wisdom he cut Rahab to pieces." (26:12)

The pages of *Job* are filled with references to pagan deities and mythological events. Already we have seen how the word "Destruction" in 26:6 is literally "Abaddon"—at that time probably the name of a pagan god of the underworld. In verse 7 the word translated "the northern skies" is "Sapon" (or "Zaphon," as in Isaiah 14:13), which was the primeval world-mountain of Canaanite creation stories. In the verse quoted above, "Yam" is the Canaanite god of the sea, while "Rahab" is the female monster of chaos, closely associated with "the gliding serpent" of verse 13. In other passages we meet figures such as "Tannin" ("the monster of the deep" in 7:12), "death's firstborn" (18:13), and "the king of terrors" (18:14), "Tehom" ("the deep" in 28:14) and many others.

This web of pagan imagery provides *Job* with a rich vocabulary, but it also lends a dark, churning, and somewhat disturbing undercurrent to the story. Unfortunately, very little of this mythological foundation survives in translation. The pagan references tend to be watered down by interpreters. Consider, for example, the oft-quoted verse, "Man is born to trouble as surely as sparks fly upward" (5:7). Rendered literally this would become, "Man is born to trouble as surely as the sons of Resheph spring up." Again, in 3:9 the expression "the first rays of dawn" should properly read, "the eyelashes of Shahar." In the complex process of translation, a great wealth of poetic and cultural resonance is entirely lost.

Yet what, we may ask, is all this steamy polytheistic language doing in a book solidly founded on moral monotheism? Scholars, comparing the pagan backdrop of *Job* with the classical Greek and Roman imagery in literary works such as *Paradise Lost*, have tended to dismiss the practice as mere poetic convention. But this may be missing the point. The writer of *Job*, unlike Milton, was not borrowing material from an ancient classical age. More likely he was reflecting the popular legends of his own time and culture. Job's contemporaries really believed in these things, and Job, his pure devotion to the Lord notwithstanding, could not help but be a part of his culture. Perhaps he had even been born into a pagan family. Did he, then, believe in the myths too? In a sense, he must have. Missionaries to primitive peoples will know that even after a strong conversion experience, converts may still retain, like a palimpsest, the outlines of their old religious heritage beneath their newfound beliefs. It is not that they have not given themselves to the Lord. But an ancient mythology, even though it may be full of lies, can still have a grasp on certain truths that may be lacking in all but the most profound Christian theology.

The conventional theology of Job's day, remember, was simply not equipped to handle the realm of experience through which this man was passing. That is the whole point of the book and of Job's struggles. Job knew instinctively that there were cosmic forces of darkness swirling all around him, but among the worshipers of Yahweh there was as yet no sophisticated demonology for explaining such things. In all probability Job resorted to the only material he had at hand, the pagan mythologies, as a way of giving expression to the chaos and darkness in which he felt entangled. As Christian readers we can now look back at these speeches and see many veiled references to " the rulers . . . the authorities . . . the powers of this dark world . . . the spiritual forces of evil in the heavenly realms" (Eph. 6:12).

As it turns out, in employing the vocabulary of pagan religion Job was in good company, for the Lord Himself does exactly the same in Chapter 41, where He devotes a full thirty-four verses of His final speech to a description of the monster He names "Leviathan." In ancient Near Eastern literature Leviathan was the serpent who represented chaos, confusion, darkness. Job, like Jonah after him, having been swallowed by the whale, is in the end brought out by the Lord, who then paints for him a hair-raising portrait of his demonic enemy in terms that make it sound like some medieval fire-breathing dragon (see 41:19-20). Do we find it strange that the God of the Bible should get Himself mixed up in primitive mythology? But does not even the New Testament speak of "an enormous red dragon with seven heads" (Rev. 12:3)? Myth or metaphor, the Bible has its monsters, and every believer must become a Saint George.

The Absence of God

"As surely as God lives, who has denied me justice. . . ."
(27:2)

As surely as the Lord lives" is the most common oath in the Old Testament, found on the lips of the godly and the ungodly alike. (See, for example, Saul's profane use of it in 1 Samuel 19:6.) Yet nowhere, perhaps, is the use of this idiom more striking than it is in the mouth of Job. "As surely as God lives," he says, and in the very next breath, "who has denied me justice. . . ." The juxtaposition is jarringly ironic. Even as Job confesses his faith in the living God, he matter-of-factly accuses this God of deserting him, of leaving him in the lurch. It is as if God, though alive, might as well be dead. Nevertheless Job appeals to this silent, absent God as one whose living reality remains absolutely beyond question, one whose existence is more certain than his own. Job does not say, "as I live," but "as God lives," even though this God has hidden His face and denied him justice.

This is faith. Faith is the ability to tolerate the intolerable paradox of God's clear and undisputed title as Lord of the universe in spite of His apparent absence. Some might prefer to see faith as an awareness of God's presence, the discerning of His hand at work in our lives. But what of all the times when we cannot see any hand at all? Sometimes the Lord touches us directly. But often He works through secondary agents—through other people, through created things, through life experiences both good and bad—and in such cases we may not be aware of His involvement until long afterwards, if at all. This is when pure faith is called for, faith reduced to simplest terms. "When you cannot practice the presence of God," wrote C. S. Lewis, "then it is something to practice the absence of God." Fallen humanity has invented many techniques for practicing (or pretending to practice) the presence of God. But the unregenerate mind cannot practice God's absence. If it could, then it would plumb the mystery of the cross and be reborn.

Job is right: believers in God are people who have been denied justice. We are the sons and daughters of the Most High; we are priestly princes and princesses in the Kingdom of Heaven. So what are we doing down here on our hands and knees, struggling along in the muck and the mire of earth? The author of Hebrews answers this way: "At present we do not see everything subject to [man]. But we see Jesus . . . now crowned with glory and honor because he suffered death" (2:8-9). In other words, we may not feel like royalty now; our present circumstances may not make us look very masterful; but we know that Jesus went through everything we are going through, including death—and look where He is now! Therefore we live by faith, not by sight. By faith we "see Jesus." By faith we have even now been "raised up with Christ and seated with him in the heavenly realms" (Eph. 2:6).

Yes, Job has been denied justice; this is the whole point of the story. Yet God's denial of justice is the very circumstance that allows for the exercise of faith, and this faith is what defeats the Devil. With a snap of His fingers the Lord could cast the Devil into the lake of fire right now and be done with him. But it is not enough for God to defeat the Devil; He wants us to defeat him too, to slay him with a word. Our Father wants His children to share His knowledge about the running of the universe. He wants to be able to entrust absolutely everything to us and know that it is in safe hands. Imagine—the Lord Almighty wants to lift us up to His own level so that we can share His wisdom and power and glory! Therefore, if He absents Himself from our world now, it is only so we can begin to fill His shoes. If He withholds justice now, it is in the interests of nurturing faith—the kind of faith that will be able not only to move mountains—who knows!—but to build whole new worlds.

With the possibility of such monumental tasks ahead, it will be good for us to have had some hands-on experience in overcoming the Devil and all his works. Our discipleship is a practicum. We learn who God is not merely through contemplation of Him, but by actually doing what He has done.

Integrity

"I will never admit you are in the right;
till I die, I will not deny my integrity." (27:5)

This is now the fourth appearance in the book of a word that with each use has accumulated new layers of significance: "integrity." The first instance of the word was in the Prologue, where the Lord testified to Satan that Job "still maintains his integrity, though you incited me against him to ruin him without any reason" (2:3). Just a few verses later comes the infamous pout of Job's wife, "Are you still holding on to your integrity? Curse God and die!" (2:9). Then in 6:29 Job pleads with his friends, "Relent, do not be unjust; reconsider, for my integrity is at stake." Note how the word comes to take on a meaning nearly synonymous with "righteousness." In fact, an alternate translation of 6:29 reads, "Reconsider, for my righteousness still stands." Finally in 27:5-6 Job speaks these two words in the same breath: "I will not deny my integrity. I will maintain my righteousness."

In contemporary terms it might seem dangerous to equate integrity with righteousness. *Integrity* is a secular word that carries about as much weight as *sincerity*. And of course one can be sincerely wrong. However, a more fundamental meaning of integrity is "wholeness," and this connotation of the word might help to explain its link with righteousness. An "integer" is a whole number; an "integral" element is something essential for wholeness; and to "integrate" means to make whole or complete by bringing together parts. Thus when Job defends his integrity, we might say that he is really arguing for the wholeness or oneness of his righteous soul.

Job sees righteousness as something indivisible, all of a piece, and for that reason it is unassailable. All along Job's friends have cast suspicion upon the soundness of Job's righteous armor, trying to find some chink in it and so bring division into his spirit. But the righteousness of a believer is a living thing; it can no more be divided or called into question than a baby can be cut in two. To be born again is to be born whole, all at once, not piece by piece. The cord to the old life has been cut, and a brand-new person complete with a new heart, a new mind and emotions, and a new body has been born into the Kingdom of God. In such a glorious Kingdom one cannot have one foot in and one foot out. But since the children of God do not appear in any worldly sense to become perfect overnight, there can be a tendency for us to assume (or at least to act as if) we are only partly cleansed, or even partly saved. This is heresy. A believer is a new creation, wholly forgiven, wholly righteous, wholly holy.

This is strange, fantastic, revolutionary teaching. But it is the gospel, and Job knows it, and therefore he insists that his good standing with God, despite all appearances to the contrary, is simply not a debatable point. Obviously this gospel of integrity is open to abuse. There are those who sincerely and adamantly believe they are righteous Christians, who are fooling themselves. And there are those who seek comfort in the idea that their sufferings are unjust, when the truth is that they have brought misery upon themselves through foolishness, unbelief, and refusal to repent. Certainly one of the reasons the gospel is hindered is that so many cling to it unrighteously. As Paul wrote, "God's name is *being* blasphemed . . . because of you" (Rom. 2:24).

Nevertheless, when righteousness is the real thing, is it not something to be clung to with a fierce and holy tenacity? "Till I die," Job maintains, "I will not deny my integrity," and this is the position that every believer under attack must assume. We must come to the place where we know that to doubt our own spiritual integrity is to doubt the integrity (that is, the wholehearted goodwill and faithfulness) of God Himself, and that to allow the slightest aspersion to be cast upon our own righteous standing would be to call God a liar. In the words of David, "May integrity and uprightness protect me, because my hope is in you" (Ps. 25:21). When God saved us He took our broken soul and mended it, restored it, put it back together into one integral whole—and "what God has joined together, *let no one pull apart*" (Mark 10:9).

Never Let Go

"I will maintain my righteousness and
never let go of it." (27:6a)

T he *Epistle to the Hebrews*, in an arresting picture of the
tenacity of faith, describes believers as those "who have fled
to take hold of the hope offered to us" (6:18). The image is
borrowed from the Old Testament, where a treasonous fugitive
could plead for mercy by fleeing into the temple sanctuary, "taking
hold of the horns of the altar" (see I Kings 1:50-53). This is the
stance Job adopts when he vows to "maintain my righteousness and
never let go of it."

The New Testament epistles, significantly, were not written to the
unconverted. Rather they were written to Christians who, in many
cases, were in grave danger of letting go of what they had believed.
These were people who for one reason or another seemed to be on
the verge of tossing the gospel aside and following something new.
Hence Paul warned the Galatians against "turning to a different
gospel, which is really no gospel at all" (1:6-7), and in exasperation
he told them, "I am again in the pains of childbirth until Christ is
formed in you" (4:19). Similarly the author of *Hebrews* advised his
readers, "We must pay more careful attention to what we have
heard, so that we do not drift away" (2:1).

Having once accepted the gospel, it seems, is no guarantee against
rejecting it. The New Testament certainly allows for this possibility.
The gospel is so simple, so homely, so unlikely a thing, that it can
be very easy to let it slip through our fingers, if not by dismissing it
outright, then by gradually and carelessly reverting to the ways of
the world. The problem is perhaps best expressed by Paul's searing
rebuke to the "foolish Galatians": "After beginning with the Spirit,
are you now trying to attain your goal by human effort?" (3:3). Or
as John warned, "Watch out that you do not lose what you have
worked for. . . . Anyone who runs ahead and does not continue in
the teaching of Christ does not have God; whoever continues in the
teaching has both the Father and the Son" (2 John 8-9). In the very
nature of the case the good news of Christ is not something we learn

once and for all and then move on to higher things. No, we never graduate from the lowly prayer of the publican: "God, have mercy on me, a sinner" (Luke 18:13).

Far from developing into spiritual experts, then, believers often find themselves in the position of having to fight for dear life just to recall the basics of their faith. As Jude wrote, we must "contend for the faith that was once for all entrusted to the saints" (v. 3). Martin Luther, so the story goes, once threw his inkbottle at the Devil—and there is a sense in which he continued to throw ink at the Devil all his life! For him, obviously, holding on to the gospel involved a daily struggle. So too with the Apostle Paul, who would not have written as urgently and furiously as he did if the gospel were an easy thing to cling to and if the case supporting it were perfectly obvious. Essentially the way of salvation, when we do see it, really is quite clear—just as plain as the nose on our face. Even so, we have a constant tendency to lose sight of it, just as we might misplace our eyeglasses and then cannot see to find them. Particularly during seasons of suffering and of fierce temptation, the simple and shining facts of our faith can grow very dim. Even to the most mature of believers the message can seem just as elusive as it was for Job. It is almost as though the Christian under attack no longer knows the good news of God's love and forgiveness and His gift of eternal life, but only senses obscurely that such things must be so. Difficult circumstances can give one the feeling of being thrown back into a pre-gospel world, a world that does not yet know the Savior but that, like Job, only dimly intuits Him.

At such times we do not see the gospel so much as smell it. That is why in our faith we must continually go back to first principles, back to square one. To quote *Hebrews* again, "We have come to share in Christ if we hold firmly till the end the confidence we had at first" (3:14). The faith we are to cultivate is the same faith we had when we first were saved, when our life lay in pieces at the feet of Jesus and He became its meaning. Considered objectively, the event of salvation is not one that ever needs to be repeated in the life of a believer, but it does need to be rehearsed, re-experienced, reenacted. Ideally the earth-shattering liberation of the gospel is something we should experience afresh every day. For each new day has its share of evil, quite enough to swamp the soul of any saint.

Conscience

"My conscience will not reproach me
as long as I live." (27:6b)

As frequently happens in Hebrew poetry, the second half of this verse is an expansion of the first. First Job says, "I will maintain my righteousness and never let go of it," and in the next breath he explains more precisely what he means: "My conscience will not reproach me as long as I live." Similarly Paul urges us to "fight the good fight, holding on to faith and a good conscience" (1 Tim. 1:18-19), and so draws a virtual equation between faith in Christ and the maintenance of a clean conscience. Peter does the same when he describes the essence of saving faith as "the pledge of a good conscience toward God" (1 Peter 3:21).

Why is the relationship between faith and conscience so crucial? Chuck Swindoll puts it this way: "What is the difference between an Indian Hindu who crawls for miles on his belly along a dusty road to expiate his sins, and a North American Christian who busies himself in a continual round of activity in an effort to salve his conscience and please God? None whatsoever." This theme is explored in depth in the *Epistle to the Hebrews*. First the author rips the rug out from under religious ritualism by telling us what ought to be obvious: all the most elaborate rites and sacrifices in the world are "not able to clear the conscience of the worshiper" (9:9). Then he exhorts us to enter into fellowship with God "by a new and living way, the blood of Jesus . . . having our hearts sprinkled to cleanse us from a guilty conscience" (10:19-22). Finally, since at the time of writing this letter the author himself seems to have been laboring under some false accusation, he ends by testifying personally, "We are sure that we have a clear conscience and desire to live honorably in every way" (13:18).

In this latter quote the word "desire" is significant, for in the maintenance of a clear conscience it is not so much the quality of one's outer life or even of one's thought-life that is the determining factor, but rather the intent of the heart. A clean conscience is not one that is without guilt, but one that is without blame. In an honest and healthy conscience there is always a sense of guilt, but blame is continually being washed away by the blood of Christ. As Richard Sibbes explained, "The blood of Christ in the conscience cries louder than the guilt of sin." So a clean conscience is not an empty conscience, but one that is active, always taking stock. In Job's case it is not that his conscience never threatens to reproach him; it does, continually. When a believer employs his clean conscience to take a good look at himself with the objective, righteous eyes of God, what else can he do but condemn himself? What else can he see but his total depravity and ungodliness? Hence he is in a predicament from which only faith can rescue him. Only faith can lay hold of sufficient grace to keep a conscience clear. Faith is precisely the activity of holding fast to the mercy of God even while condemning oneself to death.

Paul Evdokimov gives a peculiar glimpse into the mind of a mature disciple when he writes, "One part of us, being immersed in what is immediate, is always worried and distracted, while the other part observes this with astonishment and compassion." The capacity to draw back and observe oneself with wondrous compassion is the gift of a clean conscience. In fallen humanity this faculty has been critically impaired, so that strictly speaking people cannot really step apart from themselves at all, either in compassion or condemnation. Their consciences have been seared, and so they are literally trapped inside themselves. As Frederick Buechner writes, "Introspection in the long run does not get you very far because every time you draw back to look at yourself, you are seeing everything except for the part that drew back, and when you draw back to look at the part that drew back to look at yourself, you see again everything except what you are really looking for."

The only way out of this trap is faith. If we think of the conscience as being like a window in the soul, then one side of this window opens into the human heart, while the other side opens into Heaven. A person can polish and polish the window from his own side, the inside, and yet until it is cleaned from the Godward side too, it is not really clean. The only way to clean the window of the conscience both inside and out is with the blood of Jesus Christ. Only faith in Christ's atonement can cleanse and restore the human conscience so that it can be the shining window of the soul that it was meant to be.

The Power of God

"I will teach you about the power of God;
the ways of the Almighty I will not conceal." (27:11)

The thing that is so continually astonishing about Job—and this is nowhere more evident than in these first impassioned verses of Chapter 27—is how brazenly confident he can be in the very midst of his anguish. Who does this fellow think he is, covered with boils and sitting on an ash heap, that he can announce so boldly, "Now I will show you the power of God"? It is difficult to imagine a more unlikely situation from which a man might make such a claim . . . unless it would be hanging from a cross.

What is the power of God? It could hardly be plainer than Paul makes it in 1 Corinthians 1:18: "The message of the cross is foolishness to those who are perishing, but to us who are being saved it is the power of God." Or in Romans 1:16: "I am not ashamed of the gospel, because it is the power of God." To Paul "the gospel," "the message of the cross," and "the power of God" were all one and the same reality.

Reading through the New Testament, it is startling to realize how much of this writing is pointedly directed against perversions of the one true gospel. While it is gloriously true that "there is now no condemnation for those who are in Christ Jesus" (Rom. 8:1), it is also true that resounding condemnation is leveled against Pharisees and legalists, against false teachers and false apostles, against those who chronically cause division in the Body of Christ, against anyone who tries to add anything to the gospel, against those who deny the resurrection and other fundamental doctrines, and against all those who are arrogant or self-seeking in spiritual matters. The New Testament does not simply defend the truth, it angrily attacks lies. And Scripture makes it perfectly clear that half-truths can be the most damaging lies of all, since they steal from the truth in order to cloak themselves in legitimacy. Is anything more sinful than the preaching of a gospel with a little twist in it? Jesus and His apostles wasted surprisingly little breath in attacking pagan idolatry; but they went to great lengths to expose and denounce the sort of idols that imitated Christ Himself.

Job's faith, like theirs, was of the sort that rose to such challenges, that shone more brightly in darkness, that grew keener in the face of controversy. As Job disputes with his friends we are reminded of the way Paul argued against the Judaizers in Galatia, or against the spiritualizing Gnostics at Colosse, or against the "super apostles" who had been influencing the church of Corinth. For Job too, what was on the line in these dozens of chapters of long, drawn-out debate was the very essence of the gospel: "the power of God" in "the message of the cross." Though he had never even heard the words *gospel* or *cross*, he certainly knew of some good news worth fighting for. He knew that in all the world there was not enough pain or darkness or sin to disqualify the faithful from receiving the salvation of God.

With so many false and distorted gospels afoot in the world, it becomes essential to have one single, simple test to which any body of doctrine can be submitted, so as to verify whether the power of God be in it or not. That one test is the cross of Christ. Teresa of Avila issued a warning to those believers who "had made a beginning and never succeeded in reaching the end. It is, I believe, mainly due to their not having embraced the cross from the first." How important it is for the church to make certain it has a cross-centered gospel, stripped of all nonessentials. In pleasant circumstances a twisted or a padded gospel can be a fine thing. But when you are reduced to a miserable, sniveling wreck as Job was, and when all your friends turn against you, and when the Devil appears to you as an angel of light or backs you up trembling against the yawning brink of his bottomless pit, then it will mean absolutely nothing whether you are a pre-millennialist or a post-millennialist, whether you have been baptized by sprinkling or by immersion, or whether you can speak in tongues, heal the sick, or even turn stones into bread. All that will matter is that you have such a firm grip on the power of God that you can declare with Paul, "Even if we or an angel from heaven should preach a gospel other than the one we preached to you, let him be eternally condemned!" (Gal. 1:8).

Outlaw

"There is a mine for silver
and a place where gold is refined." (28:1)

In Chapter 28 Job launches into a long poem on the mystery of wisdom in which he meditates on the traditional question, "Where can wisdom be found?" (28:12). Even if people were willing to seek it (and most are not), where could they begin? There is a mine for gold, but where is wisdom hidden?

Biblical scholars are almost universally agreed that this poem on wisdom does not seem to "belong" here. It is a perfectly composed, self-contained unit, and its even tone and classical style are a marked departure from the blistering unorthodoxy of Job's other speeches. The feeling among some commentators, therefore, is that this chapter was probably interpolated into the text, either by the author at a later date, or by a subsequent editor.

Despite the best-educated guesses of the scholars, however, one question remains: why should it surprise us if Job, having exhausted all other avenues of protest and inquiry, should all at once slip quietly into a more reflective mood and begin meditating on the source of wisdom? Why shouldn't Job grow strangely becalmed here for a time and contemplate his problems from a more traditional perspective? After all, the glory of this man is that he is a human being through and through, and so by definition he is a walking bundle of contradictions. "Do I contradict myself?" Walt Whitman rhapsodized. "Very well then, I contradict myself." Why should Job not behave erratically? What is to keep him (or any of us) from stepping out of character once in a while? This man is mercurial, unpredictable, enigmatic in the extreme, and by being so he stretches our definitions of what it means to be human. Who has the right to meddle with such a character and declare that he could never have behaved thus and so, or that such and such an idea could not possibly have entered his mind or been found on his lips?

In this great book there are two great profundities, God and man, and both of them are passionately unconventional in their ways. *Job* celebrates not only the mystery of God but the mystery of a humanity that explodes all bounds, of a righteousness that escapes neat definitions, of a freedom of expression that flouts all civilized restraints. Here is a man made in the image of God, a man who, under God, does whatever he pleases. Here is someone who, simply because he is righteous, is "free indeed" (John 8:36). Who therefore is going to judge this man and tell him what he can and cannot say? He is beyond judgment; he is beyond scholarly criticism; he is beyond the law. He is an outlaw. In the words of Paul, "The spiritual man makes judgments about all things, but he himself is not subject to any man's judgment" (1 Cor. 2:15).

This same reasoning applies to the latter half of Chapter 27, where Job delivers a lecture on the woes of the wicked that sounds very much like one of the sermons of his friends. Here, too, textual critics like to claim that this speech could not possibly be Job's, and many take the liberty of moving the passage elsewhere. Yet again the question arises, Who is to say that Job should not, at this point, carefully review all the stock arguments of his friends concerning the fate of the wicked, and actually voice these arguments aloud as if they were his own? Job knows that living freely does not mean having a free ride with God. He knows the God of wrath and punishment as well as his friends do. If Job now wants to restate this conventional wisdom to show his intimate understanding of it, then what is that to the scholars? This might not make perfect artistic sense, but does it not make another, higher kind of sense? Isn't it exactly the sort of thing that could happen, at a certain juncture, in a real debate between real people?

Reality, not art, is finally what the Bible is all about. Granted, much of Scripture is artistically beautiful; but much of it is not. In the end the very artistic fabric of *Job* breaks down, falls to pieces, as if mere art, mere literature, with all its unwritten laws of proportion and propriety, finally cannot contain the message of this book. When academics try to resolve this dilemma by tampering with the Scriptural text, then the historical Job, Job the real human being, disappears beneath a sludge of airbrushed aestheticism. "What is highly valued among men," warned Jesus, "is detestable in God's sight" (Luke 16:15). Beside the colossal reality of this man Job and of his God, beautiful art is but a toy, just one more man-made idol.

Thy Will Be Done

"Man puts an end to the darkness;
he searches the farthest recesses
for ore in the blackest gloom." (28:3)

Job begins his meditation on wisdom with a fascinating account of ancient mining techniques, which he describes with such haunting poetic power as to make this one of the most memorable passages in the book. "Far from where people dwell [the miner] cuts a shaft . . . far from men he dangles and sways. . . . No bird of prey knows that hidden path, no falcon's eye has seen it. . . . Man's hand assaults the flinty rock and lays bare the roots of the mountains" (vv. 4, 7, 9). Ancient mining was a strange, lonely, dangerous occupation, involving enormous sacrifice and expenditure of energy. As the chapter progresses, we see that an ironic point is being developed: people go to such extraordinary lengths in order to dig gold and jewels out of the earth, and yet they will not walk across the street to acquire the infinitely more valuable commodity of wisdom.

Why not? Why don't people prize and pursue the pearl of wisdom above everything else? The reason is that the gaining of wisdom requires the total sacrifice of our single most precious possession: ourselves. More specifically, what is required is the surrender of our wills. To gain wisdom we must part with the very thing which, to part with, means our annihilation. And we must do this not fatalistically, not in grim resignation, but with the joyful abandonment of faith.

It is no good praying, "Thy will be done" if all we mean by it is, "Lord, I know You are going to go ahead and do whatever You want anyway, whether I like it or not." No; if the Lord's will is really going to be done on earth, let us add our approval to it. For our approval is, in a sense, the essential missing ingredient, the one thing that is lacking to make the Lord's will complete. "The Spirit and the bride say, 'Come!'" (Rev. 22:17). But what if the Spirit says yes while the bride says no? Not that He needs us at all, strictly speaking. But what is the use of God getting His way if we do not love and worship Him for it? Does He not want our blessing as much as we want His? When the Lord finished His creation He said, "It is good." But then man looked it over and said, "No, there is a flaw in it," when really the only flaw was the withholding of human approval. The refusal of our blessing is the main obstacle to the Lord's will being done upon the earth.

Coal miners used to take a canary down into the shaft where they were working. If for any reason the underground air became poisoned or dangerously thin, the canary would be the first to be affected by the change, thus warning the miners to get out. In the cold, dark mine shaft of many a professed believer's will, the canary has stopped singing. Yet people go on working, sweating, tunneling in the darkness, slaving to acquire wisdom without submitting to the Lord in wholehearted obedience. To many of the Jews who had supposedly "believed him," Jesus made it clear that they were still "slaves to sin" who needed to be "set free" by the truth: "If you hold to my teaching, you are really my disciples. Then you will know the truth, and the truth will set you free" (John 8:31-32). Mere belief is not enough. In the Bible, the knowledge of the truth comes by freely doing the will of God.

So there is nothing to be gained from accepting the Lord's will grudgingly. Rather we must thirst for it, we must ache for it, we must cherish it above all things. Without God's will we would not be able to take our next breath. That is how fundamental His will is to our lives. It is more important than food, which is why in the Lord's Prayer the sentence "Thy will be done" precedes "Give us this day our daily bread." If we do not do the Lord's will, we starve. If we do not obey Him willingly and cheerfully and with all our hearts, if we do not "run in the path of [His] commands" (Ps. 119:32), then we die. Therefore we must be prepared to lay down our lives for the sake of God's will. We must die for the will of God as readily as we would die for our own freedom. For truly, God's will *is* our freedom. Our freedom is His great desire. God's will on earth is nothing more or less than that human beings be set free.

Was this not the essence of Jesus' struggle in the Garden of Gethsemane? "Not my will, but thine be done," prayed the Son, to which the Father patiently replied, "Yes; but if You do not go to the cross as an act of Your own free will, there is no point in going at all." If Christ had given up His life with the same sullen attitude that most of us have in performing duties that are unpleasant to us, the world would never have been saved.

Wisdom Literature

"Where can wisdom be found?
Where does understanding dwell?" (28:12)

This is the traditional question of "wisdom literature," the term assigned to a distinct genre of Biblical writing. The books of the Old Testament are usually divided into the categories of law, prophets, history, and wisdom literature, with *Job* being assigned to the latter group along with *Proverbs* and *Ecclesiastes*. This is standard classification. Nevertheless, just because *Job* employs some of the language and techniques of wisdom literature, this does not mean that the book fits neatly into that pigeonhole. In fact it does not. In many ways this work is a genre in its own right, defying the tools of form criticism. At the very least, we should consider a number of good reasons for classing *Job* as much in the prophetic as in the wisdom genre.

First of all, *Job* has one great characteristic that sets it decidedly apart from the normal conventions of wisdom literature, which is that in this book *the Lord speaks*. Chapters 38—41 comprise a theophany, a direct manifestation of God in which words from the Lord's own mouth are heard and recorded. This book, in short, has a charismatic ending—something highly unusual in a standard work of wisdom literature. (This crucial issue will be addressed more fully later on.)

In the second place, there can be no denying that Job himself is not only a wise man, but a prophet. The wise man, in the Biblical sense, is one who studies and reflects upon the world around him, both the natural world and the social or moral world. His method is very much that of a scientist, collecting data, mulling it all over, and drawing profoundly logical conclusions—in the words of *Ecclesiastes*, "adding one thing to another to discover the scheme of things" (7:27). Solomon comes to mind as the prime example of this type. The intellectual activity of such a mind was, of course, carried on under divine inspiration, and yet this mode of enlightenment was very different from the prophetic mode. For the prophets, their laboratory was not so much the mind as the spirit. They were people who "spoke from God as they were carried along by the Holy Spirit" (2 Peter 1:21). In *Job* this happens repeatedly. In speech after speech Job's thoughts rise to a peak of ecstatic utterance in which he delivers some of the most amazing Old Testament prophecies about Jesus Christ. At such moments Job seems to "know" in his spirit the real answer to all his problems. Whereas his friends seem desperate to seek answers outside of Christ, Job senses intuitively that the key to everything is only to be found in the yet-to-be-revealed Messiah. At its deepest level, Job's poem on wisdom in Chapter 28 is really a mystical lament on the fact that true wisdom is as yet unattainable, since the world has not yet seen Christ, "in whom are hidden all the treasures of wisdom and knowledge" (Col. 2:3). Surely Job belongs to that select company of Old Testament heralds of the gospel—"the gospel [God] promised beforehand through his prophets in the Holy Scriptures" (Rom. 1:2). James virtually identifies Job as a prophet when he writes, "As an example of patience in the face of suffering, take the prophets who spoke in the name of the Lord," and in the very next verse, "You have heard of Job's perseverance" (5:10-11).

There are other ways, too, in which *Job* is not only radically different from the other wisdom books, but in which its message is actually a polemic *against* the conventional interpretation of wisdom literature. Nowhere is this more obvious than in the book's implicit counsel regarding the problem of pain. Where wisdom literature may seem to favor a stoic equanimity in the face of suffering, Job comes out firmly in defense of passionate expression of feelings. Job's approach has all the drama of a modern encounter group session, as opposed to the more passively analytical methods of the wisdom writers. Conventional wisdom in this book is represented by Job's friends, who appear as shallow philosophers bowled over by Job's deeper and more ardent faith. The burden of the friends' counsel could be summed up by Proverbs 4:5: "Get wisdom; get understanding." But Job's reply is, "Get love—and if you do not have love, get lost!" Job's message to his hidebound companions is that of 1 Corinthians 13:2: "If I can fathom all mysteries and all knowledge . . . but have not love, I am nothing." The great theme of the Dialogue section is that there are times in life when even wisdom runs up against a brick wall. Therefore lay hold of love, which alone comprehends all.

The Narrow Way

"God understands the way to [wisdom]
and he alone knows where it dwells." (28:23)

S mall is the gate and narrow the road that leads to life," taught
Jesus, "and only a few find it" (Matt. 7:14). What makes the
road so narrow is the fact that only one person, the Lord,
knows where it is, and therefore it is a road that cannot be found or
traveled apart from vital relationship with Him. Wisdom is not
something that can be grasped or possessed by the human intellect;
it is not a something at all, but a *way*. Does the driver of an auto-
mobile own the road on which he travels? Many drive as if they do!
Yet in reality, it would be more accurate to say that the road owns
the driver, for the driver is bound to keep to the road wherever it
goes, or else not to travel at all.

Nothing is more infuriating to the natural human mind than this
fact of the extreme narrowness of truth. Why must the way be so
narrow? It is narrow because the place in which we now find ourselves, the fallen world, is a narrow and confining place, as narrow
as the grave. The gate to salvation is narrow because the gate to
perdition was also narrow—as narrow as the thin, lying voice of a
serpent. As small as a single piece of fruit on a single tree among all
the trees in the Garden of Eden. As tiny as a single fatal act of disobedience. If humanity was capable of finding and taking the one
way *out* of Paradise, then why can we not accept the one narrow
way back in?

Amidst all our griping about the narrowness of the way, we may
tend to forget that the way is also narrow for God. Just as God is
invisible to us, so that all we see of Him is His beautiful but broken
world, so too we in our fallen state are invisible to God, making it
hard for Him to find us. "Where are you?" called the Lord to Adam
in the garden in the cool of the day, just as at the end of time He will
say to those who have not believed in Him, "I don't know you"
(Matt. 25:12). How can God reach us? How can He get *into* a world
that deliberately shuts Him out? Where is the entrance point? Yes,
even for the Lord Himself the way is narrow—as narrow as a

manger stall in Bethlehem, as slender as the shaft of a cross, as constricted as the desperately suffering yet obstinately faithful heart of a man like Job.

Essentially, the way of truth is narrow because it involves just one thing: "Only one thing is needed" (Luke 10:42). When the disciples pleaded with the Lord, "Increase our faith," His answer to them was, in effect, that increased faith was not what was needed. What was needed was faith period—the real thing, pure and simple, "small as a mustard seed" (Luke 17:5-6). When faith is real—that is, when it is living faith in the Lord Jesus Christ—then it does not matter how great it is. If it is the real thing it is already great, and it grows by itself "whether [the farmer] sleeps or gets up" (Mark 4:27). Those who are trying to "increase" their faith are like those who dig up a carrot to see how big it is. When Jesus said to His disciples, "You of little faith, why are you so afraid?" (Matt. 8:26), the words may sound to our ears like a rebuke. But suppose He really meant this: "If only you realized what a great, great thing is your little, little faith, you would not be afraid."

Today, instead of comparing faith to a mustard seed Jesus might have compared it to an electron or to the tiniest particle in physics. What He meant was that faith is the smallest indivisible unit of reality. It is the narrowest conceivable movement in the depths of the spirit. One single moment (even the moment of conception, let us say) is all the time or space a human being needs in order to experience all there is: the reality of God. In many lives the outward effects of faith may be large and dramatic, but in essence true faith is so tiny a thing as to be all but imperceptible. That is why even a person in the midst of despair or insanity may have faith, or even a dying person whose life seems to consist of nothing more than the faintest squiggle on a piece of graph paper. What a surprise it will be for the rest of us if these dying ones, these insane ones, and these littlest ones should turn out in the end to be God's greatest trophies! For "the last will be first, and the first will be last" (Matt. 20:16).

Believing in the gospel is really as simple as walking: all we need to do is one thing, and do it over and over again. The narrowness of the way, it turns out, is precisely what makes it possible for a person to follow it without getting lost.

Fear Means Fear

"The fear of the Lord—that is wisdom." (28:28)

T he fear of the Lord is the beginning of wisdom," says a key
verse in *Proverbs* (9:10). Many people are uncomfortable
with this Biblical word "fear." They feel it is too strong a
word to be applied to our relationship with a loving Heavenly
Father, and they prefer to substitute a softer term such as "reverence" or "awe." They say that this is what the Bible really means
when it talks about "the fear of the Lord," and in support of this
view they like to quote 1 John 4:18: "There is no fear in love. But
perfect love drives out fear."

How many of us, however, are perfect in love? What John is
describing here is not simply the attitude of a converted and believing soul, but of one in a state of advanced sanctification, one in
whom "love is made complete" (v. 17). Until our love for God is perfected, how shall we not continue, in varying degrees, to be afraid
of Him? So long as we are humble, this can be a healthy fear because
it will have the effect of continually driving us back into His arms.
If we are not humble, then of course our fear will keep us from
approaching God at all. So it is not the mere presence of fear that is
to be feared; rather it is the way we deal with our fear that makes
fear either good or bad, and this in turn becomes a litmus test of true
faith. As John Donne prayed, "Give me, O Lord, a fear, of which I
may not be afraid."

Is it not right and proper that we should fear to offend in any way
the One who made us? "To fear the Lord is to hate evil" (Prov.
8:13). One cannot love righteousness without hating sin, and this
includes one's own sin. We fear God because, even though we are
secure in His eternal love for us, at the same time we know very well
that there are many parts of our lives that are not yet purified and
made holy. Jesus compared the Kingdom of God to "yeast that a
woman took and mixed into a large amount of flour until it worked
all through the dough" (Matt. 13:33). In other words, the salvation
that has already taken root deep in our spirits must continue to
advance into all areas of our flesh. No doubt this is what Paul meant

when he counseled us to "work out your salvation with fear and trembling" (Phil. 2:12). We should not be surprised to find our flesh trembling and quaking before the relentless march of God's Holy-Spirited yeast inside us.

Acts 5:11 relates that at the deaths of Ananias and Sapphira, "Great fear seized the whole church." Scripture testifies overwhelmingly that there is a healthy and appropriate place for fear in the life of faith. There is a holy fear, a salutary fear, a fear not to be watered down into mere "respect." In fact the fear of the Lord cannot be escaped. To deny or repress it is to drive it underground, and this results in untold damage to the personality. Certainly, "there is no fear in love"; but wherever there *is* fear it must be courageously faced, openly expressed, and dealt with. This is exactly what Job does throughout his ordeal.

When the fear of the Lord is operating in us as it should, all the many and varied fears that we quite naturally feel in this uncertain life are being gathered together into one great fear, and this one great fear is redirected towards God. Fear of other people, fear of demons, fear of the world and of ourselves, fear of sickness and pain, fear of living and of dying—all these phobias must be rolled up into one big ball and pushed up the hill to Calvary. For like other kinds of suffering, fear will never be completely alleviated in this life. Only as we bring our fears before the cross of Christ can their sting be extracted, their poison neutralized, their utter groundlessness exposed.

Many times Jesus comforted His disciples with the words, "Fear not." But He also told us to fear: "I tell you, my friends, do not be afraid of those who kill the body and after that can do no more. But I will show you whom you should fear: Fear him who, after the killing of the body, has power to throw you into hell. Yes, I tell you, fear him" (Luke 12:4-5). Jesus is telling us not to waste our fear on anyone less than God Almighty. When we cower before the Devil we open the door to all manner of fears. But when we fear the Lord, then we have nothing to fear from Satan or from any other quarter. This is the fear that is the beginning of wisdom. It is not the end of wisdom, for wisdom's end, John tells us, is perfect love, in which there is no longer any fear. But in the meantime, let us courageously cast all our fears upon the Lord and leave it to Him to dispel them. "'Twas grace that taught my heart to fear," goes the old hymn, "and grace my fears relieved."

Dark Night of
the Spirit

"How I long for the months gone by,
for the days when God watched over me,
when his lamp shone upon my head
and by his light I walked through darkness!" (29:2-3)

As Jesus was being dragged away to trial and crucifixion He said to His accusers, "This is your hour—when darkness reigns" (Luke 22:53). The hour when darkness reigns is what John of the Cross called the "dark night of the spirit"—a phrase not to be confused with the "dark night of the soul" which, in layman's terms, could refer to any sort of season of spiritual struggle. The night of the spirit is different from the night of the soul, and the difference is this: it is one thing to walk in the darkness, so long as God's light is shining on one's path; but it is something else entirely to keep on walking when darkness reigns, when darkness becomes the only light.

Job, like Jesus, "learned obedience from what he suffered" (Heb. 5:8). We might almost say that Job's obedience was the obedience of suffering itself. It was the obedience of not knowing anything but pain, darkness, confusion, anger, abandonment. Where was Job's faith in all of this? It seemed almost to be confined to the process of struggle itself, to the sheer courage and endurance this required, and perhaps to a few rare moments of dark lucidity, moments in which the sufferer had glimpses into something far greater and more mysterious than he could grasp for long.

"Always there is struggle," wrote A. W. Tozer of the Christian life, "and sometimes there is a pitched battle with our own nature where the lines are so confused that it is all but impossible to locate the enemy or to tell which impulse is of the Spirit and which of the flesh." In the early stages of faith the intellect is usually given much to feast upon. But in later stages the mind may be darkened and understanding taken away, in order that faith might become utterly faithful by being stripped of everything except faith itself. Were not all the great believers of the Bible thrown into situations in which they were entirely out of their depth, yet where they somehow had to respond and make decisions without any real comprehension of what was happening to them? "Faith," writes Josh McDowell, "is when commitment exceeds knowledge." Under such circumstances one's characteristic feelings will be panic, helplessness, loss of control.

Even Jesus trod this path. In the prime of His ministry He was so confident that during a wild storm on the Sea of Galilee, while His disciples tore out their hair, He curled up and slept like a baby in the bow of the boat. But in Gethsemane things were different. Here the roles were reversed, and the disciples slept while Jesus sweat blood. Where was the faith of the Son of God then? Three times He prayed the same prayer, begging His Father to let Him off the hook. Is it possible that Jesus rose from His knees that night without having had any clear, definitive answer to His prayers? For already the Spirit's light was growing faint within Him; already the agony of separation from His Father had begun. Already, perhaps, Jesus was on His own, with the sin of the whole world looming over Him.

This is the hour when faith, that strange and terrible flower, blooms. This is the hour when naked trust rises in the night to perform its alien task. This is when understanding is left behind and obedience takes over. Listen: wherever there is full understanding there can be no true obedience. Consider the example of a one-year-old child whose father shouts at him to keep away from an open fire. If the child responds to his father's voice by backing away from the fire, then that response is obedience. But when a teenager keeps a respectful distance from fire, that is no longer obedience but mere common sense. The teenager understands the danger and so is motivated by the instinct for self-preservation, whereas the younger child, having little or no understanding, is motivated purely by the father's command.

The story is told of a little girl who climbed onto the main floor of a house under construction and came to the black gaping hole of the stairwell. Suddenly out of the dark basement she heard her father call up to her, telling her to jump and he would catch her. She could not see her father because it was so bright where she was and so dark where he was. But because she recognized her father's voice, and trusted him, she jumped.

This is obedience: acting without full understanding. And this is faith: not knowing anything but the sound of the Father's voice.

Uselessness

"Oh, for the days when I was in my prime,
when God's intimate friendship blessed my house." (29:4)

Suffering, like the enemy who causes it, is a many-headed beast, and one of the heads is called Uselessness. A sufferer's existence can seem so pointless, so stagnant and unworthy. Little wonder that Job's mood in this chapter is one of intense nostalgia as he longs for "the good old days" when not only was he blessed by God, but when God's blessing enabled him to bless others. Such feelings are perfectly human and understandable. We all want to be useful and productive. But one of the things we learn from the many setbacks of life is that God, in His wisdom, has a use for uselessness. The Lord Himself seems to be fond of standing around and doing nothing. When we imitate Him in this, the Bible calls it "waiting on the Lord." But just think of how God waits on us! For thousands of years He has waited for mankind to turn to Him. Right now it is just as though He were standing on a street corner outside our home, hands in His pockets, whistling a gospel tune, waiting for us to keep our appointment with Him. Are we too busy with more pressing matters? Being useless, it seems, is not an important enough activity for us, and so we leave it to God.

Of course it is true that, as Jesus taught, "My Father is always *working*" (John 5:17). But to our human eyes God's work often looks like idleness. His methods can appear so lackadaisical, so unnecessarily time-consuming, and this is particularly the case when they involve pain on our part. Suffering puts us out of commission (at least from our perspective), so that we can no longer work, no longer contribute, no longer do much of value. Without this intense feeling of uselessness, suffering and even dying might not seem half so bad. Perhaps it is even true that the very soul of suffering is not so much pain itself, in all its forms, as it is the simple humiliation of having all our plans brought to a standstill, the indignity of being made to stop and wait.

How interesting it is that when the Lord appeared to Moses, and later to Joshua, to each of them He said the same thing: "Take off

your sandals, for the place where you are standing is holy ground"
(Ex. 3:5; Josh. 5:15). Why should you take off your shoes in the
Lord's presence? Because without shoes you are not going anywhere. You might try to walk, but you will not get very far, especially in the hot sand and sharp rocks of the wilderness. Taking off
one's shoes may not be quite as drastic as cutting off one's feet, but
it amounts to the same thing. Barefootedness means immobilization,
and so it is a symbol of submission. Being immobile (in other
words, having nothing better to do) is a prerequisite for worship,
and worship is the prerequisite for all activity, all service.

Many churches today are eager to mobilize for the Lord, but
without paying much attention to the prior and greater work of
immobilization. We need to learn how to kick off our shoes and discover that the place where we are standing is holy. When Daniel saw
a vision of the Ancient of Days on His throne, "ten thousand times
ten thousand stood before him." And what was this multitude
doing? Not much. All we are told is that "the court was seated, and
the books were opened." And without anyone moving an inch four
powerful empires were destroyed (Dan. 7:10-12). In Heaven, apparently, they know the meaning of the saying, "Don't just do something—stand there!"

The people of Israel wandered in the wilderness for forty years,
and the soles of their shoes never wore out. Why not? Because they
only moved at the Lord's command. In many ways they were disobedient, but in this one point they were constrained to obey
because pillars of cloud and of fire were hanging over them. If today
we find our souls (pun intended) wearing out, it may be because we
are running around doing a lot of things that the Lord has not told
us to do. We want to be fruitful. We want to work for our church
and contribute to our society. We want to *do* something, not simply
believe. When circumstances are such that we cannot do anything,
we get restless and squirm, and just like Job we think back on our
full and productive days and we long to see them return. We long
to go back, not just so we can feel good again, but so we can get on
with our "real work," get on with making our contribution.

But listen to the words of Catherine Doherty: "If you want to see
what a 'contribution' really is, look at the Man on the cross. That's
a contribution. When you are hanging on a cross you cannot do anything because you are crucified."

The Embraceable God

"When the Almighty was still with me . . .
my path was drenched with cream
and the rock poured out for me streams of olive oil." (29:5-6)

Ｈow can the Almighty God be "with" a human being? Jesus answered this question in John 14:16: "I will ask the Father, and he will give you another Counselor to be with you forever." This "other Counselor" is not someone other than God, but it is God Himself in the person of the Holy Spirit. Job, unlike Christians today, was not able to know the constant indwelling presence of the Holy Spirit, since "the Spirit had not been given" (John 7:39). Nevertheless, Job's testimony certainly indicates that he had a rich relationship with the Holy Spirit. In the verse quoted above he describes the sweetness and goodness of this relationship in the most lavish of terms, comparing it to rivers of cream and olive oil pouring through his life. These are metaphors that have deep resonance throughout Scripture, from the Old Testament's picture of Canaan as "a land flowing with milk and honey," to Jesus' image of the gift of the Spirit as "streams of living water flowing from within" (John 7:38). Job could never have used such language if he had not had abundant experience of the Spirit's blessing and had personally "tasted that the Lord is good" (1 Peter 2:3).

For the Old Testament believer, it was possible to know almost all the same manifestations of the Spirit's presence as the Christian knows. What Old Testament believers did not know (because it would not be revealed until after the death and glorification of Christ) was how to walk with this Spirit as one walks with a friend, how to know Him as one knows any other person. How could they have known the Holy Spirit in this way when they were not even aware that the Spirit was a "He"? God Himself was a person, they knew, but the Spirit of God seemed more a kind of holy influence, an extension of divine power, perhaps even a spiritual messenger or an "angel of the Lord"—but never a full-fledged person. The Old Testament never uses personal pronouns in reference to the Holy

Spirit, whereas the New Testament (especially after Pentecost) always does. There is a profound difference. What is it?

The difference is that you can hold on to and love a person, but you cannot hold on to or love an influence, a power, or even an angel. Spiritual power slips out of the grasp; but a person can be touched, followed, stuck with, embraced. The resurrected Jesus told Mary Magdalene, "Do not hold on to me, for I have not yet returned to the Father" (John 20:17). The paradoxical implication was that once Jesus had returned to Heaven, then Mary could hold on to Him. Then all believers would have a God they could hug. "I will not leave you as orphans," Jesus promised; "I will come to you" (John 14:18). How does He do this? In the person of the Holy Spirit. "Now the Lord is the Spirit," wrote Paul (2 Cor. 3:17).

John the Baptist testified that God had told him, "The man on whom you see the Spirit come down and *remain* is he who will baptize with the Holy Spirit" (John 1:33, emphasis added). This was not a Spirit who would set down like the tail of a tornado and then take off again. No, this was a Spirit who came to stay, to indwell, to transfigure from the inside. Luke tells us that when Jesus Himself was baptized, the Spirit descended on Him "in bodily form" (Luke 3:22). This was a full-blooded, manifest Spirit who came to inhabit the believer with all the effects of full-orbed, bodily possession. As Jonathan Edwards wrote, "They who are truly converted are new men, new creatures; new, not only within, but without . . . they have new hearts, new eyes, new ears, new tongues, new hands, new feet."

Throughout the history of Christianity certain sects have tended to spiritualize or disembody the person of Jesus Christ. The Gnostics, for example, denied Christ's humanity and tried to reduce Him to a system of mystical doctrine. In the twentieth century evangelical Christians have not, generally speaking, made this mistake. But many have fallen into the equally serious error of depersonalizing the Holy Spirit. At the level of rational theology they acknowledge the Spirit's personhood, but in practice He is allowed to fade into the woodwork and become little more than an ethereal influence, more a ghost than a real person. Many see Him merely as a kind of spotlight or PR agent for Christ, rather than as a divine person in His own right whom one can know and love, and whom it is the most exquisite of pleasures to worship and to glorify.

Clean Heart,
Clean Hands

"I rescued the poor who cried for help,
and the fatherless who had none to assist him." (29:12)

From the very beginning of this book we have been told that Job was "blameless and upright" (1:1). That is, not only was he blameless before God, but he was upright before men. He had not only a righteous heart but a righteous walk. Now in his final speech Job gives concrete examples of these facts, citing many ways in which his inner faith had always proved itself genuine by issuing in practical results. "The man who was dying blessed me," he recalls; "I made the widow's heart sing. . . . I was eyes to the blind and feet to the lame" (29:13, 15). Job is not just tooting his own horn; others too have honored him for his godly life. In fact he was a man who had commanded unreserved respect from his community: "The young men saw me and stepped aside and the old men rose to their feet . . . [people] waited for me as for showers and drank in my words as the spring rain" (29:8, 23). The list of Job's saintly qualities goes on and on, and altogether it presents a remarkable portrait of a life lived well and wisely, in the pure sunshine of simple goodness.

But more remarkable still is the fact that this is the first time in the book that Job himself has drawn any attention to his external virtues. Not once before this has he pointed to any of his good deeds as evidence of his faith, but rather he has taken his stand squarely upon faith alone and not upon works. The fact that Job waited so long to introduce any hard evidence into this debate with his friends shows enormous restraint on his part—or, more to the point, enormous humility. It seems, quite frankly, not even to have occurred to him that his laudable actions and good moral qualities might be considered as admissible evidence of his righteousness. Instead his focus has been wholly an interior one; his case has been based on the integrity of his heart and the cleanness of his conscience before God.

This emphasis on faith first, works later finds a parallel in the New Testament epistles, where in most cases the practical virtues of the Christian life are not discussed or even mentioned until towards the end. By this it is made perfectly clear that right actions are the outgrowth of right faith, rather than the cause or even the proof of it. In the same way, Job's emphasis all along has been on right motivation rather than right action as the core of righteousness. Even here in Chapter 29, as he fondly recalls the godly fruit that was formerly produced so abundantly in his life, his intention is by no means to parade his good deeds as a part of his defense. No, the tone of this passage is much more one of simple lament, of sheer pining nostalgia for "the days when God watched over me" (v. 2).

Naturally it is important to remember that righteousness has two dimensions, an inner and an outer one. James is the New Testament writer we most readily associate with the message that "faith without *works* is dead" (2:26). But reading the New Testament is like following a recipe: three cups Paul, two cups John, a tablespoon of James, a dash of Jude, and so on. The proportion of the ingredients is vital. Without the tablespoon of James the recipe would turn out very bland. But if we ate nothing but James day in and day out, we might end up as constipated legalists. In the words of the psalmist, "I run in the path of your commands, for you have set my heart free" (119:32). The little word "for" is all-important: because Job was blameless, he was also upright. The latter condition flows from the former as surely as the earth is warmed by the sun and not the other way around. This same pattern can be seen in Psalm 51 where David begins by praying, "Create in me a *clean* heart, O God" (v. 10), and ends, "Then there will be righteous sacrifices" (v. 19). Unlike Lady Macbeth, David knew that he could never wash the bloodguilt off his hands. But if he had a clean heart, then he would have clean hands too.

James wrote, "Religion that God our Father accepts as pure and faultless is this: to look after orphans and widows in their distress and to keep oneself from being polluted by the world" (1:27). Is this not exactly the kind of religion Job had? Like James he knew that one could never be of any help to orphans and widows if one's heart was polluted by the world. Only those unpolluted by the world can go into the world and touch it with holy hands.

Putting on Christ

"I put on righteousness as my clothing;
justice was my robe and my turban." (29:14)

Because Jesus' teaching was often so strange and surprising, the values of His Kingdom have sometimes been called "upside-down." But perhaps the better term would be "inside-out," for being a Christian means taking the light of one's soul out from under its bushel basket and letting it shine before the world. It means, in a sense, learning to wear the heart on the sleeve. "What I tell you in the dark," said Jesus, "speak in the daylight; what is whispered in your ear, proclaim from the housetops" (Matt. 10:27). Whether in words or in deeds we are to "work out our salvation" (Phil. 2:12)—that is, we are to let the interior mystery of our redemption grow and grow so that the faith that began inside us does not just remain inside, but overflows to transform little by little the whole of our outer life.

Paul describes this process as "putting on Christ": "Clothe yourselves with the Lord Jesus Christ" (Rom. 13:14); "put off your old self" and "put on the new self" (Eph. 4:22-24). Paul clearly teaches that everyone who believes in Jesus has already put on Christ by faith: "All of you who were baptized into Christ have *clothed yourselves* with Christ" (Gal. 3:27). But the image of donning Christ as we don our clothes every morning also describes the ongoing, lifetime task of fleshing out, or incarnating, our faith. How exactly do we do this? We do it by carefully tending the root of our faith, so that all by itself this root can grow into a tree and produce fruit. "Remain in me," taught Jesus; "apart from me you can do nothing" (John 15:4-5). It is Christ we must put on, not Christian deeds.

Oddly enough, the process of "putting on Christ" is something that even Jesus must have experienced, and not just once but every day. For as He grew older He grew in the consciousness of His messianic identity, and the enlargement of this secret in Him issued in the accomplishment of more and more glorious deeds. Thus Luke tells us that "Jesus grew in wisdom and stature, and in favor with God and men" (2:52). Doesn't this imply that the Son was more favorable to His Father at thirty than He had been at twenty? But how can someone who is already perfect become more perfect? Perhaps righteousness can be compared to a priceless diamond that is being cut: all along it remains essentially the same impeccable jewel, but as new facets are continually added, it progresses from glory to glory.

All the New Testament epistles were written to people who knew the gospel, but who had not quite worked out all the details of it yet. We are regenerated overnight—in an instant—but we do not change all our ways overnight. Rome is not demolished, nor Jerusalem built, in a day. Yet in a single moment the foundation-stone of a brand-new city can certainly be laid, and in the spiritual life this turns out to be the only stone that counts: Christ the cornerstone. As Christians we see the laying of this stone in ourselves as an accomplished fact, and we can rest assured that "he who began a good work in you will carry it on to completion" (Phil. 1:6).

Strictly speaking we cannot "imitate Christ"; but by faith we can allow Him the use of our bodies to imitate Himself. When we believe the gospel, God guarantees that His laws will be written on our hearts (Heb. 10:16), so that His will is no longer an external standard we must live up to, but an internal energy that we delight to see discharged. Accordingly, there is no point in trying to "put on" any behavior or action that the Lord has not already excited our hearts to perform. As Jeremiah 17:10 states, "I the Lord search the heart and examine the mind, to reward a man according to his conduct, according to what his deeds deserve." Why should the Lord search a man's heart in order to know his deeds? Can good deeds not stand on their own and be judged in their own light? No— because however good a deed may appear on the surface, its true character can only be known by the motive behind it. It is only as good as the faith that powers it.

Jesus said, "The kingdom of God is within you" (Luke 17:21). Scholars dispute whether the preposition should be translated "within" or "among." But probably the best way to make sense of this enigmatic saying would be to omit the preposition altogether, letting it read simply, "The kingdom of God *is you*." God's Kingdom is not something you can watch, observe, analyze, or even think about; rather, it is something you *are*. You cannot see it; you can only be it.

Mockery

"But now they mock me, men younger than I." (30:1)

In the past few chapters the storm of Job's anguish may seem to have abated somewhat, as new and more positive moods have prevailed. In Chapter 26 there was Job's majestic hymn to the Lord's beauty and power in creation, and Chapter 27 was characterized by a tone of unshakable confidence. Then came the quiet meditation on wisdom in Chapter 28, followed by a mood of gentle nostalgia in Chapter 29 as Job reflected on how greatly the Lord had blessed his life in the past. By the end of this long section we may have been lulled into thinking that the worst of Job's trials are over, and that he must have gained some control over his despair and won through to a position, if not exactly of victory, then at least of greater acquiescence to his lot.

But this is not the case. Here in Chapter 30 a wave of desolation breaks over him such as we have not heard since the very beginning of the Dialogue section. "Terrors overwhelm me," he cries, "and now my life ebbs away; days of suffering grip me. Night pierces my bones; my gnawing pains never rest" (vv. 15-17). Then he accuses God: "You turn on me ruthlessly; with the might of your hand you attack me. . . . You toss me about in the storm" (vv. 21-22). As if this were not enough, we learn now of an added dimension of Job's suffering, which is the cruel mistreatment he has received not only from his three closest friends but from all the local townspeople. Had Job not "wept for those in trouble" and "grieved for the poor" (v. 25)? Yet when he himself "stood up in the assembly and cried for help," it was to no avail (v. 28). Now even the very dregs of society "detest [him] and keep their distance," and the name of Job has "become a byword among them" (vv. 9-10).

Here we discover that the scope of Job's suffering has been broader than we may have realized. The draining encounter with his three affluent and squeamish friends, it turns out, has been just one small aspect of his public ordeal. After his downfall Job did not slip away into seclusion, as some in his circumstances might have done, but rather in good faith he sought help from his community, only to be cruelly ostracized. He did not slink out of town; he was run out on a rail. Why else would he be sitting on an ash heap and scraping his pustules with a shard of pottery? Obviously his neighbors had forcibly removed him to quarantine in the town dump, where he would have been exposed to more disease, to the elements, to rats and lice—and worst of all, perhaps, to further public humiliation. Here Job was ridiculed by men who themselves were being "shouted at as if they were thieves" (v. 5). Even the skid row types avoided him and "mocked [him] in song" (v. 9).

Most authors would have outlined these sordid details of Job's ostracism at the very beginning of the story, so as to enhance the bleakness of the background against which the theological discussion takes place. But it is part of the brilliance of *Job* that many of the pertinent facts (such as the previous chapter's account of Job's charitable deeds) have been left until last. Consequently we are never allowed to become too accustomed to this man's suffering, but instead we watch it grow and take on wider and wider implications. When in Chapter 30 we learn that Job is now an outcast of outcasts, more untouchable than the untouchables, we begin to feel his isolation as being like the isolation of God Himself, who is scorned and rejected not only by the educated and the aristocratic but by the meanest and lowest. This is the isolation of Jesus Christ when He was handed over to the Gentiles. It would have been terrible enough for the Messiah to have been stoned to death by His own people. But somehow there is an added horror in the fact that the Holy One of Israel was surrendered into the hands of outright pagans to be mocked and tortured.

Certainly the scourge of public mockery is one of the fiercest of trials. Are we prepared for it? To Job it came unexpectedly and bewilderingly; but to the Christian it is promised, and its significance is explained in many Scriptures. Jesus taught, "He who rejects you rejects me" (Luke 10:16), and in the Beatitudes persecution has the final and crowning position (Matt. 5:10-12). It is one of the preeminent ways in which Christians are called upon to "share in [Christ's] sufferings in order that we may also share in his glory" (Rom. 8:17).

Disgrace

"[People] do not hesitate to spit in my face.
Now that God has unstrung my bow and afflicted me,
they cast off restraint in my presence." (30:10-11)

In this passage Job's lament once again foreshadows the crucifixion: like Christ he is mocked, spat upon, afflicted by God. In the
Old Testament as in the New, it seems, both God and men have
to find somewhere to unload their wrath. If a good person is chosen as the whipping boy, it is only because a good person can take
it. A good person, like a good God, can absorb all the hatred and
abuse you may care to throw at him, without being crushed by it.
That is just the way goodness is: it has the power to absorb or swallow up evil. In fact before evil can be conquered, it must be personally absorbed. We must take it into ourselves, like poison, with all
its dirt and shame, and then let the world watch as it passes through
us without harm. This notion is completely abhorrent to natural
religion. And yet it is the true Spirit of Christ, of whom Paul taught
that "God made him who had no sin to be sin for us" (2 Cor. 5:21).
Because the God-Man was disgraced, because He publicly suffered
loss of grace, He became the channel through which grace and goodness could flow back into the world.

This is exactly what is missing from most of our western
churches: the public disgrace of Christians. It is fine for Jesus to have
been disgraced, we feel, and it is fine when superstar charlatans get
their comeuppance. But the average faithful disciple cannot imagine how any good might come from his own public humiliation. On
the contrary, how could God possibly be glorified if we ourselves
should appear in a bad light? But really the opposite is true: if we
ourselves are busy occupying the limelight, what light can fall on
God?

Did not Jesus teach us to deny ourselves and to take up our cross?
By denial He did not mean suppression; that kind of denial leads
only to neurotic disorder. No, to Jesus denial meant annihilation. It
meant a violent public execution in which the weakness and cor-
ruptibility of our flesh were to be put on display. How conveniently

Christians today have forgotten that the carrying of a cross is not a private but a public act. Aren't most of us caught up in projecting to others an outer image of ourselves that is better than the inner truth? Instead of glorying in our weaknesses as Paul did, we like to hide them. We would far sooner busy ourselves with cultivating a saintly exterior, than be forced to live with the pain and disgrace that inevitably accompany interior sanctification. In the long run, this hypocritical playacting causes us more pain than ever, eating up enormous reserves of our energy and keeping us tied in knots. That is why we need people like Job, or like Jacob or Jeremiah, people who can help us relax by showing that God is most glorified when we are simply ourselves, warts and all. The Lord is infinitely patient and loving with a messy exterior, but an insincere heart He cannot abide.

No one can be a Christian without insisting on acquiring a pure heart, whatever the consequences might be for one's exterior life. And the consequences are bound to be catastrophic. People who are preoccupied with putting on a nice Christian veneer will die in their sins. But those who give up the pride that pours all its energy into maintaining appearances, and who openly scorn those appearances by submitting them to public disgrace, will inherit eternal life. There can be no sanctification or spiritual maturity without crucifixion with Christ, and there can be no crucifixion with Christ without some measure of public shame and scandal. Certainly disgrace is not something to be recklessly sought out; but neither is it to be frantically avoided. Denying the self, far from hiding the self, means being unafraid of having the self exposed for what it is.

Is the weakness of our flesh on display for all to see? Or do we think that being spiritual means exuding a radiant glow of saintliness? Many of us, unlike Job, have grown so terrified of appearing unspiritual in the eyes of other Christians that we no longer dare to open up our hearts, either to one another or to God. We are too afraid of what is inside. We cannot bear to confront our flesh as it really is, let alone to crucify it. What we need to realize is that only as sinners can we be disciples of Jesus. A saint cannot pick up a cross; only a sinner can pick up a cross. This is a profound mystery; but with our saintly selves, with that part of ourselves that has been sanctified and devoted to God, we cannot touch the cross. Only a sinful nature can touch the cross. It has to be bare flesh against bare wood. Mere spirit will not hold a nail.

Wrestling with God

"In his great power God clutches at my clothing;
he grabs me by the collar of my coat.
He throws me into the mud." (30:18-19)

What a testimony these words are to the immeasurable tenderness and lovingkindness of God! Of course, they are nothing of the kind. Rather they are something we have come to expect in the speeches of Job: a shockingly earthy account of a knock-down-drag-'em-out struggle against the raw power of an incomprehensible Spirit Being. Time and again Job resorts to images of war, savage aggression, and brute hand-to-hand combat in an effort to describe his relationship with God. Why? Because in his present condition this is what faith feels like for him. This is what it is like to believe in God when absolutely everything is going wrong.

One cannot help but be reminded of Jacob, another towering saint whose relationship with the Lord was so real, so physical, and so bizarre that he once got up from his prayers limping, having literally wrestled all night with his God to the point of being crippled in the hip. Perhaps what is most remarkable about this night of wrestling is that Jacob was not condemned for it, but rather rewarded. He stayed fifteen rounds in the ring with El Shaddai and walked away to tell the tale, and this sort of wiry, diehard, unholy pugnacity turns out, strangely, to be the very essence of Biblical faith. For when Jacob pinned his divine opponent to the mat and cried, "I will not let you go unless you bless me," the Lord acceded to his demand by changing his name from Jacob to Israel, and ever since then Israel has been the name for true believers. (See Galatians 6:16 where Paul refers to Christians as "the Israel of God.") And what does the name *Israel* mean? It means, "he struggles with God." So believers are called after the man who was crippled in a fight with God. We are the people who struggle with God—that is, who take God seriously enough to struggle with Him, to endure struggle for His sake. To accept this truth, and to know it better than we know our own names, is to find ourselves the recipients of God's richest blessing.

Classically there are two ways of soliciting the favor of God. One way is by trying very hard to be very very good and hoping that God will take notice. The other way is to beg God for His blessing and to refuse to let Him off the hook until He comes through. This latter way, as inelegant and impious as it sounds, is the Biblical way. It is those who refuse to give up on God who end up with His blessing. Those who utterly despair of trying to do anything good for God, yet who blindly insist that God be good to them—these are the faithful ones. These are the ones who have the grit to hold on to God through the grimmest and dirtiest of scuffles. Nothing short of this kind of faith could have carried Jesus through the ordeal of the cross. "The old rugged cross," a famous hymn calls it, and so it was. The cross was a rough, dirty, violent affair, and it was all God's idea. Why do we picture the Lord as being less rugged than we are? Just because He is holy, does that make Him milk-mannered, skittish, oversensitive, and effete? Too delicate to handle the gross crudities of real life? If we shrink from the idea of wrestling with God, is it because we are afraid of losing? But Jacob did not lose! Perhaps the real problem is our fear of offending God's refined sensibilities. Are we so afraid of seeing our nice clean God get dirt under His nails, or blood on His lily-white hands?

There is no life without fight. There is no reality without blood, toil, tears, and sweat. If you are a Christian who does not wrestle, then you may be sure of one thing: someone else is doing the wrestling for you. Jesus once said, *"The kingdom of heaven is being subjected to violence, and the violent bear it away"* (Matt. 11:12). Nobody has ever been quite sure whether Jesus was decrying the unspiritual zeal of religious rapists, or commending aggressive believers for their godly passion. But if the latter is the case, then surely the kind of people Christ had in mind were the Jobs and the Jacobs—people who would take hold of the Kingdom of God the way a dog sinks its teeth into the shank of a wild animal ten times its size, and refuses to let go. When it came to the things of God, these men were scrappers. When backed into a corner their natural vulgarity and savagery came out, and the Lord, as He loves to do, transformed these brute passions into holy stigmata.

True Prayer

"I cry out to you, O God, but you do not answer." (30:20)

In the Bible we often read of people "crying out to the Lord." But what does it mean to "cry out"? Does it mean to express oneself demurely to God, with polite restraint, using the well-worn, time-honored phrases of the conventional prayer meeting? Or do the words "cry out" suggest more the sort of sound a man might make whose legs have just been caught up in a piece of machinery? "Surely [God] will save you from the fowler's snare," sings the psalmist (91:3). A snare is a leghold trap, a contrivance designed to catch an animal and hold it until it dies of shock or starvation, condemning it in the meanwhile to hopeless struggle and horror. Is this not the sort of situation that might bring a human being to the point of crying out to God?

There is no true prayer without agony. Perhaps this is the problem in many of our churches. What little prayer we have is shallow, timid, carefully censored, and full of oratorical flourishes and hot air. There is little agony in it, and therefore little honesty or humility. We seem to think that the Lord is like everyone else we know, and that He cannot handle real honesty. So we put on our Sunday best to visit Him, and when we return home and take off our fancy duds we are left alone with what is underneath: the dirty underwear of hypocrisy.

Why do we flatly refuse to bring real emotions to our prayer meetings? Do we think that the public humbling of ourselves before the Lord should always be a pretty and an enjoyable thing? Do we think the Lord is only honored so long as our own public image and personal dignity are in no way compromised? But the truth is just the opposite: only when we ourselves are prepared to lose face can the Lord's face begin to shine through. It is for Him to exalt us; our part is to humble ourselves. "If my people, who are called by my name, will humble themselves and pray and seek my face and turn from their wicked ways, then will I hear from heaven and will forgive their sin and will heal their land" (2 Chron. 7:14).

Even in our private prayers, let alone in our public ones, we

310 □ True Prayer

Christians have a way of tiptoeing around the throne of God as if
He were an invalid or a doddering old man. But who do we think
we are kidding? The Lord always knows exactly what we are feeling. He knows all there is to know about us. There is not a shadow
of doubt or anger or hate in our hearts but God sees it. So why not
just lay all our cards on the table? Real prayer is playing straight
with God. If we have never cried out to the Lord, perhaps it is
because we have not realized the true horror of our situation. We
need to be careful that we do not grow so preoccupied with maintaining our spiritual equilibrium that we regard it as unseemly to cry
out to God.

At bottom, probably what we are most afraid of in prayer is that
no answer will come, and that then we will be left worse off than
before. But true prayer has two parts: first there is the crying out,
and then there is the waiting for an answer. If we are the sort of people who insist on having instant answers, then we shall certainly lack
the courage to cry out. Though we might continue to go through the
motions of prayer, we will have given up on the real thing.

Towards the end of the book of *Jeremiah*, the nation of Judah was
on its last legs. It had been conquered by the Babylonians, and most
of its people had been led away into captivity. Only a small remnant
was left under the puppet governor Gedaliah. But when Gedaliah
was assassinated by a rebel, suddenly even these survivors were in
peril, for everyone knew that a brutal reprisal could be expected
from the Babylonians. So what were they to do? What they did, surprisingly, was to go to the prophet Jeremiah and beg him to consult
the Lord for them. Furthermore they bound themselves to obey
God's Word no matter what. Their situation was desperate. They
were crying out. Jeremiah agreed to pray for them.

At this point, we read one of the most astounding understatements in the Bible: "Ten days later the word of the Lord came to
Jeremiah" (42:7). Imagine! *Ten days later!* Who could possibly wait
ten days under such circumstances? Did the Lord not understand
that this was a dire emergency? After ten days, naturally, the people
had already made up their minds to ignore God's answer and to do
exactly what they felt like doing: run like crazy down to Egypt.
When the pressure was on, they performed the first requirement of
prayer admirably: they cried out to the Lord. But for the second half
of prayer they had no stomach. They could not wait for an answer.

Faith and Peace

"The churning inside me never stops;
days of suffering confront me." (30:27)

M any people assume that faith means having a heart full of peace and quiet confidence in the Lord. If this were really the case, where would that leave Job? If a peaceful heart were an adequate test of the presence of faith, then Job would fail that test miserably. Or what if we were to measure the faith of blind Bartimaeus by how peaceful he was as he sat by the roadside and repeatedly screamed above the din of the passing parade, "Son of David, have mercy on me!" (Mark 10:48)? Or what about the Canaanite woman who came to Jesus crying out for deliverance for her demon-possessed daughter? Why did the Lord say to her, "Woman, you have great faith!" (Matt. 15:28)? Was it because she had total confidence that this man could work a miracle for her? No; rather than commending her for this kind of faith, Jesus at first completely ignored her. He knew it took no great faith just to believe in miracles. Was it, then, because of the serene and beatific smile on the woman's face as she threw herself before Him? Hardly. Then surely the thing that impressed Jesus must have been the cleverness of her comment about dogs licking up crumbs under their masters' table? But no, really it was none of these things. Rather what drew Jesus' attention to this woman (as to Bartimaeus) was a very unusual juxtaposition of qualities in her: it was her abject helplessness combined with her brazen persistence. Is this not exactly the attitude we have seen all along in Job? This Canaanite woman knew very well that before the Messiah of Israel she was no better than a dog, and yet she seemed convinced that she had a right to His help, and she was prepared to insist rudely on this right. Why? *Just because of who He was!* Here was someone wholly taken up, not with herself, and certainly not with her own level of faith, but rather with the Lord Jesus Christ and with His magnanimous grace and mercy.

People like this do not approach Jesus as one would buy a lottery ticket, thinking, "What have I got to lose?" Rather they seek Him out as the one conceivable answer to their anguish. Their hearts are churning, and they turn to Christ for the only possible relief. Their desperation is a part of their faith, a part of what turns them. If their souls were placid rather than turbulent, they would never come to Jesus. Even Jesus Himself did not always have peace, as He testified for example in Luke 12:50: "I have a baptism to undergo, and how distressed I am until it is completed!"

This is not to say that there is no relationship between faith and peace. There most certainly is. Paul prays, "Now may the Lord of peace himself give you peace at all times and in every way" (2 Thess. 3:16). Again he writes, "Let the peace of Christ rule in your hearts" (Col. 3:15), implying that peace is to have the same authority to govern our lives as the Lord Himself has, who is its source. Peace is to shape and determine all our activities, and any worldly goal that consistently blocks or frustrates our peace must be rejected as an idol. "First put yourself at peace," wrote Thomas à Kempis, "and then you may the better make others be at peace. A peaceful and patient man is of more profit to himself, and to others too, than a learned man who has no peace." Peace should be the hallmark of every Christian's interior life. To neglect God's gift of peace, or to make excuses for why we do not have it, is plain willfulness. Peace is one of our rights as the children of God, and we should insist upon it. We are to "seek peace and pursue it" (Ps. 34:14).

Yet at the same time, in all our seeking we must never make the mistake of directly equating peace with faith, or loss of peace with loss of faith. Peace is the fruit of a faithful life, not its root. Faith is the means to peace, but faith does not depend upon peace. Ideally peace and faith should coexist and be inseparable. But we do not yet live in an ideal state. When the ideal comes, then "righteousness and peace [will] kiss each other" (Ps. 85:10). But until then it is the lot of the righteous to endure a certain degree of restlessness, and indeed to refuse to rest until they have secured the perfect peace that God has promised. The task of faith is to hold God doggedly to His word, even during times when He might seem to be reneging. That is why every single one of the epistles of Paul begins with some form of the salutation, "Grace and peace to you." Grace is what we need when we do not have peace.

Outside the Camp

"I have become a brother of jackals." (30:29)

Mark's description of what happened during Jesus' forty days in the wilderness is, even for Mark, jarringly terse. We are told simply, "He was with the wild animals, and angels attended him" (1:12). If Job's friends and community had been allowed to witness this ordeal of our Lord's, we may safely guess that they would not have seen any angels. All they would have seen were the wild animals. In the same way, if Job's friends had somehow been able to gather at the foot of the cross, we can only presume that they would have been among the scoffers.

The *Epistle to the Hebrews* tells us that "Jesus also suffered outside the city gate to make the people holy through his own blood. Let us, then, go to him outside the camp, bearing the disgrace he bore" (13:12-13). This passage reminds us that to be a disciple of Christ is to place oneself beyond the pale of civilized society. It is to share in the loneliness and disgrace of Jesus by being quarantined on Calvary. This is exactly what happened to Job. Old Testament law commanded that everyone who had an infectious skin disease be sent "outside the camp so that they will not defile their camp" (Num. 5:3). Job had become a pariah not merely because of his skin disease, but because it and all his other misfortunes had exposed him to others as a blatant sinner. And sin was the worst kind of infectious disease. When Job's friends went to visit him in his place of quarantine, it was with the purpose of persuading him to confess his sin so he could be healed and restored to normal life. The enormity of their indiscretion only becomes apparent if we imagine the Pharisees going with a similar motive to visit Jesus in the wilderness. Or on the cross.

As Christians most of us are surprised and alarmed when we find ourselves going through times of profound isolation. We might feel alienated not only from our community and from the larger society, but even from our own church or from our closest friends and family. When this happens, it could be because we are being called apart to participate in the loneliness of God. If we do not realize this, then we will chafe and rebel against our loneliness as if it were something strange and un-Christian, as if the Bible had nothing to say about it. But wasn't this one of the trials of Job? Here was a gregarious, community-minded person who was called upon to share in the loneliness of God.

G. K. Chesterton wrote in an essay on *Job*, "The central idea of the great part of the Old Testament may be called the idea of the loneliness of God. God is not only the chief character of the Old Testament; God is properly the only character in the Old Testament. Compared with His clearness of purpose, all the other wills are heavy and automatic, like those of animals; compared with His actuality, all the sons of flesh are shadows." If we human beings are to partake of the vital actuality of God, we must first join God in His loneliness. We must pass through the great wilderness that stands between God and the world, and there, for a time, we become shadows to our fellow humans. We become brothers of jackals.

This journey into lonely desolation necessarily involves us in a crisis of identity. For that is what loneliness is: an identity crisis. We are meant to be in close relationship with other people, and when for any reason this sense of community breaks down, then essentially we are cut off from ourselves. The enigma for the Christian is that while isolation is not a good thing in itself, yet there are times when it is essential for the growth of our spirits. Since at present we do not know how to relate to others in an entirely healthy way, our old ways must die in order to make way for the new.

To go "outside the camp" with Jesus really means to leave behind us the last vestiges of our identity as we knew it. Christians are people who have given up the luxury of having any identity in this world at all—at least, of having any identity that can be known. For *"we no longer live, but Christ lives in us"* (Gal. 2:20). So who, then, are *we*? We do not know, for this is a secret that is yet to be disclosed. "The creation waits in eager expectation for the sons of God to be revealed" (Rom. 8:19). Until then, our identity is "hidden with Christ in God," so that when Christ appears, "then [we] also will appear with him in glory" (Col. 3:3-4). To insist on knowing who we are this side of glory is what Jesus calls "loving our life," and he who loves his life will lose it.

Singing the Blues

"My harp is tuned to mourning,
and my flute to the sound of wailing." (30:31)

ncient music was not written in keys but in modes. There
may have been no single standard for tuning instruments
such as there is on a modern guitar or piano, but rather tuning could be altered to achieve a variety of musical effects. Thus in
the Psalms we read instructions such as "according to *gittith*" (Ps.
8) or "according to *alamoth*" (Ps. 46), and when Habakkuk set the
third chapter of his prophecy to music he directed that it be played
"on *shigionoth*" (v. 1). The exact meaning of these terms is uncertain, but in all probability they were musical notations governing the
tuning of instruments to various modes. In conventional western
music the only modes that have been commonly preserved are the
major and the minor; but ancient music featured a much broader
and subtler modal palette. Modes were like moods, or like colors or
incense. Highly evocative, they bore a certain nostalgic correspon-
dence to the changing weathers of the soul.

When Job said that his harp was "tuned to mourning," he meant
that the circumstances of his life were such that all he could do was
mourn. He could not produce any other kind of music, any more
than a Mozart piano sonata could be played on the bagpipes. Job
knew that faith was not a matter of positive thinking, not a means
of manipulating one's moods and attitudes so as to live always in
the comfort zone. On the contrary, there is "a time to mourn" (Eccl.
3:4), and it is right and appropriate that one's emotional responses
should fluctuate according to circumstances. There are situations in
which the only authentically human reaction is sadness, gloom, confusion, or pessimism, and the person for whom this is not true is a
dangerous person. Indeed one of the marks of a soul that belongs
to God is that it grows highly sensitive to the presence of evil.
Strange chills and shadows will creep over such a soul, and while it
will not always know what these mean, it will instinctually react
with fear, horror, or pain. The fact is that believers feel pain much
more acutely than do nonbelievers—although it is also true that our

resources for dealing with pain are infinitely greater. The person who had the most pain of all was Jesus, and no one else has ever mourned as He did.

In Matthew 2:18 we read about the mothers of the slaughtered infants in Bethlehem "weeping for [their] children and refusing to be comforted." Job takes his place among those who refused to be comforted when comforting was inappropriate, just as Jesus refused comforting from the disciples when His face was set toward Calvary. The disciples' problem was that their faith was too optimistic. They were so taken up with the idea of ushering in a kingdom of this world that their faith became unrealistic. They had no room for the cross. They did not want to listen to their Master when He talked about dying; they put it out of their minds. What they needed was a good dose of the Lord's own pessimism. They needed to learn, "Blessed are you who weep now, for you will laugh" (Luke 6:21) and, "Blessed are those who mourn, for they will be comforted" (Matt. 5:4).

The Bible exalts mourning as a virtue because it is the godly counterpart of complaining. The difference between the two can be seen plainly by contrasting Job with the people of Israel under Moses. The latter murmured interminably while wandering through the desert, but unlike Job the one thing that never seemed to worry them was their relationship with the Lord. Instead they griped about the rotten food, the rotten leadership, the rotten facilities. Every day it was something new, for it is one of the chief characteristics of a complaining spirit to be restless and fickle, obsessed with things that by their very nature are transient. Job's obsession, however, was singleminded and transcendentally focused, and so his complaining achieved the status of godly mourning. Was it not the Lord Himself who, by granting Satan the permission to do anything he wanted to this man short of killing him, had tuned Job's harp to mourning?

Nothing is sadder than to see someone striving to be cheerful whose heart is tuned to mourning. Under such conditions, cheerfulness becomes ungodliness. It is a violation of the human spirit. Naturally we have many negative feelings that can and should be rejected. But often enough it is the case that our feelings just *are*; they are a part of reality, like the rocks and the trees. Let us not spurn or repress any emotion as being unspiritual in and of itself; rather, let us be real.

Job's Sermon on the Mount

"I made a covenant with my eyes
not to look lustfully at a girl." (31:1)

Chapter 31 is Job's Sermon on the Mount, for in it he touches on many of the same issues of spiritual ethics that Jesus covers in Matthew 5–7, including the relationship between lust and adultery (vv. 1, 9-12), loving one's neighbor as oneself (vv. 13-15), almsgiving and social justice (vv. 16-23), and the love of money and other idolatries (vv. 24-28). Resuming the defense of his righteous conduct begun in Chapter 29, Job not only argues his complete innocence in all these areas, but he goes even further by declaring that his conduct has exceeded mere obedience to the letter of the law, and that he has been faithful to its very spirit. This is precisely the theme of Christ's great sermon, where the emphasis throughout is not on virtuous behavior for its own sake but rather on the underlying motives of the heart, from whence true virtue springs. Job proves his grasp of this principle by pointing again and again to the vital relationship between his outer conduct and the integrity of his heart—whether that conduct involves his eyes (v. 7), his hands (v. 27), or his mouth (vv. 29-30).

Take the example of lust, that subtle business transacted between the heart and the eyes. When Job says that he has made a covenant with his eyes to abstain from lust, he does not mean that he has stopped experiencing lust altogether. What he means is that he refuses to dwell upon the lustful feelings which, as the normal red-blooded male he is, come to him very naturally. He means that he cannot tolerate such feelings without revulsion rising up within him. For in his innermost heart, he delights in God's law.

A few verses later Job elucidates his position on lust when he swears, "My heart has [not] been led by my eyes" (31:7). He knows that because of man's fallen condition his eyes are bound, to some extent, to wander. But his heart is not bound. The heart of a believer is free, free to choose and discern, free to say yea or nay to every worldly demand

and to exercise government over all the whims of the flesh. Even the best government, however, cannot entirely eradicate rebellion and law-breaking. Rather, good government takes lawlessness seriously by covenanting to punish it and, so far as possible, to reform it.

Job knows that if he made a firm resolution to control all the movements of his eyes, he could not do it. Instead he says that he has made a "covenant" with his eyes, and his use of this term is significant. For a covenant is not the same as a contract. When a contract is breached, the law has been broken, and the violator leaves himself wide open to the full consequences of legal prosecution. But when a covenant is breached, even though here too the law has been broken, nevertheless there is no need to have recourse to law for arbitration. For a covenant by its very nature contains within itself sufficient protocol for the handling of all violations in an extrajudicial manner. Law is not the bottom line of a covenant. Covenantal partners are not finally bound by law, for the covenant itself outlines a better way of settling disputes.

Today the most familiar example of a covenant agreement is marriage. When marriage partners fight, they do not run to their lawyers. They only run to their lawyers when the marriage has already fallen apart, when the covenant itself has been rejected. Only when a covenant breaks down does the law take over, and the full extent of the law's wrath can then be pressed to its bitter conclusion.

In spiritual matters God has two methods by which He carries on business with humanity: one is by contract or law, and the other is by covenant (which includes law but also supersedes it). When people accept the gospel they enter into covenant with the Lord, thereby acquiring all the rights and perquisites of a covenantal relationship, including the power to have all disputes settled in-house without recourse to law. But when people reject the gospel, automatically their relationship with God reverts to a legal, contractual basis, so that every time they breach contract by breaking even one of God's laws they automatically incur the full penalty of divine wrath. The relationship of such people with the Lord is like that of a legally separated husband and wife who communicate with each other only through lawyers. Their formal divorce may not yet be finalized, but that is only a matter of time.

Thank God that the gospel is not a contract, but a covenant. This is the great liberating truth underlying all the stratospheric moral requirements of the Sermon on the Mount.

God's Scales

*"Let God weigh me in honest scales
and he will know that I am blameless." (31:6)*

Here again is this oddly arresting little word "blameless." How many of us would dare to apply it to ourselves as freely as Job does? Of course we all know that by any human standards Job can hardly be described as blameless, for "all have sinned and fall short of the glory of God" (Rom. 3:23). Great people, in particular, have great faults, and Job is no exception. Nothing could be easier than to find fault with Job, just as his friends do, and just as the Devil seeks to do. According to their standards, Job is guilty as sin.

But the miracle of the gospel is that it is not the standards of Job's friends, nor those of the Devil, nor even Job's own standards, that count. Rather the only standards that count are the Lord's. By any other standards than those of God the whole human race would be eternally condemned. But by God's standards, those who live by faith in Jesus Christ are counted blameless.

Many people refuse to come to Christ because they do not believe God's standards are high enough. They think Christians should be morally perfect (or close to it), and if we are not, then what is the good of all our faith? Even many Christians would be surprised to discover this advice in the Bible: "Do not be overrighteous. . . . Why destroy yourself?" (Eccl. 7:16). What the Preacher means is that moral perfection is not the standard by which God accepts people. God's only standard is faith. Therefore it is foolish to work at being any more of a saint than God has already made you. Righteousness is by faith, not works. It is a gift, not an achievement.

Unbelievers (and even, at times, believers) cannot grasp this notion and find it ridiculous. They cannot believe that God would be more lenient with them than they are with themselves. Perfectionism is their bane. Since they cannot forgive themselves for being imperfect, why should they expect God to forgive them? However much they may try to pretend that somehow everything will work out in the end and they will wind up in Heaven (whatever that is), nevertheless every day their consciences condemn them, for they know very well that even by their own standards (let alone those of a wrathful God) they can never be worthy of Heaven or even come close. Striving to justify themselves, they live lives of quiet desperation. Their own impossible standards are the only ones that matter to them.

Faith, however, means accepting God's standards, not our own. God's standards are the only ones that are based on objective reality rather than on subjective fancy. When Job pleads, "Let God weigh me in honest scales," he means he will not presume to pass judgment on himself, but rather he is willing and even eager to have his faith submitted to a rigorously objective test. Like Paul he might have said, "I care very little if I am judged by you or by any human court; indeed, I do not even judge myself. My conscience is clear, but that does not make me innocent. It is the Lord who judges me" (1 Cor. 4:3-4).

By reviewing all his good deeds in this chapter, Job is not meaning to claim perfection. He is simply presenting evidence for the genuineness of his faith, knowing full well that he could never have performed such feats in his own strength. Instead of bemoaning his own obvious weaknesses, Job with astonishment and gratitude recalls all that God has done through him in the past. This is the attitude of the faithful, whose focus is not on their own performance but on God's. They are taken up with God's Word, God's decrees, God's acts, God's character. Psalm 119 uses eight different words to express this phenomenon of the solid basis of God's objective standards, repeating these words 176 times in a rapturous litany. Similarly in the letter to the Ephesians Paul refers to Jesus Christ (either by name or by pronoun) no less than forty-five times in the first forty-five verses. Everything is "with Christ" or "in Christ" or "through Christ," to the point where we may wish that Paul had paid a little more attention to the niceties of good literary style. But this is the New Testament's only message. Christianity is a faith for people who, having lost all faith in themselves, never tire of hearing the name of Jesus.

What are the "honest scales" in which Job longs to be weighed? They are the cross of Christ. In one hand the crucified Savior holds the holiness of God, and in the other He holds the sinfulness of man, and in these two hands the balance beam has come to rest. The ancient score is settled. Our sin has been fully paid for, paid on the nail.

Social Justice

"If I have denied justice to my menservants or maidservants
when they had a grievance against me,
what will I do when God confronts me? . . .
Did not the same One form us both in the womb?" (31:13-15)

Most of the good deeds that Job presents as evidence of his righteousness are simple, ordinary things: he has treated his servants justly (vv. 13-14); he has shared his food (v. 17); he has given clothing to the poor (v. 19); he has shown hospitality to strangers (v. 32). More than any one of these acts alone, it is the accumulation of them that is impressive. Job is giving the record of an entire life lived conscientiously. He was the sort of man for whom even the most mundane of daily chores was significant and worthwhile, since even the smallest matter could be handled in either a godly or an ungodly way. Northrop Frye, writing of Job's final speech, detects "a consciousness that is neither proud nor abased, but simply responsible, accepting what responsibility is there. God has clearly won His wager."

God has won His wager with Satan not because of Job's good works, but because of his good character. Character is something that is built up, like a building, through a gradual, painstaking process of placing one brick upon another. A single brick is not much. But the soundness and careful placing of each individual brick is vital to the overall result. In the same way, faith by its very nature concentrates on small things, giving its energy to the responsible completion of one ordinary task after another. True, the people of God have large visions, but those visions must be lived out one small step at a time. As Jesus said, "Whoever can be trusted with very little can also be trusted with much" (Luke 16:10). Once when His disciples were busy admiring the massive stones of the temple, the Lord redirected their attention to a widow who was dropping two pennies into the offering box, and observed, "I tell you the truth, this poor widow has put more into the treasury than all the others" (Mark 12:43). If by a stretch of the imagination we could picture Jesus standing beside us at the foot of the cross, looking up at Himself, we might hear Him make a similar observation: "You see this poor man? He might not look very great now, but I tell you the truth, this one act of His will save the world."

How is it that in God's Kingdom small and seemingly insignificant acts can turn out to be much greater than big and important acts? The answer is simple: what makes an act truly great is not its bigness, but the purity of heart of the one who performs it. Practically speaking, purity of heart is difficult to achieve on a grand scale. Rather it springs from one pure thought, one pure act, one thing done in perfect purity. Purity begins when our whole lives are narrowed to one fine focus, when the whole world falls away except for the one thing that stands before us needing to be done.

When the one thing that stands before us has to do with another person's welfare, then we have the makings of social justice. It is all very well to "practice the presence of God" in regard to all the less glamorous affairs of our private lives, from washing dishes to paying bills. But it is another kind of godliness that gives serious attention to the petty concerns of others. The essence of social justice is the assumption of personal responsibility for the quality of others' lives, especially (though not exclusively) in the case of the underprivileged. Often it happens that the underprivileged attract "helpers" who, in one way or another, are really not serving others but themselves. What drives this kind of "social worker" is the satisfaction to be found in the exercise of power over those who are weaker. But true social work begins with the surrender of personal power. Its goal is to find creative and meaningful ways of handing over power to those who lack it.

In Job's case, it was all in a day's work to hand over power even to his servants, by giving undivided attention to their trivial cares and grievances. To him such things were not trivial at all, for *"Did not the same God form us both within the womb?"* Job's sense of social justice was centered not in a committee or a task force or an impressive organization, but in his own household. There were no powerful people on his board of directors. Instead it consisted of servants, widows and orphans, and the stranger who came to his door.

Sin Boldly

"Have I concealed my sin as men do,
by hiding my guilt in my heart
because I feared the crowd?" (31:33-34)

In case we may have begun to think that the catalog of good deeds
recorded in this chapter presents a picture of implausible, superhuman virtue, Job now reminds us that he is well aware of his
sinfulness. Job's friends have been anxious to nail him with a charge
of sin, but to Job this is not even an issue. Of course he has sinned!
All along his position has been not that he has no sin, but only that
he has no *unconfessed* sin. Naturally no one can see and name every
one of his sins; sin is too deep for that. But Job is a man who had
long ago formed the habit of regular repentance, and who had
learned to place trust in its effectiveness—not because of his own
ability to analyze himself exhaustively, but rather because of the
power of the Spirit of God to search his heart. Like the psalmist he
had learned to pray, "Who can discern his errors? Forgive my hidden faults" (Ps. 19:12).

The miracle of divine forgiveness is that it covers not just particular, known sins, but sin itself. Forgiveness cannot be parceled out
piecemeal. It cannot be applied to one single behavior or incident in
one's life without also being applied to the whole life. Real forgiveness, like real love, encompasses the entire person. Such comprehensive forgiveness seems to be beyond the grasp of Job's friends.
Like so much weak theology, theirs is true as far as it goes, but it
does not go far enough. It adequately covers the total depravity of
man and the absolute righteousness of God, but it stops short of the
gospel, which is that man too can be righteous even in the midst of
his fallen condition. As the apocryphal *Book of Wisdom* expresses
this paradox, "You, our God, govern all things with mercy. Even if
we sin, we are still Yours, since we acknowledge Your dominion. But
knowing we are Yours, we shall not sin, for to be acquainted with
You is perfect righteousness" (15:1-3). Somehow it can be said of
believers that even though they continue to sin ("We all stumble in
many ways," according to James 3:2), nevertheless their true status

is that they no longer live in sin, but in righteousness. For this is a righteousness that is by faith rather than by performance.

Still, there are some who would define the sanctified life as a literal turning away from sin. True repentance, it is said, means, "stop doing it." For any believer who has felt himself deeply enmeshed in the habits of the flesh, this is a cruel oversimplification. James Houston writes of faith as "a journey through nausea, over a fearful abyss. This is because Jesus leads us through the dark tunnel of our childhood fears, our guilty secrets, and the many other things we have tried to forget and repress." Perhaps this was the situation with the desperately penitent tax collector in Luke 18, who appears to have had some sin that he longed to turn from but could not, and so he "beat his breast" and cried out, "God, have mercy on me, a sinner." Jesus' point in this parable was that the one abject prayer of the publican was more pleasing to God than all the pious thoughts and words and deeds of the Pharisee. For the essential characteristic of righteousness is not sinlessness, but rather a humble dependence upon God alone for deliverance. It is safer to be ensnared by sin and yet to trust in God, than it is to live a fine and upright life trusting in the sufficiency of one's own faith.

This is what lies behind Martin Luther's infamous dictum, "Sin boldly." It is a motto that Job would have admired. He too is a man who has learned to be at home with his sinful condition—not in the sense of making peace with sin or drifting into complacency, but in the sense of getting past the point of being shocked by his own depravity. Job knows he is a sinner; his sin holds no real surprises for him. Only proud people are taken aback by their sin; the humble know themselves too well for that. Pride might even be defined as a denial of the full extent of one's own sinfulness. As for Job, he knows his sin so well that he wears it on his sleeve for all the world to see, and this is the attitude that so scandalizes his friends. For here is a terrifying sight, a sight almost as terrifying as that of the dazzling God Himself: here is a human being who has nothing to hide. Here is someone who is naked but who is not ashamed. Job wears his depravity the way he wears his skin. It is all laid bare before the Lord and before the world, and herein lies the secret of his blamelessness.

Tāw

"I sign now my defense—let the
Almighty answer me." (31:35)

Much of what Job has said in defense of himself (including the whole of Chapter 31) has been in the form of a solemn oath or sworn affidavit. He intends his words to be taken just as seriously as a formal testimony delivered in a court of law, and in order to show that he means everything he has said and has no intention of withdrawing or altering any of it, he here declares, "I sign now my defense." To all that he has stated verbally he now puts his signature, thus rendering his testimony doubly irrevocable.

Job's statement means literally, "Here is my *taw*." Some versions translate this, "Here is my signature," since *taw*, the last letter of the Hebrew alphabet, could be used like our "X" to denote a person's "mark" or "signature." Yet even more interesting is the fact that in the ancient Hebrew script used by the author of *Job*, this letter *taw* was a cross-shaped mark. In a sense, therefore, what Job was saying is, "Here is my cross." How extraordinarily appropriate it is that this suffering man, who more than any other Old Testament figure prophetically embodies the passion of Christ, should seal all his words with the sign of the cross! Job was certainly fully literate and would have had no need to resort to scrawling his name with a crude "X." But by doing so, he showed a kind of oracular solidarity with that great statement of the Apostle Paul: "I resolved to know nothing . . . except Jesus Christ and him crucified" (1 Cor. 2:2).

Is this a farfetched theory? Perhaps. And yet isn't this tiny insignificant detail tucked away in the text of *Job* exactly the sort of hidden treasure with which Scripture abounds? The great Jewish scholar Rabbi Akiba was famous for uncovering all kinds of secret meanings in every word, every syllable, every letter of Torah. But an even greater rabbi than he, Jesus of Nazareth, put it this way: "I tell you the truth, until heaven and earth disappear, not the smallest letter, not the least stroke of a pen, will by any means disappear from the Law" (Matt. 5:18).

So when Job signs his name with a cross, it is like signing his name in blood, and in so doing he puts his hand on the central mystery of the gospel. He puts his hand on what the Bible calls "the key of David," the one key that unlocks the gates of the holy city. This key is the blood of Christ shed on the cross. For a human being is like a lock, a lock made with such wondrous precision that only one key will fit it, only one key can open it wide, and that key turns out to be the simplest, the most basic skeleton key of all: the cross. When the cross touches a human heart, that heart glides open like a great steel door swinging freely on oiled bearings. Nothing else can do this. No other sacred mystery, no other word, no other truth of Scripture, no other doctrine however glorious, can unlock the human heart. If it could—if the Word of God alone, for example, could do it—then Jesus need not have died. There was only one reason good enough for spilling the blood of the precious Lamb of God, and that was that the Kingdom of Heaven could not be opened in any other way.

Can our faith pass this simple test? Can we too, like Job, sum everything up with the sign of the cross? Perhaps the real test is how well we get along with other believers. For there is only one reason good enough for the Body of Christ on earth, His Church, ever to be divided, and that is the recognition of, or the failure to recognize, the cross. Only the issue of the cross-centered gospel, the simple gospel stripped of all nonessentials, should ever be allowed to come between Christians. For where else but at the cross is the ground upon which all of us can meet in perfect unity and love? All other theological meeting grounds, no matter how valid and true they might be, spell disunity if they are ever allowed to overshadow the cross by assuming center-stage. Only the cross holds the whole body of Christian doctrine together, giving life and light to it all. Is the cross really equal to this task? Here is what Jesus said about it: "I, when I am lifted up from the earth, will draw all men to myself" (John 12:32). It is the cross and the cross alone—not any other spiritual gift or sign or dogma or focus or strategy or theme that the church might choose to emphasize—that will call all the world to repentance and life and the unity of eternal love.

Robe and Crown

"Let my accuser put his indictment in writing.
Surely I would wear it on my shoulder,
I would put it on like a crown." (31:35-36)

The last verses of Job's final speech are filled with gloriously complex layers of sacred irony. To begin with, there is the consummate irony of Job's daring his "accuser" (whom he believes to be God) to put something in writing. Little does Job realize that the very document he is requesting will ultimately take the form of Holy Scripture, and in particular the book of *Job* itself in which the Lord, far from condemning Job, will clearly exonerate him by saying, "There is no one on earth like him; he is blameless and upright" (1:8). Of course all along the reader knows that Job's real accuser is not God but Satan. But Job does not know this. The crux of his suffering is that his oppression appears to be originating with God Himself, and for this he feels entitled to a written explanation.

Job's yearning to have something in writing from the hand of God may, incidentally, be an argument in favor of this book being the earliest of all the Scriptures. For it seems clear that at the time of the story there was no authoritative written document by which Job's case could have been judged, no Mosaic code of laws governing all relations between man and God. If such Scriptures had existed, then surely they would have been referred to in the dialogue. The friends would have quoted them to support their case, and Job too would have cited them in his defense, just as Jesus told the Pharisees, "Do not think I will accuse you before the Father. Your accuser is Moses, on whom your hopes are set" (John 5:45). In short, if any Scriptures had been extant, we may be sure that Job would have found in them the evidence of his righteousness.

This is precisely Job's point when he cries, in effect, "If only God would throw the book at me!" If only God would spell out His charges on paper, Job feels, then he is so certain both of his own innocence and of God's intrinsic justice that he knows he could take the divine indictment and wrap it around himself like a royal robe, "put it on like a crown" and then approach the throne of God "like a prince" and "give him an account of my every step" (v. 37). What a marvelous picture this is of faith placing its total confidence in the Word of God! Moreover, Job's exotic imagery hauntingly prefigures the crucifixion, hinting as it does at the purple robe and the crown of thorns which Christ's enemies intended as signs of mocking accusation against Him, but which He, scorning their shame, accepted and wore with princely humility as He ascended the steps to His throne on Calvary.

At bottom, Job's unusual choice of images in this passage suggests the way in which the believer covers himself with the blood of Christ, donning as protection from divine wrath the very blood that cries out against his own sin. For the mystery of the gospel is that the place of man's greatest treachery has become the place of his salvation. Precisely on the spot where the Son of God was brutally murdered by human hands, there opens the door to eternal life. In the same place where Adam ate from the tree of the knowledge of good and evil, there the Lord has transplanted the tree of life. Goodness was not enough for Adam; he wanted to know evil too. And in reaching for them both, he lost the simple good forever. Goodness became, in mankind, something complicated, admixed, corrupted. No longer a simple thing. No longer even good. But then the Lord set in motion a fantastic plan. He said: "All right, if people insist on choosing the one tree that I have prohibited, then I will do something that will boggle their minds once and for all. I will take that one tree, that one forbidden option, and I will make *it* the very instrument of salvation. No more shall life be found in any of the other trees of the garden, but only in this one. In the very place where My children have betrayed Me, even there will I raise the banner of life. Even there will I pour out My love on them and reconcile them to Myself."

And then the impossible thing that God had ordained actually came to pass. The very place where people had turned their faces most hatefully from the Lord became the place where the Lord's face was to shine most brightly upon them. The place of sin and indictment became the place of redemption. The tree of the knowledge of good and evil became, by God's decree, the tree of life. The two trees became one in the cross of Christ.

According to Job

Here the words of Job are ended. (31:40)

The gospel is never just the gospel: it is always the gospel *according to*. The good news of God is always filtered through an earthly medium, through a human being born into this world, and this is so because the miracle of incarnation is part and parcel of the gospel itself. Without incarnation, there is no gospel. And incarnation has two aspects to it: firstly, God became a man in the person of Jesus Christ, which is the great doctrine of the Incarnation; but secondly, man in turn must become like Christ, and this entails what might be called a "little incarnation." In the words of Martin Luther, God wants to make us into a "race of Christs."

So the Bible is not only the Word of God; it is also the word of Paul, of John, of Jeremiah, and of Job. Part of the good news is that God does not impose Himself on the world, but rather shares Himself with it. He entrusts His very Self to individual human beings, and delights in expressing that Self in different ways through the kaleidoscopic range of human character. Hence the gospel is very much the gospel *according to*, as the voice of God necessarily takes on the tone quality of human voices, and the temperament of God is colored by the many and varied temperaments of His human instruments.

No doubt this is why Paul repeatedly referred to the message he preached as "my gospel" (see, for example, Romans 2:16). He freely acknowledged that an element of human interpretation entered into revelation, and at the same time insisted that his peculiar slant did not in any way alter the essential nature of the gospel itself. Did not Paul preach the same message as Jesus? And yet, inevitably he drew upon his own experience, his own thought patterns, his own vocabulary—all of which were different from his Master's. Paul was not just a mouthpiece; he was a person in his own right, even as Jesus Himself was. Though Jesus could make the claim, "The words I say to you are not just my own" (John 14:10), still, mysteriously, they were His own too. He had His own way of putting things.

We might even go so far as to suggest that if God had, from the very beginning, chosen some other person besides Jesus of Nazareth to be the world's Messiah (as outrageous as this notion is), then the gospel would have turned out to be completely different from what it is. There would be no babe in a manger, no water baptism, no Sermon on the Mount, no Eucharist, no cross. Of course such a speculation is so preposterously theoretical as to be sacrilegious. For the glorious fact is that God did choose this Jesus—hallelujah!—and He did choose this same baptism, this Eucharist, and this cross to be the means of grace for the entire human race, and there is no other way to the Father but this way. This is the gospel according to God.

But God also chose Job. He chose this particular man, with all his crudeness and his flagrant weaknesses and eccentricities, to be held up before the Devil and before all the world as a radiant example of saintliness. Does this mean that Job was to be a pattern for all other saints? Does it mean we are to imitate him? Not exactly. For the moment we try to imitate a mere man, we run the risk of suppressing in ourselves that very individuality without which the gospel cannot be incarnated in our own lives. Paul wrote, "Whatever you have seen in me, put it into practice" (Phil. 4:9)—but to copy what we see *in* a person is not the same as copying the person himself. We cannot have anyone else's spiritual life. We can only have the spiritual life that God gives us, the life that He Himself has personally tailored for us like a suit of clothes—or, to choose a more intimate image, the life that He has molded for us like the unique features of our own face. Job is so wonderful and so radical a character that it would be impossible to imitate him. But simply by being so much himself, he sets us free too to be ourselves. By refusing to be anyone else but who, by the grace of God, he is, he gives us the courage to stand against the terrible satanic pressures of conformity. As John Chrysostom wrote, "Find the door of your heart, and you will discover that it is the door of the kingdom of God."

As Chapter 31 closes, the gospel according to Job is now complete. Job has had his say, spent all his breath, and "the words of Job are ended." Actually our hero will speak a few more words before the story is over—words of profound repentance: "I despise myself and repent in dust and ashes" (42:6). For the process of becoming a true individual, it seems, involves dying to oneself. One must, like Job, run completely out of steam, come to the end of the line, exhaust all the energy of the flesh, and disappear. One must be crucified with Christ.

ELIHU

(Job 32–37)

"Yet if there is an angel on his side as a mediator, one out of a thousand, to tell a man what is right for him, to be gracious to a man and say, 'Spare him from going down to the pit; I have found a ransom for him'—then his flesh is renewed like a child's."

—JOB 33:23-25

There is one God and one mediator between God and men, the man Christ Jesus, who gave himself as a ransom for all.

—1 TIM. 2:5-6

Elihu

So these three men stopped answering Job, because he was
righteous in his own eyes. . . . When Elihu saw that the three
men had nothing more to say, his anger was aroused. (32:1, 5)

Apart from the Prologue and Epilogue, the only prose in this
book is to be found in the first five verses of Chapter 32. This
short paragraph provides a capsule summary of the entire
dialogue with the words, "Job was righteous in his own eyes," and
it also serves to introduce the brand-new character Elihu.

As we meet Elihu, the word "anger" is used of him three times in
as many verses. This fellow must have been just about hopping out
of his skin! Elihu is angry with everybody. He is the classic angry
young man, and from the outset what we need to notice about this
kind of anger is that it puts him in a class by himself. The fact that
he is angry at both sides of the debate separates him from Job, on
the one hand, but also from the other three friends. In short, there
is something peculiar about Elihu. He does not side with Job, but
neither does he side with the establishment. He is an odd man out.
In fact next to Job himself Elihu is by far the most interesting, complex, and fully-realized character in the book.

This is not to say that readers admire him. On the contrary Elihu
is generally given short shrift and treated as though he does not
really belong. Many find him a consummate bore, and most scholars are of the opinion that the Elihu section was a later and a rather
unfortunate addition to an otherwise well-integrated manuscript.
What are we to make of this puzzling character? Here is some of the
conflicting evidence we need to sift:

1) The idea that Elihu is somehow *different* would seem to be sup-
ported by the author himself, who by saving his appearance until
last has awarded him a highly strategic position in the dialogue.
Moreover Elihu is given six full chapters of uninterrupted speech,
more than any of the other friends.

2) At the same time, it must be admitted that the actual substance
of Elihu's arguments is very little different from that of Job's other
friends. There are subtle variations in his theological bent (for

example, his view of suffering as a form of spiritual discipline is new), but essentially Elihu does not say anything we have not heard before.

3) Significantly, when we come to the Epilogue Elihu's name is omitted from the blanket condemnation that God issues against Job's other three friends (see 42:7). Elihu alone seems to be exempted from the need to repent and to apologize to Job.

4) Nevertheless, it is obvious that Elihu does have some glaring faults: he talks too much; he repeats himself; he is enormously conceited. Worst of all, like the other friends he seriously misreads Job's problem as being one of unrepented sin, and as a result he condemns a righteous man. Pastorally he misses the mark completely, so that rather than truly ministering to Job's suffering, he adds to it.

5) Finally, and most mysteriously, the last chapter of Elihu's speech is one of the most stirring and magnificent passages in the book, easily bearing comparison with the words of the Lord Himself in Chapters 38—41. The devout reader cannot help but feel this passage to be an entirely appropriate introduction to the Lord's own appearance.

All of this adds up to a mightily confusing picture. And yet, isn't this just the way life is? We want characters in a book to fit into neat schemes. We want there to be a sense of aesthetic rightness to their presence. But Elihu is not like this, and neither is life. Real people do not come in boxes. At least, there may be some people—such as Eliphaz, Bildad, and Zophar—who seem more boxed-up than others. But Elihu is definitely cut from a different cloth. With all his weaknesses, he remains an individual, and in a book that celebrates the sanctity of fierce individuality, this is saying a great deal. While it is true that Elihu makes a bad mistake in his judgment of Job, in the final analysis we might have to admit that this spirited young man actually comes much closer to sharing Job's own heart than is at first apparent. In the following chapters we shall try to examine this paradox from a few of its many angles.

Breaking the Deadlock

Elihu . . . became very angry with Job for justifying himself rather than God. He was also angry with the three friends, because they had found no way to refute Job, and yet had condemned him. (32:2-3)

Elihu is angry with Job because the only way he could find to justify himself was by accusing God, and he is angry with Job's friends because the only way they could find to justify God was by accusing Job. Elihu is angry that the debate has gone round and round in circles without producing any solution to this deadlock, for he feels instinctively that some solution must be possible. And in this his instinct is correct. For is this not the very deadlock that Jesus Christ came into the world to break? People are angry with God; God is angry with people; Christ came to make peace between the two. *Job* is a book that, like Jesus Himself, pleads both sides of the case at once.

In fact *Job* may be unique among Old Testament Scriptures in the audacity with which it takes the part of humanity just as fully as the part of God. "Everywhere else," writes G. K. Chesterton, "the Old Testament positively rejoices in the obliteration of man in comparison with the divine purpose." *Job*, however, "stands definitely alone because it definitely asks, 'But what is the purpose of God?'" Every other Old Testament saint who questions God does so with the utmost humility and tentativeness; even the psalmists do not rail against God the way Job does. The great mystery of Job is the astounding boldness of his approach to the court of Heaven. Where did he get this boldness? How does he get away with a degree of holy presumption which, strictly speaking, only became possible in the Christian era? For alone of all the world's religions Christianity teaches us to "approach God with freedom and confidence" (Eph. 3:12), and with "confidence to enter the Most Holy Place" (Heb. 10:19).

Job is so confident in defending his own righteous status that his friends, including Elihu, feel that he is defending himself over and against God. But they could hardly be more mistaken. In reality

Job's defense of his righteousness *is* a defense of God. It is a defense of God's faithfulness, and in the end this is the only leg a believer has to stand on. For our faith rests not in any personal godliness but rather in the fact that we "consider him faithful who made the promise" (Heb. 11:11). Properly speaking, righteousness is not something we possess already, but a promise we expect to see fulfilled. As Paul puts it, "By faith we eagerly await through the Spirit the righteousness for which we hope" (Gal. 5:5). Or Peter: "Set your hope fully on the grace to be given you when Jesus Christ is revealed" (1 Peter 1:13). Though perfect righteousness may not yet be present in us, we know that the One who promises it is faithful and therefore it is as good as done. By faith it is a *fait accompli*. And so as was said of Mary, "Blessed is she who has believed that what the Lord has said to her will be accomplished!" (Luke 1:45).

If we are going to defend the glorious name of our Lord, it is incumbent upon us to defend our own name too—that is, to defend to the death the fact that He has justified us. There is no way around this seeming arrogance. There is no place in Christianity for false modesty or squeamishness. God Most High has birthed us into His royal family and christened us with His own name; we are His very flesh and blood! "How great is the love the Father has lavished on us, that we should be called children of God! And that is what we are!" (1 John 3:1).

By the end of *Job* God does, of course, rebuke Job for his presumptuousness—but this has less to do with who Job is than it does with *who God is*. In this book God does not get His way merely because He has the more convincing case, but rather because He is God. Hence even after the Lord has overruled Job and Job has recanted, the latter's case still remains a weighty one. Job's arguments hang in the air, and his long ordeal of suffering still stands, like the cross itself, as Exhibit A in this strange and cosmic courtroom drama. For the suffering of the faithful is never something to be taken lightly or brushed aside. No, it is so ponderous a reality that God's ultimate response to it is not to negate it, but rather to join us in it.

Elihu's anger, like Job's own anger, is an expression of what it feels like to grapple with such deep mysteries without having any knowledge of the one key factor: the cross of Christ. To try to plumb, apart from the cross, the dual enigma of man's suffering and of God's love is like trying to take hold of the east wind in one hand and the west wind in the other and hold the two together.

The Wisdom of Youth

"I am young in years, and you are old;
that is why I was fearful, not daring to speak up. . . .
It is not only the old who are wise." (32:6, 9)

Elihu was a young man who was fed up to the teeth with being told, "Wisdom comes with age, my boy. You'll understand these things when you get to be a little older." How young Elihu was we do not know. Probably he was fresh out of seminary, so to speak. Or maybe he was the sort of fellow who would not even have bothered wasting his time in a seminary—like Jesus who had no formal training either (as we gather from John 7:15).

If we were to put a few more choice words into Elihu's mouth at this point, it might give us a better idea of his state of mind. Perhaps he would have sounded something like this:

"I know the kind of wisdom that age brings. It is a wisdom of complacency, of compromise, of disillusionment, and of weariness. Age is a number, and that is all. It is no more significant as the yardstick of a man's wisdom than is the number in his bank book. If anything, age is a measurement of the distance traveled from simplicity. When I was six years old I was so wise that I could go skipping down the street in plain view of a crowd, and singing at the top of my lungs! Now there is wisdom for you.

"What age teaches is not wisdom, but knowledge. Mere knowledge. And knowledge is no guarantee of action. Some of the most knowledgeable people in the world are practically incompetent in handling the daily affairs of their own lives, let alone in living a wise or a godly life. Never yet have I met anyone who lived a better life merely because of his great age. On the contrary, in many cases the passing of the years only causes people to relax their disciplines, to abandon their dreams, and to cease to obey their finest instincts.

"No, if you ask me, the old seem to grow more afraid of themselves and of life in general. They know they have only a little time left, and so they grow excessively cautious. They can no longer risk spontaneity or adventure. They cannot afford to make mistakes, and so they become less human. Where has the 'wisdom of their years' gotten them? It has led them into despair. And worse than that, they have lived with their despair for so long that they do not even recognize it as despair anymore."

And so on. Isn't this how Elihu would have been thinking? It is, of course, a somewhat exaggerated view. Nevertheless it must be admitted that one of the chief qualities of youth is its ability to stand apart from the status quo and to view the adult world with a certain valid and refreshing objectivity. How this is needed in the Church! Indeed it is often the case that those who see a congregation's problems most clearly are not those in the "inner circle," but rather those who are on the fringes. Youth, newcomers, ethnic minorities, the poor and the suffering—in many ways such people are on the outside looking in, and Elihu is one of this company. His youthful idealism reminds us that Jesus too was a relatively young man, who did not shrink from teaching, rebuking, healing, and discipling people often much older than Himself. From the time He was twelve years old and set the temple teachers back on their heels, Christ embodied the truth that wisdom is not always the prerogative of the aged. We see this too in the case of Paul's young protégé Timothy, whom the apostle counseled, "Don't let anyone look down on you because you are young" (1 Tim. 4:12). Timothy's example shows that age is not a Biblical criterion for the assignment of leadership in the church. Maturity counts, but age does not. Church history is full of people like King Solomon who were endowed with great wisdom in their youth but who apparently lost it in their elder years.

Jesus tells us that "anyone who will not receive the kingdom of God like a little child will never enter it" (Luke 18:17). Ironically, in the family of God to become a little child is to have attained maturity. Spiritual growth means growth in childlikeness. To grow up is to grow down.

Elihu the Charismatic

"It is the Spirit in a man,
the breath of the Almighty,
that gives understanding." (32:8)

Elihu refers to "the Spirit" no less than three times in the first
twenty verses of his speech, and he uses the word in a way
that it is seldom used elsewhere in *Job*, a way that begs for
capitalization. Job says, for example, "My spirit is broken" (17:1),
but Elihu says, "The Spirit of God has made me" (33:4). Eliphaz
asks Job, "*How is it that you turn your spirit against God?*" (15:13),
but Elihu says of himself, "The Spirit within me compels me"
(32:18). Elihu seems very conscious of the fact that the Spirit of God
is to be distinguished from one's own spirit, and that by rights the
former should have full control over the latter. In the verse quoted
at the head of this chapter, Elihu's point is that when people speak
by their own spirit they are not wise—not even if they happen to be
elders with years of experience. The truly wise person is the one,
whether old or young, whose spirit is yielded to the Holy Spirit, and
this status Elihu claims for himself. He even goes so far as to boast
the direct inspiration of the Holy Spirit when he states, "I get my
knowledge from afar . . . one perfect in knowledge is with you"
(36:3-4).

There are many other signs of a strong emphasis on "the things
of the Spirit" in Elihu's theology. To cite another example, he has a
decided preoccupation with the issue of how the Lord "speaks" to
people. "God does speak," he insists, "now one way, now another
. . . in a dream, in a vision of the night" (33:14-15). When later he
reflects upon "God my Maker, who gives songs in the night"
(35:10), one senses that he is speaking from rich personal experience, and when he exclaims passionately, "Listen! Listen to the roar
of his voice!" (37:2) we can hardly escape the feeling that this young
man really is, at that very moment, hearing the voice of the Lord.

Elihu is alert to the fact that in the lives of God's people the real
problem is not one of belief, but rather of obedience to what is
believed. In many churches all the right things are in place: these are

born-again believers who are going to Heaven and who accept on principle all the major tenets of the faith, including the divine authority of God's Holy Spirit to govern every aspect of their lives. The only catch is that little phrase "on principle." All too often the Lordship of the Holy Spirit is more a matter of principle than of practice. When the Spirit of Jesus wrote to the church in Ephesus, "If you do not repent, I will come to you and remove your lamp-stand from its place" (Rev. 2:5), He was speaking to people whose doctrinal orthodoxy was impeccable. Their problem was that the Lord did not really hold first place in their lives; His Spirit no longer swayed their wills as He had in the first flush of their conversion. If they had wanted, as happened to Paul in Acts 16:7, to do something that "the Spirit of Jesus would not allow," they likely would have barged ahead anyway. Their spirit may have been willing, but their flesh was weak.

This is the front line of the battle among evangelical Christians. Our struggle is between flesh and Spirit, between creed and living faith, between mere orthodoxy and authentic discipleship. In the *Gospel of John* we read about those to whom "Jesus would not entrust himself," even though they "believed in his name" (2:23-24). Today we face the phenomenon of entire churches to whom, if the Holy Spirit has ever entrusted Himself, no visitor would know it. Elihu is a young person who is very sensitive to the dynamics of this issue, and this is one of the keys to the complexity of his character and to understanding his place in *Job*. Unlike Job's other friends, who have fallen prey to a diehard conservatism, Elihu appears to be wide-open to the refreshing winds of God's Spirit. He is, if you like, a kind of charismatic. This does not save him from having some serious character flaws, nor from indulging his own brand of overzealous spiritualism. Nevertheless, where the other friends refuse to budge from their hardline positions, in Elihu's case we can at least detect a person whose spirituality is in flux, a person whose faith is moving in the right direction. Just how far he is prepared to move will become apparent by the end of his speech, at which point we see a transformation come over him that is nothing short of amazing. It is this spark of real openness to the Holy Spirit that redeems Elihu and makes him such an intriguing figure, and that even allows him to be the person who, like John the Baptist in a later age, "prepares the way for the Lord."

The Voice of Renewal

"The Spirit within me compels me;
inside I am like bottled-up wine,
like new wineskins ready to burst." (32:18-19)

Here Elihu unknowingly seizes upon one of the New Testament's most potent images of spiritual renewal: new wine in new wineskins. Perhaps we could best characterize the effervescent young Elihu by calling him the "voice of renewal": the fresh, radical, charismatic voice that is heard anew (praise God!) in every generation. Spiritual radicalism, of course, has both a positive and a negative side. On the one hand, such voices are to be preferred to those of the staid and musty old guard. Yet on the other hand, it is often true that they lack maturity, and their authentic giftedness and zeal does not always preserve them from making serious errors in judgment.

Essentially Elihu is like so many young charismatic Christians, who are able to see and to analyze the problems of the church with great clarity, but not always with great depth or understanding. They can tend to be reformers, not pastors—exhorters, not encouragers. To the extent that vibrant renewal movements can truly revive and invigorate a stale church, they need to be wholeheartedly embraced. But to the extent that they may lead away from the simple gospel (which, ever so subtly, they often do) and towards an unbalanced triumphalism, they need to be handled with great caution. Undoubtedly there is a certain amount of pure vinegar in what Elihu so confidently serves up as the unadulterated wine of the Holy Spirit. But the fact remains that whatever is good in the wine of reformers needs to be uncorked and shared around, and it should be possible to do this without the bottles exploding and splinters of glass flying all over the room.

The presence of Elihu serves to clarify our focus on one of the principal themes of this book: the *theologia crucis* (theology of the cross) versus the *theologia gloriae* (theology of glory). When charismatics err, they tend to err on the side of glory. They are always on the lookout for the manifest presence of the Holy Spirit. The only problem with this is that a charismatic manifestation is not the answer to all our problems. There is only one perfect answer: the cross. The cross is the place where God manifests Himself most potently. Yet paradoxically, He is hard to see there—not because the evidence of Him is so slight or small, but rather because He is so unfathomably enormous. He is much bigger than either the charismatics or the noncharismatics want Him to be. He is larger than life. Therefore He tends to inhabit depths more than surfaces, often preferring to do His work quietly and unobtrusively. Charismatics who resist this notion can be like the brothers of Jesus who tempted Him by saying, "No one who wants to become a public figure acts in secret. Since you are doing these things, show yourself to the world" (John 7:4).

Elihu truly is a bundle of contradictions—at once arrogant and sensitive, cold and passionate, brash and insecure, foolish and wise. He is, in short, exactly the sort of person whom God has often used throughout history as an instrument for revival. Why does the Lord do this? Why does He choose to work through such unrefined personalities? Why in the book of *Judges* (which is a sort of Old Testament textbook on revivalism) did God continually single out such greatly flawed and wet-behind-the-ears characters as Gideon, Jephthah, and Samson to be the leaders of renewal in their day? The answer is both obvious and obscure: it is so that all of the glory will be the Lord's. The gifts of the Holy Spirit are intended less for individuals than for the larger body. They are given not so much *to* as *through* a person, and hence there can occur the strange phenomenon of a spiritual gift passing right through an individual and blessing others, yet without doing the original recipient much good at all.

The case of Elihu may bring to mind a famous warning of Paul's: "If I have the gift of prophecy and can fathom all mysteries and all knowledge, and if I have a faith that can move mountains, but have not love, I am nothing" (1 Cor. 13:2). We may think that Paul is exaggerating merely to make a point. Is it really possible for God-given wisdom, faith, and prophecy to be uncoupled with love? Strangely, the answer is yes. Not only does this actually happen, but it happens all too commonly. Speaking by the Spirit means more than speaking the truth: it means speaking the truth in love.

The Drunken Porter

"But now, Job, listen to my words;
pay attention to everything I say.
I am about to open my mouth;
my words are on the tip of my tongue." (33:1-2)

Despite all the good that might be said of Elihu, the fact remains that he really is an astonishingly pompous little windbag. He takes his entire first chapter, for example, plus portions of the second, simply to clear his throat and announce that he has something to say. "Listen to me," he declares, "I too will tell you what I know" (32:10); "I too will have my say" (32:17); "I must speak and find relief; I must open my lips and reply" (32:20); "My words are on the tip of my tongue" (33:2). As we first meet him, Elihu is the very archetype of the self-important bore. By the time we reach 32:18 and he states, "I am full of words," no reader can be in any doubt that his estimation of himself is perfectly correct. As Proverbs 10:19 dryly observes, "When words are many, sin is not absent."

It is understandable that Elihu should be fearful of stepping in and seeming to lecture his elders. It must have taken tremendous courage for him to barge ahead and put in his two cents' worth, and in the long run we shall see how, in a very surprising way, the Lord does honor Elihu for his youthful pluck. Nevertheless, at the outset there can be little doubt that he presents all the appearance of a fool, and that this impression is deliberately set up by the author. Yet why? If we are intended to take Elihu at all seriously, why should he be made to seem even more ridiculous than the other friends?

In Shakespeare's *Macbeth* there is a memorable scene immediately following the treacherous murder of King Duncan, in which a drunken porter delivers a rollicking comic monologue. The scene is justly famous for being a preposterous anti-climax, a brilliant interlude of low-level black comedy which, even as it knocks the wind out of tragedy's dark sails, produces an eerie atmosphere of moral stupor that somehow serves to intensify the underlying horror. With the appearance of Elihu in *Job*, does something similar happen?

Certainly the dramatic effect is a subtler one, and yet just like the drunken porter in *Macbeth*, Elihu unwittingly lightens the tone. For thirty chapters we have had an atmosphere of gridlocked religious tension, and it is Elihu's privilege to begin to cut through this and break it down. While it is by no means his conscious intention to accomplish this by making a clown of himself, this is one of the ways that God uses him.

There is another important consideration in assessing Elihu's role in this play, which may be expressed by a question: what would have happened if the appearance of the Lord had followed immediately upon the heels of Job's last words? What would be the effect of this? Might it not leave the impression that a devout person could petition God and legitimately expect an immediate answer? But that would be to undermine one of the principal lessons of the book, which is the need to wait upon the Lord and persistently seek Him through times of darkness. There is a delay between human initiative and divine response, and the reality of this delay is the seed around which all of Job's hopes cluster. Without painful waiting, true faith would be impossible. As Lauren King writes, "At the victory banquet, faith sits by unneeded." No matter how advanced we may be in prayer, we cannot usually get instant results, but instead God answers in His own time and in His own way. And usually His answers take such surprising forms that the humble person of prayer is left with absolutely no basis for self-congratulation, but rather is humbled all the more.

The Elihu episode, coming as it does as a buffer between Job and God, preserves the book from being debased into a triumphalist tract. For six long chapters we scratch our heads and wonder what in the world this whippersnapper Elihu is doing—and only then does the Lord put in His appearance. God is pleased to make use of the bumptious garrulousness of the young Elihu, rather than the agonized pleadings of the mature Job, as the means of setting the stage for His theophany, and in this way God is glorified rather than Job. Revival does not come just because people get very spiritual, or because they tear out their hair, or even because they pour out their hearts as Job did.

Revival comes in the time and manner that God wills it to come.

Purity of Heart

"You have said in my hearing—
I heard the very words—
'I am pure and without sin;
I am clean and free from guilt.'" *(33:8-9)*

To set the record straight, Job did not really say the words attributed to him by Elihu in the verse above. At least, the direct quote is nowhere to be found. Certainly Job has been arguing that he is "free from guilt," but he is quite clear that this does not mean he is "without sin." The question of whether a man can be a sinner and still be "pure" and "clean" is the nub of the controversy in this book. Eliphaz had asked, "What is man, that he could be pure?" (15:14); Bildad had suggested that if Job were really pure he would not be in such a fix (8:6); and Zophar, like Elihu above, had scoffed at Job's claim, "My beliefs are flawless and I am pure in [God's] sight" (11:4).

This last statement provides a much-needed focus for the debate on purity. The basis of Job's argument is not that he is pure in any worldly sense, but that he is "pure in [God's] sight." His friends completely misunderstand this subtle but important distinction, and so they take Job's words as an outrageous form of vainglory. In today's terms, they would probably have accused him of holding to the doctrine of "sinless perfection," which he certainly did not. In fact everything Job actually says on the subject of purity may be summed up by his simple comment in 16:17, "My prayer is pure." This is really all Job is claiming. Like Paul he would have defined believers as "those who call on the Lord out of a pure heart" (2 Tim. 2:22). Job's friends seem to be much more preoccupied with the problem of purity than he is, but the purity they seek is of an external sort, not the purity of the heart.

What is purity of heart? It is the sixth Beatitude: "Blessed are the pure in heart, for they will see God" (Matt. 5:8). It is also what Jesus meant when He said, "Be perfect, as your heavenly Father is perfect" (Matt. 5:48). The Lord was not exaggerating or posing a task that is too difficult. Perfect purity of heart is difficult, to be sure. But it is not so difficult that it cannot be achieved, and in growing measure in the lives of the faithful. Perhaps purity of heart could be compared to sinking a thirty-foot putt on the golf course: it is something that feels right all the way through. When you act out of purity of heart, you know you have done something perfect. You do not know how that is possible, for you yourself are imperfect. But you know perfection when you see it. You know that this is what Paul meant when he wrote, "Love . . . comes from a pure heart" (1 Tim. 1:5) and, "To the pure, all things are pure" (Titus 1:15).

In Exodus 24:10 we read that before the throne of God the elders of Israel saw "something like a pavement made of sapphire, clear as the sky itself." If we enter into the courts of the Lord and stand in His presence, we shall find ourselves standing on this clear sky-blue sea of crystal, and then we shall know purity of heart. It is like being in a glass-bottomed boat in the middle of a perfectly limpid mountain lake. Purity means that there is no impurity. It is not a relative thing, but an absolute. "The wisdom that comes from heaven is first of all pure" (James 3:17). This is how we can recognize the voice of God and distinguish it from all the other voices that clamor for our attention: the Lord's voice is *first of all pure*. In this voice there is no admixture of impurity, no shadow of doubt nor hint of confusion. It is so pure that it makes our inner being resonate like a struck gong. As Bob Gemmell puts it, "A tastebud goes off in our heart." Suddenly we know what perfection feels like. Suddenly we catch a glimpse of what it will finally be like to be without sin. This is the purity of heart that enables us to "see God." The oftener we experience this, the more pure and sanctified we become. Doubtless we will fall back again and again into a sense of impurity, and often we will be confused and embattled. But if, in the words of Proverbs 22:11, we "love a pure heart," then the miracle of purity will always return to us, and we shall have more and more of it until gradually it will mark our entire lives. No longer will perfect purity be something mystical, laughable, or unattainable, but it will be one of the distinguishing marks of our character, as it was of Job's.

Chastening

"A man may be chastened on a bed of pain
with constant distress in his bones. . . .
God does all these things to a man—
twice, even three times—
to turn back his soul from the pit,
that the light of life may shine on him." (33:19, 29-30)

More than any of the other friends, Elihu develops the idea of suffering as a form of spiritual discipline or chastening. While the other friends do touch on this theme, there is a subtle difference in the way Elihu approaches it. Where the others view suffering as punishment for sinners, Elihu sees it as the Lord's way of correcting and healing the lives of those He is already committed to saving. His perspective is less that of Job's friends than it is of Paul who wrote, "When we are judged by the Lord, we are being disciplined so that we will not be condemned with the world" (1 Cor. 11:32).

The only problem with Elihu's assessment is that Job is not being judged by the Lord at all, and if anyone is being disciplined in this story it is not Job but his friends. How often does it happen that, in the very act of concluding that someone else is being "chastened," we bring chastening upon ourselves? From the Lord's point of view, Job's suffering has come about not because of his need for discipline, but rather as the direct result of his righteousness. Far from attracting the wrath of God, Job's quality of life has attracted the wrath of Satan. In the same way Jesus warned Peter, "Simon, Simon, Satan has asked to sift you as wheat" (Luke 22:31). Why did the Lord allow Satan's wrath to descend upon Job and, albeit in a different way, upon Peter? Because He knew that these were men who would benefit from anything and everything that happened to them, and who would glorify Him in the process. For that is the way it is with the righteous. Through suffering the Lord takes great saints and makes them greater and more saintly.

In a technical sense, of course, Elihu was correct to assume that Job was being chastened by his suffering, just as Peter was chastened. And yet, because of the kind of people Job and Peter were, it would be truer to say, not that they were being chastened, but that their suffering would inevitably have a chastening effect upon them. For *"all things work together for good to those who love God"* (Rom. 8:28). Elihu was right that spiritual discipline was a factor in Job's situation, but he was wrong that this was the primary reason behind the ordeal. In fact discipline was a relatively small part of the total picture, so small that it was hardly worth talking about. It is true that both the Old and New Testaments state clearly, "The Lord disciplines those he loves, and he punishes everyone he accepts as a son" (Heb. 12:6; Prov. 3:12). But when a believer has just lost ten children and is on the brink of mental and physical collapse, it is not the time to tell him he is being punished. On the contrary, whatever element of spiritual discipline may be involved in such a tragedy, its effect may be lost if the sufferer succumbs to dwelling guiltily on his sinfulness.

This whole problem can be clarified by a careful reading of John 9:1-3: "As [Jesus] went along, he saw a man blind from birth. His disciples asked him, 'Rabbi, who sinned, this man or his parents, that he was born blind?' 'Neither this man nor his parents sinned, but this happened so that the work of God might be displayed in his life.'" See how wonderfully Jesus shifts the entire focus of the discussion. The disciples were focused on the blind man and his sin; but Jesus was focused on what God was going to do for the man. It would have been quite easy for the Lord to reply instead, "Yes, this man is indeed a wretched sinner, and his parents are sinners too, and the entire family deserved this tragedy and brought it on themselves." Would not such a statement, as far as it went, have been perfectly true? But it does not go far enough. It spells out the utter depravity of man in his fallen condition, but it does not touch upon the gospel. Surely Jesus knew as well as the Pharisees that the man born blind had been "steeped in sin at birth" (John 9:34). But He also knew a better truth: He knew, and embodied, the sheer grace of God reaching out to heal and redeem the undeserving sinner.

Glimpses of
the Trinity

"Yet if there is an angel on his side
as a mediator, one out of a thousand,
to tell a man what is right for him,
to be gracious to him and say,
'Spare him from going down to the pit;
I have found a ransom for him'—
then his flesh is renewed like a child's." (33:23-25)

To any Christian reader these words, coming straight out of the blue, seem to erupt off the page. Where in the world did Elihu get this idea of a heavenly mediator? It is like that moment in the gospel story when John the Baptist looks at Jesus of Nazareth and exclaims, "Look, the Lamb of God, who takes away the sin of the world!" (John 1:29). All we can do is shake our heads and say, "How did John know this? And how on earth did he draw together into one simple statement so many complex strands of Biblical imagery?" The only answer is that his insight did not come from earth but from Heaven.

Elihu also exhibits an astonishing gift for prophecy, and this is one reason why we cannot dismiss him quite so easily as we can Job's other friends. Elihu has his ridiculous side, but he also reaches for and touches the sublime. Is not the passage above reminiscent of those most brilliant moments in the speeches of Job himself, when a corner of the veil covering the gospel seemed to be lifted, and by the power of the Holy Spirit Job gave utterance to New Testament mysteries? In 9:33 he had mused, "If only there were someone to arbitrate between us," and in 16:19 he apparently saw the fulfillment of his longing when he proclaimed, "Even now my witness is in heaven; my advocate is on high!" In the same way, we now hear Elihu speaking of a heavenly being who intercedes with God for human lives by offering a ransom. Elihu even designates this being as a "mediator," using a term which the New Testament freely applies to Jesus Christ.

In Hebrew the word "mediator" means literally "translator" or

"interpreter." To a modern North American audience a fair equivalent might be the term "umpire." An umpire is someone who
favors neither side, or rather who favors both sides at once by
upholding the standards of fair play. To accomplish this, the umpire
is given full authority to pass judgments. When an umpire makes a
call it matters not whether sixty thousand fans in the stadium boo
him, the call still stands. This is exactly what Job, along with every
other believer, needs—someone to wave his hands with finality over
our slide into home plate and call out incontestably, "Safe!"

To be sure, Elihu's notion of an angelic intermediary falls far short
of the personal Savior envisioned by Job. Job's friend on high is no
mere angel, but a Messiah. He is, in the full Old Testament sense of
the word, a "redeemer"—a next-of-kin with the power to redeem
or rescue fellow family members fallen upon hard times (see 19:25).
Thus while both Job and Elihu talk of a mediator, Job pushes the
implications of the concept much further. Elihu's mediator is an
angelic power, halfway between the human and the divine, who
might condescend to intervene before God on behalf of man. But
Job's mediator is one who somehow fully shares both humanity and
divinity and so is qualified "to lay his hand upon us both" (9:33).
Why is it that the author of *Hebrews* devotes his entire first chapter
to differentiating between the status of angels and that of God's own
Son? Job, we feel, would have understood why: it is to establish once
and for all that "both the one who makes men holy and those who
are made holy are of the same family. So Jesus is not ashamed to call
them brothers" (Heb. 2:11). Job would have understood why the
longed-for Messiah, when He did finally appear upon the earth,
would refer to Himself both as the "Son of God" and the "Son of
Man," giving equal weight to His divine and His human natures.

Having noted the limitations in Elihu's thinking, it is still remarkable that he should have had any insight at all into the intercessory
ministry of the second person of the Trinity. Already we have
observed his special sensitivity to the work of the third person, the
Holy Spirit, and all in all it is amazing how much primitive
Trinitarianism is present in this young man's theology. Even in the
theophany the Lord Himself gives no such glimpses into the mystery of the Triune Godhead. It is as if the Lord's answer to the
prophetic flights of both Job and Elihu was that of Daniel 8:26:
"The vision . . . that has been given you is true, but seal up the
vision, for it concerns the distant future."

Tired of Trying
to Be Good

"[Job] keeps company with evildoers;
he associates with wicked men.
For he says, 'It profits a man nothing
when he tries to please God.'" (34:8-9)

When a righteous believer has his back against the wall, he will sometimes react with behavior that is deliberately "unrighteous." He may be rude to guests; he may throw a temper tantrum; he may give his wife the cold shoulder; he may go out and buy something expensive; he may slough off work and go to the pool hall. What is going on here? Often what is happening is that the godly person has gotten sick and tired of trying to be good, and so for a little while he adopts the opposite strategy of being "bad." It is as if some profound instinct inside him had suddenly remembered that being good is, after all, not what godliness is all about. Godliness begins with faith, not with goodness, and that is why we need to be very careful about passing casual judgments on the visible actions of other believers (or, for that matter, on ourselves). When the righteous engage in behavior that appears questionable, it is possible that they are really involved in a subtle form of spiritual warfare, the real object of which is to pull the wool over the Devil's eyes. In the final analysis, there is no spiritual weapon more powerful than simply being human.

This is what Elihu, just as much as the other friends, fails to appreciate about Job. He sees this fellow full of anger and wild talk, "who drinks scorn like water" (34:7), and he thinks, "This is not the conduct of a godly man. It is the conduct of a man whose heart is rebellious and cold towards God." Yet one of the great secrets of the spiritual life is that there is a legitimate place for coldness of heart. For example, when the church of Laodicea was reprimanded, it was because their faith had become so lukewarm as to be insipid, and so Jesus told them, "I know your deeds, that you are neither cold nor hot. I wish you were either one or the other!" (Rev. 3:15). Evidently in the Lord's view it is better to be stone-cold than to be lukewarm; it is better to rebel against conventional faith than to practice that faith halfheartedly. When we are spiritually turned off, then God can revive us. But when we pretend to be turned on when really we are not, then our faith is like the emperor's new clothes and we make a laughingstock of the gospel. For this reason a boring, lifeless church service can be more sinful than drunkenness or adultery.

In a real lover of God, surface rebellion may at heart be an expression of hunger for righteousness, and in the Beatitudes Jesus taught that such hunger would be blessed and satisfied. For the true disciple it is not enough to believe that God is good and to try to lead a good life. No; what true disciples want is to have God's own goodness for themselves, to have God's goodness inside them to such an extent that it literally *makes* them good. Otherwise the practice of religion becomes merely moral effort, and to a person of integrity such effort grows unbearable. An honest soul gets fed up with it. He says, "What's the use? If I cannot be good, then why pretend to the world, or to myself, that I am? No, I want the real thing. I'm hungry for the living God."

What is the difference between the behavior of Christians and non-Christians? Are Christians any better? No, quite often they are not. There are many nonbelievers and followers of other faiths whose outward moral conduct surpasses that of the average Christian. Secular saints may be so energetic in doing good that their record of public service puts many a church to shame. What difference does it make, then, to be a believer? The difference is that as Christians we need no longer *pretend* to be better than anyone else. We don't have to put on any show of being good, for we know we are not. We are not good—we are forgiven; and so we are free to be honest before God and before others. We are free to be ourselves. We have given up trying to be good little boys and girls, and whenever we catch ourselves striving to please either God or others by dint of moral effort, we are the sort of people who react to this danger signal by falling on our faces before the Lord. For one of the secret privileges of being His child is knowing that it is all right to fail. It is all right to get tired, to throw in the towel, to give up. Did not even Jesus stumble while carrying His cross? As His followers we know that if we are ever truly to reflect His goodness or His power, it will not be by human effort but only by grace.

Shifting the Blame

"It is unthinkable that God would do wrong. . . .
Can he who hates justice govern?
Will you condemn the just and mighty One?" (34:12, 17)

What most alarmed Elihu about Job was that somehow this man had the cheek to blame God for his problems, and yet still to consider himself righteous and faithful. Certainly Elihu was correct in observing, "It is unthinkable that God would do wrong." But it was incorrect for him to conclude that God was unprepared to assume any responsibility for human error. On the contrary, it is the very linchpin of the gospel that God does in fact offer, to all those who come to Him, to take the full weight of human depravity, even though it is not His to take. This is grace. Job understood this, and that is why he was unwilling to accept any personal responsibility for the failure of his life, but instead shifted the blame onto God. After all, who else but God could carry it?

This is a maneuver that every hard-pressed Christian must learn to perform. How can we expect to be blameless before God if we persist in clinging to personal guilt? The very word *blameless* signifies that God no longer blames us for our sin, and if He does not blame us, who are we to blame ourselves? More precisely, the word *blameless* implies that someone else has taken the blame for us, and that Someone is God Himself in the person of His Son Jesus Christ. On the cross, God judged Christ instead of you and me. Jesus literally became guilty of our sins. Since He is now the guilty one, the blame belongs to him. The guilt of our sin is no longer our guilt, but His. Wasn't this the hidden meaning behind the entire sacrificial system in the Old Testament? The slaying of animals was a way of symbolically shifting the blame—not onto the animals, but onto God Himself. God takes the rap for all of our weakness and sin, and faith is that attitude which humbly allows Him to do this. So long as we retain guilt, we show that we do not really believe in the full extent of God's sacrificial love for us. To believe in Him is to take all the shame that we very naturally and properly feel for our wickedness, and to shift it onto the Lamb of God. In this way, and in this way only, we become free.

Naturally we all want to be free of guilt. But we would prefer to have our guilt just disappear, just vanish into thin air, as if it were nothing real. We do not want to be bothered by sin. We want to pretend that it does not really exist. But the act of coming to the cross and actively placing our sin on Christ establishes the overwhelming reality of personal evil. We realize then that someone has to pay, and that we cannot do it. By summoning up the incredible gall to hold God responsible for our wrongs and woes, we find amazedly that our lot becomes more bearable. Conversely, whenever we try to shoulder the responsibility ourselves, we are crushed. This pattern repeats itself over and over in the Christian life, until we come to trust more and more deeply in the Lord Jesus Christ as the God who indeed "has *borne our griefs* and carried our sorrows," so that "the punishment that brought us peace was upon him" (Isa. 53:4-5).

It is easy enough for Christians to give mental assent to those passages in Paul's epistles where he explains how our sin has been nailed to the cross. But who nails it there? You and I do. The only way for you and I to put our old natures to death is to pick up the hammer ourselves and drive in the nails, pinning everything on Christ. To blame God is not an option. It is the only way to come to the cross.

Of course there is a vindictive, rebellious way to blame God, a way to blame Him without faith. But it is one thing to blame God behind His back for all the bad in the world, and it is another thing to blame God to His face for all the bad in ourselves. Most people are too proud to bring their iniquity directly to God and let Him take it. They are quick enough to blame others for their problems— whether it be other individuals, society, life in general, or even the Devil. But when it comes to blaming God, they will not do it. They will not come directly to God and give Him their sin. Why not? Because to do so would be to surrender the freedom to go on committing it. By subconsciously resigning themselves to assuming responsibility for their sin, they retain the license to continue in it. People who do this find their identity not merely in sinning, but in performing their own atonement, and this is exactly what they will be doing for the rest of eternity in Hell. Hell is the place for those who are too proud, too religious, too self-righteous to stand up manfully before Christ and blame Him for their sin.

Free Will

"Should God then reward you on your terms,
when you refuse to repent?
You must decide, not I." (34:33)

Elihu touches here upon the question of free will—Job's power of choice over his own destiny, whether for good or for evil. The Christian teaching on this subject is highly paradoxical. Do human beings have free will? The answer is yes and no. We do have freedom, but it is the freedom to make just one choice: Christ. If we do not choose for Christ, then already we have chosen not to be free. We have thus abdicated our freedom. The Bible nowhere teaches that unbelievers are free, but rather just the opposite. In the words of Isaiah, "[God] places in the jaws of the peoples a bit that leads them astray" (30:28). According to John 3:18 unbelievers are "condemned already"; they are not free but are in the grip of something we might call fate, a kind of self-determined prison existing outside the freedom which is only to be found in Christ.

True freedom is the freedom to choose just one thing: God's will. Does this sound hopelessly narrow and confining? Really it is not. What is difficult about obeying the will of God is not how narrow it is, but how infinitely broad. For what is God's will? His will is for us to be free! The Lord does not want blind obedience; He wants sighted obedience. His will is that we make our own decisions about everything. This prospect, however, is so terrifying for us that we have to be led into it step by step. We cannot handle pure freedom all at once, and so the Lord in a sense entices us along the path by allowing us to think that He has a nice, firm, predetermined plan for our lives, like a set of railroad tracks that we need only follow along. But what freedom is there in being stuck on a track? Therefore as we mature in the Christian life, we find ourselves coming to places where the rails seem to have disappeared, and uncharted wilderness opens out before us. Where is God now, we ask? Why will He not tell us what to do, which way to turn? But He will not. He will not tell us because He wants to train us in the handling of raw freedom. He wants us to choose for ourselves, and until we do choose we will be helpless, totally unable to make progress. We will be stuck there in the wilderness with our wheels spinning in sand. "God cannot steer a parked car," goes the old saying. To move forward, we must choose. We must make a choice at the very moment when it seems most impossible to choose. We must take all the information available to us—natural, supernatural, rational, Scriptural, intuitive, the advice of others, and so on—and toss all of this data into the pot of our souls and stir it around. And then we must make a decision, a free decision based not on the drawing power of any single one of these signposts, but rather on the whole broad sweep of reality as we have come to know it in Christ. This is what it means to be human. It means to be on a set of railroad tracks whose name is Christ; and yet since Christ "fills the whole universe" (Eph. 4:10), His tracks are very broad indeed.

God led the children of Israel through the desert by means of a pillar of cloud by day and a pillar of fire by night. But this is not how He leads Christians. For us, the cloud and the fire are in our hearts. As it turns out, obedience and freedom are one and the same thing, and so we need to discover with David that "the boundary lines have fallen for us in pleasant places" (Ps. 16:6). What is hard about listening to God and obeying Him is that He tells us exactly what we most dearly want to hear. And contrary to popular opinion, the most difficult thing in the world is to choose that which we truly desire rather than what is expected of us—expected by the world, by other individuals, by ourselves, or even by "God." What we fail to understand is that the moment we give our will to God, He gives it right back to us again. Are we frightened that if we surrender our will, we shall end up without a will at all? But then we would be nonpersons and useless to God. No, the Christian secret is that the only way we can have a will at all, properly speaking, is by giving it to God, so that He can cleanse it, renew it, and restore it to us fully intact. When this has happened, then we have free will indeed. And then the exercise of our free will becomes the most powerful force in the universe—every bit as powerful as the will of God! For human freedom *is* what God wills. In the words of the prophet Samuel to Saul—those infinitely thrilling, infinitely dangerous words—"Do whatever your hand finds to do, for God is with you" (1 Sam. 10:7).

Grace Alone

"Do you think this is just?
You say, 'I will be cleared by God.'
Yet you ask him, 'What profit is it to me,
and what do I gain by not sinning?'" (35:2-3)

By now the gospel according to Job should be so clear to us that the accusations of his friends seem almost like a deliberate attack on the New Testament. Once again Elihu puts words into Job's mouth, and in the process not only misquotes him but grossly misrepresents his position. This is exactly what happened repeatedly to Paul on account of his radical emphasis on grace, as when in Romans 3:8 he stated, "We are being slanderously reported as saying, and . . . some claim that we say, 'Let us do evil that good may result.'" In the same way Elihu now accuses Job of placing so much faith in God's grace that it has made him callous in regard to his own sin. If there is any truth to this charge, it is only in the sense that the true believer is one who has given up all hope of ever being able to do anything about his sin. He can desire intensely to be free of sin, but in practice he knows that he cannot eradicate sin by his own efforts. All he can do is to wait in faith until the time when, in Job's words, he will be decisively "cleared by God." For there is no other way to be cleared. We cannot do it ourselves. There is no other righteousness except the righteousness that comes by faith.

Elihu, in attacking what he sees as a lax attitude towards sin, probably had in mind Job's flamboyant statement in 9:29-31 (or some similar passage):

> Since I am already found guilty,
>   why should I struggle in vain?
> Even if I washed myself with soap
>   and my hands with washing soda,
> [God] would plunge me into a slime pit
>   so that even my clothes would detest me.

Obviously Job was under no delusions concerning the utter depravity of his fallen nature. He had looked sin squarely in the eye.

And listen: to see sin in that way is already to have repented of it. To advise such a person that the answer to all his problems is further or deeper self-recrimination is to take the part of Satan as an accuser and provocateur. It is to deny the power of the grace of God and the effectiveness of divine forgiveness.

If Job had refused to believe that God had already forgiven him for everything, and that He was continuing to forgive him on a moment-by-moment basis, then he would have ended up flirting with the most terrible sin of all, the sin of Judas Iscariot. Judas' ultimate sin was not betrayal, but the refusal of forgiveness. For Judas realized what he had done; he knew he had "betrayed innocent blood" (Matt. 27:4); but his response to this searing self-knowledge was to go off and hang himself. In short, he punished himself for his own sin, and self-punishment is simply an elaborate method of self-justification—that is, of acting as one's own God. This is exactly what everyone does who persists in a remorseful, downcast, self-flagellating attitude before the clear revelation of the free grace of God. If the Old Testament law was binding, argues the author of *Hebrews*, "and every violation and disobedience received its just punishment, how shall we escape if we ignore such a great salvation?" (2:2-3).

This is not to say there is no reason for believers ever to be downcast or depressed. But the route through depression is not the shallow self-accusation recommended by Job's friends. Rather, the route through is . . . What? Well, read the story of Job and see for yourself. There is no better answer anywhere. Be rigorously honest, both about your sinfulness and about your righteousness; wrestle with God; and then cling for all you are worth to the sheer grace of God poured out at the cross. "For it is by grace you have been saved, through faith—and this not from yourselves, it is the gift of God" (Eph. 2:8). Job's answer to Elihu's accusations might well have taken the form of a familiar stanza from the hymn "Rock of Ages":

> *Nothing in my hand I bring,*
> *   Simply to Thy cross I cling;*
> *Naked, come to Thee for dress;*
> *   Helpless, look to Thee for grace;*
> *Foul, I to the fountain fly,*
> *   Wash me, Savior, or I die!*

Reach for the Stars

"Look up at the heavens and see;
gaze at the clouds so high above you.
If you sin, how does that affect him? . . .
If you are righteous, what do you give to him?" (35:5-7)

One of the most beautiful moments in the Bible is that scene in which God leads Abram outside at night and says, "Look at the heavens and count the stars" (Gen. 15:5). How dark the night must have been on that rural hillside some four thousand years ago, and how brilliant the starry sky! Not only was there little of our present-day air and light pollution, but in those days the whole universe would have been younger and fresher and (who knows?) perhaps even brighter. One look might have dazzled us moderns blind. When God told Abram to count the stars—"if indeed you can count them"—Abram must have looked up and seen nothing *but* stars, nothing but endless light. It was like telling him to count the whiskers in God's beard, or to weigh the gold in the streets of Heaven. No wonder "Abram believed the Lord, and he credited it to him as righteousness." Abram had seen the Lord's glory as surely as Isaiah saw Him in the temple surrounded by six-winged seraphs shouting, "Holy, holy, holy" (Isa. 6:3). Abram had lifted up the lid of the sky's treasure chest and had seen it filled—with stars? with jewels? with gold and silver? No; with the promises of God. Abram had seen the very crown jewels of Heaven, and more than that, he had seen in them his own inheritance.

How strange it is, then, that when Elihu instructs Job to "look up at the heavens," the conclusions he draws are so very different. The Lord showed Abram the stars, but Elihu shows Job the clouds. Abram had seen the stars as a picture of God's proximity; though infinitely distant and mysterious, by faith Heaven was within his grasp. But Elihu sees the clouds as a wall between Heaven and earth; to him they are a picture of God's distance from man, of His unreachability and His impassiveness. So Elihu as much as says to Job, "Who are you, to think you can influence God? Who are you to try to twist God's arm?" This very question, incidentally, might have been asked of Jacob when he wrestled with the angel and refused to let go until he was blessed. Who did these old patriarchs think they were, daring to take God as a hostage and make demands of Him?

Yet this is precisely the paradox of the gospel. For there is an answer to Elihu's rhetorical question, "If you sin, how does that affect [God]?" and the answer is: it crucifies Him. Yes, there is a wall between God and man, but the cross breaks down that wall and so produces a common ground upon which man's sin *does* directly affect God, in order that God's righteousness might also directly affect man. It is the cross that brings God close, that literally pins His shoulders to the mat and holds Him there until He blesses us. The sign of the cross announces to us that God does, incredibly, submit to being taken hostage. He lets Himself be captured by soldiers, tried by legalists and bureaucrats, condemned by a mob, scourged by mockers, and finally pinned and exhibited like a specimen insect. On Calvary God allowed mankind to torture Him, and this brutal spectacle shocks us into realizing that this same torture goes on every day. The cross spells out for us that not only is God affected by our sin, but He is as devastatingly affected by it as we are. When we hurt, God hurts. When we die, it is no greater a disaster than what God Himself has endured. This is the only basis upon which the Lord can say to us, "I love you," and make it stick. It is the cross that fledges and barbs the arrow of God's love.

The crucifixion is often explained as the satisfaction of justice for a holy God whose nature demands that He punish, or avenge Himself upon, human sin. But was it not also the satisfaction of the injustice demanded by unholy man? Good Friday was the occasion upon which man was given the one great chance of which he has always secretly dreamed: the chance to "get even" with God, the chance to avenge himself, in his own heinous fashion, upon the holiness of God. On Calvary God paid for man's sin; but on Calvary man also paid back God for His outrageous and unacceptable goodness.

So now the two are square.

Songs in the Night

"Men cry out under a load of oppression;
they cry for relief from the arm of the powerful.
But no one says, 'Where is God my Maker,
who gives songs in the night,
and who teaches more to us
than to the beasts of the earth?" (35:9-11)

There is a lovely thought in this passage, and it well illustrates the bewildering complexity of Elihu's character. On the one hand, we have seen how curiously insensitive he can be to some of the mysteries of the gospel, especially as they apply to the predicament of his friend Job. Yet on the other hand, he often seems to speak as someone who genuinely knows the voice and the touch of the Lord, and who has experienced something of the gentleness and the power of the Holy Spirit. Elihu's God is one "who gives songs in the night," who lifts the troubled spirit with strange rushes of praise and who floods the soul with peace.

The phrase "songs in the night" could refer figuratively to any form of divine encouragement given during dark times of suffering. But more probably the literal meaning of the words should be taken as the primary one. For to many believers the experience Elihu cites is not uncommon—that of being awakened in the middle of the night literally with a song of joy in the heart. It may be audible music of a kind one has never heard before, so indescribably wonderful that it could never be played by any earthly orchestra. Or it might be an ecstatic utterance that is given, or a dream or a vision, or a passage of Scripture that leaps to life, or a sudden comfort that is felt, or the inspired solution to a problem, or else simply the presence of a clear and radiant note of happiness in the soul, like the sounding of a single sustained bell tone of ineffable purity. This is what the psalmists spoke of when they wrote, "At night his song is with me" (42:8) or, "Even at night my heart instructs me" (16:7). One psalm actually puts it this way: "Let the saints rejoice . . . and sing for joy on their beds" (149:5).

The fact is that when we are filled with the Holy Spirit we can continue to commune with our Lord all night long, even during sleep. Who knows?—the worship that takes place when we are not fully awake may be the purest of all, for isn't that when God's Spirit is most likely to be given the freedom and full control that He seeks? What parents of a strong-willed two-year-old have not leaned over their child's bed at night and been overcome with waves of a tenderness that might not come so readily during the hectic daylight hours? Perhaps just so does our Lord, during certain phases of our spiritual growth, find it easiest to delight in us when we are flat on our backs.

What Elihu touches on in this passage is the importance of the subconscious and the irrational in the spiritual life. To the hyper-charismatic Corinthian church Paul wrote, "I will sing with my spirit, but I will also sing with my mind" (1 Cor. 14:15). But to a hyper-rationalistic congregation of today Paul might have put it the other way around: "I will sing with my mind, but I will also sing with my spirit." Elihu is a young man who is in tune with the Holy Spirit.

Yet now we must return to the old riddle: if Elihu really is so spiritually sensitive, then why is he so obtuse when it comes to interpreting the sufferings of Job? Why in this respect is he every bit as condemning as the other friends? There may be no good answer to this question, except to ask another question: isn't this exactly the sort of subtle twist in human nature that we often, indeed continually, run up against in real life? The wonderful warm-hearted Christian is not always warm-hearted towards everybody. The great preacher can go off on a tangent, and his sermons turn to dust. A missionary may lead a soul to Christ one moment, only to turn around and lock horns with one of his colleagues. A truly vibrant church may completely ignore or even persecute some of its most gifted people. And so it goes. The simple truth is that one can have a rich relationship with the Holy Spirit and yet still not be immune from error and judgmentalism. As an old Pentecostal saying has it, "It's not how high you jump that counts, but how straight you walk after you hit the ground."

The Impatience of Job

"You say that you do not see [God],
that your case is before him
and you must wait for him." (35:14)

In 2 Timothy 4:8 Paul characterizes the righteous as "all who have longed for [the Lord's] appearing"—surely a description that fits Job like a glove. Job is one of those who, in the poignant words of the psalmist, waits for the Lord "more than watchmen wait for the morning, more than watchmen wait for the morning" (130:6). To Elihu this attitude of waiting is suspect. It makes him uneasy. He sees it not as "waiting for" but as "waiting around." There is an insolent passivity about it, a dangerous element of what some theologians have labeled "quietism." Of course, Job is anything but a quietist; yet like the other friends, Elihu thinks Job needs to get off his duff and "do" something in order to make his peace with God.

But all Job does is wait. It's noisy waiting, but it's still waiting. For all his eggs are in one single basket: the Lord's appearing. Job's motto might have been that of Isaiah 8:17—"I will wait for the Lord, who is hiding his face." This waiting on God is so monumental a trait of Job that it has given rise to the proverbial expression "the patience of Job." This is a good, Scriptural-sounding phrase which, surprisingly, is not found anywhere in the Bible. Job is never described as having "patience," but instead, in the New Testament's only reference to him, the word James applies to him is "perseverance": "You have heard of Job's perseverance and have seen what the Lord finally brought about" (5:11).

Is there a difference between patience and perseverance? Certainly there is a difference in the connotations these words have assumed in modern English. The former word, as used in both Christian and secular cultures, hardly seems to apply to Job at all. If patience means folding the hands, biting the tongue, and pasting a beatific smile on the face, then Job was not patient. He was decidedly impatient. "Rage, rage against the dying of the light," wrote Dylan Thomas in a poem to his father. This is Job. Job is a sort of

King Lear of the Bible, famous less for his quiet endurance of life's vicissitudes than for his stormy, brazen cantankerousness. A heroic figure, perhaps, but not the kind of hero anyone would want to emulate.

We may as well admit it: if we found ourselves in Job's shoes, we would hope to Heaven to show more patience than he did, wouldn't we? Yet perhaps Job's patience is of a kind we are not used to, taking the form not of stoically containing all his pain, but rather of bearing the even greater burden of expressing to God and to others everything that is inside him. Granted, to live a life of aggressive honesty is a course fraught with danger. As Larry Crabb writes, "Emotional exhibitionists who regard the display of neurosis as a virtue make a fetish out of becoming vulnerably open." Job was not like this; but we might be if we were to try to imitate his boldness without possessing his innate humility. Job was less like the Paul who wrote from his prison cell, "I have learned to be content whatever the circumstances" (Phil. 4:11) than he was like the Paul who seized the platform one day in Jerusalem in the midst of an angry mob and demanded to be heard (see Acts 21). Is the former behavior more "mature" than the latter? Who can say? Patience today has evolved into a form of repression, of hiding one's true feelings; it is an exterior skill rather than an interior virtue. Many Christians are so preoccupied with trying to be patient that the more rugged, energetic, visionary side of patience—what the Bible calls perseverance—has been leeched out of their character.

If we had true patience, we would be less passive and intimidated. We would have more courage to be above-board with God and with people, and more active resiliency in the face of opposition. Our waiting upon the Lord would be not flat and lifeless, but dynamic and passionate, full of salt and fire. Self-control is an admirable virtue, but it can so easily degenerate into a cloak for self-confidence—that is, into pride. Like any virtue, patience can become an idol, and anyone who is able to keep cool in all circumstances has no need of God. God is for anxious sinners, not for those who are so happily reconciled to the state of things that their faces have relaxed into gassy Buddhist grins.

Knowledge from Afar

"I get my knowledge from afar. . . .
Be assured that my words are not false;
one perfect in knowledge is with you." (36:3-4)

Here is the charismatic paradox in a nutshell. Probably Elihu does have a prophetic gift to receive "knowledge from afar." But even direct revelations from God do not make a man "perfect in knowledge." There is some possibility that Elihu is referring not to himself but to the presence of the Holy Spirit in their midst (see 37:16). Nevertheless, Paul warns that "we know in part and we prophesy in part" (1 Cor. 13:9). It is precisely the imperfection of our charismatic gifts that makes us dependent on love as the supreme revelation. Prophecy is imperfect, but love is perfect. The highest wisdom on earth resides not in any gifted individual, but in the church, in the richness of loving fellowship.

Like many young charismatics, Elihu embodies both the positive and the negative aspects of a theology that leans heavily upon spiritual gifts, divine communications, and personal holiness. While all these emphases are legitimate and even vital to the continual renewing of the church, there is also a way in which an insistence upon them can lead away from the cross. When this is allowed to happen, then the charismatic gospel becomes little more than a kind of spiritualized version of the social gospel, in which manifestations of grace are exalted over grace itself.

To be sure, the first five books of the New Testament (what we might term the New Testament's "Pentateuch") are full of supernatural phenomena. But that is not their central concern. Their central concern is with the cross. The whole energy of the movement of these books is toward the cross—so much so that even the resurrection, by comparison with the crucifixion, receives rather brusque treatment. To any reader of the four *Gospels* it will be obvious what a disproportionate emphasis seems to be placed on the narrative of Christ's passion. But perhaps it is not so obvious that this same pattern is displayed in the lives of the apostles, especially Paul, as related in the book of *Acts*. The first part of *Acts* abounds in the miraculous and victorious march of the young new faith. But as the story progresses, the supernatural and the triumphant gradually take a backseat, as the shadow of the cross looms larger and larger.

Early in *Acts*, for example, we see both Peter and Paul miraculously liberated from prison cells; yet in the later chapters there are no such divine deliverances. On the contrary as Paul grows older he spends an increasing amount of time in confinement, and this is clearly in accordance with the Lord's will. All along it has been God's plan for Paul to be handed over to worldly powers so that he might bear witness before soldiers and jailers and officials, before courts and governors and kings, and in order that all the persecution against him might be duly and legally recorded just as it was in the case of Jesus. By the time we arrive at Acts 20, with its moving account of Paul's final farewell to the Ephesian elders, we even have a kind of parallel to the Last Supper. From this point on Paul sets his face relentlessly to go to Jerusalem and to die for Christ. As it turns out, he must go much farther than Jerusalem, and the last section of *Acts* (nearly a third of the book) is so entirely preoccupied with Paul's arduous journey into the very center of the labyrinth of this world's dark powers that these final eight chapters might almost be entitled "Paul's Passion."

In this way, the very structuring of the New Testament's five narrative books (to say nothing of the epistles) teaches clearly that the main highway of the Christian life is not the glory road, but the way of the cross. And the same is overwhelmingly true of the book of *Job*. Elihu claimed to have "knowledge from afar," and perhaps he did. But his knowledge may have come, in a sense, from too far away; that is, it may have been too spiritual to be practical. For if it was not rooted in the dirt of Golgotha, how could it possibly comprehend Job's passion? What Elihu did not realize was that Job, in the midst of his failure and suffering, and in the utter absence of any signs or miracles, was essentially more of a charismatic than he, Elihu, had yet dreamed of being.

Happiness

*"[God] is wooing you from the jaws of distress
to a spacious place free from restriction,
to the comfort of your table laden with choice food." (36:16)*

Elihu returns in this chapter to the theme of suffering as a form of spiritual discipline. His confusion on the subject is well illustrated by the above verse. While it is true that God may use suffering to lead His chosen ones "to a spacious place free from restriction," it is erroneous to equate this place with "the comfort of your table laden with choice food." Elihu makes the same mistake when he claims, "If we obey and serve him, we will spend the rest of our days in prosperity and our years in contentment" (36:11). As much as this turns out to be true for Job in the end, in his present circumstances it comes as a patent absurdity, just as it would to any suffering disciple today. The sober truth is, in the words of Francis Andersen, that "the gospel of Christ has not brought to any man a guarantee of less misery than Job's."

This being the case, what should be our attitude towards the pursuit of happiness in this world? Malcolm Muggeridge writes that happiness is "like a young deer, fleet and beautiful," which after the kill becomes "a piece of stinking flesh." This is not to say that happiness should be spurned. Rather we should be grateful for whatever happiness we have. But we must not fall into the trap of equating happiness with faith, or even joy with faith. In Luke 24:41 we read that when the resurrected Christ appeared to His disciples, many of them "did not believe it because of joy and amazement." So joy may actually inhibit and erode faith. Strictly speaking joy is not even evidence of faith; only faith is evidence of faith.

Joy should never be looked on as a reward for good behavior, any more than sadness or depression should be viewed as punishments. The seasoned disciple will neither congratulate himself when he is happy, nor upbraid himself when he is feeling low. To congratulate oneself is to steal glory from God, and to upbraid oneself is to give glory to the Devil. Both, equally, are insults to God's grace. If we want to have as firm a grasp on the gospel as Job did, we must surrender all thought of taking personal credit for any peace or happiness we might enjoy. Only when we have done this, only when we have truly given up on both the pursuit and the control of happiness, will we make the tremendous discovery that we no longer feel the sting of God's wrath when things start to go wrong in our lives. Instead we will simply know, whether in good times or in bad, that we are under the Lord's grace. In fact we shall come to realize that God does some of His most important work in us when we are unhappy. If we were never unhappy, we might never change. Often unhappiness merely signals that the Lord is about to open some new door for us, or to unveil some new facet to our character.

In any case happiness, like its opposite, is a symptom so easily misinterpreted as to be unworthy of trust. What we often forget is that happiness may be given to us not so much for our own comfort, as to enable us to bring relief to someone else in need. If we resent a hurting person for interfering with our comfort level, we may short-circuit the very source and purpose of our own joy. Far from being an occasion for complacency, happiness may actually be calling us to particular spiritual diligence. Sometimes it is a warning that Satan is about to attack us, and for this the Lord is giving extra grace. Thus daylight can serve as a premonition of darkness, as a way of saying, "Do your work now, for the night is coming." As Paul warns, "If you think you are standing firm, be careful that you don't fall" (1 Cor. 10:12).

Much of the work of faith consists in this: in bad times to remember the good, and in good times to remember the bad. Practicing the former gives birth to hope; practicing the latter aborts pride. It is just as important to hold oneself down in times of joy as it is to bear up in times of sorrow. The way to be happy (insofar as there is a way) is to hold happiness lightly. When the Lord gives an inch, do not take a mile. In fact, the more we experience the benefits of righteous suffering in our lives, the more we may incline to the strange view that hardship is actually preferable to comfort, and that it is better to suffer than not to suffer. We may even find ourselves not merely enduring the hard things of life, but choosing them.

Holy Babbling

"God is exalted in his power.
Who is a teacher like him? . . .
How great is God—beyond our understanding!" (36:22, 26)

The change that comes over Elihu at this point, and that continues and builds in power to the end of his discourse, is so dramatic that the reader should be bowled over by it. For here something strange and wonderful begins to happen to this young man: he opens his mouth and speaks by the unction of the Holy Spirit! Particularly startling is the fact that immediately prior to this (in 36:17-21) we have been seeing Elihu at his very worst: pompous, sententious, irrelevant, judgmental. Clearly he has run out of things to say, and what he does say is so tactless that we cringe in embarrassment for him.

But then all at once, at verse 22, the wind shifts and Elihu comes alive. He becomes incredibly enthusiastic—a word which means literally "filled with the numinous." This young fellow whose faith all along has had a certain authentic vibrancy, yet who at the same time tends to be a crashing bore, suddenly begins to speak with great beauty and power, and moreover with authority. So impressive is this latter part of Elihu's speech, clear through to the end of Chapter 37, that it stands out as one of the most exalted passages in the book, comparable in grandeur even to the speeches of the Lord Himself. It is almost as though Elihu had become a new person here, much in the way that Samuel prophesied concerning Saul: "The Spirit of the Lord will come upon you in power, and you will prophesy . . . and you will be changed into a different person" (1 Sam. 10:6).

How do we account for this sudden transformation in Elihu? Can a person really go from the ridiculous to the sublime in a single sentence? Can one be mumbling platitudes one moment, and the next be filled with the Holy Spirit? Yes, this certainly can and does happen, and the above-mentioned example of Saul suggests further that its occurrence (and the occurrence of prophecy in general) does not depend upon maturity of faith. In Elihu's case the obvious inspiration behind his words may be due not so much to his own sanctity, as to the simple fact that at this point in the book the Lord Himself is actually approaching. He is coming on the clouds of Heaven, in the appearance of a gathering storm. He is coming in His glory, and in a very few moments He is going to manifest Himself in such a way that all those who have ears will hear Him speak audibly.

God does not just come out of nowhere, however. He does not make a habit of dropping in unannounced. Rather, His coming is heralded by prophecy, and He uses frail human creatures to "prepare the way for the Lord" (Isa. 40:3). Is it not one of the boldest masterstrokes of this bold book that the coming of the Lord is prepared for by this weak little man Elihu? Flawed and immature though he be, he stands as a kind of buffer between Job's last words and the theophany, and in doing so he mitigates the idea that one man can, all by himself, storm the gates of Heaven. For the revelation of God is not given primarily to individuals, but to a community. The Lord comes "where two or three come together" (Matt. 18:20). Elihu is not the powerhouse of faith that Job is; he does not even understand Job, and so judges him wrongly. Nevertheless in the end he stands with Job and not against him, and we see that his own personal faith rings true. His theology, while flawed, is not so rigid as to render this man incapable of experiencing and exulting in the wonders of God. Indeed as soon as the Holy Spirit begins to fall on this group, Elihu catches the flame. He proves himself to be ready for the Lord's coming—and when all is said and done, is this not the essence of genuine faith? Surely here is the reason that Elihu does not come under the judgment of God at the end of the story, as Job's other friends do.

Having said this, however, it is also instructive to note the contrast between Job and Elihu, as evidenced by their different responses to the Lord's appearing. At the approach of God the more mature man of faith is silent; a holy hush falls over him, and his lips grow as still as his heart. But the young man Elihu keeps on babbling. Even if we grant that his babbling is inspired, there may yet be reason to suspect that it is, compared with the humble silence of Job, still babbling.

The Storm

"Who can understand how [God] spreads out the clouds,
how he thunders from his pavilion?
See how he scatters his lightning about him,
bathing the depths of the sea. . . .
His thunder announces the coming storm;
even the cattle make known its approach."
(36:29-30, 33)

In the final thirty-one verses of Elihu's speech there are some two dozen references to thunder, lightning, clouds, and rain. To be precise, thunder is mentioned seven times, clouds seven times, lightning five times, and rain five times. Quite obviously the weather is cooking something up, and Elihu adopts the role of providing a running commentary on these dramatic meteorological changes, and of interpreting them spiritually.

One can easily picture the scene. Job and his friends have been sitting outdoors ("on the ground" according to 2:13), probably in some remote rural area to which Job has been banished because of his disease. Gradually a storm begins to brew. Thunder boils up throatily from the horizon, dark clouds like bruises close in with premonitory swiftness, and a few raindrops the size of whale tears hurtle into the dust. Then all at once a bolt of lightning shivers the sky open like ripping silk, and a torrential downpour is unleashed. One can imagine Job and his friends jumping to their feet, tucking up their robes, and running like jackrabbits for any available cover— maybe a rickety shack nearby, or maybe just a big tree or a sheltering rock—and there they huddle together to watch the incredible power of the storm sweep over them.

Or perhaps the scenario was somewhat different. Perhaps Eliphaz, Bildad, and Zophar were the ones who scrambled for cover, while Job and Elihu (or else Job alone) remained out in the open, overcome with wonder, to bear the brunt of the storm. It may be that the Lord's words to Job in 38:3, "Brace yourself like a man" contain a reference to the buffeting winds. In any case, it is Job and Elihu who see in the storm not merely a display of God's power in nature, but a theophany. They are the ones who hear the voice of the Lord in the thunder. "Listen to the roar of his voice," cries Elihu in 37:2. Similarly, the *Gospel of John* records an occasion when God the Father spoke audibly to Jesus out of Heaven, and "the crowd that was there and heard it said it had thundered; others said an angel had spoken to him" (12:29). When the Lord speaks, it is those with the ear of faith who hear Him. Others hear only thunder, or nothing at all.

This storm scene in *Job* is in some ways reminiscent of another famous storm in literature, the one in Shakespeare's *King Lear*. For Lear is another man who has fallen from the heights and been stripped of literally everything, and whose frantic search for meaning drives him to the very limits of human endurance. Who can forget the picture of the dazed old king dressed in rags and roaming the open moors, raging in the midst of the wild tempest, with fools and madmen his only companions? In this image of nobility stripped of its robes, ejected from its own palace, and thrown out onto the mercy of the raw elements (which are not merciful at all), we see a powerful representation of the human condition without God.

Of course, it is here that the stories of Lear and Job diverge, and so have very different endings. Lear, for his part, defies both the internal storm of his own turbulent heart, and the outer storm as well, openly shaking his fist at Heaven. Yet Job, despite all his former rage, grows suddenly meek and still the moment he recognizes God in the midst of the storm. Again, while Lear in his journey into the eye of life's whirlwind finds nothing save the enormity of his own folly, Job's quest, because it has taken the form of heartfelt prayer rather than of willful striving, gains an audience in Heaven and receives an answer from the Lord. Lear began as a king and ends as a mere man; but Job, because he began as a mere man, ends as a king. For the final reward of anyone who succeeds, by faith, in gaining access to the throne of Heaven is that he himself takes on royal blood. To behold the face of the King of kings is to become a king oneself.

Elihu Prophesies

"My heart pounds and leaps from its place!
Listen! Listen to the roar of his voice,
to the rumbling that comes from his mouth. . . .
When his voice resounds, he holds nothing back." (37:1-2, 4)

With these dramatic words Elihu stakes his claim to be hearing the very voice of God, and judging by the sheer electricity that ripples along the spine of this entire speech—enough to make the hair on the back of every word stand on end—can anyone seriously doubt that these verses really are inspired? Consider the haunting grandeur of a passage such as 37:16-18:

> Do you know how the clouds hang poised,
>   those wonders of him who is perfect in knowledge?
> You who swelter in your clothes
>   when the land lies hushed under the south wind,
> can you join him in spreading out the skies,
>   hard as a mirror of cast bronze?

Throughout this latter portion of Elihu's speech we see him wholly taken up with the marvels of God. Gone now are his misguided arguments and his tendentious criticisms of Job, and suddenly his one message to the sufferer becomes the selfsame message that is to fill the speeches of the Lord Himself: "Listen to this, Job; stop and consider God's wonders! *Can you control the clouds as he does?*" (37:14-15). Even structurally Elihu's speech foreshadows the Lord's own, in the way it launches a barrage of rhetorical questions, questions that somehow manage to be devastatingly sardonic, exquisitely tender, and grandly glorious all at once. In this one chapter Elihu covers a dazzling range of emotional effects, and in this too we see one of the marks of authentic prophecy. True prophets paint with the broadest of palettes, since their colors are drawn directly from the infinite spectrum of God's own heart.

All in all this storm scene in *Job* is one of the great moments in literature—not only in the Bible, but in any literature. Perhaps what makes the scene particularly masterful is the fact that it is Elihu rather than Job who, like a human lightning rod, seems to conduct the Lord's entrance. Any ordinary writer could have penned a sublime speech purportedly from God and introduced it with a storm. But an ordinary writer would not have trusted this critical moment to Elihu. An ordinary writer would never have dreamed of letting this poor, weak little character detract from the dramatic impact of his grand storm, and effectively come between Job and God. If this were to happen in a play it would be called "upstaging," and the critics would chalk it up to bad art. But in *Job* it is spiritual genius.

Of course, many readers do not see it this way. Scholars and laypeople alike tend to dismiss the Elihu section as a piece of bumbled staging. But the author of *Job* begs to differ. From his point of view the story of the transformation of Elihu, by the power of the Holy Spirit, from a callow, excitable youth into a budding prophet, was a story well worth the telling. It was a good story in its own right, but more than that it was judged relevant enough within the larger context of the book to warrant the inclusion of six rather awkward additional chapters. Why? Perhaps the author thought it important for the reader to see how two very different men, Job and Elihu, were each affected by the manifest presence of God, and also how three other men stood by and remained ominously unaffected. When we reach the Epilogue, it may come as a shock to us to realize that Eliphaz, Bildad, and Zophar (unlike Elihu) have apparently been completely untouched by the theophany, neither seeing the Lord's glory nor hearing His voice in the storm. In the end the Lord does speak to Eliphaz too, but it is only to say, "I am angry with you and your two friends, because you have not spoken of me what is right, as my servant Job has" (42:7). Like the foolish virgins in Jesus' parable, these friends missed the Lord's coming, and it took the prayer of Job to secure mercy for them.

The Veil Is Torn

"[God] unleashes his lightning beneath the whole heaven
and sends it to the ends of the earth.
After that comes the sound of his roar. . . .
God's voice thunders in marvelous ways;
he does great things beyond our understanding." (37:3-5)

As the great storm of God breaks over the land of Uz, the entire story undergoes a fantastic metamorphosis before our eyes. Like a once-ungainly caterpillar emerging from its cocoon, suddenly the book sheds its ugly carapace of unrelieved suffering and something brand-new begins to emerge, something amazing and wildly beautiful. Why is it that a storm is used as the vehicle for this transformation? Because a storm splits the sky. A thunderstorm cracks the heavens wide open, blows them apart like an exploding safe—or, to use a more Biblical image, like the tearing of a veil. From the supernatural beginnings of this book, when the throne room of God was thrown open to public view and we became eyewitnesses to the goings-on in the heavenlies, we should have guessed that this story would have a supernatural ending as well. And now here it is. Now the heavens break open once again, and through the torn veil stream rays from the celestial throne, and the voice from on high is heard.

What a fitting conclusion this is to a protracted, unresolved theological debate. How better to break up the religious tension than with a sky-sundering, goose-bumping walloper of a storm? Yet more than that, what better introduction could there be to the appearance of the Lord Almighty? In the Old Testament a tempest or similar weather disturbance very often accompanied a theophany (see Ex. 19:16; Ps. 18:7-15; Ezek. 1:4). According to Nahum 1:3, "[The Lord's] way is in the whirlwind and the storm, and clouds are the dust of his feet." Granted, when God spoke to Elijah it was not in wind, earthquake, or fire, but in "a still, small voice" (1 Kings 19:12, KJV); and yet to Job the substance of His communication is, in a curious way, the same as that to Elijah. For what the Lord says to Job out of the whirlwind is this: "Where were you . . . while the morning stars sang together?" (38:4, 7) and, "*Have you ever watched a doe give birth to her fawn?*" (39:1). In the eye of this furious storm, what wondrous peace and gentleness gleam!

In many ways a storm serves as an ideal metaphor for the spiritual problems in *Job*. For while a storm presents all the outward appearance of chaos, of nature run amok, still throughout it all we know that the Creator remains in absolute control of every detail. As God Himself asks Job early in His speech, "Who cuts a channel for the torrents of rain, and a path for the thunderstorm?" (38:25). It is right here, in the Lord's perfect, fingertip control over the wildest primal forces, that His sovereignty is most visibly displayed. And if the Lord maintains control over the storms of nature, how much more must His hand be on the storms of emotion in the hearts of His children? The larger a body of water, the bigger are its waves, and this is true as well of the human soul. Sometimes water is calm, sometimes there are gentle lappings, and sometimes the breakers pound and rage against the restraining shore. Yet all along it remains the same body of water, and the same hand that formed it remains in charge. "Who shut up the sea behind doors?" God asks Job, and then answers, "I fixed limits for it and set its doors and bars in place, when I said, 'This far you may come and no farther; here is where your proud waves halt'" (38:8-11).

How healing it must have been for Job to see that when the Lord finally did come to him, it was on the wings of the same sort of violent desert whirlwind that in the beginning had killed all of his children. Job's fiercest trials had begun, remember, at the moment when "a mighty wind swept in from the desert" (1:19) and completely destroyed the house where his children had been feasting. Now the Lord takes this same whirlwind and, as it were, turns it inside out. He picks it up in His hand and uses it as a megaphone. What a fine stroke of cosmic, Heaven-hooraying irony this is! What's more, it would be difficult to find a more glorious picture of the salvation of Christ. For in this same way Jesus mounted a cross, a vicious instrument of torture, and by riding it into battle He destroyed forever the torture of sin and death.

Perpetual Motion

"[God] says to the snow, 'Fall on the earth,'
and to the rain shower, 'Be a mighty downpour.'
So that all men he has made may know his work,
he stops every man from his labor." (37:6-7)

The weather is everybody's favorite whipping boy. Even Christians complain openly about the weather and think nothing of the fact that they may be insulting the Lord to His face. Inclement weather is normally looked on as being, at the very least, a nuisance, and at worst a disaster. But to Elihu the weather in all its glory is the glory of God, and God stops people from their work so they can see it.

Elihu's point has a much wider application than simply the literal impediments of traffic snowed to a halt and schools and businesses closing down. For there are many more ways than the weather that God has of stopping us from our human work, in order that His divine work may take precedence. Is not the whole book of *Job* about men who have been stopped from their work? It is about an enormous work stoppage, an enormous inconvenience that has fallen out of the sky and forced five busy people to drop everything they were doing and to turn for a while to a more important task. What is this more important task? It is the work of love.

Naturally no one in this book (including Job himself) fully realizes that it is the work of love in which they have been engaged. But in the end it will be made perfectly clear to all—as it will be to all of us in whatever our own painful circumstances might be—that everything was done for the sake of love. Even "love" is almost too poor a word to describe the height and depth and length and breadth of God's real purposes for us. As Jesus put it to the woman at the well, "If *only* you knew the gift of God and who it is that asks you for a drink . . ." (John 4:10).

Significantly, Elihu is the only one of Job's counselors to make any mention of this little word "love." He does not wax eloquent upon it, but in 37:13 he simply remarks, almost in passing, that God sends the rain "to water his earth and to show his love." The word Elihu uses is that great, immensely untranslatable Hebrew word *hesed*. Its appearance here might be unremarkable if it were not for the curious fact that the word occurs only one other time in the entire book, and that is on the lips of Job in 10:12. *Hesed* thus becomes one more in the series of subtle but significant links between Job and Elihu, links which suggest that these two men may really have more in common than first meets the eye. However far apart they may seem, they are both on the track of love, the only track that counts.

Throughout history inventors have sought in vain to produce a so-called "perpetual motion machine"—a machine that would somehow have the capacity to keep on working indefinitely without any depletion of energy. Yet there is only one true perpetual motion machine in the universe, and that is love. Love is the only energy that will keep on going forever, which is why it is the mainspring of eternal life. How can love keep working forever without getting tired? The answer is simple: because the way it works is by resting. The fourth chapter of *Hebrews* consists of a strong invitation (more than that, a command) to all disciples to be sure to enter by faith into God's rest, and thereby into His love.

We know that for six days God worked to create the universe, and on the seventh day He rested. But when the Pharisees accused Jesus of doing work on the Sabbath He replied, "My Father is always at his work to this very day, and I too am working" (John 5:17). How do we reconcile these two apparently contradictory views of God, one as a worker and one as a rester? The answer lies in the relationship of pure love that exists among the members of the Trinity. The way these divine persons work is by loving one another; they work by resting in love. If for six days God rolled up His sleeves and did another kind of work, perhaps it was because for six days there was no one on earth for the Father to love, and no one to love Him back. But by the end of the sixth day there was a man, and so ever since then the Lord has been resting in His love for mankind. Just as Jesus says, "Apart from me you can do nothing" (John 15:5), so He too has restricted Himself on earth to doing His most important work through us. Therefore God rests while we work ("The earth is my footstool," He says in Isaiah 66:1), and we rest while He works ("The joy of the Lord is your strength," says Nehemiah 8:10)—and the result is the perpetual loving motion of eternal life.

Here Comes the Sun

"No one can look at the sun,
bright as it is in the skies
after the wind has swept them clean.
Out of the north he comes in golden splendor;
God comes in awesome majesty." (37:21-22)

While it is easy to see that a storm has been unfolding throughout Chapter 37, it is difficult to follow the exact progression of events. A moment ago, in 37:19, Elihu was talking about how dark it was. Now, apparently, the clouds have suddenly been swept away and the sun has come out. Is the storm over, then? But if it is, how is it that in 38:1 the Lord addresses Job "out of the storm"? Taylor Lewis sees an explanation for this puzzle in the idea of a "thunderstorm finally terminating in the whirlwind or tornado from which breaks forth the unmistakable voice of God."

Whatever the actual progression of events, it is clear that the Lord pulls out all of the stops for His interview with Job: thunder and lightning, pelting rain, driving winds and black clouds, freezing temperatures, dust storm and tornado, and finally the breakthrough of the sun and no doubt a spectacular rainbow too—and all of this in one cataclysmic display! There is so much going on here that one wonders whether all of it is to be directly ascribed to the Lord's doing. More likely, such violence in the natural order is to be explained as a kind of fallout of spiritual warfare—that is, a result of God's clash with the Devil. The Lord is invading what until now has been Satan's territory, and Satan is resisting. The Kingdom of Heaven is advancing, and the forces of darkness are fleeing in disarray. We see a similar scenario in the New Testament story of Jesus calming "a furious squall" on the Sea of Galilee (Mark 4:37). Once the Lord's boat reached the region of the Gerasenes on the other side, a key spiritual battle took place in which Jesus cast a legion of demons out of a savagely insane man. In retrospect, the storm on the lake can be interpreted as Satan's opposition to the Lord's invasion, and it is no doubt significant that Satan chose to mount his attack at a time when Jesus was sleeping.

In the story of *Job*, too, the Lord has apparently been sound asleep until now, peacefully curled up in the stern of the boat while Job has been struggling all alone with the wind and the waves. Yet consider the contrast between the Lord's response to Job's situation, and the way He dealt with His disciples on the Sea of Galilee. In the latter case He immediately calmed the storm (leaving the men even more terrified, it seems, than they had been before), while in the case of Job He let the storm rage for 37 chapters, until finally He calmed not the storm itself, but Job's heart. It is important to understand that Job's peace with God is reestablished right here, in the midst of the theophany, rather than later on in the Epilogue. It is not Job's return to normal life that finally reconciles him to the ways of God, but rather his elemental encounter with his Lord—the very thing for which he has prayed all along. Job's answer comes not out of sunny skies, but out of the heart of the storm.

Who then is the disciple of greater faith? Is it the one who in fear of the rising wind calls upon the Lord to remove the fear and its source? Or is it the one who, like Job, in the midst of fear simply cries out to the Lord?

In Matthew 14 we read about another voyage of Jesus' disciples across the Sea of Galilee, during which "During the fourth watch of the night Jesus went out to them, walking on the lake." At this sight Peter called out, "Lord, if it's you, tell me to come to you on the water." After he had tried out his sea legs and found them wanting, Jesus saved him from drowning and then gently rebuked him with the question, "You of little faith, why did you doubt?" This story is so well-known that we assume we know why Jesus rebuked Peter. Was He not saying, in effect, "If only you had more faith, Peter, you would not have sunk"? Yet what if the Lord's question actually had a very different intent? What if Jesus were really saying, "Peter, why did you doubt Me in the first place? Why did you doubt that it really was I, walking out to you on the water? Why did you have to test Me?" Perhaps the true moral of the story is that it would have shown greater faith if Peter had just stayed in the boat.

Beyond Our Reach

"The Almighty is beyond our reach and exalted in power;
in his justice and great righteousness, he does not oppress."
(37:23)

In Samuel Beckett's play *Waiting For Godot*, two absurd little men in bowler hats sit on a bench killing time and endlessly discussing the awaited arrival of a certain mysterious personage named Godot. But Godot never shows up. In fact, nothing really happens in this play at all. Whatever does happen is insignificant; whatever is done is not worth doing; whatever is said is idiotic. There is (to borrow the title of another celebrated play by Jean-Paul Sartre) *No Exit* for these men from a plight that is as meaningless as it is torturous. They are trapped inside a box called life, in which there is just enough light to see that there is nothing to be seen.

If *Job* were to end at Chapter 37—if, let us say, the closing words were those of Elihu in 37:23, "The Almighty is beyond our reach"— then the effect of this book would be very much like that of Beckett's absurdist play. Elihu's final speech, as climactic and inspired as it may be, would fall flat without a sequel. But the story of Job does not end here. Rather, it ends with what theologians call a "theophany"—that is, with God Himself appearing out of the blue and taking center-stage to have the last word. Yes, strictly speaking Elihu is right that God is "beyond our reach"; but this same God reaches out to us, and this is the essence of theophany. "Godot" shows up after all.

American astronaut James Irwin has observed that "man walking on the moon was nothing, compared with Jesus walking on the earth." Is such a God really "beyond our reach"? Or is He, to those who take hold of Him in faith, eminently reachable? As Moses taught the Israelites, "Now what I am commanding you today is not too difficult for you or beyond your reach" (Deut. 30:11). This is the God in whom Job has trusted all along, the God who ultimately reveals Himself as "Immanuel," God with us.

The word *theophany* comes from two Greek words meaning "God" and "appear." A theophany may thus be defined as an appearance, a revelation, a direct manifestation of God to man. It is the theophany that finally sets *Job* apart from the category of "wisdom literature." For in the wisdom books there are no visions or supernatural events; there is no "thus says the Lord," as there is constantly in the prophetic Scriptures. In the way of wisdom there is still divine revelation, of course, but it is a different mode of revelation. Wisdom is the Sermon on the Mount, not the Transfiguration.

Wisdom literature, then, tends not to traffic in the charismatic. But *Job*, in the final analysis, is a charismatic book. As much as the great majority of its theology may be said to be studiously noncharismatic, the ending is frankly and melodramatically supernatural. As much as we have had to focus relentlessly on the cross in order to understand Job's predicament, in the end it is as if Job is allowed to come down from his cross. He is delivered and restored, and this begins to happen through the Lord Himself speaking to him in an audible locution lasting four chapters. The very idea of the author of *Job* presuming to pen words directly from the mouth of God—this must have set the traditional audience of wisdom literature on its ear. Yet even from the opening chapters of *Job*, in which Heaven was thrown wide open, has not this book presented itself as a supernatural thriller, a classic of spiritual warfare? Right from the beginning we should have said to ourselves, If the Lord would deign to talk plainly with Satan, who hates Him, then how much more plainly will He talk with a human being who loves Him!

This is exactly what Job has been pleading for all along: a personal audience with the Lord. It is also the thing that has most infuriated Job's friends, this longing of his for some direct, charismatic, divine intervention in his situation. Job bets all of his marbles on a *deus ex machina* resolution, a bet which to his friends seems reckless and irresponsible. This same reaction, incidentally, was shared by the opponents of Jesus: the very idea that God Himself, in Person, should pay the world a visit! But just so does the book of *Job* end, with the Lord paying the world a spectacular visit and (as we learn from the Epilogue) bringing with Him a foretaste of the glories of His kingdom.

THE THEOPHANY
(Job 38–42:6)

Then Job replied to the Lord: . . . "My ears had heard of you but now my eyes have seen you. Therefore I despise myself and repent in dust and ashes."

—JOB 42:1, 5-6

I resolved to know nothing . . . except Jesus Christ and him crucified.

—1 COR. 2:2

The Lord Speaks

Then the Lord answered Job out of the storm. (38:1)

A s sensational as the ending of this book is, many readers have found the Lord's answer to Job oddly unsatisfying. In the first place, it does not seem to provide any clear response to the burning questions about suffering and evil that the book has broached. In the second place, many people feel that the content of the Lord's speeches is not significantly different from much that has gone before.

There is a sense in which these readers are right: the Lord does not say a great deal that is substantially new or earth-shattering. And yet, must not the same charge be brought against the Bible as a whole? For all that may be said in defense of the uniqueness and supremacy of Biblical religion, the fact remains that at many points the wisdom of other faiths does come very close to the wisdom of Christianity. If this were not the case, then why has so much of the world been led astray? Other gods are worshiped precisely because the secrets they impart are profound, attractive, vibrant, and powerful. Even to a highly intelligent and inquiring mind, Christianity may appear narrow and unsophisticated when compared with the fascinating religions of the East.

So let us grant that the speeches of Yahweh at the end of *Job* do not have anything essentially new or surprising to offer. This is not what makes them stand out. What does? Only one feature sets these chapters apart, and that is the simple fact that it is the Lord Himself, and no one else, who speaks them. But that in itself—just think about it—that alone makes all the difference in the world! An art critic might tell us quite a bit about the paintings in the Sistine Chapel; but it would not be the same as talking with Michelangelo—let alone with Michelangelo's Creator.

To complain that there is nothing striking about the speeches of Yahweh is a bit like saying that one human face is very much like another. This is true, as far as it goes. Generally all faces do have two eyes, two ears, a nose, a mouth, and other features in common. But only a fool would claim that because of this uniformity there is no way to tell faces apart. No, there is only one face of Jesus.

Similarly, someone might try to argue that one tree in a forest is very much like any other. But imagine, for a moment, that you are out for a walk in the woods on a lovely fall day. The sun is warm, there is a faint hint of frost in the sparkling air, and all the trees are decked in gold and crimson. For some reason, however, the beauty of the scene escapes you. Perhaps you are sunk in some dark mood, or abstractedly mulling over a problem. Although you are dimly aware of the spectacular color all around, you cannot seem to take it in. You feel cut off, trapped in your own dull thoughts. Then all at once you find that you have paused in your walk—you do not know why—and as you lift your eyes, you happen to notice one particular tree. You notice it, and then you begin to study it. More than that, you are riveted by it. For reasons you cannot explain, this one single tree has caught and held your attention in an extraordinary way. It may be a red maple, or it may be a yellow poplar. It may even be a tree from which all the leaves have already dropped. In any case, there are other trees just like it all around, and you have been seeing these same trees all day long and throughout your life. Why should this one tree suddenly catch your eye and, as it were, lift you right out of yourself? How can one tree, rather than another, exercise such power over your moods? You do not know. All you know is that you go away changed. You go away feeling as if you have just seen the most beautiful tree in the entire world, and you will never forget it as long as you live. You will never forget the look of it, but more importantly you will never forget the experience of it, the sense of revelation, of encounter. What was it that fired your imagination? What was it that made all the difference? Certainly not the tree itself. There was nothing unusual about that particular tree. What then? Surely the thing that made that tree different—the only thing—was that it was the Lord Himself who showed it to you.

If all the victims of crucifixion in the history of the Roman Empire were to be hoisted back onto their crosses and gathered together into one place, they would make a very large forest. In such a setting, would there be anything to distinguish one cross from another? No, nothing at all. Nothing, that is, except to the eye of faith.

The End of Theology

"Who is this who darkens my counsel
with words without knowledge?" (38:2)

The Lord's first words to Job contain a message that all theologians and priests, all pastors and Christian counselors, all teachers of spirituality and all writers of devotional books should have inscribed on a plaque and hanging in their studies, or perhaps even tattooed upon their foreheads for all the world to see. These words are a stark reminder that all human thinking and speaking and writing on the topic of religion, however lofty or even inspired it may be, ultimately falls short of the reality of the living God. One of the twentieth century's greatest theologians, Karl Barth, compared theology to "the turning over of a sick man in his bed for sake of change." An even greater theologian, Thomas Aquinas, had an experience toward the end of his life that caused him to cease writing altogether, and to look back over his life's work and lament, "It's all straw." Surely the best thing that could happen to any theological system or treatise, from Augustine's *City of God* to the book you are reading right now, is that it be dismantled. This is not to disparage the value (or better, call it the inevitability) of theology. But in the long run theology is no more than a crutch, and once the leg is healed, we throw the crutch away.

Many find it strange that the Lord should speak so sternly and censoriously to Job, to this man whom all along we have maintained is "blameless and upright" and whom God Himself has called the very best man in all the earth (see 1:8). Yet if God speaks this way to such a one as Job, what might He say to you or to me? Perhaps it is not so much Job and his theology that the Lord here singles out to pass judgment upon, as theology itself, the whole bumbling project of human God-talk in all its presumptuous inadequacy. God being God, how else is He to respond to all these words, words, words of ours? What other position could the Lord possibly take in regard to the thoughts of mankind, and still remain the great and awesome Holy One, matchless in majesty?

This is the very conclusion Paul reaches when he caps one of his arguments in *Romans* with the question, "Who are you, O man, to talk back to God?" (9:20). Even Scripture stops short before the deepest mysteries of God, which is why Paul at the end of Romans 11 allows the entire elaborate scaffolding of his argument simply to collapse into delirious doxology as he sings, "Oh, the depth of the riches of the wisdom and knowledge of God! How unsearchable his judgments, and his paths beyond tracing out!" If Paul could state boldly, "Christ is the end of the law" (10:4), how much more might he have argued that "Christ is the end of theology." Although Paul himself employed theology in all his writing, the essence of his gospel is not theology but rather a living relationship with Jesus. The gospel is not words and ideas, but "Christ in you, the hope of glory" (Col. 1:27).

The most remarkable feature of the Lord's speeches to Job is how free they are of theology. At least, this is like no other theology we have ever heard. For the first time in the book a character opens his mouth without any need to explain or rationalize. How refreshing this is, and how mysterious! For God is not a theologian; He is the living God. When He speaks, He does not need to justify Himself. God needs no justification; it is man who needs the justification. Therefore instead of rationalizing, God simply points. He points to the mighty works of His own creation that have been there all along for anyone with eyes to see.

G. K. Chesterton writes that the way God describes all His fabulous creatures and parades them before Job, He makes each one seem "like a monster walking in the sun. The whole is a sort of psalm or rhapsody of the sense of wonder. The maker of all things is astonished at the things He has Himself made." Chesterton goes on to conclude that "the riddles of God are more satisfying than the solutions of man," and that "man is most comforted by paradoxes."

If we find it exasperating that God never gives Job any reasons for his long ordeal of suffering, then we have entirely missed the point of these final chapters. While it is true that the Lord's answer to Job is neither logical nor theological, this is not the same as saying that He gives no answer. The Lord *does* give an answer. His answer is Himself. Naturally there is no way to sum up such an answer without sounding prosaic, pedantic, theological. There is no way to sum it up at all. It is not a formula—it is a supernatural encounter, a theophany. The Lord's answer is Himself.

Braced Before the Lord

"Brace yourself like a man;
I will question you,
and you shall answer me." (38:3)

The wind is howling like a banshee; trees are bent to the ground; dervishes of dust whirl across the landscape. Probably the wind has grown so strong by this point that Job is knocked over by it, or even swept right off his feet and carried along for a while before being sent sprawling. He must have thought, "This is it, this is the end!" And then all at once he hears someone say to him, "Brace yourself like a man." In the midst of the whirlwind, suddenly he finds himself still as a church mouse, listening. In the midst of all his turmoil, he finds something to hang on to: a voice.

If righteousness meant sinlessness, or moral perfection, or some sort of absolute "union" with God, then there would be no way to understand how Job could be a righteous man and yet still have to endure the storm of God's rebuke and correction. But the fact is that the person who is truly right with the Lord is no stranger to His rebuke. Righteousness does not negate the infinite gulf that stands between sinful humanity and a holy God; rather, it bridges it. A righteous person is not one who has arrived at perfection, but one who stands upon the bridge. And that bridge is the cross.

How can a mere man "brace" himself before the Lord Almighty? The only way is to be nailed to the cross. When an old sailing ship was heading into a storm, everything had to be tied down. The gear was stowed, the hatches battened; finally even the men themselves had to be lashed to the mast. This is what righteous suffering does to the believer: it lashes him to the mast.

"Anyone who does not carry his cross and follow me," said Jesus, "cannot be my disciple" (Luke 14:27). Have we ever wondered what Jesus' original audience must have made of such a statement?

To them, there was nothing prophetic in the image of a man carrying a cross; it was just a picture drawn from daily life. It was a sight they would have seen, probably many times, in the streets of Jerusalem: a condemned wretch trudging to his execution. This was the pretty picture of discipleship that Jesus wanted to stamp on the minds of His hearers, even before He Himself took this path. He wanted them to brace themselves—to be braced for the worst.

Only when we have faced the worst are we in a position to receive the best. Hence there is no other place but Calvary where a human being can stand still before the whirlwind of God's presence and answer His questioning. In the Old English poem "The Dream of the Rood," the cross on which Christ was crucified speaks, telling its own story:

> *I shook when His arms embraced me,*
> *But I durst not bow to ground,*
> *Stoop to earth's surface:*
> *Stand fast I must.*

Job too is shaking in his boots. He is shaking like a leaf in the storm of God's wrath. But the important thing is that he is standing fast. He is braced before the Lord. He is braced precisely because of the long ordeal of suffering that he has endured by faith, and now, like Isaiah's Suffering Servant, "*as a result of the anguish of his soul* he will see the light . . . and be satisfied*" (Isa. 53:11).

Job's situation is like that of Joshua the high priest in the third chapter of *Zechariah*. Yes, he is standing in God's presence, but Satan is still right there at his side to accuse him. Like Joshua, Job is dressed in filthy rags and has nothing whatsoever to say for himself. His one hope is in the clean robe of righteousness that only God Himself, in an act of sheer mercy, can bestow on him. And in the end this is exactly what the Lord does for Job. But He does not do it without first making it crystal-clear, both to Job and to everyone else, that it is *His* holiness that is being proffered and celebrated, not Job's. That is why Job's final humiliation in this story is to be cross-examined by his Maker and made to eat all his words. If Job is righteous, it is not because he is a fine specimen of a man, but solely because his trust is in God. If he is standing fast, it is because he is nailed to the cross.

The Big Bang

"Where were you when I laid the earth's foundation? . . .
Who laid its cornerstone,
while the morning stars sang together
and all the angels shouted for joy?" (38:4, 6-7)

T he Lord begins His cross-examination of Job by inquiring as
to his whereabouts at the time of the world's creation. Did
he have a hand in it, perchance? People like to ask where God
came from. But has it ever entered our minds that He might one day
pose the same question to us? It is a shock to have the tables turned
and to discover that the Lord, too, can ask questions about the
nature of our existence, and can express doubts about us just as we
do about Him.

In the course of this bizarrely ironical line of questioning, God lets
slip, almost as an afterthought, one of the most sensationally beautiful verses in all of Scripture. It is almost as though He Himself were
to open up the first chapter of *Genesis* and to write some new words
there. For as the creation unfolded the Lord God in His modesty
observed simply, "It is good." Yet meanwhile, according to Job
38:7, the Hosts of Heaven were letting out whoops and peals of joy!
Note too that since the text specifically reports that *"all* the angels"
(emphasis added) were celebrating, we can only presume that the
happy throng must have included Lucifer and all his future demons.
At the sight of the brand-new creation, even he who would become
the Devil was jubilant—and why not? He had just been created himself. The paint was still fresh on his wings.

So this text takes us back to a time when the universe was united
in perfect harmony, when the praise for God was so unanimous that
in all of creation there was not one dissenting voice. It is as if the
Lord were to say to Job, "You know, of course, that when everything was planned and set in motion, a cheer went up from one end
of the cosmos to the other? I mean, I'm sure I don't need to mention
this to one as well-informed as you—but you do know, don't you,
that the secret of the universe is a shout of joy? You're aware that
ecstasy is the cornerstone and foundation of absolutely everything?"

Scientists today like to talk about the Big Bang; but little do they realize that the echoes they detect may be the shouts of angels.

In *Job* this sudden mention of joy comes as something of an embarrassment—especially since elsewhere in the book nearly every other use of the word "joy" has a negative connotation. (Typical is 9:25 where Job moans, "My days fly away without a glimpse of joy.") Even for a smiling, healthy Christian, the mere mention of joy in a sermon, along with the reminder that rejoicing goes hand in hand with true faith, may toll like a great sad bell in the heart. For real joy is so scarce among us. We humans, who are slaves to sin and so do everything out of neurotic necessity and deadly pragmatism, have a most difficult time laying hold of a spirit of pure, spontaneous celebration. As much as we may value spontaneity, we can no more "be spontaneous" than we can fly. The feat is beyond us. Ecstasy is so purely a divine quality that it comes to us only by surprise, as an unexpected gift. Acts of joyful abandonment are the rare exception with us rather than the rule, whereas for God they are simply His nature, His normal mode of operating. Elan is the air God breathes. He gets a bang out of everything He does.

It is fitting that the Lord should take Job back to the beginning of the world in order to point this out, to that time of the "earth's foundation" when the very sea "burst forth from the womb" (38:4, 8). Isn't a birth the most joyous of events? Even in this fallen old world, in which a woman's "pains in childbearing" have been "greatly increased" (Gen. 3:16), what happiness can compare with that of the birth of a baby? Imagine then what it must have been like at the original birth of all things! Later in His speech the Lord returns to this theme when He asks Job, "Do you know when the mountain goats give birth? Do you watch when the doe bears her fawn?" (39:1). This is, of course, the central mystery of all: where does life come from? Where does anything come from? It is God's power as Creator of everything in the universe that first and foremost establishes His claim to be the only God. No one else can perform this feat of creation. No one else can make something out of nothing. Why not? Perhaps it is because no one else possesses the secret of pure joy.

Orders to the Morning

"Have you ever given orders to the morning,
or shown the dawn its place?" (38:12)

The Lord's answer to Job assumes something of the form of a three-ring circus. "And now, for My next act . . ." he announces, taking bow after bow. In the first ring of this divine circus are the most primal elements of the created order— such immense and unsearchable realities as the earth itself, the sea, weather, light, and darkness. The second ring contains a carnival of animals, a marvelous parade of the Lord's zoological genius ranging from the wild donkey to the soaring eagle, from the proud lion to the comical ostrich. As for the third and climactic ring, that one is reserved for the loftiest mysteries of all, the *pièces de résistance* of creation: Behemoth and Leviathan.

The image of the ring is an appropriate one, for the Lord's purpose in trooping out all these wonders is to show that He is the one who encircles and controls them all. He is the Ringmaster of this awesome circus, and these are the vast spheres of His influence. Has He not "stretched a measuring line across [the earth]" (v. 5), "shut up the sea behind doors" (v. 8), and even built "gates" for "death" (v. 17)? All those forces that from man's point of view seem so utterly wild and inscrutable, in the hands of the Lord are completely tame. He is the one who gives "orders to the morning," who leads the dawn around like a dappled pony on a bridle.

Dawn, of course, is a powerful symbol. Every morning the sun comes up to banish the shadows and paint the world anew, and this faithful, daily recurrence is a pledge of the Lord's ultimate victory over the forces of darkness. "For you who revere my name, the sun of righteousness will rise with healing in its wings" (Mal. 4:2). To Job the Lord does not explain any of this symbolism directly, but when He speaks of the dawn "taking the earth by the edges and shaking the wicked out of it" (38:13), suddenly the rising of the sun comes to signify exactly what mankind has instinctively known it to signify all along: God's final appearing, His Day of Judgment, and the renewal of all things.

Thus the Lord's question to Job, "Have you ever given orders to the morning?" becomes a way of saying, "Can you, Job, by your own efforts, do anything at all to influence the timing of My judgment and deliverance? Through all the arguing and struggling you have done, have you managed to bring about any dawning in your heart? Have you been able to bend one little ray of light in your direction?" The answer is no. It is not Job's struggling nor even the vehemence of his prayer that has brought on this visit from the Lord. Regardless of human efforts, the dawn comes at its own appointed time, and all we can do is to wait for it. Many pagan peoples have worshiped the sun, believing that their rites and sacrifices had a hand in keeping the bright orb up in the sky and calling it back every day. To us their childish folly is plain; but do we not make the same mistake when we try to manipulate our spiritual renewal? We can end up worshiping revival rather than the Lord Himself. We forget that it is up to God, and not up to us, to give orders to the morning.

This is how the Lord works with Job in these final chapters: taking the ordinary, everyday, stupendous objects of creation and parading them anew around the circus ring, He reminds Job of His sovereign power and glory. Similarly for us, when God speaks, He rarely tells us anything we have not heard before. Rather He just points to what is already there, whether in creation or in Scripture. The problems that have weighed so heavily upon us turn out to have answers that all along have been right under our noses, staring us in the face. The missing puzzle piece is one we have looked at and considered, many times, yet for some reason we have never picked it up. Before we can really see and understand the dawn for what it is, it takes the Lord Himself to point to it, much in the way that in the first chapter of *Jeremiah* He draws the prophet's attention to the branch of an almond tree (probably one bursting with blossoms) and asks simply, "What do you see, Jeremiah?" How many times before, even that same day, must Jeremiah have seen and admired the beauty of a flowering almond in spring? But now this familiar sight becomes for him the word of the Lord. Now it is the burning bush.

Meaning

"What is the way to the abode of light?
And where does darkness reside?" (38:19)

Many religious people, bearing in mind the Second Commandment's prohibition against the making of images, tend to be suspicious of art. Many more have a particular dislike for modern, abstract art. Yet one has only to look at the frost on a windowpane or at dewdrops spangled on a spiderweb, or to study a cloud or a handful of sand, to realize that our Creator God is not only an artist, but an abstract artist *par excellence*. He seems to have a passionate interest in pure color, in mere line, in sheer energy, and in the fundamentals of texture and shape. He likes geometrical patterns, but He also likes randomness. He enjoys stripes and splashes and dots and whole fields of plain paint. He appears to love form and design for their own sake. Lay down an empty picture frame on your lawn, and you have a work of pure abstraction—that is, a painting that represents nothing but itself.

True, the things of nature are not without symbolic power. Grass, which "is here today and tomorrow is thrown into the fire" (Matt. 6:30), can become a symbol of transience. But it is also simply grass. Dawn can be a symbol of renewal, but it is also merely dawn. God cannot be called a representational artist, for when He created the world and everything in it He was not copying anything. He was not depicting or representing any other reality, for there was no other reality except Himself. All his creations were but emanations of the inner workings of His own spirit.

This is the way of the abstract artist. While the representational artist attempts to show, more or less accurately, what the eye sees, the abstract artist is not so much interested in *what* the eye sees as in *how* it sees. The concern of abstraction is less with the world outside the beholder than it is with the beholder himself. Abstract art is a picture of the inner eye or heart of the one who looks. Or better: it is a picture of the looking itself.

If the abstract artist has one real point of contact with the objective world, it is his medium. The medium itself fascinates him. "Let there be light!" said God, and in the same way the artist says, "Let there be paint!" God's question to Job—"What is the way to the abode of light?"—could serve as an ideal motto for the abstract artist, whose whole preoccupation is with the inherent mysteries of light, paint, canvas. To the true abstractionist, paint is like music: precious for its own sake, quite apart from any cognitive meaning. It is like the eyes of someone we love: what do they mean? The very question is demeaning; they mean nothing but themselves. That is, their meaning is too large for expression. It is not that such meaning is vague; rather it is too powerfully particular. As Felix Mendelssohn put it, "The meaning of music is too specific for words." To look into the eyes of a lover is to have the need for meaning vanish. It is to see meaning overwhelmed by something larger than mere meaning: trust.

This is the essence of God's message to Job: "Trust Me; just trust Me. Look at the grass, look at the dawn, look at the stars, and trust Me." Can we trust the great Abstractionist? Can we believe in His art, knowing that there is nothing behind these canvases, no meaning to them, except the Artist Himself? Much of Job's pain has sprung from the chronic need (exacerbated by his friends) to try and decipher the meaning of his circumstances—to interpret, as it were, the art of God in his life. There are certainly times when this is appropriate, times when the divine art does bear a specific message for us that we can and must discern. Nevertheless, whatever God's message to us might be in any particular circumstance, it is always a message that is strictly subservient to the larger purpose of His art, which is to bear a meaning that is not really a meaning at all, but a Person—the Person of the Lord Himself.

To put this another way: of more significance than the meaning of our lives is the fact that our lives have no meaning at all except Christ. God only knows us in Christ—which is to say, Christ is God's artistic medium, His light, His paint, His only point of contact with anything outside of Himself. The Son is the way the Father sees us. It is a good thing for us to be able to see the hand of God at work in our lives; but it is a more wonderful thing simply to submit, as Mary did, when "the power of the Most High will overshadow you" (Luke 1:35).

One Hand Clapping

"Who waters a land where no man lives,
a desert with no one in it,
to satisfy a desolate wasteland
and make it sprout with grass?" (38:26-27)

The Lord's commitment to pure, abstract creativity (one might call it "art for art's sake") is so sweeping that He does not even require a human audience for His work. Torrential rain falls on "a land where no man lives"; acres of exotic flowers spring up and die with no eyes having ever enjoyed them. A few verses later an even stranger marvel is cited when the Lord asks Job, "*Who makes* the waters . . . hard as stone, when the surface of the deep is frozen *solid*?" (38:30). Here the Hebrew word for "the deep" denotes the sea, so that in Job's mind the question must have arisen, What sea? Job did not live near an ocean, did he? What are the chances that either he or his friends would ever have beheld a sea "frozen solid"?

This odd detail, if it does not quite constitute proof, is at least one of many tantalizing hints in these final chapters that this is indeed the Lord Almighty speaking, and no mere man. From the eerie vision of a wide and lonely seascape frozen in its tracks, to the rain falling where no one sees or even knows of it, to the heavenly shout of joy at the creation of the world—who else but the Lord and His angels could have witnessed such things?

For the believer in God, the famous conundrum about whether a tree falling in a forest would make any sound if there were no one around to hear it is no real conundrum at all. Of course the tree would crash! "Does he who implanted the ear not hear?" (Ps. 94:9). The One who invented sound is forever listening and hearing, even if the only noise is one of His own hands clapping. Was not the universe all in place before any human ear was put into it? Did not the sun shine, the wind blow, and the ocean breakers thunder and freeze, all without human help? And it was good; it was very, very good. Nothing at all was missing. The Lord did not make man because He had any need of him, any more than He had need of a warthog. The creation of humanity was an act of sheer, uncalled-for extravagance, wholly unnecessary. That is just the way the Lord is, doing nothing out of personal need but only out of His own abundantly overflowing life.

Still, it seems strange to us that God should send rain where no one can use it, and at the same time withhold His blessings from Job who could have used them very well, thank you. Yet just so, whole nations may starve even while food abounds in places where no one can harvest or eat it. It is like the cat Jesus lets out of the bag when He tells the town of Capernaum, "If the miracles that were performed in you had been performed in Sodom, it would have remained to this day" (Matt. 11:23). Why then, one wonders, did the Lord not perform those miracles in Sodom, in order that that town, at least, might have been saved? Why give the miracles to those who could not appreciate them, and withhold them from those who could?

Once again, the only answer is that the Lord, from our point of view, is like some eccentric modern artist who lines up a row of empty canvases against one wall, positions himself on the far side of the room, closes his eyes, and proceeds to hurl great gobs of paint with both hands, willy-nilly, and has the time of his life doing it. If anybody else but God were to behave in this way, he would be a crank. But because this crazy paint-thrower is the Lord, His works are glorious and majestic, and neither His methods nor His ends are to be questioned. If His art is so wildly abstract and avant-garde that one cannot even get a frame around it, it is because the subject of all His work is the awesome enigma of His own incomparable Self. Would we put Jesus in a frame? Would we hang Him on the wall? Would we analyze Him, interpret Him, write Him up in the newspaper or in a Ph.D. thesis? Well, inevitably we will, and perhaps we must. We are only human. But we should never mistake our human interpretation, our theology, for the living Person. To cling to the former is religion; to embrace the latter, come what may, is faith.

Weather

"Does the rain have a father?
Who sires the drops of dew?
From whose womb comes the ice?" (38:28-29)

Much of the Lord's first discourse to Job concerns the weather or, to use an earthier term, the elements. Can we human creatures bring on a rainstorm? Can we make sunny skies to order? Can we, as the Lord asks Job in 38:35, "send the lightning bolts on their way"? Of course we cannot. Ever since we were kicked out of the Garden of Eden we have longed to learn the secrets of such things. But we never have. We call them the elements because they are just that: so elemental as to be, like God Himself, unfathomable. Even in our scientific age the weather is so far beyond human control that it might better be classed as a spiritual than as a natural phenomenon. The rain, for all we really know about it, might as well fall directly out of Heaven rather than from clouds, and thunder might as well be God's own voice and lightning the snapping of His fingers.

Insurance companies refer to natural disasters as "acts of God." But is not the sunshine also an act of God? Is dew any less a miracle than manna? And if the secret of a simple thing like dew is entirely out of our reach, how much more awesome are the deeper mysteries of God! Why not admit, then, that if it rains it is only because God has opened the clouds; and likewise, if we have any understanding of God it is only because He Himself has opened our hearts. Consider the words of Micah 5:7—a terrible verse in which even the dew, so delicate and innocent, becomes a symbol of something far more powerful than all the world's armies and nuclear weapons, for the day is coming when the army of the Lord "will be in the midst of many peoples like dew from the Lord, like showers on the grass." And then "all [God's] foes will be destroyed" (v. 9).

Why do people flap their jaws so much about the weather? Why does it often seem to be the only thing to talk about, the one topic we all have in common? Isn't it because an awareness of the weather is the closest many people ever come to being spiritual? Regardless of our beliefs, weather is one of the most conspicuous ways in which the divine continues to manifest itself in secular lives. Chatting about this phenomenon is one means for a godless society to satisfy its natural yearning to be godly. It is a way of talking about the Lord without the embarrassment of having to mention Him by name. Don't people's attitudes toward the weather tell much about their feelings toward God? For many, God will always be either too hot or too cold, too wet or too dry.

Pagan religions revere the elements so highly that they think of them as causes rather than effects, and so give them personal names and worship them as gods. There are gods of snow and of the west wind, and goddesses of dew and of the dawn. Weather is more than the home of these gods; weather's different manifestations form their very bodies and personalities. At least pagans have a healthy sense of the force behind the elements as being a "who" rather than a "what," whereas modern meteorology has depersonalized creation. Listening to a weather report can be a bit like hearing an autopsy on someone you love who is still very much alive. As much as this daily barrage of information may give us an illusion of prognostication, is it really the case that nature is any less primitive or unpredictable than it was for Abraham? While the science of meteorology is certainly of great benefit when properly used, it can also have something occultish about it, like astrology or physiognomy. People can give more credence to weather forecasts and thermometers than they do to sticking their own noses out the front door. We can be so curious about what the future will bring that we lose sight even of the present. Rain gauges can be our phylacteries, fancy barometers a kind of modern rosary, and isobars like the entrails of animals.

Concerning all this Jesus warned: "When you see a cloud rising in the west, immediately you say, 'It's going to rain,' and it does. And when the south wind blows, you say, 'It's going to be hot,' and it is. Hypocrites! You know how to interpret the appearance of the earth and the sky. How is it that you don't know how to interpret this present time?" (Luke 12:54-56).

Wildness

"Who let the wild donkey go free?
Who untied his ropes?" (39:5)

C hapter 39 is the Lord's carnival of animals, the second ring of His grand circus. From the dramatic eight-verse poem on the horse to a lovely one-line cameo of the hawk, this chapter consists of a series of portraits of the wild kingdom. One is reminded of the time in the Garden of Eden when God paraded all the beasts before Adam, so the man could marvel at them, give them names, and realize the full extent of his dominion. Job does no naming here; in fact he does nothing at all except to look and to be amazed. For part of the Lord's point in trooping out this menagerie is to remind Job that, while it is true that humanity exercises God-given dominion over all the things of nature, our dominion has never implied full power either to control or to understand these things. That is not the sort of dominion it is. On the contrary, there remains something beautifully elusive about everything that God has laid His hands on, something that utterly escapes human grasp.

"Not only is My world wild," God says in effect, "but it is wilder than you have yet imagined." Consider the wild donkey, who "laughs at the commotion in the town; he does not hear a driver's shout" (39:7). The picture is that of a creature who is totally oblivious to the all-important hustle-bustle of human commerce, and who somehow manages to get along quite nicely without even hearing man's voice, let alone heeding it. The very wildness of this beast is his glory. He is free in a way that people only dream about.

Annie Dillard, pondering the mystery of wildness, asks, "What goes on in a weasel's brain? What does he think about? He won't say. His journal is tracks in clay, a spray of feathers, mouse blood and bone: uncollected, unconnected, loose-leaf, and blown." In this enigma of pure savagery there is something of the enigma of God Himself, whom we must go out to meet in the wilderness. God is, after all, not who we think He is. His thoughts are not our thoughts. He is a wild, alien God. A poem by Richard Trench puts it this way:

If there had anywhere appeared in space
Another place of refuge, where to flee,
Our hearts had taken refuge in that place,
And not with Thee.

Significantly, when the Lord Jesus was preparing to ride in triumph into Jerusalem, He sent two disciples on ahead to locate a certain donkey "which no one has ever ridden," instructing them to "untie it and bring it here" (Mark 11:2). In this way the Messiah came riding into the holy city on wildness itself. Psalm 18:10 tells us that the Lord "soars on the wings of the wind." Why does tradition like to picture a donkey as being among the creatures who knelt in the straw beside the cradle of the baby Jesus? Because the donkey, more than being a symbol of lowliness, is a symbol of stubborn wildness. Genesis 16:12 prophesied of Ishmael that he would be "a wild donkey of a man." Similarly in Job 39:9 the Lord draws attention to the wild ox and asks, "Will he consent to serve you? Will he stay by your manger at night?" (39:9).

Is all of nature wild, then, except for man? No; perhaps the truth is really the reverse. While even the wildest animals obey their Creator, human beings do not. The Apostle James, having observed that "all kinds of animals, birds, reptiles and creatures of the sea are being tamed and have been tamed by man," adds the stinging sentence, "But no man can tame the tongue" (James 3:7-8). *Homo sapiens*, he means, is the wildest creature of all—yet with a wildness not of glory but of sin. "The ox knows his master, the donkey his owner's manger," opens the book of *Isaiah*, "but Israel does not know, my people do not understand" (1:3).

How then do we fulfill our Lord's bidding to exercise dominion over the wilderness, whether inside or outside of ourselves? We do it by bowing before the One who created and controls all wildness. We do it by worshipfully submitting to a higher wildness than our own.

Comedy and Absurdity

"The wings of the ostrich flap joyfully." (39:13)

Of the eight animal portraits that make up Chapter 39, probably the most striking is the one devoted to the unlikeliest creature of all: the ostrich. The mighty eagle merits four verses, but the ostrich gets six. While the poem on the horse is one verse longer, the poem on the ostrich is more brilliantly unusual, even outlandish, and forms the centerpiece of the chapter. The horse may be a fast runner, but when the gangly ostrich "spreads her feathers to run, she laughs at horse and rider." Yet this silly flightless bird, the Lord notes with some wryness, "lays her eggs on the ground . . . unmindful that a foot may crush them," and moreover "she treats her young harshly, as if they were not hers . . . for God did not endow her with wisdom or give her a share of good sense" (39:13-18).

This passage is remarkable in that it constitutes the first and only real humor in the book of *Job*. Leave it to God to pull a stunt like this, forcing a smile out of Job at a time when the poor fellow has been so intent on his misery. Maybe Job even laughed out loud at this picture of the dumb, clumsy ostrich, without a grain of sense in her tiny head, who in terms of aviation looked like a dirigible assembled in a plumbing factory. Who can consider the duck-billed platypus or the blue-footed booby without thinking, "What a joker God is!" No doubt such touches of humor were an essential part of the healing of Job's traumatized emotions.

The Lord's quirky sense of humor, however, is more than just a laughing matter. It also poses some rather profound questions. In the world of animals it is fine to give a creature feathers and wings and two legs like a bird, and yet withhold from it the power of flight. But what about when the Lord allows this sort of thing in a human being? What about the disabled child who will never learn to walk, or perhaps never grow up at all? Do we laugh about this too? Or do we conclude that God is cruel?

Clearly, the comedy in the Lord's description of the ostrich is more than just joking around. It is comedy of a higher order, of the sort Dante understood when he entitled his great and serious epic poem *The Divine Comedy*. This is comedy that is the opposite of tragedy. Such a comedy presents an ordered and purposeful worldview, as opposed to the grievous disorder, the senseless waste, of tragedy. Even though life's underlying order might not always (or often) be humanly comprehensible, nevertheless the comedic perspective believes and trusts that order is there, and so comedy always moves toward a point of resolution, toward that inevitable conclusion in which the hidden scheme of things rises to the surface and becomes manifest. For this reason the book of *Job* is really not a tragedy but a comedy.

Even in the best of times our world can appear, on the surface, chaotic and absurd. But comedy takes this very absurdity and puts it to work. In classical literature the device of absurdity was used to reflect the natural limitations of the human mind. Since the reality of life itself is always bigger than the mind is able to assimilate, our view of any given event is bound to be somewhat absurd. In the literature of the twentieth century, however, this truth came to be turned upside-down. To modern writers the device of absurdity usually reflects the essential meaninglessness (as they see it) of life. But this is not at all the case with *Job* or with any of the other great literature of antiquity. Classically, it is not life that is absurd, but ourselves. If reality seems meaningless to us, it is because we are not dealing with a full deck.

In His response to Job the Lord does not supply any of the missing cards. All He does is to say, in effect, "Here is the deck; learn to play with it. Learn to live without knowing everything. What does it matter whether I give you great wisdom or only a little? Compared to all there is to know, it is still only a pittance, and therefore many things are going to strike you as preposterous or even insane. So get used to it. Get used to My absurdity, and live by faith rather than by sight. Be like the ostrich: though you cannot fly, you can still flap your wings joyfully!"

Zen

"Is it by your wisdom that the hawk soars?" (39:26)

"A Zen line in *Job*," commented Thomas Merton on this verse. Merton was certainly right in detecting a Zen-like quality that runs throughout these speeches of the Lord. How like a koan is the question in 38:22, "Have you entered the storehouses of the snow?" Or consider this from 38:24: "What is the way to the place where the east winds are scattered over the earth?" There is an eccentricity here, an oddness of perspective, an angle of vision that is slightly skew. It is hard to pin down what this quality is, exactly, except to say that we are seeing things through the eyes of Someone who is somehow different from ourselves—Someone we might call a "real character," and yet also Someone just ordinary enough that if we were to pass Him on the street during the course of a normal day, we might not give Him a second glance.

In a couplet of indifferent poetry that has become strangely famous, Robert Louis Stevenson wrote, "The world is so full of a number of things, / That we all should be as happy as kings." But we are not as happy as kings. Even when God spills open His treasure chest at our feet, still we seem to squint and grimace at all the jewels, as if they were too bright, or not quite bright enough, for our liking. Or as if they were not even there, really, though we may end up tripping over them and falling on our faces. How can we be so shortsighted in the face of all God's glories? It is because we are living in a cloud of sin. We literally have scales over our eyes, just as Paul did after his experience on the Damascus Road. Is it possible that Paul's scales had been there all along, and the reason he went blind was that he had never seen them before? Three days later the Lord healed him, and the scales fell from his eyes (Acts 9:18). Yet even then, apparently, the apostle continued to struggle with eye trouble for the rest of his life.

Surely what the Lord is aiming at in these final chapters of *Job* is to pull the wool from over our eyes. To do this, He hurls images like thunderbolts. Essentially He speaks to Job, and to all of us, just the way He has all along in creation: by bombarding us, almost indiscriminately, with the most ordinary of things, and at the same time showing us how wonderful they are. Are not even the crumbs that fall from the Lord's table glorious? And so He keeps inundating us with crumbs until one day, inexplicably, one of the crumbs comes crashing through our scales like a bombshell. Finally one little image impinges on our clouded screen: the picture of the hawk, let us say. And all at once something perfectly ordinary splits our hearts wide open and becomes for us what it was meant to be all along: a love letter from our Creator, an original work of art signed by the Master of the Universe and hanging on our very own living room wall. But the Lord does not stop there. He keeps after us, trying out one lavish image after another, saturating us with marvels until the day comes—hallelujah!—when we can no longer think our own thoughts anymore, but only His.

How loving and gentle is our God as He hurls His thunderbolts of reality! And just think: all through the harrowing experience of Job's trials the hawk was still there—still leaning his small weight against the great smooth wind, still circling lazily in the eye of the sun, his taut wings every bit as golden and diaphanous as they had been all along. For God had not changed. Job's circumstances had changed; but God remained the same, His power and love undiminished.

Deep within us, no doubt, there is buried a kind of psychic memory of what it must have been like for Adam to live in the Garden of Eden without sin. And even deeper than that must lie the memory of that very first morning of creation, just after the Lord had breathed His own life into Adam's nostrils and the man had opened his eyes on a brand-new world. Is this what Zen is? Is "enlightenment" a kind of echo of this moment? If so, then western Christianity, so inordinately pragmatic and rationalistic, could stand to learn something from the Zen masters.

At the same time, it should be clear that this is just one aspect of the Lord's message to Job, and that a full-orbed faith in Christ involves much more than this. The gospel is more than just a return to Paradise; it is entry into eternal life. More than just an awakening to the reality that already is, it is the forging of a brand-new reality, a brand-new creation. To be born again is to add something new to reality that was never there before. This is the true Zen, the true Zion to which no one comes except through faith in Jesus Christ.

The Great Banquet

*"The eagle's young ones feast on blood,
and where the slain are, there is he." (39:30)*

There is something peculiarly arresting in this verse—so much so that it causes the Lord Himself to break off, to come to an abrupt halt, so that His discourse is divided into two distinct halves at this point. Indeed the pause may have been a very long one, as both Job and God stopped to consider this strange image of baby eagles eating blood.

What makes this verse doubly remarkable for us is that the last line of it is found twice on the lips of Christ. Both in Matthew 24:28 and in Luke 17:37 the Lord says, "Where there is a dead body, there the eagles [or vultures] will gather," and although the two settings of this saying are somewhat different, in each case its effect is abrupt and discordant, and its meaning so obscure as to be almost impenetrable. Are there any other verses in the *Gospels* more difficult to interpret? The context itself is hard, as the Lord is discussing the mystery of His second coming, the details of which are not fully understood even by Himself, but only by His Father. Perhaps Jesus quoted these words from *Job*, then, as a shorthand way of referring to His Father's entire enigmatic discourse in that book, in the same way as His quotation from the cross of one verse in Psalm 22 pointed to that entire psalm.

Still, what did Jesus mean by it? What does the gathering of birds of prey around dead bodies have to do with the coming of the Kingdom of God? Consider the following passage from *Revelation*: "And I saw an angel standing in the sun, who cried in a loud voice to all the birds flying in midair, 'Come, gather together for the great supper of God, so that you may eat the flesh of kings, generals, and mighty men, of horses and their riders, and the flesh of all people, free and slave, small and great'" (19:17-18). This is a startling prophecy. It seems that even as the children of God sit down to a great banquet in the Kingdom of Heaven, so all the birds of the air will gather too at the Lord's table and, in a kind of ghastly parody of the Eucharist, proceed to devour the bodies and blood of the wicked. In a still more graphic passage in Ezekiel 39:17-20, we read that not only birds but all animals are to participate in this great feast, when the tables will finally be turned upon the wicked and when the New Earth, possessed of an infinitely greater capacity for self-cleansing than the old earth, will rid itself once and for all of sinful human flesh. Then the baby chick will eat the ruthless dictator, a family of field mice will wolf down a line of kings, and even the silly stork will gobble up a batch of terrorists.

Do we find this imagery too gruesome and offensive for our taste? If so, perhaps it is because we have not yet been offended enough by the cross of Christ and by its mystical carrion that unceasingly feeds a sinful and hungry world. If we are repulsed by the idea that all of nature might one day sit down in the Kingdom of God and feast on the bodies of sinners, then what about the fact that Christians now live on the body and blood of Christ? Is this not even more repulsive? Or have we never really thought about what we are doing when we consume little bits of bread and wine at church— what it really means? Do we realize that we are living off His death? We have all heard stories of missionaries who have ended up in cooking pots. But how many civilized people regularly cook and eat Jesus Christ, and think they are doing Him a favor by showing up at church?

Perhaps we have taken this mysteriously satisfying little ritual of the Eucharist too much for granted. Perhaps it has never shamed and horrified us as it ought to: that the spotless Lamb of God should have to sit and stew in the world's grimy pot; that He for whom sin was something utterly alien should have had to go to such revolting lengths in order to save and satisfy our souls.

Wherever there is a carcass, there the eagles will gather, and even their little ones will feast on blood. Truly this is a hard saying. Yet perhaps our difficulty lies not so much with understanding as with accepting it. Surely these words would have meant something to Job, to this man who had come to know what it was to take evil into himself, evil that he did not deserve, and who in fact had licked up and eaten this evil like dust until he was sick of it, sick to death. Yes, no doubt he would have understood something of the Last Supper and of the Marriage Feast of the Lamb, he who himself had been devoured on the groaning banquet tables of Satan.

Dialogue with God

The Lord said to Job. . . .
Then Job answered the Lord. . . .
Then the Lord spoke to Job. . . . (40:1, 3, 6)

While the Lord has a lot to say to Job, and while He continues to say it for two more chapters, gradually it dawns upon us that this is not just a lecture from on high, but a dialogue. The entire book of *Job* is not a series of soliloquies but a conversation among friends. In this section the conversation is between Job and God. The Lord speaks to Job, and Job answers. How astonishing! Is this not the secret, burning desire of every human being—to speak face to face with God "as a man speaks with his friend" (Ex. 33:11)?

We have seen already that one of the great differences between Job and the other people in this story is that Job talks not just *about* God but *to* God. There is hardly one of his speeches that does not move at some point into prayer. Prior to this, of course, the Lord has not answered these prayers. He has been silent, silent as death. Job might as well have been talking to the ceiling for all the results he gets. But now, beginning with Chapter 38, something different happens: now the Lord speaks back. Here is something unusual. There is nothing very unusual, really, about prayer. Most of the world prays; even atheists pray now and then. But it is one thing to pray, and it is another thing to get answers. It is one thing to call up the White House and ask to speak to the President; it is another thing to get through.

In prayer, getting through to God is essential. If prayer is all one-way it is not prayer. It may be thinking, daydreaming, or imagination, but it is not prayer. Prayer is dialogue with God. God may, as in *Job*, be silent for agonizing periods of time. But if He does not answer eventually, all is lost. If God does not speak, and if people do not hear Him, then there can be no true religion. The word *religion* means "linking"—really it's just a synonym for relationship or friendship. True religion is friendship with God, the linking of Heaven and earth. It means that the lines are always open. God's telephone number is J-E-R-E 33:3: "Call to me and I will answer you and tell you great and unsearchable things you do not know." This is what happens for Job. It is also what must happen in the life of every believer. For there is no other way to grasp the things of the Spirit except by direct revelation, and this is as true for ordinary people today as it was for the Biblical prophets and apostles. Saying prayers, going to church, even reading the Bible are not enough. There must be direct, personal, experiential contact with the living God. Yes, the Bible is God's Word; but a person can study the Bible all his life and never hear from God. How pathetic it is to see fine human minds poking and prodding the Scriptures to try and force some meaning out of them, when the fact is that God's Word can only be understood by hearing God speak it all over again into your very own heart, so that the Word becomes as new and as fresh as the day it was first heard and written down. The apostles were great because they were the first to be told the mystery of the gospel. But doesn't every Christian today have the same experience of God's grace as they did? Every Christian receives a personal revelation of the gospel directly from Christ. Every Christian, in effect, has a Damascus Road experience. Every Christian meets Jesus personally, walks with Him and talks with Him, and the result is spectacularly life-changing.

Is personal experience, then, a higher authority than Scripture? Absolutely not. While personal experience is vital, it is only valid insofar as it does not in any way contradict Scripture. If an experience of God is authentic, it will be fully in accord with what God has already revealed about Himself in His Word. In this way, Scripture validates experience, and experience brings Scripture alive. In authentic spirituality there is no disharmony between the two.

Granted, one can receive by faith things that have not been imparted to one personally by any dramatic supernatural experience. Indeed such faith is the normal means of God's revelation to His people. But the great secret about faith is that, all by itself, it *is* a supernatural revelation that both includes and surpasses all others. How else could the least Christian be greater than John the Baptist (see Matt. 11:11)? This is why "anyone who receives a prophet because he is a prophet will receive a prophet's reward" (Matt. 10:41), and why Paul could promise that "you can boast of us just as we will boast of you" (2 Cor. 1:14). The revelation of the gospel of faith is the key revelation that surmounts all other visions and prophecies.

Silence

Job answered the Lord:
"I am unworthy—how can I reply to you?
I put my hand over my mouth.
I spoke once, but I have no answer—
twice, but I will say no more." (40:3-5)

Certain bodily gestures seem naturally to accompany profound worship: kneeling, bowing, lifting the hands, falling prostrate. Yet perhaps one of the most worshipful gestures of all is the uncommon one that Job here performs: covering the mouth with the hand. This act is a demonstration of total submission. One can fall on one's face and yet continue to blubber and babble. But to yield the tongue is to yield everything. Job's response of humble silence before the presence of the Lord is echoed in some of the best-known verses of the Bible: "Be still, and know that I am God" (Ps. 46:10); "The Lord is in his holy temple; let all the earth be silent before him" (Hab. 2:20).

It is tempting to speculate on the nature of the great whirlwind at the beginning of the theophany in *Job*. Where did all this wind come from? Did the Lord bring it with Him? Or might it be better explained as the immense accumulation of stale air from the long-winded dialogue between Job and his friends? How the Jews loved these grand debates! How Christians love them! But the judgment of this book is that, while such discussions may serve a certain end, in the final analysis they are just so much empty wind to be whisked away before the coming of the Lord.

This is not to say, of course, that there is anything wrong with talking. There is a time for silence, and there is a time for speech. In Psalm 39:1-3 David described how he determined to "keep my tongue from sin; I will put a muzzle on my mouth. . . . But when I was silent and still, not even saying anything good, my anguish increased." Looking back over Job's passionate tirades, surely we must concede that he was doing what he had to do, pouring out his heart in bitter complaint rather than holding everything inside to grow more bitter still. Even Jesus, "during the days of his life on earth, offered up prayers and petitions with loud cries and tears to the one who could save him from death, and he was heard because of his reverent submission." This statement, tucked away in Hebrews 5:7, offers a surprising glimpse into the private prayer life of our Lord. Since when are "loud cries and tears" to be equated with "reverent submission"? But this is the kind of reverence we see in Job. In pain and confusion, he cries out to the Lord. Yet as soon as the Lord answers him, Job instantly grows silent and humble. Where before he was all mouth, now he is all ears.

Nevertheless, many readers find it strange and contradictory when Job suddenly claps his hand over his mouth and seems to recant everything he had formerly said so fervently. Doesn't this suggest that maybe he's not quite so righteous as he's been claiming to be? Not at all; for to say that Job maintains a status of perfect righteousness throughout the book is not to say that his faith undergoes no change. On the contrary, the spirituality of the righteous is continually in flux as a result of the experiences they undergo. One of the marks of mature faith is this versatility of response, this willingness to contradict oneself, this ability to change and grow and so to react appropriately under different circumstances. Our characters are not static and unbending, but moldable, which means that we are subject to being regularly melted down and refashioned.

It is easy to idealize the life of faith. But the reality is that during those seasons when the Lord seems distant or absent to the soul, its conduct is bound to be very different from its conduct during the Lord's felt or manifest presence. Isn't this just as it should be? Granted, the practical goal of faith is to behave in every situation just as though the Lord were immediately present—which of course He is, whether we feel it or not. But Revelation 1:17 tells us that even John, the beloved disciple, the man who had been Jesus' best and closest friend on earth and who had lain his head on the Master's breast the night before He died, even this man, when the glorified Christ actually appeared to him from Heaven in dazzling splendor, "fell at his feet as though dead." The Lord's manifest presence makes a difference—all the difference in the world.

Behemoth

"Look at the behemoth,
which I made along with you
and which feeds on grass like an ox." (40:15)

Now we come to the final ring of the Lord's three-ring circus, the ring that contains (next to man) the grandest and most mysterious of all His creatures: Behemoth and Leviathan. We all know that when we go to the zoo we will see lions, tigers, bears, and elephants. But what if we heard about a zoo where we could see living dinosaurs? Or a zoo where wildness itself—the very spirit of savagery—had been caught in a cage and put on visible display for human eyes to inspect? Or what if all the most spectacular features of all the world's greatest animals had somehow been lumped together and combined into one magnificent beast? Wouldn't that be a sight worth seeing?

Perhaps this is something of the effect the Lord intends by His description of the Behemoth. Traditionally this beast has been assumed to be either the hippopotamus or the elephant, the most formidable of the land mammals, and the chapter can easily be read in this light. And yet, can it really be said of either of these creatures that its "tail sways like a cedar" (40:17)? The Hebrew word *behemoth*, rather than being the name of any particular species, is actually the plural of the word for "beast." Thus "behemoth" could almost be understood as a kind of "Mother Nature," a figure containing in herself the essence of all the Creator's power and genius in nature. Is this why, as big as Behemoth is, "the lotuses conceal him in their shadow," while "the hills bring him their produce, and all the wild animals play nearby" (40:20-22)?

The Nicene Creed opens with the words, "I believe in one God the Father Almighty, Maker of heaven and earth, and of all things visible and invisible." In the portrait of Behemoth (and even more in the portrait of Leviathan) the Lord appears to be moving Job gently out of the visible realm and into the invisible—that is, into the realm of mythic or supernatural beasts, of which there are many other examples in the Bible. The pages of *Ezekiel*, *Daniel*, and

Revelation teem with strange and otherworldly creatures who have no real or visible existence in the natural order. Concerning these apocalyptic beasts the question can fairly be asked, Are they *real*? Do they literally exist in the heavenly realms? Some would argue that these creatures have primarily a symbolic value, such as the ones in *Daniel* who represent world powers or periods in history. Yet what about the "four living creatures . . . covered with eyes" who, according to Revelation 4:6-8, stand in the inner circle around the very throne of God and constantly give Him glory and praise? Do mere symbols inhabit the throne room of Heaven and open their mouths in ecstasy? However we may interpret the meaning of these heavenly creatures, one fact seems clear enough: our Lord God has some mighty strange friends!

It also seems clear that the Lord's main purpose in shifting the focus of His talk from the natural to the supernatural order is to remind Job that here too He is Lord. Can anyone capture the Behemoth or "trap him and pierce his nose" (40:24)? Certainly not. Yet to the Lord even this colossus is as tame as a little lap dog, for he "feeds on grass like an ox" (v. 15). Though Behemoth "ranks first among the works of God, yet his Maker can approach him with his sword" (v. 19). The very docility of this beast is counted as one of his finest features. "When the river rages, he is not alarmed; he is secure, though the Jordan should surge against his mouth" (v. 23). With perfect tranquillity and royal magnanimity the Behemoth stands unperturbed in the midst of the world's swirling current. He is a kind of buddha of the beasts, cosmically unflappable, and surely here the Lord is dropping a rather broad hint to Job. For if the Behemoth has no fear of anything, it is because of his position of absolute preeminence over nature. And yet, how much more reason does Job have to be unafraid! For just as the Behemoth stands far above every other wild creature, so does Job, in the mystery and dignity of his human frame, stand head and shoulders above the Behemoth. There is a quiet yet robust irony in the fact that the Lord's one glaring omission from His dazzling three-ring circus, His festive catalog of "God's Greatest Hits," is the human being. As Jesus taught, "You are worth more than many sparrows" (Matt. 10:31)—more too, He might easily have added, than many behemoths.

Leviathan

"Can you pull in the leviathan with a fishhook?" (41:1)

C hapter 41, the climax of the theophany, is entirely devoted to a long poem on an outlandish creature named Leviathan. "Nothing on earth is his equal," boasts the Lord as He leads into the ring this monster who "makes the depths churn like a boiling caldron" (vv. 33, 31). Leviathan, it seems, is God's trump card, His ace in the hole, His final answer to all of Job's perplexity and pain. After seeing this, Job instantly repents "in dust and ashes," confessing meekly, "I know now that you can do all things; no plan of yours can be thwarted" (42:6, 2).

What is going on here? What is it about the Lord's description of Leviathan that Job finds so completely convincing? For in all fairness, many readers do not share Job's reactions. Many are unimpressed by this final word from the Lord; they find it unsatisfying and bafflingly anticlimactic. Is this God's answer to all the world's suffering? Is this the resolution to all the complex problems discussed in the dialogue? Are these words suitable to be read aloud to the sick, the depressed, and the dying?

If there is a key to this chapter, it must lie in the correct interpretation of this bizarre image of Leviathan. Most scholars identify this creature as the crocodile, pointing to his jaws "ringed about with fearsome teeth," his back scaled with "rows of shields tightly sealed together" (vv. 14-15), and so on. But can it really be said of the crocodile that "firebrands stream from his mouth," "smoke pours from his nostrils," and "his breath sets coals ablaze" (vv. 19-21)? This sounds less like the description of a crocodile than of a fire-breathing dragon. Even more than in the case of the Behemoth, it seems clear that we are here in the presence of no mere earthly beast but of some otherworldly, supernatural entity. Yet how are we to understand this image? What—or whom—could it represent? Who could this possibly be whom the Lord in His parting shot calls "king over all that are proud" (v. 34)?

Who is the King of Pride? Who else but . . . Satan?

Those who find the conclusion of *Job* unsatisfying are the same ones who complain that Satan, following his two brief appearances in the Prologue, is never mentioned again. Not only is his name never spoken, but no one in this book seems even aware of his existence. Neither does the Lord ever reprimand or discipline Satan for his brutal attacks on Job, nor offer one word of explanation as to the satanic origin of all of Job's sufferings. Instead the Devil gets off scot-free, while Job takes all the flak. At least, that is how it appears. God can talk all He wants to about the beauties and marvels of His creation, but as long as Satan is at large in it, alive and well and able to wreak havoc at will, there is a fly in the sacred ointment. This one loose end unravels the whole garment.

Chapter 41 is the Lord's answer to this very dilemma. It is His answer to the problem of evil. While it is true that Satan is never named outside the Prologue, this does not mean that the Lord never deals with him. He deals with him here in the form of Leviathan, describing him to Job with the same sort of symbolic picture-language He uses in *Revelation*, where the Devil is also portrayed as a great dragon who is to be "thrown into the Abyss" (20:2-3). The connection between Satan and Leviathan can be seen too in *Isaiah*, implicit in God's promise that on the Day of Judgment He "will punish with his sword . . . Leviathan the gliding serpent, Leviathan the coiling serpent; he will slay the monster of the sea" (27:1). Job himself, mysteriously, had testified back in 26:13 that the Lord's "hand pierced the gliding serpent"—suggesting that he already had some rudimentary understanding of the personal nature of evil and of the Lord's sovereign power over it.

Accordingly, when God begins to enlighten Job further on this subject of Leviathan, Job would have understood exactly what was meant. He would have understood that the same God who made the silly stork also made the "king of terrors" (18:14), and therefore when all is said and done there is no real difference between Satan and a little mouse or a flea, for Satan too is nothing more than a created being. For all his breathtaking power, the Prince of Darkness is merely a creature, just one more lowly lump of dust in the hands of his omnipotent Creator. So what does it matter if Job cannot "put a cord through his nose" (41:2)? Man cannot tame this fiery dragon—but God can, and has, and will. And this is the message that finally pierces Job's heart.

Christianity
Doesn't Work

"Any hope of subduing [Leviathan] is false;
the mere sight of him is overpowering." (41:9)

In our incredible human presumption, we have all felt that there must be some way to tame the evil that both surrounds and permeates us. We have all clung to the hope that there must be some method, if not to avoid suffering entirely, then at least to get the upper hand on it. And from time to time we seem sincerely and ardently to believe that we have found it, this master key to life. We think we have hit upon some secret, some answer to the riddle of pain, some formula that can be applied to all of our problems. And it works! It really does. It works, perhaps, for quite a while. For a good long time we may find that we have a goodly measure of peace and happiness in this world. Hurray! We have discovered the secret!

Christians, of all people, may be the most prone to this foolishness. After all, the claims of the gospel are so extraordinarily lavish. No other belief or philosophy promises what Christ does, nor comes even close. So it can be most disheartening for the Christian to come face to face with the enemy of our souls, with manifest evil, and to plead earnestly to the Lord for help, only to receive the answer that Job received in 41:9: "Any hope of subduing him is false." At such times it is as if the Lord were to say to us, "With all your theology, with all your faith, with all the spiritual secrets you know, still you cannot lead the Devil around by the nose." Not only that, but "if you lay a hand on him, you will remember the struggle and never do it again!" (41:8).

Most of the world's religious and philosophical systems are advanced by people who, in one way or another, appear to be on top of life's problems. In reality nobody is ever on top for very long; nobody leads Satan by the nose. But for a brief while, someone may seem to have discovered the "secret." Someone finds something that "works," and then he writes a book, founds a cult, starts a movement. He is on top, and so he preaches to those who are still on the bottom, working their way up.

But this is not the Christian way. No, the central message of

Christianity is not preached by someone who is on top. Rather, it is preached by someone who is at the very bottom of the heap: hanging on a cross. The gospel is the message of a loser, not of a winner.

To be sure, Christ wins in the end. He conquers death and rises from the grave to live forevermore (something which, incidentally, no other religious leader has ever done, nor even claimed to do). And yet, it is not primarily on the basis of the resurrection that the gospel is preached. Christ's victory over death is vital, and without it His teaching would be worthless. But the fundamental platform of Christianity is not the platform of success, but of what appears to be total defeat: the cross. The cross is the pulpit in which God stood to preach His greatest sermon, and it is also the only pulpit where anyone else may stand and rightfully preach to others. As disciples of Christ we stand on our weakness, not on our strength.

Of all the answers to the world's problems, the gospel is the only one whose primary claim is not that it works, but that it doesn't work. No doubt it works better than anything else, for "we know that in all things God works for the good of those who love him" (Rom. 8:28). But built into the gospel is a frank admission that (at least in worldly terms) it cannot work perfectly, because the world itself is unworkable, defunct. It doesn't work because human beings are no longer viable creatures, no longer operable in their fallen state. It cannot work because humanity stands condemned and so is not worth a plugged nickel. Other theologies try to do something with the plugged nickel. But Christianity throws the worthless thing away, nails it to a cross. A Christian's life is good for nothing except crucifixion.

This is why true faith is not something that runs along smoothly and efficiently. Rather, it has a built-in tendency to fall apart at the seams. According to Paul faith regularly finds itself "hard pressed," "perplexed," "struck down" (2 Cor. 4:8-9). The very fact that faith looks to a power beyond itself means that it is continually subject to loss of control. So if you're looking to get control of all your problems, forget Christianity. If you're looking for success, happiness, or freedom from pain, forget Christ. The way of Christ is the cross, and the cross spells weakness, poverty, failure, death. This is what stands at the center of this "system"; this is the door at which Jesus knocks. If you want to follow Jesus, give up any idea of trying to control Leviathan. If you want to follow Jesus, get it through your mind that you are going to suffer unspeakably at the hands of evil. Get that one little thing straight, says the gospel, and the rest will be smooth sailing.

Giving the Devil
His Due

"How can I resist speaking of his lineaments,
his strength and his graceful form?" (41:12)

God does a very mysterious thing in this chapter: He boasts about Satan. He magnifies the powers of darkness. He vaults the Devil's majesty and supremacy as second only to His own. With rhapsodic abandon the Lord sings the praises of this "creature without fear" who "looks down on all that are haughty," who "treats iron like straw" and "laughs at the rattling of the lance," and who *"makes the sea fume like a scent burner . . . as though the deep had white hair"* (41:27 ff.).

What is going on here? What possible motive could God have in extolling this horrific monster Leviathan, making him appear so awesome and invincible? This question is like one that was forced upon us at the very beginning of the book: how is it that Satan has ready access to the very throne room of God, and why is the Lord so quick to hear and to grant his outrageous demands? Why has God chosen to bestow upon Satan, His own bitterest enemy, powers and favors that overwhelmingly surpass those of any other creature in the universe? And why does God seem so pleased about this? Why is God content to let Satan run amok through the beautiful garden of His creation?

In his novel *Moby Dick* Herman Melville describes the enormous white whale's "broad firmament of a forehead, plaited with riddles; dumbly lowering with the doom of boats, and ships, and men. . . . In that full front view, you feel the Deity and the dread powers more forcibly than in beholding any other object in living nature." For Melville, apparently, "the Deity and the dread powers" were virtually one and the same, and similarly for Job it was precisely this sense of confusion between the two that had been his problem all along. In fact, for all of us is this not the central problem of faith? In Job's words, "God assails me and tears me in his anger and gnashes his teeth at me" (16:9), and "If it is not he, then who is it?" (9:24).

In Chapter 41 God finally reveals to Job who it is who has been torturing him. Moreover the Lord here makes a distinction once and for all between His own power, which is uncreated and therefore unlimited, and the power of Leviathan which, as sweeping and unparalleled as it may be, is nevertheless a created power and therefore one with strict limits. By painting metaphorically so sublime and impressive a portrait of the Devil, God is only doing what He has done all along with Job, and all along throughout the history of the world: giving the Devil his due. God allows evil, for now, to have its day, and even to gain the upper hand and grow greater and greater, to the point where it may seem to have completely obscured the very memory of everything that is good. Why does God do this? He does it so that in the end, when He finally steps in and crushes Satan's head, His victory over evil will be all the more astounding and glorious, and so that all those who have put their faith in Him will be filled with an exceedingly greater joy than would have been possible in any other way.

What the Lord is trying to show us, in this elaborate puffing up of Leviathan, is that God's good is ultimately so much greater than the Devil's evil that there is really no contest between the two. A contest will be waged, to be sure, but only because people do not believe. The longer this contest goes on, and the bigger and stronger Satan appears to grow, the more his utter powerlessness will be exposed in the end, and the more the mystery of simple faith in God will be vindicated. What does it matter if "the mighty are terrified" (41:25) by the tumultuous thrashing of Leviathan? How much more shall the faithful be overjoyed at the coming of Christ! "Everything under heaven belongs to me," exults the Lord, and since "no one is fierce enough to rouse [Leviathan], who then is able to stand against me?" (41:10-11).

How magnificently ironic it is that when the Lord Himself praises to the skies the spectacular qualities of His archrival, the final result is that the latter is reduced to nothing. Just so, each nail that was driven into the hands and feet of Christ was a nail in Satan's coffin.

Jonah Swallows
the Whale

"When leviathan rises up, the mighty are terrified;
they retreat before his thrashing." (41:25)

Evil, when we are in the midst of it, can seem so overwhelmingly convincing. Not only is it powerful, but it can even
appear so right and so good. And yet when the Lord arises,
He is so much more convincing than the Devil that there is really no
comparison between the two. The merest touch from God, and
Leviathan deflates like a balloon. One taste, one glimpse, of the Lord
Almighty is enough to dispel all the world's evil in a moment. This
is one of the Lord's qualities that we come to count on: His power
to engulf sin and evil completely in the blink of an eye. When we
believe in Jesus, all the problems of yesterday, all those shadows that
may have loomed so large for us in the past, need no longer haunt
us. They can vanish like the dreams of night when the morning
comes. They are gone, whisked away by the mighty and merciful
hand of the Lord, whose "compassions never fail. They are new
every morning" (Lam. 3:22-23).

Certainly there are many things that will continue to trouble us
in this life, and new problems are bound to emerge to take the place
of the old ones. But the day is coming—make no mistake!—when
all our earthly trials will be gone, gone like a mist at the rising of the
sun. More than that, "the former things will not be remembered,
nor will they come to mind" (Isa. 65:17). How is this possible? God
alone knows. But we Christians are people who have already experienced firsthand something of God's power to consume and anni-
hilate evil; we have seen this power at work so consistently in our
own and others' lives that we develop an implicit trust that the Lord
will not fail to honor His Word, but that evil will ultimately be so
wholly eradicated that no one will give it so much as a passing
thought anymore. It will be like that Monday afternoon when we
were two years old and we fell and skinned our knee: it simply will

not be remembered. It will not be significant enough to be remembered. The damned will be able to think of nothing else but Hell; but the blessed will not give it a thought. The Lord "will wipe every tear from their eyes" (Rev. 21:4).

Nevertheless, perhaps we harbor a nagging feeling that we might never really be happy in such a Heaven, knowing that other people (including, no doubt, some whom we had known and loved in the world) were at the same time being tormented eternally in Hell. But this is a bit like thinking that we could never enjoy a sunny day because then the shadows are darker. To those whose own choices have condemned them to live in the shadows, darkness is everything. But to those who live in the light, shadows are nothing at all.

As Christians we trust that even now God has not only forgiven our sin, He has forgotten all about it. We believe this even though we cannot grasp it. How, we wonder, could God ever really forget anything? But He has, He has! He forgot all our sin when He took it into Himself on the cross. He forgot it when He said, "I'm thirsty," and instead of cool water the bitter cup of evil was raised to His lips and He drank it down to the dregs. And then He died with all of the world's shadows inside Him. He took them down to Hell and left them there. And now the Lord is teaching us, too, to drink this cup, to swallow the poison of Hell without being hurt by it at all, to swallow it down until not a trace of it is left, not even in our memories.

Jonah was swallowed by a whale; but the believer in Jesus Christ swallows the whale. We eat Leviathan for breakfast. It takes a very big God, and a very big faith in God, to be able to absorb so much evil. Leviathan seems so endlessly sprawling, gargantuan, invincible. But the essence of the gospel is that the love of God is greater than any evil—and not just a little bit greater, but infinitely greater. When John assured us that "the one who is in you is greater than the one who is in the world" (1 John 4:4), he was making one of the Bible's most fantastic understatements. Can our souls enlarge to the point where the God who lives inside our own little hearts is this big—big enough to down Leviathan in one gulp? Then in truth we will be able to shout, "Death has been swallowed up in victory" (1 Cor. 15:54).

Unknowing

"Surely I spoke of things I did not understand,
things too wonderful for me to know." (42:3)

T he best way to comment on Job's final response to the Lord
may be simply to quote from one of the shortest and loveli-
est of all the psalms, Psalm 131:

> My heart is not proud, O Lord,
>   my eyes are not haughty;
> I do not concern myself with great matters
>   or things too wonderful for me.
> But I have stilled and quieted my soul;
>   like a weaned child with its mother,
> like a weaned child is my soul within me.

There is a strange thing that happens at the point when we finally,
somehow, manage to give up wrestling with matters that are too
complex, too lofty, too wonderful for the human mind to understand. What happens is this: suddenly, inexplicably, we do understand! For there is a knowledge that is beyond mere knowing. We
can "know this love that surpasses knowledge" (Eph. 3:19), and
there is a "peace of God, which transcends all understanding" (Phil.
4:7).

Paul wrote, "The man who thinks he knows something does not
yet know as he ought to know. But the man who loves God is known
by God" (1 Cor. 8:2-3). Real knowledge of God involves not so
much knowing Him, or knowing anything about Him, as it does
being known by Him. Paul began a sentence to the Galatians, "Now
that you know God," but immediately corrected it to read, "Or
rather, are known by God . . ." (4:9). Jesus warned about those who
pretend to know Him but to whom He will say in the end, "I never
knew you" (Matt. 7:23).

Many Christian mystics have testified that the highest form of
prayer consists simply in being with the Lord, in a state that is somehow beyond words, beyond images, beyond concepts. If this teaching sounds dangerous and extreme to us, it is because so much of

the work of rationalistic theology involves wrestling God out of the arena of the ineffable and reducing Him to propositions that the human mind can handle. But isn't the work of Jesus rather different? His work is to lead us out of ourselves, out of the stale confines of our minds, and into the arena of mystery and of spirit, of tears and of blood, of thunder and of the great silence of God. His work is to engage our souls in that most terrifying of all human ventures: trust.

Where there is full understanding, trust is not needed. Paul tells us to "offer the parts of our body to God as instruments of righteousness" (Rom. 6:13). But probably the last of all the parts to be wholly offered is our intellect, our compulsive need to comprehend everything, to create a sense of reasonable order where none is apparent. Yet why should we expect life to be reasonable? It is the Lord who is sovereign, not human reason. While faith is not contrary to reason, it does greatly surpass it. The Spirit must control the mind, not the other way around. As Paul puts it, "The mind controlled by the Spirit is life and peace" (Rom. 8:6). When this state is achieved, the result is that paragon of Christian maturity whom Paul calls "the spiritual man" (1 Cor. 2:15).

When the baby Jesus was first brought into the temple, how did the prophet Simeon recognize Him as the Christ? Was it by some intellectual process? Not at all. Neither did Simeon believe because of anything Jesus had done, for so far He had done nothing. Rather, this old man's faith sprang from a supra-rational revelation of the Holy Spirit. One might say that just as the Christ, at this point, was a tiny baby, so Simeon's intellectual faculty had to be reduced to that of a tiny baby in order to know Him for who He was. In the words of the anonymous author of *The Cloud of Unknowing*, "By love God can be caught and held, but by thinking never."

If Jesus Christ is our Lord, we must allow Him not only to inform our thinking, but to override it. If we are never prepared to take a step without a clear understanding of where we are going, and if we have no experience of folding the wings of the intellect and of doing things for no other reason than that the voice of God is speaking in our hearts, then as much as we may think we know the Lord, we are still hanging back from what it means to be known by Him.

The Holy of Holies

"You said, 'Listen now, and I will speak.'" (42:4)

During the last four chapters we have been witnessing the central mystery of faith: a man listening to God. No one can believe in God who has never heard Him speak. For faith does not come from outward observances, but from hearing God. It comes from sitting at the feet of the living Christ, meeting and touching Him in the innermost recesses of one's spirit. So Paul tells us, "Faith comes from hearing the message, and the message is heard through the word of Christ" (Rom. 10:17). Faith without hearing is dead.

Christianity had its beginnings in a second-story room behind locked doors, and from there it spread into the whole world. Just so, the Kingdom of God is like a small amount of yeast that permeates a large batch of dough. The yeast, the smallest ingredient of all, is the active ingredient. Without it the whole recipe falls flat. In the spiritual life this active ingredient is the hearing of the Word of God in the inner sanctuary of the heart.

In Old Testament religion the Holy of Holies, the secret inner sanctuary of the temple where God dwelt, was cut off from the people. No one ever went in there except the high priest, and that only once a year, and even then he had to dress up like some fancy technician performing a highly dangerous maintenance task on the core of a nuclear reactor. In Christianity, however, the inner sanctum, the reactor core, is wide open. When the Jewish high priest went into the Holy of Holies he had to take blood with him. But now the blood is freely supplied. Now when an ordinary person first enters the sacred precinct, blood pours out and covers him—the blood of Christ. In this room pure radioactivity is flowing all over the place, and yet no one inside gets hurt. The rest of the world, to be sure, is in an advanced state of meltdown—a situation so perilous that the New Testament warns us to "*hate* even the clothing stained by corrupted flesh" (Jude 23). But in the inner sanctuary, in the core of the reactor itself, there—and there only—one is safe. That is what *sanc-*

tuary means: safety. This is where Christians live, in the safety of holiness. A Christian's life and work flow out from this home base. Christianity begins in the sanctuary of the deep heart's core, and reaches out from there. It never works the other way around.

What exactly goes on in this inner sanctuary? What is in there, apart from a sea of blood? The Old Testament tells us that the Holy of Holies contained a chest called the Ark of the Covenant, and in this chest there were three objects: a jar of manna preserved from the days of the Israelites' wanderings in the wilderness, Aaron's staff that had budded, and the two stone tablets of the law that Moses had received from God. For the Christian these objects symbolize, respectively, the body of Christ, His cross, and the Word of God.

In 2 Samuel 6:6-7 we read that when a man so much as touched the Ark of the Covenant accidentally, the Lord was so angry that He immediately struck the man dead. How amazing, then, that under the New Covenant the secret of righteousness actually consists in this very act of drawing near to the sacred Ark and touching it. More than that, believers now are told not merely to touch this mystery but to maintain continuous, living contact with it. One can have any number of religious rituals, sacrifices, good deeds, or good moral intentions, and yet never touch God, never enter the one place where He lives. But the child of God stays in this inner sanctuary all the time, and if he moves it is only as the Holy of Holies moves with him, in order that its fragrance may spread into all the world.

The believer knows he has no life apart from what goes on in this smallest and most secret of rooms with its three simple, hallowed objects. Whenever the Christian gets up off his knees to go somewhere or to do something, his sole motive is to push out the four walls of this little room to the very ends of the earth. But he must never leave the room itself. For this tiny, holy sanctuary in the depths of the heart is the only safe island in a doomed and dying world. It is the floating ark that rides above the waters of destruction, and everything that matters—everything that is worth saving—is inside it.

No Time for Coasting

*"My ears had heard of you
but now my eyes have seen you.
Therefore I despise myself
and repent in dust and ashes." (42:5-6)*

In every season of suffering there comes a turning point. The turning point is not usually the point at which the suffering itself is alleviated. Rather, it is that time when it begins to dawn upon the sufferer that there may actually be a meaning to his pain.

Many commentators make much of the fact that Job's final words are words of repentance—as if somehow this proves that all along he has been in the wrong. But Job's repentance proves nothing of the kind. On the contrary, it proves his righteousness! For wrong though he may have been in some of his behavior and attitudes, his very capacity to repent shows that in his heart of hearts (where righteousness is calculated) he was right. Here is a man who is accustomed to walking uprightly with his God, whose entire bent is towards putting things right with God on a moment-by-moment basis. As soon as the Lord speaks to him, therefore, Job repents. But he did not repent when the Lord was silent. How could he? Repentance itself is a divine grace, a gift of the Holy Spirit. Humanly speaking, it cannot be done. And it certainly must not be done simply as a means of ingratiating oneself with an austere Deity, nor out of neurotic perfectionism, nor as a response to peer pressure. To one of the greatest Old Testament prophets the Lord said something that takes on profound significance when considered against the background of Job's struggle with his friends: "If you repent," God told Jeremiah, "I will restore you that you may serve me. . . . Let this people turn to you, but you must not turn to them" (Jer. 15:19).

If the Lord Himself is not calling a person to repentance, but rather to some other form of obedience (whether cheerful service, patient suffering, peaceful repose, or spiritual warfare), then to become mired down in repentance at such a time would be a sinful waste. Like other affections or moods of the spirit, repentance has

its proper place, and Job resists the artificial, trumped-up, bargaining sort of repentance that his friends have been urging upon him,
and instead he calls on the Lord to shed more light on his situation.
Thus his very repentance, and the manner of it, points not so much
to his sin as to his fundamental uprightness of heart. Has Job been
sinful? Yes; everyone is sinful. "There is not a righteous man on
earth who does what is right and never sins" (Eccl. 7:20). But the
glorious thing about the story of Job (and the story of every true
believer) is that the real point of the story is not Job's sin, but his
righteousness. How wrong it is to rivet our attention on human sin
when we ought to be focusing on the glory of God!

What has really been happening to Job throughout his ordeal is
that his God has been getting bigger. God does not change, of
course, but our human perception of Him does. There is a popular
little Christian maxim that goes, "Does God feel far away? Guess
who moved!" The implication is that the believer is responsible for
maintaining intimacy with God. But this is only a partial truth, for
faith is a relationship, a two-sided thing, and the Lord bears far
more responsibility than we do for the maintenance of it. We speak
of our "daily devotions"—but is the Lord not infinitely more
devoted to us than we are to Him? If He feels far away, it may be
because He has suddenly moved closer to us than ever before—so
close that He fills our field of vision and we can no longer see Him.
Perhaps significant growth never takes place without our temporarily losing sight of God. Before we can begin to feel close to Him
again, our hearts must expand in order to accommodate His new
intimacy with us.

For the disciple of Jesus, then, the ongoing work of repentance is
not so much a sign of sin as it is of normal, healthy spiritual growth.
In the words of Harry Robinson, "God's purposes for us are so
unlimited that there's no time for coasting." The Apostle Paul told
his Corinthian congregation, "We will be ready to punish every act
of disobedience, once your obedience is complete" (2 Cor. 10:6).
The Lord's correction of Job, and Job's ready repentance, are signs
that this man's obedience has been complete.

THE EPILOGUE
(Job 42:7–17)

And so Job died, old and full of years.

—JOB 42:17

I have fought the good fight, I have finished the race, I have kept the faith.

—2 TIM. 4:7

Revival

After the Lord had said these things to Job, he said to Eliphaz the Temanite, "I am angry with you and your two friends, because you have not spoken of me what is right, as my servant Job has." (42:7)

The Epilogue of *Job* reads almost like a textbook on revival. In this brief section of the Old Testament we find listed in quick succession, verse after verse, examples of at least seven vital marks of genuine revival in the church of Christ. Here they are:

1) One of the surest signs that revival is breaking out is that God begins to speak to those whose hearts have been hard, and they are broken down. This is exactly what we see in the verse quoted above.

2) The repentance of Job's friends is preceded by Job's own repentance in verses 5-6. For the beginning of revival is a deep humbling and breaking of the people of God—even of the best!

3) In verse 8 we learn that Job was to pray for his friends, and that through his prayers they would be saved. A revived church is one in which powerful and effective intercession is taking place—so effective that the world begins to fall all over itself trying to get into the Kingdom of Heaven.

4) The inevitable climax of revival is described in verse 11: a jubilant communal celebration in which both old and new believers join hands and weep and laugh and feast together in joyous fellowship. (This is in marked contrast to the apparently rather coarse gatherings of the Job clan mentioned in 1:4-5.)

5) Healing and restoration flow like a river. Not only was Job's body healed, but in every way "the Lord blessed the latter part of Job's life more than the first" (v. 12).

6) True revival is accompanied by liberation for the oppressed. In a lovely touch of gospel grace, verse 15 records that Job gave his daughters financial equality with his sons, showing that even an old patriarch can become open to women's rights.

7) Finally, the most significant mark of revival is that the people of God are filled with the joy of their salvation. Surely Job in his later years must have been the happiest man on earth! The final verses

give almost the feeling that his passing from this world was less a
death than an assumption into Heaven.

What a strange book this is. After spending forty-odd chapters
hammering home the decidedly uncharismatic message of the cross,
suddenly it breaks out in a sweeping charismatic revival. Of course,
the issue here has nothing to do with whether or not Holy-Spirited
renewal is needed in the church. The real question is, What is the
route that leads dependably to it? Everyone agrees that revival is
needed and is a wonderful thing. But some so-called revivals have
borne less resemblance to Acts 2 than they have to Luke 19, which
records the first Palm Sunday when Jesus went riding into Jerusalem
to shouts of "Hosanna!" In itself this was a stirring event. But where
was that same crowd a week later when it came to accompanying
their Lord to the cross? It was great to be filled with exuberant emotion and to be counted with Christ when He was on top. But the less
savory aspects of discipleship were not for them. What sort of
revival is that?

The key to genuine and lasting revival is the cross. Throughout
history revivals have flared and died out, but only the cross can keep
revival going. Only those whose lives are profoundly marked by the
odor of death and the consciousness of their utter inadequacy will
come to possess the secret of continuous revival. They will know
that revival is not a destination but a journey, and so they will realize how vain it is to try to cling to spectacular public evidences of
the work of the Holy Spirit. At times the Kingdom of God does
make dramatic advances, but it is dangerous to look upon these as
the normal operational mode of the church. Without time for con-
solidation, the fruits of revival will be lost. That is why whenever
Jesus enjoyed public success His tendency was quickly to move on.
His eyes were continually on the cross. He knew how to sustain
revival.

The revival that breaks out at the end of *Job* is thrilling, but it is
only a small part of the fuller picture of God's ways as presented in
this book. In *Job* we learn that the road to revival never departs from
the way of the cross. This is not a road for those who put happiness
and excitement first.

Satisfaction Guaranteed

"So now take seven bulls and seven rams and go to my servant Job and sacrifice a burnt offering for yourselves."
(42:8a)

The fact that Eliphaz, Bildad, and Zophar, after all they have said against Job, should now do a complete about-face and come to him virtually on bended knee, bringing not only apologies but ritual sacrifices and humbly begging him to intercede for them with his God—is this not astounding? This could only be the work of an unusual outpouring of the Holy Spirit. Ironically, Eliphaz himself had prophesied this very turn of events back in 22:29-30, when he told Job that if he repented, "When men are brought low and you say, 'Lift them up,' then God will save the downcast. He will deliver even one who is not innocent, who will be saved through the cleanness of your hands." Little did Eliphaz realize how exactly his words were to be fulfilled!

Adding to the wonder of this occasion is the fact that as yet there has been not one iota of change in Job's outward circumstances. For it was only "after Job had prayed for his friends" that "the Lord made him prosperous again" (42:10). The prayer that moves mountains does not happen in the midst of prosperity. For all we know, at the point when Job's friends brought him sacrifices his body was still covered with boils and he was still sitting on his ash heap swatting flies. What a comeuppance it must have been for these three proud pillars of society to have to pay homage to a man in this condition. But just so is the time approaching when the whole world will have to bow before a crucified Savior.

Reading the Epilogue of *Job*, we are reminded of these words of Isaiah:

> Surely he took up our infirmities
>   and carried our sorrows,
> yet we considered him stricken by God,
>   smitten by him and afflicted.
> But he was pierced for our transgressions,
>   he was crushed for our iniquities;

> the punishment that brought us peace was upon him,
> and by his wounds we are healed. (53:4-5)

Perhaps more than any other Old Testament character, Job through his unmerited suffering becomes a reflection of Jesus, a Christ-figure. For it is not simply through sacrifice and prayer that Job's friends gain their forgiveness, but rather through the entire mystery of Job's suffering which, by sending its relentless roots deep into their hard hearts, has been invisibly breaking ground for the living God. Thus those who had considered Job "stricken by God, smitten by him and afflicted" in the end receive healing through his wounds. Healing for what? Healing for wounds less visible than Job's, wounds they did not even know they had: the wounds of lovelessness. When the powerful come to the powerless for help, there the door to the Kingdom of God swings open.

Nothing, really, could ever have made up for the pain that Job's friends caused him by kicking him when he was down. But when he saw these same persecutors turning to him as to a priest (or, these days, as to a psychiatrist) something in Job must have been wonderfully satisfied—not in any priggish I-told-you-so sort of way, but rather in the way that only humility can be satisfied. Perhaps the key word in understanding the Biblical concept of atonement is this word *satisfaction*. On Calvary, the all but insatiable thirst of Almighty God for righteousness among men was perfectly satisfied, in a manner that somehow did not require human beings becoming outwardly perfect. Righteousness is by faith and not by works, and the same is true of holiness and of everything else in the Christian life. Just as Job was satisfied by his friends' gesture of coming to him and, in effect, saying "Sorry," so our holy God is fully satisfied simply by our coming to Him through the One whom He has chosen, yet whom we have despised and rejected, Jesus Christ. In fact there is no other gesture of ours that will satisfy God—no other apology or recompense or sacrifice or virtue or sincerity or good intention—except this one gesture of freely offering ourselves, full of sin as we are, at the foot at the cross. We can claw at the sky until our fingers bleed, yearning for holiness. But until we let the Lord Jesus Christ do our bleeding for us, we will never be satisfied. Atonement implies satisfaction on both sides, on the part of God first, but also on the part of man. At the cross, and only at the cross, both parties are eternally delighted by the amazing solution.

Intercession

"My servant Job will pray for you, and I will
accept his prayer and not deal with you according
to your folly." (42:8b)

What an extraordinary revelation it must have been for Job that instead of trying to talk sense into his friends, he could simply pray for them, and that where all of his arguments had failed, his prayers would prevail. How much Job may have prayed for his friends before this we do not know. But just as there is a time for repentance, there is a time for intercessory prayer. There is a time when intercession is effective, and there is a time when the skies may as well be brass. Intercession is a form of spiritual warfare, and as in any battle strategy, timing is vitally important. A raid behind enemy lines is not to be undertaken lightly. The Lord is the one who leads intercessory prayer, and so the proper way to undertake it is with specific instructions from Him and by the power of the Holy Spirit. Is it not a strange policy to assume that we can pray for others by our own energy, according to our own whims and opinions concerning their needs? At best such intercessions may be a waste of breath. Even Jesus confessed, "The Son can do nothing by himself; he can do only what he sees his Father doing" (John 5:19).

Is intercession so straightforward, then, that it is simply a matter of rubber-stamping the divine will? And does this mean it was easy for Job to pray for his friends? The answer is yes and no. When we know what to pray for, it is not difficult to pray. What is difficult is the process of being brought into the knowledge of the Lord's will, especially where it touches upon the lives of other people. It is a dread business to presume to see, however imperfectly, into God's will for the life of another. Yet without such insight, how much real intercession can take place? Certainly the Holy Spirit groans within us and interprets our inarticulate longings (Rom. 8:26). But mature, effective, intercessory prayer is not a hit-and-miss affair, like throwing darts blindfolded and hoping that one might hit the target. Rather, intercession is fueled by spiritual discernment, and it is the acquisition of this discernment, along with the necessary humility and compassion, that can make this prayer a painful labor. Back in the Prologue we saw how Job regularly prayed for his children, pleading with the Lord for their lives to be clean and pure (see 1:5). But did he also pray this way for Eliphaz, Bildad, and Zophar? Before his trials it may never have occurred to the humble Job that his peers were in fact not his peers, that their sanctity fell far short of his own, and that without his specific prayers for them they might be in real spiritual danger. This is weighty knowledge for a man to bear about his friends, and Job might never have faced this hard truth, nor developed the spiritual muscle to pray through it, without first enduring his long night of suffering and persecution.

Who knows but that the whole reason for Job's ordeal was precisely this—that in the end his friends might be saved through his prayers. For the normal position of the intercessor is to be the lowest of the low. Like Jesus Himself, the intercessor is one who in a sense has "descended to the *depths* of the earth" (Eph. 4:9), and it is precisely because the Lord has brought him so low that he can identify with the pain of others. Their pain becomes his. Yet more than that, their pain eventually *displaces* his, and herein lies the great secret of intercessory prayer. As we pray for others, we ourselves are first afflicted, then healed. For there is an actual exchange of burdens that must take place, a transfer of weight. It is hard to take up someone else's burden; perhaps there is nothing harder in the world. But the hard part, ironically, is not the carrying of the other's burden, but the fact that before we can do it we must first set down our own. Significantly, it is only after Job prays for his friends that the Lord finally heals him and makes him prosperous again.

The word "intercede" means literally "going between." What does it take to go between a holy God and a fallen world? An old Jewish legend runs like this: When the children of Israel were about to leave Egypt, Satan rushed to God, protesting, "Master of the Universe, think! Only yesterday these men and women were infidels, idol-worshipers, and You plan to perform miracles on their behalf? Will You really part the waters of the Red Sea for them? And give them Your law? How can You trust them?" In order to get rid of him, God pointed to Job and said, "Go and take care of him first; we'll talk later." And while Satan was busy torturing his victim, God managed to free His people from bondage.

True Riches

After Job had prayed for his friends, the Lord made him prosperous again and gave him twice as much as he had before. (42:10)

It is surprising how many readers tend to sneer at this restoration of Job's fortunes—as if there were something too saccharine and happy-ever-afterish about such an ending. But didn't Jesus say, "Everyone who has will be given more, and he will have an abundance" (Matt. 25:29)? People who really know the Lord do not get jealous or upset over His lavish generosity. They know that this is just the way He is. Perhaps it is the people who do not know Him, the spiritual have-nots, who cry sour grapes at the way *Job* ends.

Naturally the Lord's liberality does not always take the form of material riches. That has been one of the chief lessons of the last forty chapters. But technically speaking, there is really no direct connection between Job's righteousness and the final restoration of his wealth. After all, the story did not have to end this way. The fact that it does is simply and purely a demonstration of the Lord's gracious magnanimity. If we try to draw some necessary connection between righteousness and worldly prosperity, we have missed the whole point of the book. The Lord's giving is just as gratuitously unpredictable as His taking away.

Then too, it is not as if Job's newly acquired wealth had fallen out of the sky. That is not how the Lord chose to give it to him. Rather we are told that all of Job's friends and family rallied around him, and "each one gave him a piece of silver and a gold ring" (42:11). This is how Job was able to purchase new livestock and get back on his feet, and even then it would have been a slow process. How wise it was of the Lord to accomplish Job's healing and restoration not through some supernatural zap, but by surrounding him with people. How the love of these folks must have warmed and filled Job's lonely, aching spirit!

So Job's real wealth was in his friends. The increase of his worldly estate has no real significance in itself, but rather is a sign of the love and honor that both God and people lavished upon him. In the same way, the baby Jesus was given gifts of gold and frankincense and myrrh, but His true wealth lay in the souls behind these gifts, the royal souls of human beings who had been given to Him by His Father. Only God can give to all His children the ultimate Christmas gift: other people, one to another, in love. Only God can give people away.

Another fact that tends to be overlooked by those who are unhappy with the happy ending of *Job* is that for Job himself this turn of events would not have been all peaches and cream. Surely his reentry into the whirl of business and society would have been terribly difficult for him—perhaps, in some ways, as painful as the trials he had just endured. For when a man has been stripped of everything, and yet found that in his dire need he met the Lord face to face, why should he want riches and a "normal life" again? It is not as though anything in this present world could ever really reward him for his faith, nor compensate him for past troubles. In fact the great irony in the ending of this story is that even now there is no real justice for Job. Just think: this man is a son of the Almighty King; by rights he should be sitting on a golden throne in Heaven! So what is he doing tending sheep and donkeys down on earth? To the eye of faith, all the gold in the world looks like so much rust. If we look for God to be just—to "make everything right"—in this life, we shall always find Him unjust.

No, the Lord does not give to us as the world gives. Rather He pays us in love, which is real wealth. He pays us by the enlarging of our heart. During the night of tears and sorrow the believing heart cannot help but swell, so that like a growing plant it comes to hold more and more of the sap of eternal life, which is love. The true nature of this spiritual wealth is expressed with beautiful simplicity in a little hymn by Bishop Kingo:

> *Break forth, my soul, with joy, and say*
> *How rich I have become this day!*
> *My Savior dwells within my heart!*
> *Thanks for the joy Thou dost impart.*

Community

*All his brothers and sisters and everyone who had known
him before came and ate with him in his house. They
comforted and consoled him over all the trouble the Lord
had brought upon him, and each one gave him a piece of
silver and a gold ring. (42:11)*

It may surprise us to learn that Job had brothers and sisters.
Where were these folks when he needed them? Apparently they
too deserted him when the chips were down. Yet now that his
fortunes are on the rise again, they and other hangers-on come
crawling back to rally around, kowtowing and currying favor.

How easy it would be to be cynical about this. But listen: this is
not a time for cynicism. Will we dare to be cold and critical when
the Kingdom of Heaven is breaking out and when others all around
us are melting at the touch of God? How do we know whether Job's
relatives were even believers? All the more reason to rejoice that now
they are being drawn to their God-fearing brother as moths to a
light.

What was it that drew them? Possibly it was the simple fact that
in this man's presence the Holy Spirit was so real you could reach
out and touch Him. The power of God was resting on Job, and
everybody knew it. This is not to say that Job was suddenly transformed into some miracle-working guru. Quite the contrary; we are
told that other people "comforted and consoled him," making it
clear that he did not recover from his ordeal overnight, and that he
needed lots of help. Job's restoration took time, and it happened not
in solitude but in the context of community. In fact the Lord used
this period of recuperation for the blessing of many, many people.
In Job's home there was something going on that nobody wanted to
miss. It was like Christmas or a wedding; there was feasting and gift-
giving. But more than that, people were ministering to each other.
Job was praying for his friends and relatives, and they in turn were
comforting him. It was a two-way street. It was, in a word, love.
People were loving each other. How amazing! Love is what happens
when the Kingdom of God breaks forth, and in this respect Job

42:11 is a kind of Old Testament Pentecost that came about, like the New Testament Pentecost, not because believers were intent on praying for revival, but because they were all together in one place and were one in spirit.

The greatest miracle of Pentecost was the one that preceded the fireworks. For it is one thing for the power of Heaven to be displayed on earth in the form of signs and wonders; but it is another and a far greater thing for the humble power of earth to be displayed to the heavenlies in the form of faith, hope, and love. It is primarily this latter, more mysterious power that filled Job's household at the end, and that also happens to be the principal mandate of the Church of Christ. This is how we are to become "a spectacle to the whole universe, to angels as well as to men" (1 Cor. 4:9), so that "through the church, the manifold wisdom of God should be made known to the rulers and authorities in the heavenly realms" (Eph. 3:10). As mere human beings we are prone to suppose that there is nothing very special or unusual about being human. But to the heavenly powers mere humanity is the greatest of mysteries. To an angel (whether a good angel or a demon) there is probably nothing spectacular about seeing people perform miracles, for the supernatural is the very air that angels breathe. But simple acts of love performed on earth for the building up of a community—to an angel such deeds must appear awesomely powerful and baffling. To the good spirits they are beautiful beyond words, and to the evil they are sheer torture.

Given his choice, Satan would far rather see people exercising supernatural power than loving each other. Weakness is a more disturbing phenomenon to him than strength; perseverance troubles him more than victory; and prayer that requires long waiting is far more enigmatic to him than prayer that receives immediate answers. To the Devil and all his demons, just as to the ungodly among men, patient waiting is something incomprehensible. Hope and peace of heart are qualities so dark to them as to be utterly impenetrable. And love? Holy, heavenly love between brothers and sisters? Ah! To the legions of darkness, love is so maddeningly alien a power that it literally drives them crazy, disarming them of every last particle of strength.

A Thousand Donkeys

The Lord blessed the latter part of Job's life more than the first. He had fourteen thousand sheep, six thousand camels, a thousand yoke of oxen and a thousand donkeys. (42:12)

After thirty-nine chapters of passionate poetry, the return to prose in the Epilogue comes as something of a relief. One cannot live continually on the level of intensity represented by poetry. Returning to ordinary life after a mountaintop experience of God is largely what faith is all about. The gospel is not fully the gospel until it is fleshed out in the world of daily affairs. The good news cannot go naked; it must be clothed. And where else to obtain clothes for Heaven except on earth? To dress the gospel one must go into the world. One must enter the alleys and marketplaces of sin and woe and purchase there the robes and sashes and crown-gear for His Majesty. This is what Jesus did. What would have happened if the Son of God had balked at His Father's plan of sending Him into the cold, crass world? No, Jesus was born in a barn, and He never forgot it. When He entered Jerusalem in triumph He did not ride merely on the wind of the Spirit, but on a donkey. Just so, God's plan of redemption depends upon the disciples of Christ getting down off their high spiritual horses. The willingness to come down from a direct encounter with the living God is just as important as the willingness to enter into one. How pitiful it is to see people frantically trying to maintain a certain aura of spirituality when the proper season for that has passed.

In Job's case the return to business as usual meant sheep, camels, oxen, and donkeys, together with all the million and one practical details involved in the care and feeding and productive employment of twenty-two thousand livestock. Job, like Jesus, knew something of hay and manure. Being responsible for a thousand donkeys is no picnic. Such facts, together with the primitive style of prose that describes them, suggest to us again that Job would have belonged to the era of the patriarchs, those dinosauric grand old men of faith. When we consider the daily lives of these men, what is most astonishing about them is not any inherent greatness in their characters but rather, as with the disciples of Jesus, just how ordinary they were. A plainer bunch could hardly have been found, and this is precisely the point. These were not great men, but they had a great God.

Take Isaac, for example. He was the promised child, the boy wonder, and yet there appears to have been very little in his character to distinguish him. He was so run-of-the-mill that Scripture almost glosses over him, as if unable to find much to say. Or look at Jacob. If ever there was a man who barely squeaked into the Kingdom of Heaven, it was Jacob. Was he the sort of fellow always on his toes trying to please God? Not a bit of it. A schemer, a money-grubber, an incurable worrywart, he just blundered his way through life and was blessed for it, almost in spite of himself. The earthy humanness of such fellows is wonderfully refreshing, providing a vivid contrast to the self-conscious spirituality of many modern Christians.

One of the principal fascinations of *Job* is the behind-the-scenes glimpse it gives us into the patriarchal psyche, into the very heart and mind of one of the earliest believers in Yahweh. Because the faith of these patriarchs dates from a time long before there was any law, it is faith with a mystically raw, wild edge to it. While it is important to read the New Testament in light of the Old (and vice versa), it is something else again to see the whole of salvation history against the background of the faith of the patriarchs. Isn't this exactly what Paul loved to do? He loved to get back to pre-Exodus days and meditate on what made old Abe tick (see Romans 4, etc.). In a sense, people like Job and Abraham belong to neither Testament; they had their own deal with God, their own covenant. Religion without any basis in law is a fearsome thing.

How we need these patriarchs! How we need their rough-hewn example so that we will not fall into the terrible error of being super-spiritual—that ugly caricature of real, living faith. Even the disciples of Jesus, it is painfully obvious, were far too preoccupied with trying to be religious. But for the patriarchs it was just the opposite: if anything, they were busy trying *not* to be religious. About all you can say for them was that they could not get away from God. Unlikely, stubborn, coarse, and even savage men, they prove to us just how radical is the grace of the gospel.

Job's Daughters

*Job also had seven sons and three daughters. The first
daughter he named Jemimah, the second Keziah and the
third Keren-Happuch. Nowhere in all the land were there
found women as beautiful as Job's daughters, and their
father granted them an inheritance along with their
brothers. (42:13-15)*

In the old days, when wishing still worked," begins a tale by the
Brothers Grimm, "there lived a king, and his daughters were all
beautiful; but the youngest was so beautiful that the sun itself,
although it had seen so many things, wondered whenever it shone
into her face." Job had not just one daughter like this, but three—
three daughters whose beauty was so radiant that, more than natural, it was supernatural. It was one of the signs of the grace of God
poured out upon Job's life.

This is very nice to know. Yet still, with all that might have been
said about the glory of Job's latter days, why was this information
about his daughters singled out for special mention? The very odd-
ity of the passage may be a clue to its importance, for at the time it
was written (and for long afterwards) it must have struck its readers as being not just odd but outrageous. That the names of Job's
daughters should be specifically mentioned while those of the sons
are omitted, and furthermore that the daughters should be given
equal inheritance with the sons—this was not conventional Old
Testament protocol. Indeed to most of the societies of the ancient
world such treatment of women would have seemed not merely
eccentric, but politically subversive. To give women a landed inheritance is to give them equal status; it is to take them out of the
kitchen and make them managers, owners, merchants, voters, and
finally lawmakers and rulers. How far ahead of his time Job was!
He was like Caleb, another unusual Old Testament saint, who having conquered his portion of the promised land, promptly awarded
his daughter Acsah a slice of its very choicest real estate—an act so
unconventional as to earn conspicuous mention in two separate
books (see Josh. 15:18-19 and Judg. 1:14-15).

So the phenomenal beauty of Job's daughters is not the real point of this passage. Rather, their physical beauty is but a sign of something even more beautiful—the fact that they brought the true spirit of women's liberation to their father's household. Perhaps more than any other passage in the book this one shows how deeply Job, both inwardly and outwardly, had already been transformed, as it were, from an Old Covenant to a New Covenant man. On the surface his life was restored to the status quo, but at heart he had become more boldly nonconformist than ever. No doubt his treatment of his daughters would have drawn harsh criticism—not least, we may imagine, from his sons, who must have felt cheated out of a large portion of their inheritance. But Job's action was motivated not by favoritism or doting love for his daughters, but rather by a revolutionary love, a prophetic love which pointed to the gospel era when there would be "neither slave nor free, male nor female, for you are all one in Christ" (Gal. 3:28).

Even in the Christian age, some eighteen centuries were to elapse before the Church finally took any initiative in addressing the problem of human slavery. And yet getting around to the emancipation of women, even within the Church's own ranks, has taken longer still. "Slaves, obey your earthly masters" was Paul's clear-cut command (Eph. 6:5)—and yet what Christian today would think seriously of citing this verse in defense of the institution of slavery? To this day, however, many cling to texts such as "Wives, submit to your husbands" (Eph. 5:22), and "Women should remain silent in the churches" (1 Cor. 14:34) as evidence that Scripture supports what is arguably (at least in some circumstances) the oppression of women. Interestingly, whenever the church undergoes revival, disputes about gender roles tend to fade into the background. It is the dead church that gets bogged down in sexual politics.

Job, obviously, was a man full of the reforming effervescence of the gospel. In his home, when the celebration began it was for everyone. Like Jesus he simply went ahead and began treating women as though their liberation had already taken place. Wasn't it a woman who first announced the resurrection to the unbelieving male disciples? How fortunate we are that "Mary Magdalene, Joanna, Mary the mother of James, and the others with them" (Luke 24:10) had not been told that women were to remain silent in church!

Full of Years

*After this, Job lived a hundred and forty years; he saw his
children and their children to the fourth generation. And
so he died, old and full of years. (42:16-17)*

Since we do not know what age Job was when his trials began,
neither can we say exactly how old he was when he died. If the
Septuagint is right in saying that he lived 240 years in all, then
he would have been seventy at the outset. This is probably a reasonable estimate (if anything is reasonable when it comes to the ages
of the patriarchs). What does seem clear is that Job's unusual length
of years is yet another detail placing him in the patriarchal era, and
probably somewhere in the period between Noah who died at the
age of 950 and Abraham who died at 175.

In any event, when Job died he was "full of years," a Biblical
expression signifying not merely longevity but fullness of wisdom
and godliness. To be full of years is to have seen everything there is
to see and to have done everything there is to do, to the point that
now one is so full of it all that there is no room for anything else.
There is no room for any more time or any more world; one is
crammed to the gills with it. There is room only for eternity and for
God. If Job was "blameless and upright" before his ordeal, then
think what he must have been like 140 years after it. He must have
had so much holiness that his flesh would have been practically
crawling with it.

Is that not exactly the way it is with old saints? Even their physical bodies seem to take on an aura of sanctity. Their very skin, wrin-
kled and blotchy as it is, glows translucently, like a great dripping
tallow candle lit from the inside. You can see God in the lines of
these faces, in the wattles of the neck, in the creases around the eyes
and on the mottled hands. These folks are still sinners just like everybody else, and yet one can almost see the sin falling off them. Evil
no longer frightens them; they eat it for breakfast. Death does not
terrorize; they run swiftly toward it like Olympic youths. Such people have their feet firmly on the ground, and yet they are almost in
Heaven. Their bodies are falling apart, but about the persons them-

selves there is something fantastically young and ageless—one might even say sexy! They are like the very first glistening little shoots of tender green pushing their way up through the mud and the snow on a February day that is both winter and spring at once. What business do these decrepit, dying old folks have being so brazenly radiant, so totally and profanely *themselves*, so full of a hair-raising God-awful wildness of pure liberty? Never have their bodies so held them down, and yet never have they come so close to bumping their fool heads on the sky, so lightsome are they. (Why else do you think they walk around stooped and bent over?)

We young folks, still bound on the wheel of time and worldliness, can barely stand the stench of sanctity around these old saints. It unnerves us. These people are like ancient and unimaginably dangerous gangsters, like Mafia godfathers. Long ago they hung up their sawed-off shotguns, and now their weapons are of an entirely different order; now they transfix you with only their eyes and the gravel in their throats. One sits utterly transparent, X-rayed, in their presence. One has the feeling that they can do literally anything they want and get away with it. Their faith has made them untouchable. The blood of Christ has made them incorruptible. Even as they lie on their beds breathing their last, the mighty power of the resurrection is fairly jumping out of their mouths. Flat on their backs, they are dancing a jig with Jesus. They have linked hands with the Lord and are dancing a tarantella on top of their own graves, and their feet are as nimble and irreverent as the hooves of satyrs. When you go to view their bodies in the church or funeral parlor, if you stand very quietly and listen very closely, you might even be able to hear them singing—singing at the top of their lungs while swinging their steins like shameless beerhall revelers. And then, if you press your ear close against the cool, hollow wood of the coffin, perhaps you will make out the words of their song, for they are the same words sung centuries before by a man named Job: "I know that my Redeemer lives, and that in the end he will stand upon the earth. And after my skin has been destroyed, yet in my flesh I will see God" (19:25-26).

A Last Word

L et's give the last word to Dostoyevski—or rather, to one of that novelist's characters, Father Zossima. Zossima is the wise and saintly old monk who forms the spiritual center of gravity in Dostoyevski's last and greatest novel, *The Brothers Karamazov*. On his deathbed, in the climactic scene of the first half of the book, Zossima reflects on his childhood and on the story of *Job*, in the following words:

> Even before I learned to read, I remember how I was first moved by deep spiritual emotion when I was eight years old. My mother took me alone to church, to morning mass on the Monday before Easter. It was a sunny day, and I recall now, just as though I saw it again, how the incense rose from the censer and floated slowly upwards and how through a little window from the dome overhead the sunlight streamed down upon us and, rising in waves toward it, the incense seemed to dissolve in it. I looked and felt deeply moved, and for the first time in my life I consciously received the first seed of the word of God in my soul, as a boy stepped forth into the middle of the church carrying a big book, so big that I thought he could hardly carry it, and laying it on the lectern he opened it and began to read. It was then that I suddenly understood for the first time, for the first time in my life, what it is they read in church: "There was a man in the land of Uz, and that man was perfect and upright. . . ."

As Father Zossima retells the ancient tale in his own words and reflects on it, we can almost see his thoughts blending into those of Job himself, as if these two saintly old patriarchs were somehow being mystically united, just like the incense and the sunlight:

> Since then—even yesterday I took it up—I have never been able to read this sacred tale without tears. And how much that is great, mysterious, and unfathomable there is in it! Scoffers say: How could God give up the most loved of his saints to Satan to play with, take his children from him, smite him with sore boils so that he scraped the corruption from his sores with a potsherd—and for what? Just to be able to boast to Satan, "See how much My saint

can suffer for My sake!" But the greatness of it all lies just in the fact that it is a mystery—that the passing earthly show and the eternal justice are brought together here, and in the face of the earthly truth the eternal truth is accomplished. Here the Creator, just as in the first days of creation He ended each day with praise—"What I have created is good"—now looks upon Job and again boasts of His creation. And Job, praising the Lord, serves not only Him but all His creation for generations and generations and for ever and ever, since for that he was ordained. Lord, what a book it is and what lessons it contains! What a book the Holy Bible is! What a miracle and what strength is given with it to man! It is just like a sculpture of the whole world and all its human characters, with everything named there and everything shown for ever and ever. And what mysteries are solved and revealed: God raises Job again, gives him wealth again, and many years pass by and he has other children and he loves them. Good Lord, but how could he love those new ones when his old children are no more, when he has lost them? Remembering them, how could he be completely happy with the new ones, however dear they might be? But he could, he could! The old sorrow, through the great mystery of human life, passes gradually into quiet, tender joy; the fiery blood of youth gives way to the gentle serenity of old age. I bless the rising sun each day, and my heart sings to it as of old, but now I love its setting even more, its long slanting rays and the quiet, gentle, tender memories that come with them, the dear images from the whole of my long and blessed life—and over it all Divine Truth, tender, reconciling, and all-forgiving! My life is drawing to a close. I know that, I feel it. But I also feel every day that is left to me how my earthly life is already in touch with a new, infinite, unknown but fast-approaching future life, the anticipation of which sets my soul trembling with rapture, my mind glowing, and my heart weeping with joy. . . .